MEDICAL ANTHROPOLOGY

GEORGE M. FOSTER
University of California, Berkeley
BARBARA GALLATIN ANDERSON
Southern Methodist University

John Wiley & Sons

New York
Chichester
Brisbane
Toronto

Production was supervised by Joseph P. Cannizzaro.
Text and cover design by Mark E. Safran.
Cover illustration executed by Small Kaps Associates.

Library of Congress Cataloging in Publication Data:

Foster, George McClelland, 1913-
Medical anthropology.

Includes bibliographical references and index.
Medical anthropology.
1. Medical anthropology   I. Anderson, Barbara Gallatin, joint author.
II. Title

GN296.F67   362.1   78-18449
ISBN 0-471-04342-7

Printed in the United States of America

10 9 8 7 6 5 4 3 2

Preface

In *Medical Anthropology* we discuss a number of the themes that have attracted biological and social anthropologists as they have turned their attention to matters of health and illness during the past generation. A comprehensive treatment of all of the work that has been done is not our objective; even if this achievement would be possible, which we doubt, it would make for dull reading. Instead, we have contented ourselves with a general overview of the field of medical anthropology as we see it, concentrating on the topics that we know firsthand from research, consulting activities, and teaching, and that we have found to be of interest to our students. Although—as the reader will note —we neither ignore nor underestimate the importance of the more purely biological side of medical anthropology, the sociocultural orientation of most of the chapters that follow make clear the debt we owe to our sister discipline, medical sociology. There are very real differences in subject matter, conceptual framework, and research methods between medical anthropology and medical sociology, and the validity of separate disciplines is not in doubt (Cf. Foster 1974; Olesen 1974). But there are also important similarities and common ground. Anthropologists interested in the social and cultural dimensions of health and illness can no more ignore the data and models that come from sociology than they can ignore the data and models that come from biological anthropology.

Two basic anthropological points of view underlie the chapters that follow. First, we believe that health-related behavior, in Western and Third World countries alike, past as well as present, tends to be "adaptive"; consciously and subconsciously it is designed to promote the survival and increase of the members of each society. We view health behavior, too, as a rational response (given the world view or cognitive orientation of the members of every group) to the perceived causes of illness. Second, we believe that the comparative method of anthropology gives the greatest insight into the structure and dynamics of health behavior. Consequently, we stress a cross-cultural perspective, emphasizing the common elements that underlie all aspects of medical systems, regardless of cultural context. In the chapters that deal primarily with the Western world, it is implicit, in the sense that the culture-specific medical institutions of the West provide an obvious and striking contrast to those of other parts of the world.

The organization of the chapters that follow, while eclectic, emphasizes these points of view. In Part 1 we first consider the general characteristics of the new field of medical anthropology. We next consider the relationship between disease and culture as they appear to have influenced human evolution, drawing particularly on the findings of paleopathology. Continuing the theme of disease and its relationships to culture and human behavior, we discuss some of the principal ecological themes that have interested anthropologists and their colleagues. We then discuss medical systems, which we find to be adaptive responses to the biological threat of disease. The concept of medical system also provides an appropriate backdrop for later chapters since, in one way or another, almost all of the work done by medical anthropologists ultimately relates to specific systems.

Part 2 deals primarily, but not entirely, with the traditional materials of ethnographical research: ideas about the nature and causes of illness, mental illness in non-Western societies (and especially the so-called culture-specific illnesses such as *pibloktoq*), the behavior and roles of indigenous curers, and the strengths and weaknesses of traditional medical systems.

In part 3 we turn our attention to the West to consider some of the major topics that have interested medical sociologists and medical anthropologists: role behavior and symbolic interaction as evidenced in the relationships between patients, doctors, nurses and other medical personnel, hospitals as small societies, and the question of professionalism. Our focus to this point is descriptive and theoretical.

In Part 4 we emphasize the applied side of medical anthropology, the roles anthropologists have played (and might play) both in our own country and in the developing world in helping to find answers to health needs. The concept of change is inherent in all of these chapters, although in slightly different ways. In the first four chapters our approach is in the tradition of American applied anthropology (i.e. the social-aspects-of-technological-change model), as evidenced in classic works such as Saunders' *Cultural Difference and Medical Care* (1954), Paul's *Health, Culture, and Community* (1955), and in a wide variety of articles appearing in Human Organization, Science, and other journals. In the final chapter we suggest the role of the medical anthropologist as a constructive critic of American medicine, one who asks questions about our doctor-dominated health care delivery system and about the ethical dilemmas that science and technology have forced on us. We speculate as to whether there are not lessons about birth, old age, and dying that we can learn from practices in other less complex societies.

Here we must enter a professional caveat: we generalize, we paint with a broad brush. It is impossible to do otherwise in a relatively short book of broad scope. We recognize that the "Bongo-Bongo" don't conform perfectly to our generic descriptions, and that we fail to recognize all their peculiarities. Yet we prefer seeming oversimplification to that common anthropological disease, inability to see the forest for the trees. In health behavior viewed cross-culturally, as in all other kinds of behavior, we find patterns, trends, and regularities that transcend the unique. We believe there is more to be learned by searching out common patterns than by making sure that every minor variation is footnoted. We ask readers who feel that we go too far mentally to insert about the statements they question, "Except, of course, among the Bong-Bongo." They will do no injustice to our meaning, and we will all be happier.

At the editorial level we have followed a policy of full and complete citations; we feel strongly that scientific writing should—among many other things —lead interested readers to additional source materials and permit them to check on the accuracy with which authors have presented the views of others. Illustrations without specific citations are based on our field research. Those from the Mexican peasant village of Tzintzuntzan, Michoacán, and from other parts of Latin America, Spain, and Indonesia, are from Foster's work. Uncited references to Europe (especially France and Denmark), Africa (especially Morocco), and India are from Anderson's field observations.

In a gender-conscious era, the use of personal pronouns often presents difficulties. We hope that readers will realize that when "he" is used in a generic sense, "she/he" may be read at one's discretion.

Many groups and individuals have been helpful to us, particularly in reading and criticizing draft chapters. Several chapters were presented at monthly dinner meetings of the social anthropology staff at the Department of Anthropology, University of California, Berkeley. Also at Berkeley, doctoral candidates Ann McCawley, Pamela Meyer, Jennie Joe, Jeanie Kayser, and Barbara Koenig read and criticized early drafts. At Southern Methodist University this role was played by faculty and graduate students of the Ph.D. program in Medical Anthropology. Nancy Hazam, Cahlene Cramer, and Debra Schumann, doctoral candidates in medical anthropology, greatly facilitated all phases of research and writing. David Stewart of Southern Methodist's faculty aided in the painstaking organization of the book's index. And in the Summer the faculty of California State University at Hayward made facilities available for continuing work on the manuscript. To the secretaries who worked solicitously on the many drafts, especially Jane Taylorson and Jane Girard, we express warmest appreciation of their skill and for their patience with us.

George M. Foster
Barbara Gallatin Anderson

Contents

MEDICAL ANTHROPOLOGY

part 1

ORIGINS AND SCOPE

chapter 1

The New Field of Medical Anthropology

Since the end of the World War II, anthropologists, both sociocultural and biological, have turned in increasing numbers to the cross-cultural study of medical systems and to the bioecological and sociocultural factors that influence the incidence of health and disease now and throughout human history. In part their interests have been theoretical, sparked by the desire to understand man's health behavior in its widest manifestations; and in part their interests have been applied, motivated by the belief that anthropological research techniques, theories, and data can and should be used in programs designed to improve health care in both developed and developing nations.

Today anthropologists with these interests work in schools of medicine, nursing, and public health; in hospitals and health departments; and in traditional university anthropology departments. They do research on topics such as human evolution, anatomy, pediatrics, epidemiology, mental health, drug abuse, definitions of health and disease, the training of medical personnel, medical bureaucracies, hospital organization and operations, the doctor-patient relationship, and the processes of bringing scientific medicine to communities that previously have known only traditional medicine. These anthropologists are usually called "medical anthropologists," and the field they represent is the new anthropological subdiscipline, "medical anthropology."

As can be seen from the kinds of activities in which medical anthropologists engage, the field embraces many perspectives and foci of concern. Conceptually these may be ranged along a continuum, one end of which is marked by a biological pole, and the other, by a sociocultural pole. Toward the biological pole we find those anthropologists whose dominant interests include human growth and development, the role of disease in human evolution, and paleopathology (the study of diseases of ancient man). Anthropologists with these interests find much common ground with geneticists, anatomists, serologists, biochemists, and the like. Toward the sociocultural pole we find those anthropologists whose dominant interests include traditional medical systems ("ethnomedicine"), medical personnel and their professional preparation, illness behavior, the doctor-patient relationship, and the dynamics of the introduction of Western medical services into traditional societies. Medical anthropologists with these concerns find overlapping interests with medical sociologists, medical educators, nurses, public health specialists in health education and administration, and other behavioral scientists who work in the field broadly labeled "modernization." Midway along the continuum, and looking in both directions, we find those anthropologists interested in epidemiology and cultural ecology. They may share interests with almost any of the above, but their relationships are especially close with medical epidemiologists, ecologists, and the emerging group known as medical geographers.

But medical anthropology should not be thought of as two loosely joined fields — the biological and the sociocultural — because at innumerable points the problems of both require the intrusion of data and theory from the other. Mental illness, for example, cannot be studied solely in terms either of physiological and biochemical factors, or as a psycho-sociocultural phenomenon stemming from stress; both kinds of data are essential to the clearest comprehension of what is involved. The same is true of diet, where food habits and preferences are intimately tied to nutritional levels. And epidemiological theory is based on the knowledge that human behavior greatly influences the vectors that transmit much disease.

Even the past may be tied to the present, often in the most unexpected fashion. Some years ago two University of California anthropologists — an archeologist and an epidemiologist — examined a series of more than 50 reconstituted coprolites left by the prehistoric population that lived in Lovelock Cave, Nevada. They found no eggs or larvae of parasitic helminths and, because of the excellent state of preservation of the coprolites, concluded that this population was, in fact, free of scourges such as tapeworms, hookworm, flukes, and *Ascaris* (Dunn 1968:222). More recently a zoology graduate student at Berkeley, and a member of a medical anthropology seminar, confirmed these conclusions. Finding that Chenopodium seeds constituted an important item in the diet of these long-gone Indians, he hypothesized that Chenopodium acted as a vermifuge that kept them free of parasites. The attractiveness of this hypothesis, biological in origin, was heightened by cultural evidence supplied by an ethnologist who reported that in a Mexican village he knew well, the local variety of Chenopodium — *epazote* — was widely regarded as treatment for intestinal parasites![1]

In short, medical anthropology is viewed by its practitioners as a biocultural discipline concerned with both the biological and sociocultural aspects of human behavior, and particularly with the ways in which the two interact and have interacted throughout human history to influence health and disease. The biocultural nature of medical anthropology is made clear in a series of review articles that have appeared during the last 25 years (Caudill 1953; Polgar 1962; Scotch 1963a; Fabrega 1972; Lieban 1973; Colson and Selby 1974), and by looking at what we call the "roots" of the modern discipline. In discussing the origins of medical anthropology we are concerned with "roots" in the fairly narrow sense of how the contemporary field has come into being. We are less interested in the history of individual anthropologists and their interest in medicine and medical problems, or in the contributions of physicians to physical anthropology topics. It is possible, as Hasan recently has done, to argue that "the roots of contemporary medical anthropology . . . are traceable to the development of anthropology itself " (Hasan 1975:7).

If we are to take this approach, we must begin with the great German pathologist Rudolf Virchow, who in 1849 wrote, "In reality, if medicine is the science of the healthy as well as of the ill human being (which is what it ought to be), what other science is better suited to propose laws as the basis of the social structure, in order to make effective those which are inherent in man himself ? *Once medicine is established as anthropology,* and once the interests of the privileged no longer determine the course of public events, the physiologists and the practitioner will be counted among the elder statesmen who support the social structures. *Medicine is a social science in its very bone and marrow . . .* " (Quoted in Rather 1958:66. Emphasis added).

Yet in spite of these prophetic words, Virchow really had nothing to do with the origin of the contemporary field; a new field requires more than a brilliant flash of inspiration to bring it into being. New fields develop slowly; sciences constantly expand, and little by little areas of research previously ignored are taken up. When a sufficient number of researchers focus on the same, or related, topics, and as significant new data begin to appear, the stage is set for the emergence of a new discipline or subdiscipline. But some spark is essential to coalesce these emerging interests around a common focus; usually, it seems, an appropriate name supplies this spark.

We see this clearly in the history of medical anthropology. The first major survey of emerging anthropological (and other behavioral science) interests in the health field, published in 1953, was titled "Applied Anthropology in Medicine" (Caudill 1953). It was a brilliant *tour de force* but, for all the enthusiasm it inspired, it did not "create" a new subdiscipline. It was not until a decade later, when Scotch entitled a major survey article "Medical Anthropology" and Paul spoke of "medical anthropologists" in an article on medicine and public health (Scotch 1963a; Paul 1963), that American anthropologists fully appreciated the implications of health and illness research for anthropology.[2] Further legitimizing the new subdiscipline was the appearance the same year of the anthropologically oriented *Medical Behavioral*

Science (Pearsall 1963); the 3000 entries in this bibliography left no doubts about the importance of medical systems to anthropology.

THE ROOTS OF MEDICAL ANTHROPOLOGY

We trace contemporary medical anthropology to four rather different sources, each of which developed in relative (but not absolute) isolation from the others: (1) the interest of physical anthropologists in topics such as evolution, adaptation, comparative anatomy, racial types, genetics, and serology; (2) the traditional ethnographic interest in primitive medicine, including witchcraft and magic; (3) the "culture and personality" movement of the late 1930s and 1940s, with collaboration between psychiatrists and anthropologists; and (4) the international public health movement after World War II.

1. Physical anthropology

Long before there were "cultural" medical anthropologists, physical anthropologists taught and did research in schools of medicine, usually in departments of anatomy. Almost by definition, physical anthropologists are medical anthropologists, since their concern with human biology parallels and overlaps many of the interests of medical doctors. In fact, a significant number of physical anthropologists *are* medical doctors. By interest, and by association, physical anthropologists of an earlier period, as today, devoted much of their attention to topics of obvious medical significance. Hasan and Prasad (1959) list a number of these areas, including nutrition and growth, and the correlation of body build and a wide variety of diseases such as arthritis, ulcers, anemia, and diabetes. Anthropological studies of human growth and development are as much medical as anthropological, as is the study of serology.

Underwood and others have sought a broader understanding of disease processes by looking at the influences of human evolution and the differential exposure of populations affected by cultural factors such as migration, colonization, and the spread of urbanization (Underwood 1975:58). Fiennes goes so far as to argue that disease, as encountered in human populations, is a specific consequence of a civilized way of life, dating from the time when agriculture began to provide the basis for the rise and growth of expanded, heavily settled communities (Fiennes 1964:23-26).

For many decades physical anthropologists have engaged in "forensic medicine," an area of medico-legal problems involving identification as to age, sex, and race of human remains where foul play is suspected, and through blood types the determination of possible paternity when there is disagreement as to who the father of a child may be. Albert Damon, for example, served on the team of scientists appointed by the attorney general of the State of Massachusetts to act as an advisory board in the apprehension of the Boston Strangler.

In the development of preventive medicine physical anthropologists have contributed to research on the recognition of high-risk groups such as persons with sickle-cell anemia and carriers of hepatitis. They have also utilized their knowledge of human variation to aid in the field of "biomedical engineering," contributing to the development of appropriate arctic and tropical clothing and gear for American servicemen and for U.S. field stations. The astronauts' clothing as well as work spaces were built to anthropometrical specifications. "Measurements, norms, and standards derived from a host of anthropological studies are used in such areas as general and pediatric medicine and dentistry and in surveys of nutritional levels and etiology of disease in diverse populations as well as within a population. The list for applied biological anthropology is almost endless" (Damon 1975:366).

2. Ethnomedicine

The subdivision of medical anthropology today called "ethnomedicine" [i.e., "those beliefs and practices relating to disease which are the products of indigenous cultural development and are not explicitly derived from the conceptual framework of modern medicine" (Hughes 1968:99)], is the lineal descendant of the early interest of anthropologists in non-Western medical systems. Beginning with their earliest field research, 100 years or more ago, anthropologists routinely have gathered data on the medical beliefs of the peoples they studied, in the same way and for the same purpose that they have gathered data on all other aspects of culture: to have as complete an ethnographic record as possible. The diligence of early anthropologists, and of explorers and missionaries who also gathered data on the peoples whom they discovered, or among whom they worked, is well illustrated by the first comparative worldwide survey of beliefs about disease causation — now nearly half a century old — that cites 229 sources, a high proportion of them ethnographic (Clements 1932). Prior to Clements, the noted British physician/anthropologist W. H. R. Rivers published an epic-making study in the field of medical anthropology, titled *Medicine, Magic and Religion* (Rivers 1924). To Rivers we owe important and basic concepts, especially the idea that indigenous medical systems are social institutions to be studied in the same way as social institutions in general, and that indigenous medical practices are rational actions when viewed in the light of prevailing causation beliefs (cf. Wellin 1977:49). Counterbalancing this positive legacy, we may also note that it is Rivers, more than anyone else, who bequeathed to us the unfortunate stereotype that has dominated studies of primitive medicine almost to the present, the idea that religion, magic, and medicine are always intimately linked together, so that one can be studied only in terms of the others. This stereotype, uncritically accepted by a majority of anthropologists during the last half century, has severely limited us in our understanding of non-Western medical systems.

Needless to say, neither Rivers nor Clements nor any of their contemporaries engaged in collecting data on primitive medical systems had any idea that they were doing "medical anthropological" research, and they seem to have been unconcerned with the possible significance of their findings to the health of the people they studied. Consequently, we cannot say that medical anthropology has developed out of early research on primitive medicine; rather, it is the other way around. Anthropologists who today work in the health fields have "recaptured" and given a formal name — "ethnomedicine" — to the traditional study of non-Western medicine and made it a part of their specialty. As medical anthropology has developed, especially in the broad areas of international public health and transcultural psychiatry, the practical as well as theoretical importance of knowledge about non-Western medical systems has become apparent. This recognition has sparked renewed interest in ethnomedical research, elevating it to major importance in medical anthropology.

3. Culture and personality studies

Except for ethnomedical studies, done largely as a part of tribal studies, most health related publications by anthropologists prior to 1950 deal with psychological and psychiatric phenomena. Beginning in the mid-1930s, anthropologists, psychiatrists, and other behavioral scientists began to ask questions about adult personality, or character, and the sociocultural environment in which this character was displayed. Were adults what they were largely because of the infant's plasticity and its receptivity to the childhood conditioning that it received, as well as later life experiences? Or is there an inherent psychic constitution based on biological factors that plays a major role in determining culture and hence personality? These questions were triggered by a variety of observations about human behavior in different parts of the world. How, for example, could "arctic hysteria" in polar America and Asia be explained in the apparent absence of these symptoms in other societies? Or "running amok" in Southeast Asia? How could apparent "norms" of personality, so different in distinct cultures, be accounted for? Behavioral scientists, too, were interested in the possibilities of new "projective" tests, such as the Rorschach inkblot cards and the Thematic Apperception Test, shedding light on the functioning of the human mind, and thus affording clues to the answers of the questions being raised.

The range of topics that interested anthropologists and other behavioral scientists in this new field is illustrated by the titles of representative publications: "Anthropological data on the problem of instinct" (Mead 1942); *Doll Play of Pilagá Indian Children* (Henry and Henry 1944); "Sibling rivalry in

San Pedro" (Paul 1950); "Schizophrenia among primitives" (Demerath 1942); "Aggression in Saulteaux society" (Hallowell 1940); "Primitive psychiatry" (Devereux 1940); "Elements of psychotherapy in Navaho Religion" (Leighton and Leighton 1941); "Some points of comparison and contrast between the treatment of functional disorders by Apache shamans and modern psychiatric practices" (Opler 1936). Interestingly, almost all of this "medical" anthropology appears in psychiatric journals; very little is found in standard anthropology sources.

Although the great bulk of culture and personality research was theoretical in nature, a few anthropologists who were leaders in this movement were concerned with the ways in which anthropological knowledge could be used to raise levels of health care. Thus, Devereux studied the social structure of a schizophrenic ward with an eye to determining its therapeutic fitness (Devereux 1944), and the Leightons wrote a marvelous book showing the conflict between Navaho culture and society and the problems of introducing modern medical services to the Navahos (Leighton and Leighton 1944). At the same time, Alice Joseph, a physician and anthropologist, described the problem of interpersonal relations between white physicians and Indian patients in the American Southwest, showing how role perceptions and cultural differences prevented the most effective therapeutic interaction (Joseph 1942).

4. International public health

Although the Rockefeller Foundation had been engaged in international public health work since the early years of this century (e.g., Philips 1955, on the 1916-1922 hookworm campaign in Ceylon), it was only in 1942 that the U.S. government initiated cooperative health programs with the governments of a number of Latin American countries as a part of a broader technical assistance program. With the end of the war, with the extension of U.S. technical aid programs to Africa and Asia, and with the founding of the World Health Organization, major bilateral and multilateral public health programs in developing nations became a part of the world picture. Health workers in cross-cultural settings came to see far sooner than those working within their own cultures, and particularly those involved in clinical medicine, that health and disease are as much social and cultural phenomena as they are biological. They quickly realized that the health needs of developing countries could not be met simply by transplanting the health services of industrialized countries.

The corpus of data on primitive and peasant medical beliefs and practices that had been gathered by cultural anthropologists in earlier years, their information on cultural values and social forms, and their knowledge about the dynamics of social stability and change provided the needed key to many of the problems encountered in these early public health programs. Anthropologists were in a position to explain to health personnel how traditional beliefs and practices conflicted with Western medical assumptions, how social factors influenced health care decisions, and how health and disease are simply aspects of total culture patterns, which change only in the company of broader and more comprehensive sociocultural changes.

Beginning in the early 1950s, anthropologists were able to demonstrate the practical utility of their knowledge (and of their research methods) to international public health personnel, many of whom welcomed anthropologists with open arms. Anthropology provided insight into why many programs were less successful than had been hoped and, in some instances, anthropologists were able to suggest ways to improve programs. The anthropological approach was acceptable to public health personnel, too, because it did not threaten them as professionals. They saw it as a safe approach, in that it defined the problems of resistance to change as lying largely with the recipient peoples. Representative studies dealing with the early participation of anthropologists in cross-cultural and international health programs include Adams (1953), Erasmus (1952), Foster (1952), Jenny and Simmons (1954), Kelly (1956), Paul (1955), and Saunders (1954). We believe that it is this fourth, and last, of the "roots" of contemporary medical anthropology that, more than any other, precipitated the realization that here was a new, and major, subfield within anthropology, one whose potential at the time was only beginning to be sensed.

THEORETICAL AND APPLIED DIMENSIONS

As pointed out on page 1, the development of anthropological interest in health and disease problems in part has been theoretically motivated; since medical beliefs and practices constitute a major category in all cultures, a full account of any culture requires that the same attention be given to health institutions as is given to political, economic, social, religious, and all other institutions. Much of the research, too, in biomedical anthropology, has been theoretical in orientation. But in growing measure the anthropologist's interest in health and disease has had practical dimensions as well: much research has been "applied," carried out in conjunction with the medical personnel of health programs and projects, directed toward the end of improving health services, or toward the understanding of the behavioral components in the incidence of various diseases. By some, medical anthropology has been viewed as essentially an applied science. This was particularly true during the formative period of the 1950s, when public health physicians and anthropologists were jointly concerned with improving health levels in the developing world. It will be remembered that the first major survey of the field was, in fact, entitled "Applied Anthropology in Medicine" (Caudill 1953). A few anthropologists still see the applied dimension as the most significant. Weaver, for example, believes that "Medical anthropology is *that branch of applied anthropology* which deals with various aspects of health and disease" (Weaver 1968:1. Emphasis added).

Most medical anthropologists, however, at least implicitly subscribe to the model of the sociologist Straus. He speaks of the "sociology *of* medicine," the study of all aspects of medical institutions, "best carried out by persons operating from independent positions outside the formal medical setting." This is the theoretical side of the field. In contrast, "sociology *in* medicine" involves collaboration with medical personnel in research and often in teaching, activities in which concepts, techniques, and personnel from a number of disciplines are integrated (Straus 1957:203). Following Straus, we can speak of the *anthropology of medicine,* the theoretical side, and *anthropology in medicine,* the applied side.

Straus feels that the theoretical and applied branches of medical sociology are incompatible, that "the sociologist of medicine may lose objectivity if he identifies too closely with medical teaching or clinical research while the sociologist in medicine risks a good relationship if he tries to study his colleagues" (Straus 1957:203). In contrast, in our experience the distinction between the theoretical and the applied is largely analytic, a way of viewing the several aspects of the work, or of writing up research results. We find that, as with other applied work, research undertaken in an applied setting feeds basic data back into our corpus of culture theory, and that purely theoretical research (e.g. the study of the medical system of a Mexican village) has immediate value in practical programs, such as introducing new government health services in that village.[3]

Colson and Selby correctly note that while the field of medical anthropology grows rapidly, and there is a heightened sense of group identity among its members, there is "neither a widely shared definition of the field nor an agreement about its boundaries" (Colson and Selby 1974:245). In a pioneering definition Hasan and Prasad suggest that medical anthropology is "that branch of the 'science of man' which studies biological and cultural (including historical) aspects of man from the point of view of understanding the medical, medico-historical, medico-legal, medico-social and public health problems of human beings" (Hasan and Prasad 1959:21-22). A much later definition also makes explicit the biocultural dimension of the field: "Medical anthropology is concerned with the biocultural understanding of man and his works in relation to health and medicine" (Hochstrasser and Tapp 1970:245). Lieban simply says that medical anthropology "encompasses the study of medical phenomena as they are influenced by social and cultural features, and social and cultural phenomena as they are illuminated by their medical aspects" (Lieban 1973:1034). Fabrega defines the term on the basis of the content of the work performed. He defines a "medical anthropological inquiry" as one that "(a) elucidates the factors, mechanisms, and processes that play a role in or influence the way in which individuals and groups are affected by and respond to illness and disease, and (b) examines these problems with an emphasis on patterns of behavior" (Fabrega 1972:167).

We believe medical anthropology is best defined as formal anthropological activities concerned with health and disease. As a working definition, we suggest the following.

Medical anthropology is the term used by anthropologists to describe (1) their research whose goal is the comprehensive description and interpretation of the biocultural interrelationships between human behavior, past and present, and health and disease levels, without primary regard to practical utilization of this knowledge; and (2) their professional participation in programs whose goal is the improvement of health levels through greater understanding of the relationships between bio-sociocultural phenomena and health, and through the changing of health behavior in directions believed to promote better health.[4]

NOTES

[1] Coprolites are desiccated excrement specimens that, after chemical reconstitution, can be analyzed in much the fame fashion as fresh stool samples. The archaeologist was Professor Robert F. Heizer of the Department of Anthropology, University of California, Berkeley; the epidemiologist was Professor Frederick L. Dunn of the Department of International Medicine of the University of California, San Francisco. At the time these words are being written, the graduate student, Michael Kliks, is investigating the prevalence of intestinal parasites among *epazote*-eating peoples in Latin America.

[2] These are not, however, the first uses of the term "medical anthropology." In 1956 P. T. Regester used the expression to mean the study of the influence of social, genetic, environmental, and domestic factors on the incidence of human disease and disability in any population. Regester's orientation was clearly biocultural; he noted that such studies "include some aspects of physical and social anthropology" (Regester 1956:350). In 1959 Hasan and Prasad used the term "medical anthropology" in an important article in an Indian medical journal (Hasan and Prasad 1959). Since neither of these articles became widely known in the United States, their potential influence in crystalizing the concept of medical anthropology was not realized.

[3] See Foster 1969, Chapter 2, for discussion of the relationships between theoretical and applied anthropology.

[4] For a comparison between medical sociology and the social aspects of medical anthropology, see Foster (1974) and Olesen (1974).

chapter 2

Medical Anthropology and Ecology

ECOSYSTEMS AND SOCIOCULTURAL SYSTEMS

During recent years more and more anthropologists have become interested in biocultural-environmental health problems that are best studied from what Bates has described as the "ecological point of view" (M. Bates 1953:701). It is not surprising that the ecological point of view has proven congenial to anthropologists since, in reality, it is nothing more than the extension to all environments and their biotic communities of anthropology's fundamental approach: concern with systems. A "system," as defined in Webster's Second Dictionary, is "an aggregation or assemblage of objects united by some form of regular interaction or interdependence; a group of diverse units so combined by nature or art as to form an integral whole, and to function, operate, or move in unison."

In anthropology, of course, the "integral whole" is a sociocultural system or, to use the more common term, a culture. In ecology the integral whole is an *eco[logical] system,* "an interacting group of plants and animals, along with their nonliving environment" (Hardesty 1977:289). As Geertz points out this environment or "habitat" may range in size, complexity, and duration from a single drop of pond water with its microorganisms to the entire earth with all of its plant and animal life (Geertz 1963:3). More commonly the ecosystems studied by ecologists are things such as the Kalahari Desert with its plant, animal, and human life, the Arctic tundra, the Amazon rain forest, an Alpine meadow, or a tidal pool.

In both disciplines, as the dictionary definition points out, two primary questions underlie all enquiry. First, how are the diverse units that make up the system organized with respect to each other (i.e., what is their structural

11

arrangement, and what are their functional interdependencies)? Second, when the system is in motion (as it always is), how do these structural arrangements shift to form new alignments, and what are the consequences of these new alignments for the continued functioning of the system? The first question has to do with form and function; the second is a matter of dynamics.

To continue to function without grave disruption, both an ecosystem and a sociocultural system must maintain a minimum level of integration and inner consistency, a level sufficiently high so that the discrete units within the system can play their contributory roles toward each other. But integration cannot be complete for change, inevitable in nature, is possible only because the parts in its systems are not permanently locked into unchangeable positions. They change, impelled by a variety of dynamics, in form and in function and, in so doing, they bring changes, in form and function, to the elements to which they are functionally tied. To students of ecosystems and sociocultural systems this fact is of greatest importance, for in both disciplines scholars are primarily concerned with the systemic alterations that follow change and innovation.

THE ECOLOGICAL INTERESTS OF MEDICAL ANTHROPOLOGISTS

A considerable variety of terms has been used to describe the ecological themes that have interested anthropologists and their colleagues in related fields, pathologists, geographers, epidemiologists, sociologists, and a great many more. Thus we find human ecology, medical ecology, social ecology, ecology of disease, epidemiology, social epidemiology, and the like all used often in different and overlapping senses. The important thing, however, is topics, or areas of interests, and here we find fairly general agreement in the anthropological literature.

Medical anthropologists, almost by definition ecologically oriented, are concerned with the interrelationships between man's natural and social environments, his behavior, his diseases, and the ways in which his behavior and diseases have influenced his evolution and culture through feedback processes. Paleopathology, the study of the diseases of ancient man, tells us much about how our ancestors were influenced by the environments in which they lived and about their way of life. Knowledge about their diseases in turn helps us to understand human evolution, the ways in which succeeding generations of man adapted biologically (as well as culturally) to the health threats they encountered. In the contemporary world the ecological approach is basic to the study of epidemiological problems, the ways in which individual and group behavior bears on levels of health and the incidence of different diseases in different populations. The ecological point of view is especially useful in studying health problems in international developmental and modernization programs, for often, as we will see, narrowly conceived technological change projects are initiated without awareness that the changes, if achieved, will set in motion a long series of other changes, many of which will adversely affect health.

In ecological studies we begin with environment. Insofar as man is concerned, environment is both natural and sociocultural. All groups must adjust to the geographical and climatic conditions that prevail in the places they live, and they must learn to exploit the resources available to meet their needs. All groups, too, must adjust to the man-made milieu they create and within which their members live. It is an oversimplification, however, to say that there are two different types of environment; elements of the two often blend so that we are, in fact, dealing with a single environment. Disease, for example, is a part of the human environment. Disease involves pathology and, at one level, it is obviously biological. Yet sociopsychological and cultural factors often play roles in triggering disease, while the way in which a patient's environment is altered while he is undergoing care is purely cultural.

Disease, viewed as an element in man's environment, has influenced human evolution, as we will see shortly in the example of the proliferation of the sickle-cell trait among West Africans, an adaptive evolutionary change that gave its carriers relative immunity against malaria. Disease also plays a role in cultural evolution as, for example, in the cultural form of "little angels"; these are children in Catholic countries who are believed to go directly to heaven without passing through purgatory when they die young. Since to escape purgatory is viewed as good fortune, the little angel's wake and funeral may be marked by music, singing, dancing, and other manifestations of happiness. In traditional societies, where up to half of all children die before the age of five, this cultural form may be viewed as adaptive, assuaging in some degree the grief of parents and relatives.

Nutrition may also be viewed as a biocultural feature of environment. Nutrition cannot, of course, go beyond the limits of what is provided by the natural environment. But what parts of the nutrients available in a given environment that are defined as "food" — and are hence edible — is a matter of culture. Nutrition is also a part of the sociocultural environment in those situations where, for example, men eat first and receive most of the protein-rich foods, while women and children take what is left, often at great nutritional cost to them. The ways in which infants are fed may also be viewed as environmental. In many developing countries packaged infant formulas have had great commercial success, often replacing breast feeding in significant degree. Human milk, doctors agree, is the ideal infant food, always fresh, properly mixed, and easily kept sanitary. In contrast, packaged formulas are frequently improperly mixed, or contaminated water is used, causing diarrhea and other gastrointestinal upsets. Bottle or breast, an infant's food is very much a part of his environment.

In the following pages we will discuss a number of the principal topics that have drawn the attention of ecologically oriented anthropologists.

PALEOPATHOLOGY

Pathologists, anatomists, and physical anthropologists have learned a great deal about the diseases and injuries of prehistoric man. But there are limitations that will perhaps never be transcended that prevent us from knowing all we would like to know. For the most part, only diseases that produce visible evidence in bones can be identified. Deformities or abscesses in bones such as those resulting from syphilis, tuberculosis, yaws, osteomyelitis, poliomyelitis, leprosy, and the like are the only kinds of infectious diseases that can be recognized, for example. And even in cases like these, there are uncertainties: pathologists still argue whether syphilis was a pre-Conquest American disease brought back to Europe by Columbus' sailors, or whether it is of Old World origin (Kerley and Bass 1967:640-642). Arthritis, dental caries, rickets, and a number of other diseases can also be established from skeletal remains.

The soft tissues of artificially and naturally preserved mummies can tell us a good deal about infectious diseases. After early work on Egyptian mummies, with relatively primitive analytic techniques, this approach has lapsed. Cockburn recently has called for fresh studies, pointing out the kinds of evidence that ought to be encountered (Cockburn 1971:53) as a consequence of improved histological techniques. The newest technique in the analysis of the diseases of ancient man is the use of fecal matter (coprolites) which when reconstituted give invaluable information about the presence or absence of intestinal parasites. Coprolites are also giving exciting information about the diet of ancient man, particularly about the seeds and other grains he consumed. Paleopathologists likewise make use of art forms such as cave paintings, pictures on pots, human figures, wood, stone, and pottery, and the like. And, for much more recent times, the works of early medical writers and historians are highly useful, even though it is often impossible to be certain what diseases they are describing.

Returning to skeletal materials, the kinds of injuries found in ancient bones tell us about possible cannibalism, warfare, and other aspects of daily life. Wells, for example, points out how Peruvian skulls from early sites often show up to a dozen round depressed fractures, almost certainly caused by sling stones, which frequently are found in burial grounds (Wells 1964:19). Since the injuries are almost always well healed, it looks as if this form of battle, while painful, was not necessarily lethal. A more serious "double or triple depressed fracture of the cranial vault" resulted from the use of six-pointed "star-headed" maces as a favorite weapon (*Ibid.,* 49).

Although weapon wounds are among the most common of injuries to be found in skeletal materials, types and distributions of other injuries also enable us to infer cultural forms of a more prosaic nature. Anglo-Saxon burials reveal frequent leg fractures, often only of the fibula, a type of break characteristic of a fall in which the foot is twisted. Today, tripping over a curbstone is a common cause of such a break. Wells interprets this break in Anglo-Saxon burials as resulting from falls incurred while breaking and cropping rough ground. Clumsy footware may have contributed to frequent tripping. The frequency of an associated fracture of the arm about an inch from the wrist lends credence to this hypothesis, since this fall typically is produced by falling forward onto outstretched arms (Wells 1964:51-52).

A comparison of these Anglo-Saxon fractures with those of ancient Egyptian Nubians reveals different environmental and, presumably, cultural forms. Among the latter leg fractures were much less common than among the former, accounting for only about 10 percent of fractures in a series of nearly 6000 skeletons. Wells believes this low frequency compared to Anglo-Saxon farmers indicates that Egyptian lands were less rough and furrowed and, therefore, less likely to trip the unwary, and that barefoot people are more surefooted than those with heavily shod feet. Forearm fractures are found in 30 percent of the Nubian specimens. But, unlike the Anglo-Saxons, most are not wrist fractures, but midarm breaks of a type typically incurred in protecting the head against a blow. These breaks, says Wells, "point to short tempers and aggressive conduct being a common feature of the society and as many of them occur in females wife-beating or a generally low status of women may be implied. The mummy of a teenage girl has been found in which both forearms had been shattered in this way. When her efforts to protect her head proved unavailing her skull was crushed with a powerful blow. The fact that she was four or five months pregnant might have been the motive for this assault upon her" (Wells 1964:53).

Something about the diseases of ancient man and his adaptation to his environment can be inferred from the study of surviving hunting and gathering peoples such as the Bushmen of South Africa and the Australian aborigines. While it is true, as Polunin warns us, that primitive peoples should not be regarded as surviving examples of ancient peoples, nevertheless "it can be stated with some confidence that present day primitive men live under conditions which are more like those which were widespread in ancient days than those in advanced communities, and their disease patterns are probably more like those of ancient men, than those of modern sophisticated men" (Polunin 1967:70).

Perhaps the most important conclusion to be drawn from these studies, in conjunction with other evidence such as the behavior of genes and viruses, is that many of our modern diseases did not exist in ancient populations, and that "the spectrum of diseases that afflicted man through most of his development may have been much smaller than that to which we have been subject in historical times" (Black 1975:515). This is not to say that ancient man was healthier than modern man; in all likelihood the opposite is true. It is simply that ancient man's ills were caused by fewer varieties of pathogens and environmental factors than those of modern man. Measles, rubella, smallpox, mumps, cholera, and chicken pox, for example, probably did not exist in ancient times.

Cockburn (1971), among others, has summarized the evidence that leads to this conclusion. Many infections, he says, require minimum host populations for permanent maintenance, so the infections die out if sizes fall below a given threshold. For those diseases in which the infectious stages are brief and rapid transmission of the agents from one host to another is required, maintenance of the disease needs large numbers of susceptible persons to support the chain of transmission. The diseases listed in the previous paragraph are among those in this category. In the absence of a sufficiently large population to maintain the chain of transmission, any diseases of this type that are introduced will run their course and then die out.

In prehistoric times, hunting-gathering populations were small — bands of, at most, 200 to 300 persons. They were far too small to constitute reservoirs for the maintenance of infectious diseases of the types described. From the standpoint of the existence and survival of pathogens, a different kind of pathogen is needed, one that can survive for a long time until new hosts appear. "Natural selection will, therefore, favor those pathogens that can live in a kind of commensal relationship with their hosts and those that can continue to live away from their hosts. In a small population there would be no infections like measles, which spreads rapidly and immunizes a majority of the population in one epidemic, but many like typhoid, ameobic dysentery, pinta, trachoma, or leprosy, in which the host remains infective for long periods of time, and many like malaria, filaria and schistosomiasis, where the infection not only persists in the host for a long time but also has an outside vector or intermediate host to serve as an additional reservoir" (Cockburn 1971:50).

The health of hunting-gathering peoples is also affected positively by their nomadic habits; a people few in numbers and constantly on the go is less likely to reinfect itself from its fecal and other matters than is a large, settled population where, once infection is endemic, it is almost impossible to eradicate it, short of the most modern environmental sanitation practices.

Oddly, it was the invention of agriculture that appears to have done the most to multiply the kinds and frequencies of diseases suffered by man. As Neel puts it, " . . . the advent of civilization dealt a blow to man's health from which he is only now recovering" (Neel 1970:818). Although the more assured food supply that was made possible by agriculture (and the domestication of animals) resulted in great population growth, it was only at the cost of a vast upsurge in infectious diseases. In part this is because large populations provide reservoirs of infection not possible in small populations. And in part this is because intimate association with animals likely introduced new pathogens. As Cockburn points out, the smallpox virus is very similar to the cowpox virus, the measles virus belongs to the group containing dog distemper and cattle rinderpest viruses, and the influenza virus is closely related to viruses found in hogs (Cockburn 1971:51). Again, "Settled life, and the problem of sanitation in settled communities, must certainly have increased the rate of parasitism as the occasion for repeated reinfection and contamination with human wastes increased" (Underwood 1975:59).

The contrast between the potential for infectious diseases in hunting-gathering and agricultural populations has incited speculation with respect to population control. Throughout history a high infant mortality has been the most common explanation of the relatively slow growth of world population. Yet research among hunting-gathering peoples suggests that very high infant mortality among primitive peoples is not necessarily the rule. Neel, drawing conclusions from health research among the Xavante, Makiritaré, and Yanomamö Indians of the Amazon Basin, believes that the very slow increase in world population prior to the invention of agriculture "was probably not primarily due to high infant and childhood mortality rates from infectious and parasitic diseases . . . We find that relatively uncontacted primitive man under conditions of low population density enjoys 'intermediate' infant mortality and relatively good health, although not the equal of ours today" (Neel 1970:816). Neel believes that man's equilibrium with the resources of his environment was maintained by cultural forms, especially intercourse taboos, prolonged lactation, abortion, infanticide, and the like, all of which, combined, reduced the average *effective* birth rate to one child every 4 or 5 years (Neel 1970:816). To this list Bates adds homicide: "The effect of constant, attritional warfare among many primitive peoples is easy to see, and such warfare, through much of human prehistory, may have been the actual check on population growth" (M. Bates 1959:72).

But with the appearance of agricultural economies "more densely populated settled communities of humans would have proven more susceptible to the effects of infectious disease as a primary means of population control" (Underwood 1975:61). Foster's unpublished demographic data for the peasant village of Tzintzuntzan, Mexico, substantiates this conclusion. The average *effective* live birthrate is one child approximately every second year for women in the childbearing years, and crude birthrates as high as 50 per thousand have been the rule as recently as 1950. Traditionally intercourse taboos have been few, abortion seems to have been rare, and infanticide has been almost unknown. Homicide, while not infrequent, is limited to males, and warfare, except for the Mexican revolution early in the present century, has had no apparent effect on population. But infectious diseases have been the great killers, especially whooping cough, smallpox, and gastrointestinal ailments. In some years, as recently as the beginning of this century, up to 10 percent of the entire population of the village (including, of course, adults) has been wiped out by diseases, largely infectious! Only since about 1940 has there been a significant population increase in Tzintzuntzan, brought about by smallpox vaccination, other immunizations, a pure water supply, antibiotics, and other curative and preventive measures.

DISEASE AND EVOLUTION

Infectious diseases have been an important factor in human evolution for 2 million years or longer; it is through the mechanism of the evolution of "genetic protection" that our early ancestors were able to triumph over disease threats to individual and group life (Armelagos and Dewey 1970). The appearance of genes that provided resistance against malaria in a West African population is one of the most dramatic examples of this evolutionary process. In recent years Americans have read about a disease new to most of them, known as sickle-cell anemia, which is more likely to afflict blacks than other racial groups. This disease, marked by red corpuscles that take a falciform or sickle shape instead of the normal disc shape, is genetic in origin. Most individuals who develop the disease die young, and there is no known cure for it. Far more numerous than those who die are the blacks who carry the trait, or gene, in recessive form, which they may pass on to their children, but which does not affect their own health. Sickle-cell trait is coming to be recognized as a serious health threat to black people in the United States; through testing and genetic counseling, efforts are being made to control the spread of the gene.

In other environments, far from being a health threat, the sickle-cell trait is a desirable characteristic, since in malarial areas it confers a high degree of protection on individuals exposed to the bites of the *Anopheles* mosquito. Research in West Africa during the past generation has revealed how this protection against malaria has resulted in genetic selection in favor of individuals with the sickle-cell trait. This is of interest to medical anthropologists as perhaps the most striking example of how a specific disease — an environmental threat to health — can affect human evolution. In greatly simplified form, the evidence that led to this conclusion follows.

In many parts of West Africa the sickle-cell trait is found in up to 30 percent of the indigenous populations. There is a strong positive correlation between endemic malaria and sickle-cell trait; among all populations with trait frequencies greater than 15 percent, malaria is endemic. There are, however, groups with low frequencies of the sickle-cell trait. This seems particularly to characterize the remnants of the earliest known peoples of West Africa, many of whom have been forced into peripheral areas of deep forest by later migrants from the east. True forest-dwelling peoples appear to suffer very little malaria. This is because the *Anopheles gambiae,* the most important malaria vector in West Africa, cannot breed in very shaded water such as that found in undisturbed tropical rain forests.

But with a settled agricultural population and the felling of the forest for planting, ideal conditions for *A. gambiae* are created. In West Africa, agricultural peoples coming from the east began to replace the original inhabitants about 2000 years ago. Until this time the tropical rain forest was agriculturally unattractive, both because of difficulties in clearing it with stone tools and because of the low yields of the first African cultigens, millet and sorghum. But with the simultaneous introduction of iron working and a high-yielding yam, the *Disocorea latifolia,* perhaps domesticated in Nigeria, the stage was set for a dramatic environmental change. Forests were felled, villages became permanent, and the *A. gambiae* multiplied. The sickle-cell trait, already present in the Bantu-speaking populations that took advantage of these new techniques, thus had a selective advantage over the non-sickle-cell gene because of the relative immunity it conferred and, presumably, its frequency increased significantly. "Therefore," concludes Livingstone, from whom most of the foregoing is drawn, "the spread of this agriculture is responsible for the spread of the selective advantage of the sickle cell gene, and hence for the spread of the gene itself" (Livingstone 1958:555). On a broader theoretical level, he concluded that "The sickle cell gene thus seems to be an evolutionary response to this changed disease environment. Hence, this gene is the first known genetic response to a very important event in man's evolution when disease became a major factor determining the direction of that evolution" (*Ibid.,* 557).[1]

In a later article Wiesenfeld describes the sickle-cell trait as a "biological solution to a cultural problem." From this he draws a general proposition of the widest significance: "Where a socioeconomic adaptation causes a change in the environment, the frequency of a gene will change in proportion to the survival value the gene confers on the carriers in the new ecosystem. Increasing frequencies of an adaptive gene remove environmental limitations and allow further development of the socioeconomic adaptation" (Wiesenfeld 1967: 317).

DIET AND EVOLUTION

Like disease, diet is also an environmental characteristic that influences human evolution. Stini has described some aspects of this process as it affects body size. Our primate ancestors, he points out, were tree dwellers, largely but not entirely herbivorous, who reached a weight of about 70 pounds prior to the time when, perhaps 2 million years ago, they descended to earth to become omnivorous hunter-gatherer-scavengers. During these 2 million years, man spread over most of the habitable earth and increased significantly in body and brain size, presumably at least partly in response to the animal protein that had become a part of his diet. Only a diet adequate in quantity and balance would have favored this growth. But with agriculture and with frequent reliance on a limited number of vegetable nutrients, nutritional imbalances may lead to shortages of some of the amino acids essential to growth and development of tissue. Among children one common result is the protein-calorie deficiency disease known as kwashiorkor. Other consequences are a slowing of the rate of growth; in the peasant agricultural village of Heliconia he studied in Colombia, Stini found men did not attain their maximum stature until 26 years of age (Stini 1971:1025). Although both males and females retained normal body proportions, the population was marked by a "general miniaturization." "The proportional reduction in body size in all members of a population where protein resources are severely restricted," writes Stini, "would be adaptive in the sense that more individuals could survive on the available resources, each individual possessing a proportionately small amount of metabolizing tissue with a concomitant reduction in nutritional requirements" (*Ibid.,* 1027). In time these reductions would become genetically fixed by natural selection, continues Stini, just as a large, robust body was genetically fixed by 2 million years of man's career as a hunter-gatherer-scavenger. But, he says, the reduction in body size found among many tropical agricultural peoples "is more likely an example of evolution in process, i.e., an example of man's adaptability or plasticity, rather than a true adaptation in a genetic sense" (*Ibid.,* 1027). Eight to ten thousand years, Stini feels, is insufficient time for the multiple genetic changes to take place that would produce a reduced body size.

Another interesting study that shows a possible relationship between nutrition and man's capacity to adapt in his evolutionary course has to do with adult consumption of milk. Anthropologists long ago noted that adults in agricultural Japanese and Chinese populations, among other groups, usually did not drink milk. This they attributed to "custom," a culturally based aversion comparable to the usual American repugnance at the thought of eating rattlesnake. Yet recent research suggests the possibility that most adult nonmilk drinkers are such for good reason: to drink milk causes physiologically induced gastric discomfort in the form of diarrhea and stomach cramps. Since most Europeans and their descendents in other parts of the world, as well as cattle-herding East Africans and numerous other peoples, tolerate milk as adults, this aversion cries for explanation. McCracken recently has suggested an intriguing hypothesis.

Lactose (or milk sugar), he points out, is the only significant carbohydrate as well as the predominant solid in milk, itself a complex natural food composed of water, fat, proteins, enzymes, vitamins, and other ingredients and trace elements. Milk, like other foods, must be metabolized in order to be used by the body. Some simple carbohydrates can be absorbed, or metabolized, directly by the human body; other more complex carbohydrates must be converted into the simple form before this can be done. Lactose falls into this second category, and its conversion is made possible by the presence of lactase, a genetically controlled enzyme. All normal human infants produce sufficient lactase to metabolize the lactose in milk and milk products, but many adults lose this ability. These are the ones who suffer upset stomachs when they consume milk and milk-based foods. McCracken (and other researchers) suggests a genetic interpretation to account for some if not all of this variation in lactase levels. According to this interpretation lactase deficiency in many adults represents a genetic survival from a time before adult humans began to drink milk (i.e., throughout human history prior to the invention of dairying). Adult humans, the reasoning goes, like other adult mammals, were naturally lactase-deficient. Since this trait would not adversely affect their survival, there was no selective evolutionary pressure to develop increased lactase production. But, where dairying developed beginning more than 5000 years ago, through the forces of natural selection adults began to develop the capacity to continue to produce lactase throughout their lives. "In those environments," he writes, "where lactose constitutes a significant portion of the adult diet, the lactase-deficient individual is at a selective disadvantage in comparison with the lactase-producing individual. In such environments, over long periods of time, adult lactase-producers will tend to be established at the expense of the lactase-deficient, and the dominant gene for adult lactase production will significantly predominate numerically over the recessive gene for adult lactase deficiency. *Thus dietary habits and traditions may generate selective pressures which favor one genotype over another*" (McCracken 1971:484. Emphasis added).

EPIDEMIOLOGY

In the biocultural-environmental themes we have dealt with so far in this chapter, we have been concerned with the work of anthropologists in conjunction with that of pathologists, biochemists, medical doctors, and ecologists. When we turn to epidemiological studies, in the present and in the recent past, we must take note of the work of medical sociologists who, more than any other group of behavioral scientists, have made this their special field. Briefly defined, epidemiology deals with the distribution in space and the prevalence or incidence of diseases as influenced by natural and man-made environments and by human behavior. The variables most commonly dealt with by sociologists and medical epidemiologists in their studies are things such as age and sex differences, marital status, occupations, ethnic affiliation and social class, individual behavior, and natural environment.

All of these, and many other factors, have been demonstrated to bear importantly on the distribution and prevalence of different diseases. Young American males, for example, are much more likely to die as the result of accidents than are young females or older people of either sex. Workers in asbestos industries run high risks with respect to pulmonary asbestosis and lung cancer; university professors do not. Cigarette smokers are far more likely to die of lung cancer or cardiovascular diseases than are nonsmokers. Inland areas, particularly mountainous ones, are particularly apt to have a high incidence of goiter, as compared to populations that live near the sea and have access to iodine-rich seafood.

The epidemiologist, says the sociologist Clausen, views his task as "establishing the correlates of disease incidence in order to secure clues to the complex patterns of disease causation or to possibilities of disease control" (Clausen 1963:142). The correlates of disease are established primarily by means of population surveys to discover the relationship between the occurrence of disease and the presence of biological, physical, and social factors. "The kind of 'proof' that it tries, for the most part, to obtain is statistical association between the presumed 'causal' factor and the occurrence of the disease" (Suchman 1968:98).

Epidemiology is goal oriented in that its primary purpose is to raise levels of health, to reduce the incidence of all health threats. In its history it has had notable successes. Goiter, for example, was early determined to be the result of a dietary deficiency of iodine, a deficiency easily remedied by iodized commercial salt. As far back as the 1850s, in the famous Broad Street pump incident in London, John Snow demonstrated that typhoid fever was spread by contaminated water and that people who drank pure water were unlikely to come down with the disease. And current research more and more leads to the conclusion that a high proportion of cancers are caused by environmental factors, many of which can be altered or controlled to lead to lower incidences of this dread disease (Cairns 1975). The "practical" end of epidemiological studies is evidenced by the fact that it is the scientific base for a large part of the profession of public health.

In contrast to sociologists, anthropologists have been more interested in the epidemiological characteristics of the diseases of non-Western peoples including, often, the so-called "culture-specific" syndromes such as arctic hysteria, amok, Canabis or *ganja* psychoses (e.g., Rubin and Comitas 1976), *koro, latah, windigo,* and the like. Although population surveys and statistical analyses are appropriate in these studies when possible, as in much anthropological research, samples that would be considered statistically valid by other social scientists are hard to assemble. Many of the conclusions, therefore, are drawn from observations of behavior and from knowledge of cultural forms. Sometimes, as in the case of *kuru,* research takes on the characteristics of detective work, the search for the elusive variable that is the key to explanation.

Anthropologists have also been greatly interested in what may be called the "epidemiology of development," the health consequences — often deleterious — of technological development projects. Increased incidences of "river blindness," which often follow in the wake of man-made lakes, and the spread of bilharziasis (or schistosomiasis) as the consequence of irrigation schemes, are illustrative of the kinds of epidemiological problems studied by anthropologists in developing countries. Since readers who are interested in more information about classical epidemiology, its history, and its present practice in the United States can find good information in almost all medical sociology texts, we propose in the pages that follow to concern ourselves with the more purely anthropological concerns just mentioned.

THE MYSTERY OF KURU

In the mid-1950s a new disease — *kuru* — previously unknown to medical science, was discovered in a single linguistic group, the South Fore, of the Eastern Highlands of New Guinea, with a population of about 15,000. The South Fore people conform to the general culture patterns of other indigenous groups in the Eastern Highlands. A striking feature of this pattern is marked separation between the lives of men and women. The former live, eat, and sleep in a men's house, spending most of their time in legal disputes, feuds, raids, and ceremonies. While they do the initial clearing of fields, most of the agricultural work is carried out by their wives, who live in small round huts with their children and the family pigs. In the mid-1950s South Fore women, like the women in neighboring tribes, practiced ritual cannibalism, eating the bodies, and especially the brains, of their deceased kinswomen. After government pacification of the Eastern Highlands, strenuous and successful efforts were made to stamp out this aspect of native life.

Kuru showed unusual epidemiological characteristics. It is limited almost entirely to women and to children; although young men occasionally come down with it, it is not a threat to adult male health. In contrast, in some villages nearly half of all adult female deaths, and most of the deaths of children between the ages of five and sixteen, were due to kuru. Kuru is not found among any tribesmen from adjacent groups, even those with whom there is a good deal of contact. Neither has it ever been passed on to a European. South Fore young men working away from their homes occasionally developed kuru, but their workmates from other areas remained unaffected. Through government genealogical tables it was apparent that kuru strongly followed family lines.

Kuru is marked by progressive deterioration of the central nervous system, leading to complete incapacitation and, often, inability to swallow. Death, usually within 6 to 12 months of the first symptoms, but occasionally delayed for up to 2 years, results from complications such as starvation, pneumonia, or bed sores. No known treatment will arrest, must less cure, kuru. Here, obviously, was a mystery crying for a solution.

The solution was worked out over more than a decade by combining field observation and laboratory experiments and the insights of scientists representing many fields. The virologist-anthropologist Carleton Gajdusek stands first among these researchers; he dedicated most of his professional life to this problem for many years following his first 10-month visit to the South Fore in 1957. Recognition of the importance of his contribution came when, in 1976, he was awarded the Nobel Prize for Physiology of Medicine. The various hypotheses first put forward to explain kuru "read like the players' repertoire in *Hamlet* — genetic, infectious, sociological, behavioral, toxic, endocrine, nutritional, immunologic" (Alpers 1970:134), with the genetic explanation seeming most plausible in the light of the tendency of the disease to run in family lines and to be restricted to the South Fore people. This explanation, however, had one very serious limitation: it required that a dominant or partly dominant mutation that must have arisen in a single individual centuries before had such a selective advantage that it would spread to several thousand descendants of the original carrier. Yet a highly lethal gene, such as that hypothesized to explain kuru, could hardly have had such an advantage. Moreover, according to local accounts kuru had first appeared only about 50 years earlier, well within the memory of the older men of the tribe.

The breakthrough came in 1959 when another epidemiologist noted pathologic similarities between kuru and a sheep disease known as scrapie. Scrapie was found to be caused by a filterable agent transmissible to sheep but which, unlike most viruses, produced the disease only after a long incubation period, of a year or more. "Slow virus infections" is the term now applied to diseases that conform to this pattern. The fact of scrapie's transmissibility suggested a laboratory experiment, the inoculation of chimpanzees with brain suspensions from natives who had died of kuru, which was carried out beginning in 1963. After a long incubation period, the chimpanzees succumbed to the disease. Later various species of New and Old World monkeys developed the disease after similar inoculations and even longer incubation periods. Kuru thus has the distinction of being the first human illness known to be caused by a slow-acting virus.

The laboratory evidence of nonhuman primates, however, did not explain a curious development among the South Fore; kuru, in full bloom in the 1950s, began to decline rapidly in the 1960s, so that by 1970 preadolescent children no longer fell ill. Nor did it explain the curious age-sex distribution of kuru. It is here that the ethnographic work of a pair of social anthropologists, Robert and Shirley Glasse, enters the picture. They found that, according to local traditions, cannibalism among South Fore women was a relatively recent introduction, first appearing about 1910 (i.e., at the same time the disease made its appearance). This custom, borrowed from neighboring tribes, was soon ritualized as a part of the mourning ceremonies: surviving women relatives were expected to cook and eat the brains of their deceased kinswomen, with leftover tidbits going to children of both sexes. But since the brains often were not thoroughly cooked, the virus present in the woman who died a victim of kuru was transmitted to her female kin and to children in the family. The recent rapid decline in new cases of kuru is explained as due to the success of the Australian government in eliminating cannibalism. In other words, with the cessation of cannibalism we can assume that eventually kuru will die out. This explanation today is accepted by virtually all epidemiologists who have worked on the problem; remaining to be answered is the question of where the virus came from and how it was harbored prior to 1910.[2]

ECOLOGY AND DEVELOPMENT

The recent American ecology movement to the contrary, for most of the world's people the word "development" has a positive connotation. It is, they believe, through "development," the rational utilization of a nation's human and physical resources, that poverty will be eliminated, education become universal, disease be brought under control, and standards of living made acceptable. The concept of development implies man's technological intervention in the balance of nature: the building of dams, the clearing, leveling, and irrigating of fields, the construction of highways, schools, and hospitals, the drilling of oil wells, the opening of mines, and the erection of factories. In the broad sense man's developmental activities are not new; they can be traced back at least to the Neolithic period when agriculture first began in major fashion to modify the ecological balance that had underlain a hunting-fishing-gathering type of subsistence. With the coming of the industrial revolution in Europe, the pace of man's intervention in nature rapidly stepped up, and air pollution first became known. With impure air, lack of sanitation, and crowded living, the first city slums that accompanied the industrial revolution had health consequences that we have not yet fully solved. But however note-worthy these early forms of development, in scale and complexity they cannot compare to the contemporary worldwide rush to "modernize."

Development, of course, is here to stay; there is no reasonable alternative in a crowded world. But there is "good" development, and there is "bad" development, the former that in which a given population is, on balance (if such a balance can actually be measured), better off than before development, and the latter that in which a population is worse off. This is because, as noted at the beginning of this chapter, changes do not occur in isolation. Cultures are delicately balanced systems which do not change piecemeal, and seemingly beneficial innovations in one area (e.g., agriculture) may turn out to produce secondary and tertiary changes in another area (e.g., health) that may out-weigh the anticipated benefits narrowly viewed. Almost always there are "un-foreseen consequences of planned innovation" (Foster 1962:79-86), some of which may be good, but many of which turn out to be undesirable.

DuBos has phrased the culturally oriented "unforeseen consequences" model in ecological terms. "All technological innovations," he writes, "whether concerned with industrial, agricultural, or medical practices, are bound to upset the balance of nature. In fact, to master nature is synonymous with disturbing the natural order" (DuBos 1965:416). While DuBos, like many others, believes that it is "desirable in principle" to maintain a balance of nature, he recognizes that it is extremely difficult to define an operational meaning of the idea. "Nature is never in a static equilibrium because the interrelationships between its physical and biological components are endlessly changing. Furthermore, man placed himself apart from the rest of nature when he began to farm the land and even more when he became urbanized" (*Ibid.,*

416). The die was cast millenia ago; the problem is not whether we will upset nature but, rather, how to change it so that innovations will be beneficial and not deleterious.

Hughes and Hunter express the same ideas in slightly different words. Any programs, they write, that change preexisting relationships between man and his environment must be looked at within an ecologic framework. "They must be viewed as the forging, as it were, of a new 'ecological contract' between man and his surroundings, a contract which usually has hidden costs" (Hughes and Hunter 1970:479).

From the very beginnings of their discipline, anthropologists have been interested in how cultures change. In the post-World War II era much of this interest has had to do with the "social consequences of technological change," the hidden costs as well as the obvious benefits of developmental programs. The ecological point of view provides an ideal perspective for studies of developmental change, since most of the projects analyzed involve intervention in nature. The concept of "hidden costs" applies to all kinds of change, of course, but in the present context we are concerned primarily with health costs. Here we are in the mainstream of epidemiology, for we find that the critical variables that concern us are environment and human behavior. The environment that draws our attention is not primarily an unadulterated natural environment, but a natural environment massively worked over by man to the extent that a major new "ecological contract" must be drawn up. Cities and their factories and slums are a major element in this environment; so are man-made lakes and resettled populations, newly cleared agricultural lands, and highways. Although we tend to think of development as essentially a physical process, it is also social and economic, involving things such as mass migrations, cash cropping, credit facilities, and many more activities that influence human health and well-being. In the pages that follow our purpose is not to give an overview of what may be called "developmental epidemiology," but to illustrate with a few examples the kinds of health problems that are related to development.

We begin by noting what is fairly obvious: low health levels in general, and some specific diseases, seriously inhibit development. In the case of the Panama Canal it was yellow fever that defeated the French engineer DeLessup in his first attempt to dig a canal; only after American doctors discovered the cause of yellow fever, and after the mosquito vector was eliminated, was it possible to finish the canal. Until recent years endemic malaria has left many fertile, tropical lowlands almost uninhabited, and sleeping sickness caused by the tsetse fly severely limits the exploitation of much of Africa. And, in a chronically ill population, absenteeism from factory and field takes a serious economic toll.

Hence, disease itself is a major instigator of many developmental programs; plans for its eradication are primary elements in many of them and sometimes, as in the smallpox eradication program, the main project itself.

Finally, successful development often significantly increases the incidence of certain diseases, creating health problems formerly absent or relatively minor. Paradoxically, success in control or elimination of infectious diseases has its hidden health costs. It is just this success that has led to the population explosion which, many of us believe, is the greatest of all threats to the future of humanity. It is quite possible, too, that because of population growth, for all of modern medicine's success in controlling disease, there is just as much illness on a worldwide scale as there was a century ago.

We are thus faced with a disease-induced circular chain of events. Disease inhibits development; it therefore acts as a stimulant to produce the development of health services and disease control, which permit other kinds of development; in the wake of these developmental "successes" often come overpopulation and more disease, and the cycle begins again.

DISEASES OF DEVELOPMENT

Not all diseases are equally influenced by development, although it is likely that all illness equilibriums are influenced by developmental changes to some degree. There are, however, a few diseases whose prevalence has been so greatly expanded through developmental activities that Hughes and Hunter suggest calling them "diseases of development" or, using the analogy of "iatrogenic" diseases that result from medical treatment, "developo-genic" diseases (Hughes and Hunter 1970:481). Among the important diseases that would fall into this classification are trypanosomiasis (sleeping sickness), bilharziasis (also called schistosomiasis), river blindness (ochoncerciasis), filariasis, malaria, poor health resulting from malnutrition, and perhaps tuberculosis and chronic illnesses in general. These result from relatively few causes, chief among which are man-made lakes, irrigation agriculture, road building with resultant labor migration and trade, the shift from subsistence to cash crop farming, and rapid urbanization. In the following paragraphs we will examine briefly the epidemiological implications of some of these activities, as reflected in disease incidences.

1. River basin development

Since World War II no developmental projects have so changed the face of the earth as have the enormous man-made lakes, such as Lake Nasser on the Egypt-Sudan border, that have appeared on all of the inhabited continents. The rationale for these lakes and the dams that make them possible is much the same: flood control, hydroelectric power, irrigation agriculture and, perhaps, lesser benefits such as fishing and other water-related activities. Laudable as these goals are, many projects have had highly deleterious health consequences, of which the most serious have been the increase in bilharziasis and ochoncerciasis.

Found particularly in Africa, but also in South America, the Near East, and the Orient, bilharziasis is caused by any one of several species of a parasitic blood fluke of the genus *Schistosoma,* vectored by a water snail. The life cycle of the schistosome is complex and exceedingly difficult to break at any point. After adult schistosomes breed in the veins around the human bladder and bowel, their fertilized eggs pass to the urine and feces. If excreted fertilized eggs reach water they hatch into larvae that can survive up to about 6 hours. If they come into contact with a snail of the right species during this time, they make the snail their abode for about 6 weeks, after which they emerge in a second larval form that is able to penetrate the skin of any human they encounter in the water. After 2 months of further development in the human host, and now adult schistosomes, they again reach the veins around the bladder and bowel where they mate, and the cycle starts anew. Bilharziasis, while extremely dehabilitating, is usually not a killer in its own right. Instead, it attacks various organs of the body, such as the bowel, genitourinary tract, kidneys, liver, spleen, heart, and lungs, and causes progressively more serious malfunctions, so that death may be recorded under any one of a number of causes. Bilharziasis is curable, but the treatment is lengthy and often accompanied by unpleasant side effects. Moreover, the disease confers no immunity to subsequent exposure, and reinfection rates are high.

In recent decades the number of sufferers from bilharziasis has grown rapidly to a worldwide total of perhaps 200 million. One authority believes it is "probably the fastest spreading and most pathogenic parasitic disease of man" (Heyneman 1971:301). This spread is almost entirely the result of newly irrigated lands made possible by high dams and their stored water. For example, within 3 years of the completion of the Nassar High Dam in Egypt, the infection rates in children in the areas affected between the ages of two and six rose from a range of 5-25 percent to 55-85 percent (Miller 1973:15). Similarly, in the construction area of the Volta Dam in Ghana, the host snails for the *Schistosoma* parasite had yet to be found in the early 1960s. Yet the ecological balance was upset so rapidly by this dam that by 1972 more than 70 percent of a sample of 1000 children in a lakeside study area within 10 miles of the dam were infected (Scudder 1973:50). These, and other similar rapid increases in the incidence of bilharziasis, stem from the fact that the slow-flowing and semistagnant waters of irrigation ditches and irrigated fields provide the ideal environment for the snail vector. Through irrigation nature forges a new "ecological contract," but it is a contract whereby man sometimes is the loser.

Although its impact is much less than that of bilharziasis, ochoncerciasis (or "river blindness") increasingly threatens the well-being of many peoples living along the banks of tropical rivers and lakes. The fly vector that thrives in this environment bites the victim on the back of the neck, depositing eggs that hatch into larvae that destroy the optic nerve. Blindness can be prevented if the cyst that results from the bite is surgically excised but, with the limited medical resources of developing countries, this control is only modestly effective, and reinfection is always a likelihood.

2. Land reclamation

Land reclamation and "rational" agriculture, often a part of river basin development projects, sometimes have deleterious health effects. Miller (1973) gives a number of examples. In the Caribbean littoral systematized agriculture provided the conditions for an increase in the breeding of the *Anopheles* variety that transmits malaria; the sunlit waters provided by rice plantations, irrigation canals, and water troughs were, from the standpoint of the mosquito, preferable to its natural environment. In Malaya rubber plantations were established in malaria-free areas but, after clearance of the native forest, ideal conditions were established for the breeding of *Anopheles maculatus,* with a consequent introduction of malaria. The same thing occurred in a south India area where clearance of native cover in uninhabited hills encouraged the breeding of *A. fluviatilis,* followed by the introduction of malaria. Clearly, the cultural innovations postulated by Livingstone to explain the sickle-cell trait in prehistoric West Africa are being repeated today.

3. Road construction

Some diseases which were localized or spread slowly in an earlier time are propagated to previously free areas as a result of rapid mass communication made possible by roads, railroads, and air travel. Trypanosomiasis (sleeping sickness) is one such disease in large parts of Africa. A tsetse fly vectored protozoal disease, it affects not only man, but has immense natural reservoirs in domestic and wild animals. The flies prefer waterways and brush-covered country. With new roads, river crossings are attractive stopping points for travelers to drink, bathe, and otherwise refresh themselves; here they run the risk of tsetse fly bites and sleeping sickness infection. Migrant labor, made possible by roads, plays a major role in the dissemination of this disease. In Ghana migrant laborers from the north of the country passing through the tsetse fly belt on their way to work in the Ashanti area spread the disease so thoroughly that Ashanti came to have higher rates of infection than the north, where the disease was endemic (Hughes and Hunter 1970: 452-453). "Roads are thus linear-type transmission sites, and modern roads built for economic development consequently may constitute a major health hazard in endemic regions, their very purpose being to encourage movement and mixture of peoples and goods but having, as implicated effects, the facilitation of man-vector contacts for several different kinds of insect-borne diseases" (*Ibid.,* 453).

4. Urbanization

The migration of village peoples to crowded urban slums causes a variety of health problems. In the shanty towns surrounding the core cities in almost all Third World countries living conditions are crowded, dirty, and unsanitary. Frequently there is no potable water system, and water-borne diseases, particularly dysentery, are endemic. As in early industrial England, tuberculosis rates are often very high. Frequent malnutrition also contributes to lowered resistances to many diseases. Traditional peoples long settled in the same environment usually acquire an unconscious folk wisdom insofar as exploiting the nutritional resources of their homeland is concerned. But in an urban context, tempted by soft drinks, candies, and high-carbohydrate packaged foods, this folk wisdom means very little. The nutritionally wise allocation of food money is not something that is easily learned; consequently, new urban dwellers often suffer significant nutritional deficiencies.

A nutrition-based urban health problem that is attracting increasing attention from public health personnel is the widespread and growing use of patented infant formulas in developing countries. Sometimes mothers work in factories, and they have no alternative but to leave their infants with grandmothers and other women for bottle feeding. And some mothers, of course, perhaps badly nourished themselves, simply do not have sufficient milk for their babies. More often, however, mothers seem to be the victims of overzealous advertisers who seek to persuade mothers that bottle feeding is the "modern" and "progressive" thing to do, and that commercial formulas are nutritionally superior to human milk. Whatever the motivation for bottle feeding, the consequences frequently are deleterious to the health of the child. Illiterate nurses may use too much or too little formula, or the water in which it is mixed may be contaminated. In all these cases, the infant suffers.[3]

5. Public health programs

As we have already noted, and paradoxical as it may seem, environmental sanitation and other programs designed to control disease may actually worsen the situation or simply shift the problem from one disease to another. In northern Malaya house spraying largely eliminated the indigenous vector mosquito that lived in houses, on walls, and in thatched roofs. This opened the way for forest-dwelling species of *Anopheles* to move in on a new human source of blood, feeding on people without alighting on walls, and then returning to the jungle, where no spray could reach them. New outbreaks of malaria from an uncontrollable haven of infection was the result (Heyneman 1971:-305). Attempts to persuade desert-dwelling villagers to construct "sanitary" latrines have been known to backfire. In Iran in the early 1950s American public health consultants insisted, in the face of visible evidence to the contrary, that defecation in the open air would produce flies. In fact, the dry atmosphere quickly dries fecal matter, and flies do not breed. The advisers, however, insisted that latrines must be built which, when installed in numbers and poorly maintained, became fly breeders (Foster 1962:180). In 1959 a yellow Cuban maize was introduced into the eastern lowlands of Bolivia. This maize, nutritionally superior to the indigenous variety, seemed to be an excellent device to improve the diet of both humans and animals. Unfortunately, its hardness, desirable from the standpoint of storage, made it difficult to grind, and the people were unwilling to take the time to haul it to commercial mills in towns. The maize, however, makes excellent alcohol in home stills, so that a seemingly desirable innovation promoted alcoholism instead of better nutrition (Kelly 1959:9-10).

A final example of a well-intentioned project going awry comes from the Ryukyu Islands. Trachoma, an infectious disease that leads to blindness, is caused by a virus thought to spread from person to person by direct contact or indirectly by water, towels, or clothing. With good environmental sanitation and pure water, trachoma prevalence is low or absent. This is true in the Ryukyus in areas with pure water and good environmental sanitation. But incidences run as high as 40 percent where these conditions do not prevail. Scarcity of water, particularly, and the subsequent use of a single bowl for washing by a number of people is an easy way in which the virus is passed on. In an effort to control trachoma, schoolchildren in water-abundant areas are required to wash their hands and faces before being allowed to eat. But, since the schools lack funds for individual paper towels, handkerchiefs are pressed into service; a single one is used by as many as ten children to dry their hands and faces. "Thus it is almost certain that trachoma is transmitted from child to child in this manner" (Marshall 1972:11).[4]

There are other important ecological topics and health problems associated with development that quite properly might be included in a more comprehensive review of the field. One such topic, for example, is the implication of increased stress that often characterizes people who are undergoing rapid urbanization; in cultures as different as the Zulu (Scotch 1963b) and western North Carolina (Tryoler and Cassel 1964), it has been found to be associated with increased hypertension and/or coronary disease. The epidemiology of psychosocial disorders in situations of rapid change also merits discussion; a good deal of evidence indicates that an increase in such disorders is the consequence of stressful living conditions (e.g., Hughes and Hunter 1970:-474-479). Although we have not been able to cover all the points that ideally should be considered in a discussion of medical ecology, other relevant themes such as the nutritional consequences of migration from country to city and additional health problems in development are dealt with in chapters 14 and 15.

NOTES

[1] Thalassemia, or Mediterranean anemia, is a similar genetically caused condition that also gives protection against malaria. In Europe and the Near East it is found in former areas of endemic malaria; it is also found in a belt across Asia to India, Indonesia, and Japan. Paleopathologic research on skeletal materials going back to Bronze Age farmers in the eastern Mediterranean lead Angel to believe that malaria was endemic long before 2000 B.C. in this area, and that thalassemia represents a selective advantage in human evolution in that it conferred greater protection on human beings than would be had by those lacking the trait (Angel 1964).

[2] There is an extensive literature on kuru. In preparing this summary we have drawn especially on Alpers (1970), Alpers and Gajdusek (1965), Burnet and White (1972: 256-261), Fischer and Fischer (1961), Gajdusek (1963, 1973), Gajdusek and Gibbs (1975), Gibbs and Gajdusek (1970), and Zigas (1970). Hunt recently discussed kuru to illustrate an ecological-epidemiological approach useful in searching for the causes of disease. His *cascade model* "analyzes health problems through the successive elimination of possible explanations." He shows how in kuru studies explanations such as sorcery, malnutrition, environmental toxicity, and heredity were successively discarded, thus clearing the field for the slow virus hypothesis now generally accepted (Hunt 1978).

[3] This, and other nutritional problems associated with rapid urbanization, are further developed in Chapter 15.

[4] A similar impasse in the treatment of trachoma was reached in the health care experiment at the Navajo community of Many Farms. Treatment of active cases had little impact on the endemic problems. Transmission was readily recognized as taking place by way of the contaminated fingers of those afflicted — usually children. However, "To decontaminate their fingers (and the communal towels and vessels) would have necessitated a permanent change in such household habits . . . as hand and face washing, the use of soap, individual towels and precautions in their handling" (McDermott et al. 1972: 28).

chapter 3

Medical Systems

MEDICAL SYSTEMS AS SOCIOCULTURAL ADAPTIVE STRATEGIES

In the preceding chapter we considered within a biocultural-ecological frame of reference broad matters of diseases and some of their roles in human evolution, viewed as biological adaptive strategies. Our emphasis was on disease itself, not on people as individuals, and on the ways in which human behavior bears on the presence, absence, or incidence of specific diseases. In this chapter we turn to a sociocultural-institutional frame of reference; we focus on the problems of sick people who, as cultural beings, have over time developed social institutions, etiological theories, and therapeutic techniques to enable them to cope with the social and other dislocations occasioned by illness-induced disability. And, just as we can speak of biological adaptive strategies that underlie human evolution, so too can we speak of sociocultural adaptive strategies that bring into being medical systems, the culturally based behavior and belief forms that arise in response to the threats posed by disease. The adaptive nature of a medical system is apparent from Dunn's recent definition: "*the pattern of social institutions and cultural traditions that evolves from* deliberate behavior *to enhance health, whether or not the outcome of particular items of behavior is ill health* (Dunn 1976:135).

Disease, with its pain and suffering, is the most predictable of human conditions; it is a biological and cultural universal. In prehuman times, as among animals today, disease was almost entirely a biological phenomenon. With rare exceptions a diseased animal is of no concern to its mates; usually they shun or abandon the sufferer. Jane Goodall describes this animal pattern when a poliomyelitis epidemic struck the chimpanzee community she was studying in Tanzania. A group of healthy animals observing a cripple struggling to reach the feeding area made no attempt to help him. Instead, they kept their distance, stared nervously at the invalid, grinned in fear, and embraced and patted each other in gestures of reassurance. A second animal, badly paralyzed and dying, struggled to keep up with the troop as it moved up the valley. "But whether he dragged himself on his belly, or hitched himself backward, or laboriously somersaulted, he could move only very slowly, and the rest of the group were soon out of sight" (Lawick-Goodall 1971:223).[1] In the absence of curing skills avoidance or abandonment is adaptive behavior, a kind of preventive medicine in which a primitive "quarantine" reduces the danger of exposure of healthy individuals to contagious germs and viruses.

As our primate ancestors evolved into man, their diseases, many of which they brought along with them, and the new ones they acquired along the way (e.g., Cockburn 1971:45-46) ceased to be purely biological phenomena; they acquired social and cultural dimensions as well. For with man, unlike other forms of animal life, disease threatens in major fashion not only the biological safety of the sufferer and his fellows but also the social and economic life of the group. As with animals, an infectious individual exposes his companions to epidemic illness, and history is replete with cases of decimation of human populations when sufferers from smallpox, tuberculosis, or plague were brought into contact with peoples who previously had not known these diseases. In attempting to protect himself from these threats, man sometimes has followed the mammalian pattern of outcasting, or flight from the sick. In the West, from Biblical until modern times, lepers were condemned to live outside city walls and to warn all who approached them with the cry "Unclean! Unclean!" On the opposite side of the globe the primitive forest-dwelling Kubu of Sumatra, when threatened by an epidemic, simply abandoned their afflicted fellow tribesmen and moved deeper into the forest, thus condemning them to a social death even prior to physical death (Sigerist 1951:148).

Far more often, however, man has sought to cure the sufferer. As Rubin has written, "By necessity man has undoubtedly always been concerned with questions of health and survival, and has sought, within the framework of his knowledge, solutions to problems of illness" (Rubin 1960:785). This concern is not alone humanitarian, although in most societies there is a strong urge to nurture the sick; rather, it also represents a new and distinctively human form of adaptive behavior, one based on logic as well as compassion.

Activities in all human societies, to a far greater extent than those of animals living in groups, are organized around age, sex, and occupational specializations that we call "roles." Basic roles in simple societies include parent, child, husband, wife, cook, housekeeper, hunter, fisher, gatherer, herbalist, religious specialist, and the like. Every human being fills a number of roles: a husband may also be a father, a son, a hunter, a craftsman, a religious leader, or many other things. And his wife is a daughter, a mother, a cook, a clothesmaker, and perhaps an herbalist, all at the same time. Whatever the role, the person who fills it — the "incumbent" — assumes certain rights and expects certain forms of behavior from those people with whom he or she interacts. A husband has sexual prerogatives in relation to his wife and, at least in traditional societies, he expects her to cook his food, discipline his children, and perhaps make his clothing. In her absence he would be hard put to exist. Equally important, the incumbents, the occupants of every role, have obligations, or duties, toward their fellows — and these are often reciprocal. The husband must meet his wife's sexual needs (i.e., she also has sexual prerogatives), and he is to provide game, fish, or other foods for her and their children. Without his contribution life for them would be exceedingly difficult. Role obligations and role expectations also extend well beyond the primary family to include kinsmen, friends, and neighbors. In short, even the technologically most simple societies are characterized by an interlocking network of mutually supportive and dependency relationships.

This network of supportive action is well illustrated among the Iban of Borneo, where healing ceremonies often involve not only the family of the patient, but also the entire longhouse of as many as 12 separate family units. All co-dwellers "become directly involved with the patient's problem, may have responsibilities for preparations needed for the healing ceremony, and often must observe certain taboos after the ceremony to keep the patient well. *It is also in their best interest for the patient to get well since a community as interdependent as a longhouse misses any sick member*" (Torrey 1972:97. Emphasis added).

Clearly a sick human being signifies something quite distinct from a diseased animal: to the extent the patient is unable to fulfill his normal obligations to others, he jeopardizes their well-being, since they depend on him for many things. Faced with the crisis of serious illness of one of their members, the other members of the group must decide what to do. In an analytic sense they have polar choices: like animals they can leave their sick comrade to his own resources, to recover or to die without their help. If he recovers, the victim can resume his former roles; if he dies, a substitute will be found for him, and the life of the group will go on as before. Alternatively, the members of the group can attempt to restore the sick person to health so that he can again fulfill his normal role obligations. In human societies the second alternative is the one that is usually selected, except in those rare instances — as with leprosy in past centuries — when it is recognized that recovery is impossible.

To a point, people usually are willing to gamble time, resources, and an extra work load (in caring for the patient and in temporarily fulfilling his basic role obligations) in order to avoid the greater social disruption and costs that inevitably accompany death. But, with the possible exception of the most affluent societies, "cost-benefit" factors always seem to be considered. The estimate of time and other expenses necessary to probable recovery and the perceived likelihood of recovery itself are consciously and subconsciously balanced against the perceived utility of the patient to the group that is making the decision. Great effort will be made to save a father or mother in the prime of life, with small children needing care, and contributing to the social and economic well-being of other members of the group. But less value will be placed on trying to save the life of old people, now of limited value to family and community; and infants and small children, still major drains on parents' time and resources and all too easily replaced, may receive nothing beyond the simplest home remedies.

Thus we see that the emergence of human societies created a new adaptive strategy in the face of disease, a strategy that forced on man a major concern with the prevention and treatment of disease. In learning to treat disease man has developed "a vast complex of knowledge, beliefs, techniques, roles, norms, values, ideologies, attitudes, customs, rituals, and symbols, that interlock to form a mutually reinforcing and supporting system" (Saunders 1954:7). This "vast complex," and all of the other items we might think to add to the list, constitutes a "medical system." The term properly embraces the totality of health knowledge, beliefs, skills, and practices of the members of every group. It should be used in a comprehensive sense to include *all* of the clinical and nonclinical activities, the formal and informal institutions, and any other activities that, however tangentially, bear on the health levels of the group and promote optimum functioning of society.

Frequently, however, the term is used in a much narrower sense. We sometimes hear health problems discussed — particularly when "American medicine" is under attack — as if a medical system consisted largely of how a doctor treats (or mistreats) his patients. Some people express surprise when it is suggested that environmental sanitation and nutrition education and the scientific knowledge that underlies these activities are just as much a part of our medical system as is the physician's practice. Some critics, loath to concede any merit in modern medical practices, give credit for indices of medical success such as increasing longevity and lowered morbidity rates to "rising standards of living," without realizing that rising standards of living historically have included potable water, sanitary sewage and refuse disposal, more numerous varieties of fresh foods in local markets, outdoor sports, and many other things known to bear directly on health levels. The skills and knowledge involved in manufacturing and fitting eyeglasses, hearing aids, artificial dentures, and prosthetic devices, which contribute so greatly to the health and well-being of contemporary peoples, must also be considered a part of a medical system.

In short, *we view every medical system as embracing all of the health-promoting beliefs and actions and scientific knowledge and skills of the members of the group that subscribe to the system.*

DISEASE THEORY AND HEALTH CARE SYSTEMS

At this most comprehensive level it is correct to conceptualize a single medical system for every society, and so we frequently speak of the medical system of the contemporary United States, of a Mexican village, or of the Zulu. It is one thing to conceptualize an all-embracing medical system, but it is quite another thing to analyze it and study it. In practice, therefore, we must identify subsystems or multiple institutions within a single medical system in order to deal with it in any systematic manner. In the United States, for example, we customarily divide our formal medical system into component parts such as a medical education system, a medical research system, a health care system, a public health system, and many more similar categories. In technologically simpler societies many of these subsystems are lacking or exist only in attenuated form. Hospitals, medical schools, formal public health institutions, research laboratories, and the like are not found. Yet the medical systems of all groups, however simple some may be, can be broken down into at least two major categories: (1) a "disease theory" system, and (2) a "health care" system.

A *disease theory system* embraces beliefs about the nature of health, the causes of illness, and the remedies and other curing techniques used by doctors. In contrast, a health care system is concerned with the ways in which societies organize to care for the sick and to utilize disease "knowledge" to aid the patient. Disease theory systems deal with causality, the explanations given by people to account for loss of health, explanations such as breach of taboo, theft of the soul, an upset in the hot-cold balance within the body, or the failure of a human organism's immunological defenses against pathogenic agents such as germs and viruses. A disease theory system is thus an ideational, conceptual system, an intellectual construct, a part of the cognitive orientation of the members of the group. It deals with classification, explanation, and cause and effect. All disease causality systems are, in large part, rational and logical, in that curing techniques are functions of, or stem from, a distinctive conceptual organization of ideas about causes. Disease causality systems can be thought of as irrational only by people in other societies who believe that the premises underlying explanation are wholly or partly contrary to fact.

A *health care system* is a social institution that involves the interaction of a number of people, minimally the patient and the curer. The manifest function of a health care system is to mobilize the resources of the patient, his family, and his society to bring them to bear on his problem. A health care system obviously reflects the logical and philosophical characteristic of the disease causality system with which it is linked, in that the latter dictates many of the decisions that are made and the actions taken by the participants in the sick room drama. Yet the two systems, for all their closeness, are not the same. For analytical purposes they can be kept separate, and the characteristics and functions of each can be studied without immediate reference to the other. Each of the two systems fulfill specific functions beyond their joint role in caring for the sick.

The distinction between disease theory and health care systems is useful for a variety of reasons. For one, it helps us to see more clearly the strengths and weaknesses of total medical systems. Today the "American medical system" is much criticized, and growing numbers of people are turning to "alternative" forms of medical care to meet their clinical and psychological health needs. Although we recognize the iatrogenic consequences of some clinical measures and the inevitable errors of judgment inherent in even the most skillful medical practice, we believe that in considerable measure this criticism reflects discontent with the health care rather than the clinical side of medicine.

The distinction between disease theory and health care systems also has advantages in certain action situations: it enables us to cope more wisely, more sensitively, with the challenge of introducing change in medical practices among peoples who previously have known only their traditional systems. In such societies, we have found, traditional disease causation ideas often persist long after Western innovations in health care become attractive. The members of such societies are, however, often faced with a dilemma; the conflict between their deep-seated health beliefs and the obvious success of the physician in treating much illness. Many medical personnel feel that good health practices must be based on comprehension of the scientific theories that underlie these practices. Yet this does not necessarily follow, and there is strong evidence that in developing societies the physician's ability to reintegrate contrasting systems from distinct cultures into a single viable unit greatly aids him in his work. The Leightons have pointed out how this synthesis of contrasting systems promotes health among the Navaho. "If an Indian is told to take digitalis every day he will probably munch a few tablets and then forget about them. If he is told that his green medicine comes from the leaves of the foxglove, that his body must never be without it any more than his mind without a good song, and that he must take it every morning of his life when the first brightness of the day is in the east, one stands a much better chance of having the instructions carried out" (Leighton and Leighton 1941:523).

Finally, the separation of health care from disease theory systems is helpful as a pedagogic and research device. It enables us to concentrate, in turn, on major bodies of data for analysis and cross-cultural comparison. This dichotomy is implicit in much of the discussion in this and following chapters.

SOME UNIVERSALS IN MEDICAL SYSTEMS

Although the medical practices and beliefs of, say, the Eskimo would appear to have little in common with those of the inhabitants of a large American city there is, in fact, an underlying structure of universals in all medical systems that facilitates comprehension and study. Some of these universals have to do with roles and their obligations: there are always, at a minimum, patients and curers. These will be discussed in subsequent chapters. Other universals are more general, having to do with things such as the definition of illness, attitudes toward health and illness, the integration of medicine into the general cultural framework, and the like. Some of these more common universals follow.

1. Medical systems are integral parts of cultures

The major institutions of every culture are related to each other and fulfill specific functions in relation to each other. Each institution is essential to the normal functioning of the culture in which it is found and each, in turn, draws on the others for its own continued existence. Medical institutions are no exception. For example, disease beliefs in many societies are so intimately related to magic and religion that it is impossible to separate them. Mythology may be important in explaining cosmology and the supernatural deities and other beings who are thought to bring illness. Social institutions are reflected in the roles of curers and their relations to patients and their families. Legal forms may come into play in determining responsibility for sickness if, for example, witchcraft is involved, and economic factors are significant in payments to shamans. In short, medical systems cannot be understood solely in terms of themselves; only when they are seen as parts of total cultural patterns can they be fully appreciated.

To say that medical systems are integral parts of cultures is to view them at a basic, but fairly obvious level. But medical systems are parts of cultures at a more abstract level, in that in content and form they reflect patterns and values that are less obvious. Pellegrino has caught the spirit of this level when he writes that "Medicine is an exquisitely sensitive indicator of the dominant cultural characteristics of any era, for man's behavior before the threats and realities of illness is necessarily rooted in the conception he has constructed of himself and his universe. Every culture has developed a system of medicine which bears an indissoluble and reciprocal relationship to the prevailing world view. The medical behavior of individuals and groups is incomprehensible apart from general cultural history" (Pellegrino 1963:10).

In the Mexican mestizo village of Tzintzuntzan, for example, health is defined in terms of an equilibrium between the "hot" and "cold" forces inherent in the body and in the surrounding world. This view, in turn, is found to be merely a special statement of a much broader view of life, that the healthy community is also one in which equilibrium prevails, in which there is a balance, an even distribution of good of all kinds, in economics, in justice, in power, and the like. In traditional Chinese medicine, says Pellegrino, we see how world view influenced medical ideas and practice: disease was thought due to a disharmony or "lack of ebb and flow" between yin and yang forces. Man was thought to be a microcosm of the universe, made up of the same five elements — wood, fire, earth, metal, and water — which in turn correspond to the five viscera, five senses, five colors, and five tastes. "Such an assured view of the constitution of man," says Pellegrino, "strongly discouraged the study of anatomy. Chinese medicine was characterized by the vaguest notions of human anatomy. Its thereapy was directed to providing the missing Yang element by the administration of some animal organ presumed to have a high content of that material" (*Ibid.,* 12).

Consistency in culture patterns is manifest in still other ways. In many tribal societies, for example, much medical belief and practice is magical, conforming to a more comprehensive pattern in which magic is invoked to explain all misfortune, and in which it is used to control the social environment. In contrast, in Western countries formal medicine is predominantly scientific, reflecting the scientific orientation that has characterized these countries during the past three centuries. In many non-Western communities group consensus is the basis on which decisions are made. In these societies major medical decisions are reached in the same fashion, and only after extended consultation among those relatives and friends who are directly affected by the illness will the decision as to what to do be taken. In the United States, where independent decision-making ability is highly valued, major medical decisions are made by fewer people, sometimes by the patient alone in consultation with the doctor. In both cases, decision-making behavior can be understood only against the background of wider cultural patterns.

2. Illness is culturally defined

In the United States we are so accustomed to think of illness in terms of germs and viruses that we assume it is a biological constant, a pathological condition that is verified from laboratory tests or other forms of clinical examination. From a cultural point of view, however, illness is quite a different thing: it is the social recognition that a person is unable to fulfill his normal roles adequately, and that something must be done about the situation. In other words, we must distinguish between *disease,* a pathological concept, and *illness,* a cultural concept. We speak, for example, of plant and animal diseases, quite divorced from culture. But man's diseases become socially significant only when they are identified as illness, a physiological malfunctioning that is seen to threaten the individual and his society. Another way to point out the distinction is to say that a medical doctor wishes to *cure disease* but he *treats illness,* for it is usually the impairment of function and not the presence of disease pathogens that causes us to seek aid.[2]

Societies define illness in different fashions, and symptoms that are accepted as evidence of illness in one society may be ignored in the next. Definitions within the same society may also change over time. Today malaria is recognized as one of the most dangerous of all killing diseases and, since the early 1950s, the World Health Organization has made strenuous efforts to eliminate it from the globe. Yet in the Upper Mississippi Valley in the nineteenth century it was so common that it was not regarded as pathological. As the frontier was pushed westward, the cutting of forests, travel by riverboat, settlement in river bottoms, poor sanitation, and stagnant water increased the incidence of the

Anopheles mosquito and man's exposure to it. "In the beginning the 'chills' were regarded as a necessary element of the inevitable 'acclimatization' and after having 'shaken' for years people got so used to it that they hardly paid attention to a little 'ague.' This is a classic example of how an objectively dangerous and burdensome bodily condition can subjectively, by social convention, even lose the character of disease" (Ackerknecht 1945:4).

Other examples also illustrate how culture defines what is and what is not illness. As in the Upper Mississippi Valley in the last century, malaria is prevalent among the Mano of Liberia. Although most people have some immunity to it (presumably because they carry the sickle-cell gene that is believed to provide significant protection), many adults suffer. Yet they do not consider this to be illness (Harley 1941:44). Nor do the Mano view yaws as illness: "Oh, that is not a sickness," they say. "Everybody has that" (*Ibid.*, 21). In rural Greece cases of measles, mumps, chicken pox, and whooping cough are rarely reported in government morbidity records, since they are considered to be "compulsory diseases," an inevitable and perhaps normal part of the process of growing up (Blum and Blum 1965:53).

3. All medical systems have both preventive and curative sides

In the United States the formal dichotomy between preventive (public health) and curative (clinical, largely private sector) medicine tends to make us feel that those simpler societies that do not recognize this division are lacking in preventive concepts. It is true that, insofar as preventive medicine is based on legal foundations (public health in its narrowest sense), most non-Western peoples lack the *institution* of public health. Among tribal and peasant peoples one looks in vain for public officials who can require or prohibit behavior known or believed to be causally connected to health levels. Things such as quarantine, compulsory immunization, minimum standards for potable water, and communitywide sanitary disposal of sewage and waste require legal mechanisms normally associated only with well-developed governmental systems. This is not to say that such systems by definition are modern; in ancient China there were well-developed institutions to promote public health.

But among most non-Western peoples preventive medicine consists of personal acts rather than legal functions, personal behavior that follows logically from disease causation concepts which, by explaining why a person falls ill, simultaneously teach what must be done to avoid illness. When people believe that illness is sent by angry gods or resentful ancestors who are punishing sin, "the obvious procedure to prevent it is confession or, even better, the meticulous observation of social taboos and the careful execution of rites and ceremonies owed to the gods and the ancestors" (Aguirre Beltrán 1963:196). For those who attribute illness to witchcraft, it is wise to avoid offending neighbors who might resort to nefarious acts. If illness is thought to follow the entry of cold air into the body, the cautious person tries to avoid situations in which cold air may strike him. Where it is feared that babies will sicken because of the envious glance of a barren woman, careful mothers place the appropriate amulet around the infant's neck or wrist to ward off the evil eye. These and countless similar individual acts, although quite distinct from modern public health ideas and programs, are nevertheless properly viewed as preventive medicine, since they aim to prevent illness. The extent to which we can speak quite properly of preventive medicine in traditional societies is illustrated by Colson's long monograph dealing entirely with Malay acts and rituals designed to prevent illness (Colson 1971).

Although many indigenous "preventive" practices are little if any more than superstition, some actions undoubtedly benefit, even if not for the reasons assumed. Many traditional peoples, for example, keep their living areas scrupulously free of fecal matter: although they do this because of the fear that enemies may practice sympathetic magic against them with their excrement, the reduction in flies resulting from this practice is almost certainly beneficial. And the Mano of Liberia, many of whose health practices are far from ideal from a medical viewpoint, are clean in their personal habits; they take a hot bath every evening at sunset, their food is clean and well cooked, and defecation takes place in the bush instead of in towns, which are remarkably free of vermin (Harley 1941:73-74).

4. Medical systems have multiple functions

At first thought the answer to the question, "What is the function of a medical system?" is obvious: to restore the patient to health, if at all possible. This certainly is a basic reason, and perhaps the most important of all. Yet, as with other complex cultural systems within a society, medical systems fulfill a number of functions essential to the well-being of the culture of which they are a part, functions which often are not recognized by members of the group themselves, but that are adaptive in the sense that they in some way promote the well-being of the group. A health care subsystem serves not only to care for the patient but also, as will be discussed in Chapter VIII, as a backdrop against which the social roles of illness can be played out: temporary release from psychological and social pressure, a wish to gain attention, a device to control the behavior of others, and the like. Similarly, disease theory systems go far beyond simple explanation of illness causality, as the following paragraphs will show.

(a) A DISEASE THEORY SYSTEM PROVIDES A RATIONALE FOR TREATMENT

If illness is defined as due to the intrusion of an object by a sorcerer, extraction of the object is essential to returning the patient to health. Treatment may also be designed to placate or neutralize the sorcerer in order to ensure that the illness will not return. If illness is explained as due to a wandering soul that had no time to return from its dream world when its owner awakened, the curer will attempt to trap or otherwise lure the soul back to the body. And in Western medicine, if laboratory analysis of a throat culture reveals a streptococcus infection, the modern physician prescribes the appropriate antibiotic.

(b) A DISEASE THEORY SYSTEM EXPLAINS "WHY"

In all societies patients are concerned about recovery. But, important as it is in this context, the function of a disease theory system is not limited to providing a guide to therapy. There is always the nagging question, "*Why* did it happen to *me,* at *this time,* in *this place*?" If a good answer to this question is not forthcoming, the patient fears the return of the illness. So a disease theory system not only diagnoses cause and provides the logic for treatment, but it deals with the much wider question of what has happened to disturb the patient's social relationships, what harmony inherent in nature may have been disturbed, and why, with apparent capriciousness, fate has dealt this individual a blow. Both traditional and civilized people find it difficult to live with uncertainty. They want to know "why?" Why do the rains come and the crops mature one year and not the next? Why does one villager prosper and acquire wealth, while his neighbor remains poor? Why does one girl suffer repeatedly from a sore throat, while her sister rarely does? In traditional societies, at least, disease causality systems go far beyond explaining what has happened; they also account for why, thus helping to satisfy a basic human need to know.

(c) DISEASE THEORY SYSTEMS OFTEN PLAY A POWERFUL ROLE IN SANCTIONING AND SUPPORTING SOCIAL AND MORAL CULTURAL NORMS

This is particularly true when illness is attributed to sin, taboo violations, and other forms of wrongdoing. In the Judeo-Christian tradition illness historically has been explained as God's punishment of man for his moral lapses, for his sins. Individual illness represented personal transgressions, while great epidemics signified major social moral failures. In either case, repentance and adherence to God's law was the way to recovery and the avoidance of future affliction.

Illness, seen as a penalty for disapproved conduct, is widespread in non-Western societies. Or, stated differently, the *threat* of illness as a consequence of socially unacceptable behavior plays a major role in many societies in maintaining the moral order. The Lugbara of the Congo believe that "the dead hear the words of the living and then send sickness to show the offender, whose offence is that of disobedience to his elders, the error of his ways" (Middleton 1970:54). Lieban describes fear of illness as a social control in his account of *ingkantos* in a village on Negros Island, in the Philippines. Ingkantos are spirits, normally invisible, which sometimes assume human form. When they do so they usually are physically attractive and obviously wealthy and powerful; they are also extremely dangerous. Lieban believes ingkantos symbolize all of the good things in the world that the villagers know about, from their contacts with the extravillage world, that they would like to have but know they are unlikely to obtain. "The individual who sees and interacts with an ingkanto can, through fantasy, bring temptation within reach, or succumb to it. However, such experiences are considered hazardous and often are thought to lead to illness or death. This pattern of thought and behavior associated with beliefs about ingkantos and their influence appears to support social equilibrium in the community by dramatizing and reinforcing the idea that it is dangerous to covet alluring, but basically unattainable, wealth and power outside the barrios. In this way, the value of accepting the limitations of barrio life, and one's part in it is emphasized" (Lieban 1962a:309).

Hallowell, in describing the world view of the Ojibwa Indians of central Canada, says that their "central values are reinforced by the belief that sickness is a penalty for bad conduct" (Hallowell 1963:266). "Any serious illness," he writes, "is associated with some prior conduct which involved an infraction of moral rules; the illness is explained as a penalty for bad conduct. It is a consequence of behavioral deviation from expected patterns of interpersonal relations, whether between human persons or between a human being and an other-than-human person . . . Thus, causes of illness are sought by the Ojibwa within their web of interpersonal relations, rather than apart from it" (*Ibid.,* 277). Among the Ojibwa one of the most important forms of "bad conduct" is refusal or reluctance to share food with others, a failure to display hospitality. In a society of hunters, fishers, and gatherers, where not all families have access to the same amount of food every day, food reciprocity is ecologically a sound device to ensure the survival of the group. But not all sharing, says Hallowell, was based on this principle; often individuals were motivated to be hospitable for fear of witchcraft from those with whom they refused to share. Refusal of hospitality might be interpreted as a hostile act toward the supplicant. Thus, fear of illness from witchcraft of angry fellows reinforced the norm of widespread generosity and sharing (*Ibid.,* 294-296).

So struck was psychiatrist John Cawte with the role of medicine as a sanction against social nonconformity among the Australian aborigines that he titled his book *Medicine is the Law.* "Aboriginal Australian societies . . . " he writes, "take advantage of the polarization that disease creates in society: the power of doctors and the dependency of patients. This domination-submission reciprocity is exploited by native doctors as an inducement toward social conformity. The native doctor says, in effect: conform lest you become ill. He may take a similar advantage of misfortune, utilizing its occurrence or threatened occurrence to persuade dissident parties toward compromised courses of action, so that kin live better together. In the native doctor's philosophy, *medicine is the law . . .* " (Cawte 1974:xxii).

(d) A DISEASE THEORY SYSTEM MAY PROVIDE THE RATIONALE FOR CONSERVATION PRACTICES

Among some hunting, fishing, and gathering, and simple horticultural peoples, disease explanations play powerful roles in the husbanding of scarce food supplies. The Colombian anthropologist Reichel-Dolmatoff has described one such case among the Tukano Indians of the Colombian Amazonas. The Tukano derive much of their sustenance from manioc gardens, but most of their protein comes from game animals and fish. All game animals and fish are subject to the Master of Animals, a dwarflike spirit who jealously guards his flocks of deer, tapir, peccary, agouti, and other animals and fish that are a food resource. He and his charges live inside steep rocky hills and at the bottom of deep pools in rivers. To obtain the Master's permission to catch fish or kill game, hunters must undergo rigorous purification rites that include bathing, sexual abstinence, and food restrictions. A man can hunt, not when the fancy strikes him, but only after this anxiety-charged period of preparation, "the purpose of which is to avoid over-hunting" (Reichel-Dolmatoff 1976a:313).

Game animals are thought to take revenge on hunters by causing illness and, among one Tukano group, the Desana, "the malevolence of game animals is believed to be the largest single cause of illness" (Reichel-Dolmatoff 1976b:158). They can cause illness, however, only through the Master. Hence the Tukano, working under the guidance of their shaman who visits the Master in a trance, strive to hunt only those animals, and in numbers, for which they have the Master's permission. Illness beliefs clearly promote sound conservation of game practices.

Remarkably similar beliefs, serving essentially the same ecological ends, are found among the Popoluca Indians of Veracruz, Mexico. These horticultural people also derive a significant amount of protein from hunting and fishing. Three-foot dwarfs known as *chanekos* play the role of game masters, who grant or withhold luck to hunters and fishers. Deer are their "cattle," which they let out to graze by day, but call back at night to underground safety. As with the Tukano, elaborate purification rites designed to obtain the favor of the *chanekos* are essential to hunting luck. A hunter who kills too many animals or who carelessly allows wounded animals to escape is punished by a *chaneko* who kidnaps his soul; unless he relents and returns the soul, the hunter sickens and dies (Foster 1945:181). One myth tells of a hunter spirited away to the underground home of a *chaneko* where he was shown all of the deer he had wounded but not killed. "If you want to return home you must cure all of these deer," he was told. Only after much supplication and because of extenuating circumstances, was the hunter released (*Ibid.,* 200). Myths such as this impress on all young hunters the need to kill only when food is necessary, and to make sure that wounded animals do not escape, later to die, uneaten.

(e) A DISEASE THEORY SYSTEM MAY SERVE TO CONTROL AGGRESSION

Spiro has described the *alus* — malevolent ghosts — who are believed by the inhabitants of the tiny Micronesian atoll of Ifaluk to be causes of illness and misfortune. "The *alus* cause worry, fear, and anxiety, as well as sickness and death; and by causing the death of individuals they can, potentially, destroy the entire society. From the point of view of the people, it would be better if there were no *alus*" (Spiro 1952:498). Why, asks Spiro, does such a dysfunctional belief continue to survive? The answer involves demography, ecology, and psychology. Aggressive drives, in some degree, probably characterize everyone. In large, open societies a certain amount of overt aggression can be absorbed without threatening the community. But in tiny, circumscribed communities, overt aggression is an intolerable threat to the survival of the community; it must be repressed and redirected. Ifaluk is an atoll of 250 people (at the time of the study) occupying a square half mile of land surrounding a lagoon double in size. Not surprisingly, Ifaluk culture is characterized by strong sanctions against overt aggression in interpersonal relationships. But the aggressive drives are there; they must somehow be given vent. One possibility would be to turn them inward, which would, of course, be destructive of the individual personality. Another possibility — that found on Ifaluk — is to displace the aggression onto some object outside the human community. Spiro feels that the extreme fear and hatred of the *alus* felt by the Ifalukans is sufficient to displace aggressive drives away from humans and to dissipate them in culturally sanctioned, aggressive culture patterns.

(f) THE NATIONALISTIC ROLE OF TRADITIONAL MEDICINE

Traditional medicine often plays an important role in the development of nationalistic pride, since it may symbolize the antiquity of the country concerned, and the high levels to which culture had evolved in ancient times. In countries with ancient, documented, medical systems there is frequently an urge to elevate the indigenous system to "separate but equal" status with contemporary Western medicine, basing the argument both on the antiquity of medical knowledge in the country concerned and the putative effectiveness of traditional treatments. Recent descriptions of ancient Chinese medicine, for example, stress the important medical techniques that were known and used long before they appeared in the West (e.g., Huard and Wong 1968). And in South Asia, Hindu Ayurvedic and Moslem Unānī Tibbi medicine are recognized and supported by national governments (Opler 1963:32).

In 1945, in urging the establishment of an Institute of the History of Medicine in India, Sigerist recognized the powerful role of traditional medicine as a symbol of nationalism. He noted that India was in a period of transition, awakening to a new life, and looking into the future. "At such an historical moment," he wrote, "the people look back with pride to their cultural history. It is the common ground on which they stand." He pointed to the publication of classical literature in new editions, the cinematographic use of ancient epics instead of gangster stories, and the reenactment of old dances as examples of a renewed interest in the past. "And when it comes to medicine, they remember their history also. Just as we look to Hippocrates as the father of medicine, they look to their own classics, to Caraka, Suśruta, Vabhata, who collected and preserved the medical lore of their time . . . Indians remember with pride that in the third century B.C. Aśoka, the great Buddhist Maurya king, had provided medical services for rich and poor . . . throughout his empire, that he had hospitals built in town and country . . . at a time when there was not a single hospital in the Western world" (Roemer 1960:276-277).

In summary, medical systems are rich and complex organizations that serve many roles and goals. Ostensibly concerned only with the problems of disease and illness, narrowly defined, they in fact reflect the fundamental patterns and values of the cultures of which they are a part. Only when viewed in the broad context of a total sociocultural milieu can the health behavior of the members of any group be fully understood.

NOTES

[1] The same chimps, however, on other occasions removed offending splinters from one another, were observed pulling the diseased teeth of friends, and often huddled with discomforted members of the group. Also, the brother of the dying polio-ill chimp initially did attempt to aid him; however, the general reaction of the group to their seriously stricken members evoked in Lawick-Goodall what she reported as among the most negative reactions of her entire field experience.

[2] Or, as Eisenberg recently has said, "patients suffer 'illness'; physicians diagnose and treat 'diseases'" (Eisenberg 1977:11).

part 2

THE NON-WESTERN WORLD

chapter 4

Ethnomedicine

In this and the following three chapters we direct our attention to the traditional subject matter of anthropology: tribal, peasant, and other preindustrial peoples. We ask questions about the nature of illness as it is conceived in these societies, and about its causes and its cures. We enquire into the types of therapists that seek to alleviate illness, and about their skills and social roles. Then, in the final chapter in this section, we examine the evidence that bears on the effectiveness of non-Western medical systems, asking the question, "How satisfactory are these systems in meeting the health needs of the people they serve?" Although our primary concern is with non-Western peoples, many of the topics discussed can be most fully comprehended only from a comparative perspective. To provide the contrast that most sharply illuminates salient aspects of the medical systems we are describing, we therefore — where it seems to us enlightening — compare features of these systems with their analogs in the contemporary world.

We begin our exploration of non-Western medical systems with ethnomedicine. This is an appropriate starting point for, as we saw in Chapter 1, the curiosity of anthropologists about the medical beliefs and practices of the members of the traditional societies they have studied is the oldest of the "roots" of medical anthropology. Ethnomedicine, the contemporary term for the vast body of knowledge that has resulted from this curiosity and the research methods used in adding to it, is of interest to anthropologists for both theoretical and practical reasons. On a theoretical level, medical beliefs and practices constitute a major element in every culture; consequently, they are interesting in their own right and also for the insights they give into other aspects of the culture of which they are a part. On a practical level, a knowledge of indigenous medical beliefs and practices is important in planning health programs for, and in delivering health services to, traditional peoples. As we will see in Part 4, one of the major roles of medical anthropologists has been to explain prevailing medical beliefs and practices to health planners and to suggest how they can be integrated with the modern practices that characterize the formal health plans of all countries. In this chapter, however, our interest lies at the theoretical level, the nature of indigenous medical systems and, particularly, the ideas of causality that underlie them.

TERMINOLOGICAL PROBLEMS

In describing medical systems other than our own anthropologists show increasing embarrassment over the problem of terminology. All terms commonly used imply a qualitative gap between "modern" medicine and medicine that is the product of indigenous cultural developments, a dichotomy emphasized by contrastive terms such as "scientific" versus "primitive," "Western" versus "non-Western," and "modern" versus "traditional." Although (as we point out at the end of this chapter) the qualitative gap exists, in an era of extreme cultural relativism many people are disturbed by terms that suggest evaluation. Earlier writers were not bothered by these problems. They were studying "primitive" peoples, so quite naturally they talked of "primitive medicine." Writing in the 1940s Erwin Ackerknecht, a physician-ethnologist who might well be described as the "father" of medical anthropology, unabashedly speaks of "primitive medicine," which he describes as *primarily magico-religious, utilizing a few rational elements*" (Ackerknecht 1971:21). When, after World War II, studies of peasant communities became fashionable, following Redfield's early terminology these peoples often were described as possessing a "folk culture." Not surprisingly their medical systems usually were described as "folk medicine," a practice that frequently causes confusion, since the popular medicine of technologically complex societies is also often called "folk."

Because of tradition and frequency of use in the literature it is tempting to adhere to a terminology derived from the traditional anthropological categories of "primitive," "peasant," and "modern." Yet we are more and more reluctant to speak of "primitive" peoples because of the pejorative implications of the word. Euphemisms — "primitive" first appeared as a nondenigrative substitute for "savage" — ultimately outlive their usefulness and take on the disagreeable connotations of the words they have replaced. Ackerknecht himself recognized the need for change; in a 1971 collection of his essays, most titles were changed to eliminate the word "primitive." Contemporary anthropologists, in their endeavor to avoid criticism, often resort to mouthfuls such as "the vocabulary of Western scientific medicine," "culture specific illnesses," "nonscientific health practices," "indigenous or folk medical roles," and "native conceptual traditions about illness."

If, however, we turn from a framework of societal types to one of etiology, of disease causality concepts, we can largely avoid the pejorative implications of earlier terminologies and the circumlocutions of later times. We cannot easily eliminate terms such as "Western," "scientific," "contemporary," "non-Western," "traditional," "indigenous," and the like, but we believe that used within the context of classificatory systems labeled with relatively neutral terms, they should be offensive to no one.

DISEASE ETIOLOGIES

In surveying the ethnomedical literature dealing with causality concepts, we are struck by how few cognitive frameworks among non-Western peoples are necessary to "explain" the presence of disease. We find, in fact, that a dual division is sufficient to distinguish major categories, or systems. We suggest that these be called *personalistic* and *naturalistic*. Although these terms refer specifically to causality concepts, they can also conveniently be used to speak of entire medical systems (i.e., not only causality, but all of the associated behavior that stems from these views).

1. Personalistic medical systems

A personalistic system is one in which illness is believed to be caused by the active, purposeful intervention of a *sensate* agent who may be a supernatural being (a deity or a god), a nonhuman being (such as a ghost, ancestor, or evil spirit), or a human being (a witch or sorcerer). The sick person literally is a victim, the object of aggression or punishment directed specifically against him, for reasons that concern him alone.

2. Naturalistic medical systems

In naturalistic systems illness is explained in impersonal, systemic terms. Naturalistic systems conform above all to an equilibrium model; health prevails when the insensate elements in the body, the heat, the cold, the humors or *dosha,* the yin and yang, are in balance appropriate to the age and condition of the individual in his natural and social environment. When this equilibrium is disturbed, illness results.[1]

Similar dichotomous classificatory systems with varying terminologies have been used by other anthropologists. Seijas' "supernatural" and "nonsupernatural" categories, for example, correspond very closely to our personalistic and naturalistic categories, as the following passage makes clear: "Supernatural etiological categories refer to those explanations that place the origin of disease in suprasensible forces, agents, or acts that cannot be directly observed. Explanations of disease such as sorcery, witchcraft, spirit intrusion, *susto,* evil eye, and the like fall into this category. Nonsupernatural explanations of disease are those which are based entirely on observable cause-and-effect relationships, regardless of whether or not the relationship established is mistaken because of incomplete or faulty observation" (Seijas 1973:545).

Nurge, discussing the medical beliefs and practices in a Philippine village, speaks of "supernatural" and "natural" causes of illness. The former are "agents of disease" such as spirit-gods, witches, and sorcerers. The latter include indigestible foods, sudden changes in temperature, strong winds, and blood or air "trapped in the body" (Nurge 1958:1160-1162). For Simmons the contrast is between "magical" and "empirical" etiologies, terms he uses to describe the folk medical beliefs of mestizo peoples in coastal Peru and Chile (Simmons 1955).

"Natural," "nonsupernatural," and "empirical" are appropriate equivalents to our "naturalistic" label. "Supernatural" and "magical," however, are much less precise, since they require the lumping of agents that are quite distinct conceptually. The term "supernatural" refers to an order of existence beyond nature or the visible and observable universe that includes beings such as deities, spirits, ghosts, and other nonmaterial entities. Witches and sorcerers do not belong to the supernatural world. Sometimes they draw on the supernatural, but their powers are best thought of as magical, consisting of spells, charms, and black magic. To classify witches and sorcerers as supernatural — as Seijas and Nurge must do — seems to us to do violence to the concept. Simmons falls into the same dilemma, but from the opposite side: "magical" is the appropriate terminology for the work of sorcerers and witches, but it is inappropriate for the actions of deities, spirits, and ghosts. The common denominator in the supernatural and the magical is the sensate "agent" who causes a victim to fall ill. For this reason we prefer "personalistic" to other terms that have been used for the supernatural-magical etiologies.[2]

Personalistic and naturalistic etiological systems are, of course, not mutually exclusive. Peoples who invoke personalistic causes to explain most illness usually recognize some natural, or chance, causes. And peoples for whom naturalistic causes predominate almost invariably explain some illness as due to witchcraft or the evil eye. Yet in spite of much overlap, most peoples seem committed to one or the other of these explanatory principles to account for most illness. When, for example, we read that in the Venezuelan peasant village of El Morro 89 percent of a sample of reported illnesses are "natural" in origin, whereas only 11 percent are attributed to magical or supernatural causes (Suárez 1974), it seems reasonable to say that the indigenous causation system of these people is naturalistic, not personalistic. Conversely, when we learn of the Melanesian Dobuans that all illness is attributed to envy, and that "Death is caused by witchcraft, sorcery, poisoning, suicide. or actual assault" (Fortune 1932:135, 150), it is clear that personalistic causality predominates.[3]

CAUSALITY CONCEPTS IN PERSONALISTIC SYSTEMS

The essence of causality in personalistic systems is captured by Glick in writing about the Gimi of highland New Guinea: "Illnesses are caused by *agents* who in some way bring their powers to bear against their victims. Such agents may be human, 'Superhuman' . . . or nonhuman; but always they are conceived as willful beings, who act not indifferently but in response to consciously perceived personal motives" (Glick 1967:36). The central role of the agent is also found among the Abron of the Ivory Coast, where it is believed that people sicken and die because some power has acted against them. "Abron disease theory contains a *host of agents* which may be responsible for a specific condition, each of them associated with a set of possible reasons for spreading sickness. These *agents* cut across the natural and supernatural world. Ordinary people — equipped with the proper technical skills — sorcerers, various supernatural entities — such as ghosts, bush devils, and witches — or the supreme god *Nyame,* acting alone or through lesser gods, may all cause disease" (Alland 1970:161. Empasis to "agents" added).

In descriptions of systems in which personalistic causality ideas predominate, it is remarkable how often one reads that all, or almost all, death and illness is caused by agents, that "causes" Westerners would consider to be natural are viewed as conforming to this model. The Melanesian Dobuans, as we have seen, are among those who attribute all illness to agents, and particularly to their envy. "*There is no concept of accident.* Falling from coconut palms or other trees is due to witchcraft; similarly other accidents" (Fortune 1932:135, 150. Emphasis added). Similarly, the physician Harley, who practiced medicine for nearly 15 years among the Mano of Liberia, found that among these people "Disease is unnatural, resulting from the intrusion of an outside force" usually directed by magical means. Disease and early death "are thought to be caused by external forces, or witchcraft" (Harley 1941:7, 20). Harley lists 16 nonnatural causes of illness and death, including witchcraft, poisoning, broken taboo, fetish power, and were-animals. "Natural" causes are limited to simple ailments treated with herbal remedies, old age leading to death (an event he describes as rare), and sacrifice of a slave or child (*Ibid.,* 35-36).

Personalistic disease causation beliefs predominate in the medical and health data recorded in classical ethnographic monographs on "primitive" peoples. These include groups such as the indigenous inhabitants of the Americas, of much of Africa south of the Sahara, of Oceania, and of the tribal peoples of Asia. Most of these groups are (or better, were) relatively small, isolated, nonliterate, and lacking contact with ancient high civilizations. There are important exceptions, however, as illustrated by the indigenous, complex civilizations of West Africa and by the Aztec, Maya, and Inca of America.

Causality Concepts in Naturalistic Systems

In contrast to personalistic systems, naturalistic systems explain illness in impersonal, systemic terms; sensate agents play no role. In these systems, health conforms to an equilibrium model: when the basic body elements — the "humors," the yin and yang, and the ayurvedic *dosha* — are in the balance appropriate to the age and condition of the individual, health results. When this balance is upset from without or from within, by natural forces such as heat, cold, or sometimes strong emotions, illness follows. Although the equilibrium principle in naturalistic systems is expressed in a number of ways, contemporary descriptions reveal the primary role of heat and cold as the principal threats to health. The words sometimes refer to actual temperature, but more often they describe qualities not directly related to heat or cold. In the Latin American variants of this system, foods, medicinal herbs, and many other substances, conditions, and events (such as ice, menstruation and pregnancy, and an eclipse) are classified as hot, cold, or neutral in the sense of innate qualities. The conceptual principle is similar to that used in the United States in "hard" and "soft" water, "hard" and "soft" beverages, and "dry" and "sweet" wines. We know that liquids are not hard, soft, or dry in the usual sense of the words, but the ethnologist from Mars would be puzzled by our terminology.

Contemporary naturalistic systems resemble each other in an important historical sense: the bulk of their explanations and practices represent simplified and popularized legacies from the "Great Tradition" medicine of ancient classical civilizations, particularly those of Greece, India, and China. Unlike personalistic systems, known largely through modern anthropological studies, historical records describing naturalistic systems reach back as far as 2500 years ago. Knowledge of the origin and development of these systems enables us to understand the many modern variants with a degree of clarity that would be impossible if we had to rely only on contemporary ethnographic accounts. The three systems summarized here are humoral pathology (found today in Latin America), Ayurvedic medicine (found in India and adjacent countries), and traditional Chinese medicine.

1. Humoral pathology

Humoral pathology is based on the concept of bodily "humors." Its roots are found in the Greek theory of the four elements (earth, water, air, and fire) already recognized by the sixth century B.C. By the time of Hippocrates (born about 460 B.C.), this theory had been augmented by the parallel concept of four qualities — hot, cold, dry, moist — which, when integrated with the original theory, produced the concept of the four "humors" with their associated qualities: *blood* (hot and moist), *phlegm* (cold and moist), *black bile,* also called "melancholy" (cold and dry), and *yellow bile,* or "choler" (hot and dry).

Although Hippocrates is certainly a historical figure, the collection of medical treatises that bears his name — the *Hippocratic Corpus* — has multiple origins. Since the earliest surviving manuscript of the *Corpus* is probably from the tenth century A.D. (Chadwick and Mann 1950:5), we will probably never know precisely what writings are those of the real Hippocrates and what comes down to use in his name only. It is convenient, however, to describe classical Greek medicine as if the *Corpus* were written by Hippocrates.

That the equilibrium theory of health was well developed in ancient Greece is evidenced by "Hippocrates' " description of disease: "The human body contains blood, phlegm, yellow bile and black bile. These are the things that make up its constitution and cause its pains and health. Health is primarily that state in which these constituent substances are in the correct proportion to each other, both in strength and quantity, and are well mixed. Pain occurs when one of the substances presents either a deficiency or an excess, or is separated in the body and not mixed with the others" (*Ibid.*, 204).

The four humors, writes Hippocrates, "have specific and different names because there are essential differences in their appearance. . . . They are dissimilar in their qualities of heat, cold, dryness and moisture" (*Ibid.*, 205). Although Hippocrates appears to specify precisely in no place the qualities of the humors, he clearly comprehended these qualities and noted that they varied in quantity over the year, depending on climate and weather. Phlegm increases in the winter, he wrote, because as the coldest humor, it is most in keeping with the winter. During the spring the quantity of blood increases, stimulated by the wet and warm days of the rainy season. Because it is moist and hot, this part of the year is most in keeping with the blood. During the summer, although blood remains strong, the bile gradually increases, ruling the body during the summer and autumn. The hot and dry summer weather is conducive to yellow bile but, as the cool and dry autumn comes on, the bile is cooled, and black bile preponderates (*Ibid.*, 206-207).

Because of these annual seasonal variations it is reasonable, said Hippocrates, to expect most diseases to occur only during certain times of the year and, hence, in applying his remedies, "The physician must bear in mind that each disease is most prominent during the season most in keeping with its nature" (*Ibid.*, 208). In addition, treatment should aim at opposing the cause of the disease: "Diseases caused by over-eating are cured by fasting; those caused by starvation are cured by feeding up. Diseases caused by exertion are cured by rest; those caused by indolence are cured by exertion. To put it briefly, the physician should treat disease *by the principle of opposition* to the cause of the disease according to its form, its seasonal and age incidence, countering tenseness by relaxation and *vice versa*. This will bring the patient most relief and seems to me to be the principle of healing" (*Ibid.*, 208. First emphasis added).

Since the most important organs of the body (the heart, brain, and liver) were thought in classical Greek times to be respectively dry and hot, moist and cold, and hot and moist, the normal, healthy body had an excess of heat and moisture. But this balance varied with individuals, so that their temperaments, or "complexions," varied: the *sanguine* (ruddy, cheerful, optimistic), the *phlegmatic* (calm, composed, sluggish, apathetic), the *bilious* (choleric, ill-tempered), and the *melancholic* (depressed, sad, melancholy). Good medical practice thus consisted of knowing the natural complexion of the patient, in establishing which humor or humors were momentarily excessive or deficient in quantity, in matching these findings with the dominant humor of the season, and in deciding how the normal humoral balance could best be reestablished. This was accomplished by means of diet, internal medicines, purging, vomiting, bleeding, cupping, and like forms of treatment.

The routes whereby classical Greek medicine has come down to our times to produce contemporary folk humoral pathology are too complex to discuss in detail. Greek medicine was preserved, and manuscripts were copied and recopied in the great library at Alexandria founded in the third century B.C.; it is from that source that Galen (ca. 130-200 A.D.) acquired the bulk of his vast knowledge. Although a Greek, Galen practiced for most of his life in Rome, adding to and refining the earlier Greek writings, giving the theory of humors its final shape, and assuring its supremacy (Sarton 1954:54). Through Byzantine civilization Galen's influence was transmitted to the oriental Christians and to the Moslems. Some of his writings were translated into Syriac, and then into Arabic, while others were translated directly into Arabic.

Much of the early work of translating Greek sources was done by Nestorians at Edessa, in Mesopotamia. When they fled Edessa at the end of the fifth century, they settled at Gundê-Shāpūr in southwest Persia where, until the middle of the ninth century, the medical knowledge of classical Greece and Galen was translated into Arabic, thus giving rise to the Arab version of humoral pathology. At Gundê-Shāpūr, too, Ayurvedic medicine from India came into contact with humoral medicine, but we know little about the form and extent of the interchange of ideas that certainly took place.

During the latter half of the ninth century, the school for translations at Baghdad replaced that in Persia; it was here that the greatest physicians of the Eastern Caliphate — most of them Persians by birth — flourished: Rhazes (ca. 865-925), Haly Abbas (died 994) and, best known of all, Avicenna (980-1037), whose *Canon of Medicine* sums up medical knowledge as of that time (Gruner 1930).

Simultaneously, other Moslems pushed west along the north coast of Africa, conquering Spain and Italy and carrying with them the medicine of classical Greece and the eastern Arab world. Those Spanish-born physicians who most influenced European medicine included Avenzoar (1113-1162, or 1196), Averroes (1126-1198), and the Jew Maimonides (1135-1204), a resident of Cairo for most of his life.

These combined medical legacies began to be translated from Arabic into

Latin, especially in Toledo after the expulsion in 1085 of the Moors, and in Salerno (Sicily) and Monte Casino (Italy).

Thus the ancient doctrine of humors became the basis for medieval Christian medicine, where it remained dominant until the discoveries of Vesalius (1514-1564), Harvey (1578-1657), and Sydenham (1624-1689). From the writings of Christian physicians until this time we see that Hippocrates, Galen, and the Arab physicians, especially Avicenna, were the principal authorities for medical theory and practice. Even after its dethronement by scientific medicine, humoral pathology remained influential at the popular level until well into the nineteenth century in the form of herbals and home remedy books. From England colonial United States also acquired the doctrine of humors and, as Snow recently pointed out, more of it survives at a popular level, particularly among low-income blacks and poor white Southerners than has usually been assumed (Snow 1976).

It is, however, in Latin America that humoral medicine, first in an elite and then in a popular form, has had its greatest modern impact. With the discovery and conquest of America, it came to the New World as part of the cultural baggage of the *conquistadores* and later settlers. As it had been in Spain, so in the New World it remained the scientific medicine well into the eighteenth century. Simultaneously, and by paths that have not been well worked out, parts of humoral pathology filtered down to the folk level replacing, among mestizo peasants and acculturated Indian groups, a large part of pre-Conquest medicine and blending with those parts that have survived. Conforming to the processes whereby simplified parts of an elite culture gradually sift down to folk and peasant levels, humoral pathology lost the qualities of moist and dry (Foster 1953a, 1953b).

Today in large parts of Latin America, from Mexico south through Hispanic and Portuguese South America, the folk variant of humoral pathology is the most important explanatory element in the medical systems of rural — and to some extent urban — peoples. Although it has been suggested that the hot-cold dichotomy in Mexican folk medicine has its roots in Aztec beliefs (e.g., López Austin 1974:209, 218-219), this explanation would not account for the nearly universal Latin American distribution of the system, which is much better explained by the historical antecedents just described.

In contemporary Latin American humoral pathology, illness is ascribed to invasion of the body by excessive heat or cold. Sometimes actual temperature is involved, as when a woman explains hand and arm cramps as due to her carelessness in washing them in cold water when they were temporarily heated from ironing clothing. More often heat and cold are viewed metaphorically: a man who suffers hand and arm cramps may explain them as due to his carelessness in washing them when they were temporarily heated by the mineral lime he was using in whitewashing a wall. Cold may enter the body in the form of "aire," or air, from the ingestion of "cold" foods, from stepping on a cold floor barefoot, and the like. Body heat rises from exposure to the sun, a potter's kiln, or a cooking fire, from bathing in warm water, from sleeping, from reading (the eyes become heated), from being pregnant or during the menses, from ingesting "hot" foods and beverages, and from experiencing "hot" emotional experiences such as fright, anger, or grief. In theory illnesses believed to have hot causes are treated with cold herbal remedies and foods and with cold treatments (such as some kinds of skin plasters). Illnesses believed to come from cold causes are treated with hot herbal remedies and foods and hot treatments (such as mustard plasters and cupping). In fact, most remedies are mixtures of a number of elements in which a hot or cold balance predominates.

Representative descriptions of contemporary Latin American humoral pathology are found in Cosminsky (1975, 1977); Currier (1966); Foster (1953a, 1967:184-193); Harwood (1971); Ingham (1970); Logan (1973); Madsen (1955); Mazess (1968); McCullough (1973); Molony (1975); Orso (1970); the Reichel-Dolmatoffs (1961); Ryesky (1976); Simmons (1955); and Suárez (1974).

Greek humoral pathology, in its Galenic form, also diffused eastward carried, as in the movement to the west, by the expanding Moslem civilization. The Moslems called the medicine of Galen *Tibb-i-Yunānī* (or *Unānī Tibbi*), and in Persia, Pakistan, and other southwestern Asian countries it has demonstrated remarkable vitality at both sophisticated and folk levels. Browne recalls how, when he attended the meetings of the Persian Council of Public Health in Tehran in 1887, he was astonished to find that a majority of the physicians knew no medicine other than that of Avicenna (Browne 1921:93). Today humoral pathology underlies much folk medicine in Malaysia, Java (where *masuk angin,* or "wind entry," is viewed as the principal threat to health), and the Philippines. In the Philippines these beliefs appear to be the result of Spanish influence, by way of Mexico and the Manila galleon (Hart 1969:62). In contrast, Malaysian humoral pathology is clearly the result of Moslem influence, partially in the form of direct translation of Arabic works into Malay (*Ibid.,* 45), and partially as a legacy of earlier Moslem invaders. The Javanese hot-cold syndrome, too, appears more nearly to correspond to Moslem patterns than to indigenous south Asian influences. Thus, propelled eastward and westward by Moslem and Spanish movements, the basic classical Greek medical beliefs have encircled the earth.

2. Ayurvedic medicine

In contemporary India many foods are thought to have heating or cooling qualities and, as in humoral pathology, the right combinations of foods and herbs can restore the proper balance when the body equilibrium has been disturbed. *Garam* (hot) foods include eggs, meat, milk, dahl, honey, and sugar; *tonda* (cold) foods include fruit juices, yoghurt, acid buttermilk, rice, and water (Jelliffe 1957:135). These beliefs have their origin in Indian Ayurvedic medicine, an indigenous system that first appears in the Vedic writings of the early years of the first millenium B.C. These early texts, however, are "Couched in terms of imprecations against demons, sorcerers, enemies; of charms for expelling diseases wrought by demons or sent by the gods as punishment for man's sin" (Zimmer 1948:1-2). It was not until significantly later that classical Ayurvedic medicine appears in surviving Sanskrit documents: the *Caraka Samhita* of the first century A.D., the *Susruta Samhita,* about the fourth century A.D., and the *Vagbhata,* about the eighth century A.D. (Leslie 1968: 562). The theories found in these sources, however, certainly predate them by several centuries.

According to Ayurvedic theory, the universe is composed of the same four elements recognized by the Greeks (earth, water, fire, air), plus a fifth, ether. The arrangement of these elements in the body, each of which possesses five "subtle" and five "material" forms, is a microcosm of the universe. The human body also has three humors, or *dosha* (hence the term *tridosha* theory): phlegm, or mucus; bile, or gall; and wind, or flatulence. Good health exists when the three dosha are in equilibrium; ill health manifests itself when one or more of the dosha are not functioning properly (Leslie 1969; Opler 1963). The dosha also are associated with age and the seasons: phlegm with youth and the growing season, bile with middle age and the rainy season, and wind with old age and cold and dry weather (Beck 1969:562).

The similarities shared by Ayurvedic medicine and humoral pathology point to significant interrelationships between the two systems. Yet the historical record is such that mutual influences are difficult to prove until fairly late in time. Beginning early in the twentieth century, Ayurveda has become more and more important among Indian nationalists as a symbol of the antiquity and greatness of Indian civilization. In 1920, for example, more than a generation prior to independence, the Indian National Congress passed a resolution to the effect that, "having regard to the widely prevalent and generally accepted utility of the Ayurvedic and Unani systems of medicine in India, earnest efforts should be made by the people of India to popularize schools, colleges, and hospitals for instruction and treatment in accordance with these indigenous systems" (Udupa 1975:54). Subsequently, schools of Indian medicine were opened in Madras, Bombay, Delhi, Bengal, and in other cities "to train competent practitioners of Indian medicine with a good working knowledge of modern medicine so that they could render comprehensive medical service to the rural population" (*Ibid.,* 55).

Because of the symbolic role of Ayurveda in India, there is some tendency on the part of authors to make sweeping, undocumented, statements. Udupa, for example, writes that "At the beginning of the Christian era, Ayurveda had spread far and wide and had influenced the systems of medicine in Egypt, Greece, Rome, and Arabia" (*Ibid.,* 54). Since the first of the great Ayurvedic writers, Caraka, lived at the end of the first century or the beginning of the second century A.D., this statement obviously is overdrawn.

In 1947 the Department of Health of the newly independent government of India named a committee to consider ways to increase the usefulness of Hindu Ayurveda and Muslim Unānī Tibbi medicine. A "Scientific Memorandum" in the appendices of the Committee's 1948 report begins by saying of Ayurvedic medicine, "It has been the product of the genius of this country and has not been borrowed from outside . . . The humoral theory of the Greeks was, perhaps, a bad adaptation of the *Tridosha* theory" (Opler 1963:32). Again, there is no evidence to support such a statement. The evidence for a major interchange between humoral pathology and Ayurvedic medicine is far better at Gundê-Shāpūr. Basham reports that the court physician to a Persian emperor early in the sixth century (i.e., shortly after the Gundê-Shāpūr school was founded) visited India and brought back Indian medical texts and Indian physicians who practiced at the school. "Later, at least fifteen Indian medical texts were translated into Arabic" (Basham 1976:39).

The direct traces of humoral pathology in India are far stronger than the other way around. Unānī Tibbi medicine, widely practiced by Muslim hakīms in India today, is classical Greek medicine, as modified by Arab scholars. The word *Unānī* (or *Yunānī*) is a corruption of the Arabic word for "Ionian" (i.e., Greek).

Whatever their historical relationships, humoral pathology and Ayurvedic medicine have had distinct culture histories. Whereas humoral pathology was developed and elaborated by a series of famous doctors in renowned medical centers, who have left us a massive written record, "Hindu medical lore has been handed down through generations, not by faculties and bodies, colleges, or research centers, but through the individual training of pupils by skilled practitioners, masters of their craft" (Zimmer 1948:75). Yet today humoral pathology is folk medicine and an historical curiosity, while Auyrvedic medicine receives major Indian government support. By the mid-1970s 91 Ayurvedic medical colleges and 10 Unānī colleges were admitting about 7000 students a year, and had already trained about 50,000 "institutionally qualified" Ayurvedic physicians (Udupa 1975:64-65). In addition, there are about 150,-000 "noninstitutionally qualified" but "registered" practitioners of Ayurvedic and Unānī medicine, and perhaps another 200,000 unregistered Ayurvedic practitioners. This contrasts with 107 "modern" medical colleges admitting about 13,000 students annually. Beyond this, national and state governments support about 9000 Ayurvedic dispensaries and 195 hospitals offering Indian medicine. Ayurvedic — and to a much lesser extent Unānī — medicine clearly plays a major role in contemporary Indian health care.

3. Traditional chinese medicine

"Ancient" traditional Chinese medicine is best known through the *Huang Ti Nei Ching Su Wên,* the Yellow Emperor's "Inner Classic," or book of internal medicine. *Huang Ti,* the Yellow Emperor, was in Chinese genealogies the third of China's first five rulers; the precise dates 2697-2597 B.C. are assigned to him (Veith 1972:5). In fact, the book, while old, is considerably more recent. After sifting the evidence, Veith concludes that "a great part of the text existed during the Han dynasty (202 B.C.-221 A.D.), and that much of it is of considerably older origin, possibly handed down by oral tradition from China's earliest history" (*Ibid.,* 9). In other words, ancient China's medicine began to turn to naturalistic explanations at about the same time that the process took place in Greece and India.

Traditional Chinese medicine represents a special case of the central concept of Chinese cosmology, "the dual forces of *yin* and *yang,* whose continuous interaction lies behind all natural phenomena, including the constitution and functioning of the human body" (Croizier 1968:17). As previously pointed out, the proper balance within the body of yin and yang is essential for good health. "This principle of harmony, which views disease as essentially due to its impairment through external or internal, physical or mental causes, has remained central to all of later Chinese medicine" (*Ibid.*).

Since yin and yang are thought to be the primordial elements from which the universe evolved, it is not surprising that they are endowed with innumerable qualities. Their earliest meanings — cloudy and sunny — have been expanded to produce a philosophical duality that can accommodate almost any concept. Thus, yang represents heaven, sun, fire, heat, dryness, light, the male principle, the exterior, the right side, life, high, noble, good, beautiful, virtue, order, joy, wealth — in short, all positive elements. Yin represents the opposite: earth, moon, water, cold, dampness, darkness, the female principle, the interior, the left side, death, low, ignoble, bad, ugly, vice, confusion, and poverty — in short, all the negative elements.[4] Because of its heat, excessive yang causes fever; because of its coldness, excessive yin produces chills. Diseases believed caused by external forces are yang diseases, and those believed caused by internal forces are yin diseases. Yet yin and yang have always been conceived of as a single entity combining, in any being or situation, both positive and negative elements.

Chinese philosophers (including doctors) recognized the five elements of water, fire, metal, wood, and earth, all contained in the human body and all linked to physiological processes and to specific internal organs. The number five was, in fact, the basis for an elaborate system of numerical concordances that described and integrated the entire universe, including man, so that most phenomena were thought to occur in sets of five: seasons, directions, musical notes, colors, emotions, bodily orifices, food flavors, internal organs, and many more. The linkage between the human body, health, and the universe is also found in the concordance of the number of days of the year with the 365 drugs of the earliest surviving pharmacopoeia (Croizier 1968:20) and the 365 bodily surface points recognized for insertion of acupuncture needles (Veith 1972:62). This preoccupation with philosophical elegance unquestionably stultified medical advances by means of empirical observations and experimentation.

"Such an assured view of the constitution of man," says Pellegrino, "strongly discouraged the study of anatomy. Chinese medicine was characterized by the vaguest notions of human anatomy. Its therapy was directed to providing the missing Yang element by the administration of some animal organ presumed to have a high content of that material" (Pellegrino 1963:12). Croizier has noted the same thing. Despite some precise knowledge apparently derived from earlier human dissection, the anatomical and physiological principles of the *Nei ching* "tended to become exempt from empirical modification as they became philosophically more elaborate, so that they ended up true to their larger cosmological system but often far removed from material reality" (Croizier 1968:18).

The antiquity and importance of the hot-cold dichotomy in traditional Chinese medicine is more difficult to determine than in the case of humoral pathology and Ayurvedic medicine. This is partly because ethnologists working in Chinese societies until recently have been little interested in popular medicine. Until less than a decade ago anthropological reports on China said nothing whatsoever about a hot-cold classificatory system, and even today the occurrences — which appear to be widespread if not universal — are just beginning to be described. Moreover, these recent accounts deal with the hot-cold dichotomy in the context of food and food habits that promote health rather than in the context of medicine *per se*. The concepts of hot-cold, wet-dry dichotomies are, of course, implicit in the yin-yang duality. Yet in the *Nei ching* we find no specific references to this belief. Instead, foods are classified according to five flavors (pungent, sour, sweet, bitter, and salty), and proper manipulation of these foods to benefit the affected organs was carried out in much the same way as balancing hot and cold in the other two systems.

Scattered bits of evidence extracted from various sources by Chu and Ch'iang appear to push a specific hot-cold dichotomy back as far at 180 B.C. For example, heat and cold "condensed with moisture" in the intestines is a common explanation for intestinal worms (Chu and Ch'iang 1931). Far better evidence comes from Chia Ming's *Yin-shih-hsü-chih* (*Essential Knowledge for Eating and Drinking*), dated 1368 A.D. This remarkable treatise describes 43 kinds of fires and water, 50 kinds of grains, 87 kinds of vegetables, 63 kinds of fruits and nuts, 33 "flavorings" and condiments, 68 varieties of fish, 34 kinds of fowl, and 42 kinds of meat! The entry for each of these 460 entries tells to which of the five flavor categories it belongs, its "character" (specified degrees of hotness or coolness), and the other foods that should not be eaten with it. The character of natural rainwater, for example, is cold, while that of water from a stalactite cavern is warm; the flavor of both is sweet. Glutinous rice is said to be warm, and eaten in excess it causes fever. Soybeans and fragrant leeks are warm, vinegar is "slightly warm," and distilled spirits are "very hot." Spinach, persimmons, and milk are cold (Mote 1977:227-233).

Whatever the time of the formalization of the hot-cold dichtomy in the Chinese dietary and medical systems, recent ethnographical research shows that the belief is widespread and pervasive today. Topley's Hong Kong work shows that a balance between heat and cold is believed essential to physical well-being, and that foods and medicines have hot or cold qualities that must be considered in maintaining a proper balance in diet and in treating illness (Topley 1970:425-426). Moreover, acupuncture (the insertion of fine needles along the lines of the body's "meridians") is a "cold" operation, hence especially suited to diseases due to an excess of yang, while moxibustion (the burning of tiny cones of dried leaves of mugwort on the skin) is a "hot" treatment, particularly suited to diseases caused by an excess of yin.

The Andersons, describing diet and health beliefs and practices in Chinese villages in Hong Kong and Malaysia, include as hot foods strong alcoholic beverages, spicy and fatty foods, protein-rich dishes, and foods prepared by long cooking at high heat. Cold foods include herbal teas, bland and low-calorie vegetables, beer, and the like. A few items such as crabs, mollusks, and catfish are both hot and wet; venereal diseases are "wet" and hot (Anderson and Anderson 1975:146-148, 1977:366-370). From Taiwan we also now have good data about the hot-cold bodily equilibrium that spells health and the relationship of food to it (Ahern 1975; Pillsbury 1976). This and similar evidence, such as that of Linda Koo for Chinese in America (Koo 1976), lead us to believe that the relative absence of good information on the hot-cold dichotomy in Chinese health beliefs is a consequence of past research neglect and not absence of the trait.

EMOTIONAL ELEMENTS IN CAUSATION THEORY

In suggesting that most non-Western medical etiologies can be subsumed under the rubrics of personalistic and naturalistic, we are, of course, generalizing. And, as with all generalizations, there are loose ends that do not neatly fit into grand schema. The widespread belief that strong emotional experiences such as envy, fright, grief, and shame can cause illness does not fit into either major category. Or perhaps we should say that, depending on situation and circumstance, these beliefs may fit into either category. *Susto* — illness caused by fright — widespread in Latin Amefica, is illustrative (e.g., Gillin 1948; Kearney 1972:54-58; O'Nell 1975; O'Nell and Selby 1968; Rubel 1964; Seijas 1972; Uzzell 1974). A person may be frightened by a ghost, a spirit, an encounter with a devil, or by something as simple as stumbling near water and fearing death by drowning. If the agent *intended* harm, the etiology certainly is personalistic. But accounts of such encounters often suggest chance or accident and not purposive action. And, in fearing death by drowning, no agent is present.

The problems inherent in attempting a too-tight classificatory system are also apparent in Potter's account of soul loss (the common explanation as to *why* fright causes illness) among Cantonese village children. The souls of small children, the chief victims, are believed to be loosely attached to their bodies; they may be dislodged either by fright or by a hungry or malicious ghost that enters the body and "steals" the soul (Potter 1974:222). In the former instance the cause is naturalistic; in the latter it is obviously personalistic.

In Mexico and Central America *chipil* may strike small children about the time they are weaned. Western physicians explain the crying, whining, and apathy that are symptoms of the condition as primarily due to loss of protein when the child is removed from the breast. But the folk explanation attributes illness to the knee-child's jealousy of its mother's affection and its envy and resentment of its sibling-to-be, which it senses in its mother's womb. Is the fetus an intentional and calculating agent, already looking out for itself? It could be perceived either way.

The evil eye is also difficult to categorize. In the Near East, the Mediterranean, Latin America, and other parts of the world, it is thought by many that a human agent, as a consequence of envy, consciously or unconsciously produces illness in another person or causes damage to some possession of the individual envied. Most commonly the envied object is a beautiful, healthy child, but domestic animals, automobiles, or almost any other object that one might desire is a potential victim of the "eye." The glance of the envious person is believed to cause the child to fall ill, the animal to sicken and die, or the automobile to break down. If the envy actually exists (often people simply suspect, or fear, that they are being envied) and it respresents symbolic aggression, then the evil eye would conform to a personalistic model. Yet people accused of having the evil eye may not intentionally cast a spell; they may have the power in spite of themselves, and it is sometimes unknown to them. In the absence of intent, it is harder to classify the cause as personalistic.

Obviously a dual taxonomy for phenomena as varied as non-Western beliefs about illness causes will leave some questions unanswered, and it will often encounter borderline cases, as in the following example reported for Sri Lanka by Obeyesekere. In that country naturalistic causes are those of Sanskritic Ayurveda, involving disturbances in the equilibrium of the three humors, the *tridosha*. Personalistic causes take the form of demons, mean spirits, and gods, who cause all kinds of misfortune, including illness. Ayurvedic doctors treat symptoms and restore humoral balance with medicine. Possession by demons or spirits, in contrast, requires placation and banishment of the disease-causing agents. The distinction seems simple. Yet "demonic incursions, as well as incursions by any external spirit, cause in turn the upsetting of the three humors, so that the symptoms of demonic illness may be similar to the symptoms of physical illness" (Obeyesekere 1969:175). Since the identical disease may be caused by either naturalistic or demonological factors, it is difficult to classify some Ceylonese illness. But a taxonomy is not an end in itself, something to be admired for its elegance. Its utility lies in clarifying our understanding of relationships among the phenomena with which it deals.

CORRELATES OF CAUSALITY

Disease causality systems, like all subcultural systems, reveal a basic harmony within themselves, a rational integration of their many parts. And, like all subcultural systems, disease causality systems reflect the basic structural principles, the patterns, and the premises of the cultures in which they are imbedded. Speaking specifically of non-Western medical systems, we believe that the greatest utility of the personalistic-naturalistic classificatory system is that it makes possible a reduction of the welter of curers, curing techniques, divination, and all other medical elements described for the world's societies to some semblance of order.

If we look at medical beliefs and practices in terms of causality concepts, we see that the other major aspects of a given medical system stem logically from these concepts. It is not going too far to say that if we are given a clear description of what a people believe to be the causes of illness, we can in broad outline fill in the other elements in that medical system. To elaborate, personalistic etiologies logically require a particular kind of curer, a shaman or other diviner, to determine not only the immediate cause of illness but, more important, to find out *who* lies behind the cause. Naturalistic etiologies require a different kind of curer, such as a physician or herbalist who knows the medicines and other treatments that will restore the body's equilibrium. Neither personalistic nor naturalistic causality explanations can really handle the concept of contagion; only with the development of the scientific concept of pathogens can the transmission of disease from one person to another be easily explained.

One of us (Foster 1976b) recently has discussed the principal contrasting correlates of personalistic and naturalistic etiologies, which we summarize here.

1. Comprehensive and restricted etiologies

Personalistic medical etiologies are parts of more comprehensive explanatory systems, while naturalistic etiologies are largely restricted to illness. In other words, in personalistic systems illness is only a special case in the explanation of all misfortune. In societies in which personalistic explanations for disease prevail, we find that the same agents, the same beings, also lie behind *all* misfortune, such as blighting of crops, financial reverses, theft, and family quarrels. Illness is not a separate category from misfortune in general.

In contrast, naturalistic etiologies are restricted to disease as such; they are not invoked to account for drought, bad luck in hunting, disputes over land, or other irritants in life. Where the hot-cold dichotomy is found, its role is restricted to explaining illness and guiding treatment. Conversely, while false friends and natural-born troublemakers may lie behind much misfortune, they are not accused of causing illness.

2. Disease, religion, and magic

Glick has written, "We must think about how and where 'medicine' fits into 'religion'. . . . In an ethnography of a religious system, where does the description of the medical system belong; and how does it relate to the remainder?" (Glick 1967:33). Similarly, in writing about the Bomvana Xhosa of South Africa, Jansen says that "religion, medicine and magic are closely interwoven . . . The Bomvana himself does not distinguish between his religion, magic and medicine" (Jansen 1973:34).

Medicine, magic, and religion are so often discussed as though they are inevitable parts of one system that one rarely asks, "When do they *not* go together?" Yet when we relate religion and magic to etiological systems, it becomes clear that they correlate with personalistic systems and are largely lacking in naturalistic systems. In the latter, curing procedures are rarely ritual, and religious and magical elements play a small part in them. Never do we hear of the curer described as a priest or priestess as, for example, in much of Africa. When religious elements are found in illness treatment in naturalistic systems, these elements are conceptually distinct from those found in personalistic systems. In one way the practices and beliefs of the two systems are mirror images of each other. When, in Latin America and the Mediterranean, victims of illness place votive offerings on or near "miraculous" images of Christ or the Virgin, they are engaged in religious acts intended to work cures. But — and this is the important point — these supplications are not directed at beings responsible for the illness but rather to supernatural beings who, as advocates for man, can intervene to help the sufferer in *any* extremity. In contrast, in personalistic systems sacrifices and offerings are made to propitiate the beings held responsible for the illness.

3. Levels of causation

Generalizing from his research among the LoDagaa of Ghana, Goody concludes that among most nonliterate peoples disease explanations that Westerners would regard as natural are not in themselves sufficient to account for illness and death. They recognize that a snakebite can cause a man to die, but the snake is seen as an intermediary agent; surviving relatives want to know who or what had grounds for hostility toward the dead man and sent the snake to bite him (Goody 1962:208-209). Goody's use of the term "intermediary agent" points to an important contrast between personalistic and naturalistic systems. In the latter, disease usually is explained by a single cause such as excessive heat or cold in the body which has upset the natural equilibrium. The patient may reflect back to determine what careless act on his part permitted the heat or cold to attack him, but he does not ask "Who put the heat (or cold) in me?"

Personalistic systems are more complex in that two or more levels of causality can be distinguished and, in curing, these levels must be taken into account. At a minimum we can distinguish the personal agent (the witch, ghost, or deity) *and* the technique used by this agent (such as intrusion of a disease object, poison, theft of the soul, possession, or witchcraft), but this act alone usually is not seen as sufficient. The agent who lies behind the act must be identified and propitiated or otherwise rendered harmless if recovery is to be permanent. Differing levels of causality, as we will see, is critical to an understanding of basis differences in curing techniques found in the two systems.

4. Shamans and other curers

Personalistic systems recognizing multiple levels of causality logically require curers with supernatural or magical divinatory powers, because the primary concern of patient and family is "who?" and not "what?" The shaman, with his direct contact with the spirit world, and the witch doctor (to use an outmoded but still useful term from the African literature), with his magical powers (both of whom answer the questions "who?" and "why?") are logical answers to the needs of multiple causality concepts. After these questions have been answered, treatment for the immediate cause can be administered by the diviner, or the task may be turned over to a lesser curer.

Shamans and witchdoctors are usually not found among peoples whose primary etiologies are naturalistic. Both patient and doctor usually agree what has happened, and the problem is to determine the appropriate treatment to restore the lost equilibrium. In naturalistic systems curers tend to be "doctors" in that they have learned their skills through observation and practice and not acquired them through divine intervention.

5. Diagnosis

Personalistic and naturalistic etiological systems also are distinguishable on the basis of diagnostic techniques. In the former, as we have just seen, powerful shamans or witch doctors are desirable, to identify the causative agent. Treatment of symptoms may be of secondary importance. In contrast, as far as the curer is concerned, diagnosis is of very minor importance in naturalistic systems; the determination of cause is made by the patient himself or by members of his family. The patient seeks aid from a curer for relief of symptoms, and not to find out what has happened.

Self-diagnosis in societies with naturalistic etiologies is illustrated by what is done in Tzintzuntzan, Mexico. To illustrate, when a person feels unwell, he thinks back to an experience the preceding night, the day before, or even a month or a year earlier, when an event transpired that is believed to cause the symptoms that are distressing him. Did he awaken with a sore throat? He remembers that on going to bed the night before he carelessly stepped on the tile floor in his bare feet. This, he knows, can cause cold to enter the feet, compressing the normal heat of his body into the upper chest, throat, and head. Thus, he suffers from "risen heat." *He* tells the doctor what is wrong and merely asks for a remedy. Similarly, a woman who suffers an attack of rheumatism in her arms may remember that, after ironing and thereby heating her hands, she washed them in cold water without allowing them to cool first. She needs no diviner to tell her why she is suffering. In theory, at least, any patient, upon reflection, should be able to identify every cause of illness that may afflict him.

AMERICAN FOLK MEDICINE

By and large American popular medical beliefs and practices have not been studied within the conceptual framework of ethnomedicine. Until recently most research on the topic has been done by folklorists instead of anthropologists, and particularizing description, not theory, is the dominant note in publications. But with the growing interest of anthropologists in American society and ethnic cultures this situation is changing, and anthropological accounts of contemporary American folk medicine are more and more common. From these it is clear that the concept of ethnomedicine (i.e., medical beliefs and practices not explicitly derived from modern medicine) is as useful for an understanding of American folk medicine as for non-Western medical systems.

At the most general level we can speak of a single American folk medical system, defined as all those beliefs and practices that are not a part of orthodox, scientific medicine. At the most specific level we can argue that there are as many folk medicines in the United States as there are ethnic groups. But to focus on either level in discussing American folk medicine is to oversimplify the picture vastly. There are, obviously, distinct folk medicines: Mexican-American traditional practices are quite different from those of the Pennsylvania Dutch. At the same time, ethnically distinct folk medical systems often share common historical origins to some degree. This is particularly evident in the influence of humoral pathology on Mexican-American, Cuban, Puerto Rican, and other Spanish-American folk medicines. Furthermore, elements of humoral pathology are found in black folk medicine, the legacy of mixing Spanish, French, and Negro cultures in the Caribbean. And on a more remote and still largely unexplored level, the folk medicine of European ethnic groups unquestionably incorporates remnants from the time when humoral pathology was scientific medicine in Europe and colonial America (e.g., Snow 1974:83, 1977a:34).

1. Euro-American folk medicine

We use the term Euro-American to refer to the folk medical beliefs and practices of European immigrants and their descendants in the United States. This is not a homogeneous system (as is, for example, Mexican-American folk medicine), since many different countries and time periods are represented, but only with the license of "lumping" of categories is it possible to compare and contrast major patterns. Particularly in the nineteenth century, Euro-American folk medicine, regardless of the country of origin of settlers, was shaped by the common experience of a frontier life: doctors were scarce, their talents were limited, Indian "powwow" doctors were highly respected, and self-reliance and dependence on family resources were essential to survival. It was also shaped by another factor that sets it off from all other folk medicines: to a very great degree it was a *literate* phenomenon in which the printed word as well as oral tradition played a major role in shaping and maintaining belief and practice. It was in the United States where, for the first time in history, the great majority of people who depended on their own resources and those of the local curer could read. And read they did; it was a rare family that did not, along with its bible, carry with it one or more home remedy books and read in local newspapers the extravagant, usually fraudulent, claims made by local "doctors" and patent medicines.

In the early years of the frontier Indian influences on folk medicine were strong: "In some western communities in the earlier years there were Indian doctors who were held in quite as high repute as regular white doctors" (Pickard and Buley 1945:36). Even after native American medicine men ceased to play a direct role in popular medicine, their mystique remained strong, as evidenced by the titles of the "powwow" guides to curing and health that flooded the United States in the first half of the nineteenth century: Peter Smith's *The Indian Doctor's Dispensatory* (1813), Dr. Richard Carter's *Valuable Vegetable Medical Prescriptions for the Cure of All Nervous and Putrid Disorders* (1815), Dr. S. H. Selman's *The Indian Guide to Health* (1836), Dr. William Daily's *The Indian Doctor's Practice of Medicine* (1848), James Cooper's *The Indian Doctor's Receipt Book* (1855), and many more with similar titles.[5]

Interestingly, the Indian mystique remains strong in contemporary American spiritualism. "The names of more than a dozen mediums, men and women and their Indian controls, appear in the *Encyclopedia of Psychic Science*. Such historic figures as Red Jacket, Black Hawk, and Tecumseh are on the list, as well as spirits with such names as White Feather, Bright Eyes, and Moonstone" (Macklin 1974a:409). Indian controls usually are viewed as benevolent and beneficent, if at times a bit rambunctious in séances.

In addition to those works that played on the reputed power of Indian curers, the literate frontiersman had access to an equally impressive number of home remedy books, many of which were the product of legitimate physicians who, however, often found themselves in opposition to the profession at large. Books with titles like *The Family Physician* and *Travellers Pocket Medical Guide* went through uncounted printings. Perhaps the best known, Dr.

John Gunn's *Domestic Medicine or Poor Man's Friend, in the House of Affliction, Pain and Sickness,* first published in 1830, had gone through 213 editions by 1885, not counting German translations (Pickard and Buley 1945:93).

The nineteenth-century American in need of medical help could also turn to "sectarian" medicine, as manifest in the German import, homeopathy, or the homegrown "botanic" medicine of Samuel Thomson, and its offshoots, "Eclecticism" or "Reformed" botanic medicine, and other systems of "curing" such as hydropathy, phrenology, and Mesmerism.

But even in the face of literacy, genuine oral-tradition folk medicine also flourished; perhaps the most influential, and certainly the best studied, is that of the Pennsylvania Dutch, German immigrants who came to the United States late in the eighteenth and early in the nineteenth centuries, settling first in Pennsylvania and later sending sons and daughters to the Midwest as it was opened up to farming. In this and other American oral traditions, we find that, just as much folk culture reflects the sophisticated culture of an earlier generation, so are many folk beliefs and practices survivals of orthodox medicine of an earlier time. Thus, the popular saying "Feed a cold and starve a fever," long since medically rejected, but still widely believed in this country, dates back to Celsus (ca. A.D. 50) (Gebhard 1976:95). Similarly, vinegar, a sovereign remedy since classical times, is an essential element in folk pharmacopoeias (Hultin 1974:199), and the use of cobwebs to staunch the flow of blood goes back at least to Galen.

Other items, particularly pertaining to the supernatural, witchcraft, and magic, while lacking classical antecedents, were important in Euro-American folk medicine. "Especially in Pennsylvania we get reports of the pow-wow-doctors drawing a magic circle around the house in which the patient lay and another around the bed of the patient and then sometimes describing a circle around the injured or diseased part. Gradually by incantation and the use of various kinds of verbal formulae they drove the evil spirit out from within these circles" (L. Jones 1949:484). "Bloodstoppers" had (and have) the power to stop bleeding, simply by prayer; laying on of hands, or physical treatment, was not necessary nor, in fact, did the patient have to be in the presence of the curer at all (Dorson 1952: Chap. 7).

As in all folk medical systems, belief in witchcraft was and is a part of the Euro-American tradition. The word "hex," in fact, comes to us from the German *hexerei* through the Pennsylvania Dutch (L. Jones 1949:481; Dorson 1959:85). Later European immigrants, and particularly those from the Mediterranean, brought with them a strong belief in the supernatural, as manifest in the fear of witchcraft and the evil eye (e.g., E. Smith 1972:97).

At the same time, Euro-American folk medicine has always been remarkably naturalistic in its etiologies; even though illness is often explained as due to God's punishment, the striking thing is the frequency with which nonsupernatural, nonmagical causes are invoked. This is particularly true of the nineteenth-century home remedy books, and it is true of much folk medicine today.

To illustrate, among the contemporary Amish "A mysterious ailment called 'livergrown . . . ' " is common among infants. It is believed to be caused "by too sudden exposure to the outside atmosphere, or by being shaken up by a buggy ride" (Hostetler 1963-1964:272). And in Detroit a southern Appalachian migrant reported that "Quick TB" was a dreaded disease in her family that afflicted menstruating women who took a shower or were caught in a rainstorm (Stekert 1970:137). The latter example strongly suggests residual humoral pathology, which says that menstruation is marked by greater-than-normal body heat, thus making the woman especially vulnerable to attacks by "cold" in any form.

2. Black folk medicine

In contrast to Euro-American folk medicine, the traditional popular medicine of American Negroes is a legitimate folk medicine in that it represents a pure oral tradition. Although this ethnic medicine has existed since the first slaves were brought to the United States, the best-known variant, commonly called "voodoo," "hoodoo," or "conjure," took shape in the early nineteenth century around New Orleans. When Haitian slaves rebelled and threw out their French masters, thousands of blacks, mulattos, and whites fled to New Orleans, the nearest French port (Hurston 1931:318). Tinling has described voodoo as "a mixture of European Catholicism and African tribal religions" (Tinling 1967:-484) which, as it spread beyond Catholic Louisiana into the Protestant south, lost its "Catholic trappings." It seems highly likely, as Snow has pointed out (1977a:34), that elements of humoral pathology accompanied voodoo when it reached the United States; the hot/cold dichotomy is to this day well marked in Haiti (Wiese 1976). But these elements are attenuated; the hot/cold dichotomy itself seems entirely lacking, replaced by a strong fear of "cold" as a cause of illness, including especially menstrual disorders which, as we have just seen, in a full-blown humoral pathology are associated with greater-than-normal heat.

Black folk medicine also includes elements that have crossed the Atlantic directly from England. Whitten, in a study of North Carolina "malign occultism," is impressed by the extent to which, in that state, contemporary occult practices represent the assimilation of seventeenth- and eighteenth-century European occultism, a fact that he explains as due to the use of English rather than African languages, membership in European churches, and — in North Carolina — relatively close contact between slaves and white masters (Whitten 1962:318-319).

Perhaps because of its multiple origins, black folk medicine has given us some of the most graphic and widely used terms to describe curers and their methods: "root" medicine (and its derivatives "rootwork" and "root doctor"), "mojo," "conjure" (and "conjure man") and, of course, "voodoo" and "hoodoo." Snow has classified black etiologies as "natural" and "unnatural": the former include things such as failure to protect the body against inclement weather (again suggestive of attenuated humoral pathology) and divine punishment for sin; the latter "have to do with the individual's position as a member of society" (Snow 1973:272) (i.e., they reflect social instead of physical pathology). Although some of the latter are explained as stemming from worry and other forms of stress, fear of witchcraft seems particularly important: "Nothing else in the [read "my"] fieldwork elicited so much emotional response as questions about witchcraft. Whether answers were negative or affirmative, the vehemence was often startling" (*Ibid.,* 274).

From the beginnings of black folk medicine, belief in the supernatural, magic, and witchcraft seem to have played a more important role than in Euro-American folk medicine. Not surprisingly, then, the successful curers are those who have occult powers as well as herbal skills. Speaking of North Carolina, Whitten writes that "Central to the whole occult complex . . . is the conjurer. This is the professional diviner, curer, agent finder, and general controller of the occult arts" (Whitten 1962:315-316).

Snow believes that folk medical beliefs, and especially those of blacks, reflect three major world view themes: the world is a hostile and dangerous place, the individual is liable to attack from external sources, and the individual must depend on outside aid to combat such attacks (Snow 1974:83). Clearly, such a world view is congruent with a high degree of belief in witchcraft and a folk medical system designed to protect and cure a person of witchcraft and witchcraft-induced illness. But black folk medicine is far from limited to witchcraft and the occult. Writers speak with admiration of the unlettered rural "granny" women, skilled midwives who (until recently) delivered most black infants in the South and who also had a wide knowledge of herbal lore. The variety and richness of traditional black medical lore is fully equal to that which has been recorded for the other major ethnic groups in America.

3. Spanish-American folk medicine

The study of Spanish-American folk medicine differs from that of Euro-American and black folk medicines in that anthropologists rather than folklorists have given us our best accounts. In view of the fairly comprehensive coverage that anthropologists have given of Mexican and other Latin American folk medicines, extension of this interest to Spanish-Americans in the United States is a logical development. Spanish-American folk medicine differs from the other folk medicines that concern us here in a number of ways; we call attention to two of them. First, it can be argued that it is a more integrated "system" than the other two, in that in theory and therapy a great deal of it conforms to an "equilibrium" model of health. Equilibrium is expressed first and foremost in the attenuated humoral pathology belief that the healthy body maintains a balance between "hot" and "cold" *calidades* — qualities or elements — and that illness results when an excess of "heat" or "cold" strikes or enters the body and destroys this equilibrium. The equilibrium model is also expressed in the belief that parts of the body, especially the fontanelle, the womb, and "nerves" (or tendons), can be displaced; recovery then depends on manipulation and other treatment to restore these parts to their normal position.

Second, Spanish-American folk medicine, in contrast to black and Euro-American folk medicine, is much more obviously a direct transplant from the mother countries, especially Mexico, Cuba, and Puerto Rico. In most instances the time factor is so short that the local variants characterizing the other two folk medicines have not developed. This is not to say that Spanish-American folk medicine is completely homogeneous, but only in the case of Hispanic folk medicine in New Mexico and Colorado, which has existed largely on its own since the end of the eighteenth century, do we have a distinctly "local" Spanish-American form (cf. Schulman 1960; Samora 1961).

Thus, to understand Spanish-American folk medicine fully, it is almost essential to understand the popular medicine of the countries from which it is derived; for example, contemporary Mexican-American folk medicine makes little sense unless the reader understands its humoral antecedents, and Catholic ritual and belief having to do with supernatural patrons, petitions for help, and the fulfillment of vows.

According to Spanish-American humoral beliefs, the "cold" and "heat" that disrupt the equilibrium of the healthy person can enter the body in a number of ways. As *aire,* or air, cold may strike the head, causing *punzadas* — shooting pains in the eyes and ears — and headaches and common colds. Cold also enters the body when a person gets his feet wet or steps barefoot on a cold floor. This may lead to "risen heat," a condition in which the normal body heat is compressed into the upper part of the body, the source of fevers, bronchitis, tonsillitis, and a number of other respiratory ailments. Heat threatens particularly from foods thought to be *caliente* or *irritante,* which may cause diarrhea and other kinds of stomach troubles. Although in most English accounts of the hot/cold system illnesses are said to *be* hot or cold, more properly, as in classical humoral pathology, an illness *comes from* a hot or cold source. Depending on the hot or cold "quality" of the source of an illness, a patient is treated with herbal remedies of the opposite quality, with purges, cupping, enemas (which draw off the heat of fever), and *chiquiadores* — hot or cold herbs or plasters stuck to the temple of sufferers from headache, to draw off the heat or cold, as diagnosed.[6]

In addition to common ailments, whose Spanish names have equivalent English forms (headache, toothache, bronchitis, tonsillitis, tuberculosis, pneumonia, colic, dysentery, etc.), a half dozen "folk" illnesses that correspond to no English-language illnesses are well described in the literature. The most common of these are *caída de la mollera* (fallen fontanelle) and *caída de la matriz* (fallen womb), which conform to the displaced-parts-of-the-body etiology. The former afflicts children (and occasionally adults) and comes from a shock to the system, such as fright, or a blow on the head. The latter is the result of lifting a heavy weight after childbirth or of a fall or shock. Many Mexican-American women believe that it can be prevented if, beginning at puberty, they swaddle themselves with a tight sash for the rest of their child-bearing years.

Empacho is a clogging of the stomach and upper intestinal tract (*not* consti-pation) from too much food or from the wrong kinds of food, such as green fruit. *Bilis* is a jaundice-like condition believed to result from anger or fear; it is treated with bitter herbal coctions. *Susto,* or fright, is viewed in some places as an illness in its own right; often, however, as with *bilis,* it is the cause or beginning of another illness. Finally, we have *mal puesto* [or *brujería* (i.e., witchcraft)], the belief that a witch has worked sympathetic or contangious magic against a victim, usually occasioned by *envidia* or envy of the person so afflicted by a less fortunate individual, and *mal (de) ojo,* the evil eye. In contrast to witchcraft, which is conscious and planned, the evil eye more often than not is unintentional, and some people about whom it is whispered that they can "eye" are unaware of their power. To be on the safe side, the culturally aware person who admires a child is always careful to slap it lightly on the cheek to neutralize the possible *ojo.*

It is interesting to note that the etiologies of these "folk" illnesses lie largely outside the hot/cold syndrome. Some would appear to be of New World origin as, for example, *susto,* which implies soul loss, a widespread New World indigenous etiology. Others, such as the forms of witchcraft (sticking pins in dolls) and the evil eye, are probably brought from Europe.

Best known of Spanish-American folk curers is the *curandero(a),* in classic form a male or female herbalist who has learned the "qualities" of herbal and nonherbal remedies and their proper combinations for each illness. Curan-deros also rub, massage, and otherwise manipulate the body (e.g. "lifting" the fontanelle back into place). Still other *curanderos* have occult powers, includ-ing the ability to bewitch as well as to cure. Such curers usually are known as *brujos(as),* and they arouse ambivalent feelings because of the dual nature of their calling.

Much Spanish-American curing involves neither *curandero* nor home reme-dies. Or, put in another way, God is the ultimate healer. For many illnesses (and for misfortune in general) Spanish-Americans frequently seek the inter-vention of saints, the Virgin, or Christ, lighting candles and praying at their altars. Often vows or solemn promises are made to "miraculous" images of Christ or the Virgin; if the request is granted, the petitioner must fulfill his or her part of the bargain, which often involves a lengthy pilgrimage to the town or city where the image has its cult. But Christ and the Virgin are merely advocates who intercede for their human clients; God, in the final analysis, decides on the outcome.

The pilgrimage as a part of curing is also manifest in a less ancient pattern, in which a sufferer travels to the shrine of a charismatic folk healer who, before or after his death, has taken on many of the qualities of a Church saint. Best known among folk saints in the United States is Don Pedrito Jaramillo, who came from his birthplace, Guadalajara, to Los Olmost Creek, Texas, about 1880, already a recognized curer. Here his cures, based largely on hydrotherapy, brought him statewide and then international fame. After his death in 1907, visitors began to place candles and flowers on his grave; over the years it became a veritable mecca for the sick. Written petitions for help and expressions of gratitude for cures achieved continually are placed in the present small shrine, and Don Pedrito is viewed, like real saints, as a powerful intermediary with God. Many petitioners come from as far away as central Mexico (Romano 1965). Mexico also has its folk saint, El Niño Fidencio in Nuevo León, who enjoys greater popularity than Don Pedrito and who draws thousands of petitioners from among Mexican-Americans (Macklin 1974b). Folk saints may also extend their influence far beyond their shrine graves since, at least in the case of El Niño Fidencio, he has been "captured" by at least one Mexican-American spiritualist who practices in a small Indiana town; he speaks through "Mrs. A.," and is recognized by her patients — many of whom come from distant states — as her source of power (Macklin 1974a:394-402).[7]

AMERICAN FOLK MEDICINE VIEWED AS ETHNOMEDICINE

Drawing on the three systems of folk medicine we have briefly sketched, we see how beliefs and practices of the present and the past conform to the correlations noted earlier in this chapter for non-Western medical systems. First, it is apparent that the personalistic-naturalistic dichotomy of etiologies fits American folk medicine as well as other systems. Personalistic etiologies cover the very widespread belief in witchcraft, the evil eye, and illness as God's punishment for sinning. Naturalistic etiologies include the belief that cold in many ways causes illness, as well as perhaps the common childhood illnesses, and injuries such as sprains and broken bones (although these may also be explained as caused by witchcraft).

The same correlations we noted with respect to types and roles of curers also emerge from American folk medicine. Speaking particularly of personalistic etiologies, it is striking that, as in similar non-Western etiologies, and in contrast to naturalistic etiologies, "Good health is classed with any kind of good luck: success, money, a good job, a peaceful home. Illness, on the other hand, may be looked upon as just another undesirable event, along with bad luck, poverty, unemployment, domestic turmoil and so on. The attempted manipulation of events [by individuals] therefore covers a broad range of practices that are carried out to attract good, including good health, and to repel bad, including bad health" (Snow 1974:83).

Personalistic etiologies in American folk medicine, as in their non-Western counterparts, often reveal dual causation levels. Thus, among Sicilian-Americans in Buffalo, a physician, usually unknowingly, often "works in conjunction with a *spilato*, a curer, or even a witch, since the patient and/or his family may believe that there is more than one level at which a cure must be affected" (E. Smith 1972:095).

The qualities of many curers are remarkably similar to those described for the non-Western world. Conjurers, for example, like witch doctors and Alaskan shamans, work both good and evil; they are "bad" only insofar as they work evil (Whitten 1962:318). Many contemporary healers are remarkably like classic shamans. Thus, "Mrs. M.," a 65-year-old Connecticut Yankee possession trance-medium, suffered from a spiritual illness at the age of nineteen. When "called," she protested that she did not want to be a medium, that she wanted to live a "normal" life. But she was told by the medium who was attending her that "it was not what *she* wanted, it was what 'they' wanted" (Macklin 1976:43). In short, Mrs. M. acquired her power through "divine election," just as Siberian shamans do. Speaking of the contemporary American pattern in which "the Lord selects an individual on whom to confer special powers of healing," Snow compares recruitment "to that of the shaman described in the anthropological literature" (Snow 1977b:35).

Finally, it is striking how in much contemporary folk medicine the distinction between religion, magic, and medicine is blurred. One has the feeling, in surveying American folk medicine, that personalistic etiologies and the therapies that are associated with them are gaining at the expense of naturalistic etiologies. The anthropologist starts out to study folk medicine, but is quickly — almost forcibly — drawn to the personalistic and supernatural. Smith writes, for example, of her Sicilian-American research, "Though the study was undertaken to learn about folk medicine . . . (and not witchcraft) . . . the informants tended to stress the supernatural approach and showed little interest in herbalism and the old pharmacopoeia on which I had intended to focus" (E. Smith 1972:92-93). As far back as 1946, Withers spoke of "a new and recent wave of curing by prayer and other religious techniques" (Withers 1966:233). Snow, too, writes of recent research on poor southerners, black and white alike: "My research has *not* been directed to religion *per se;* rather, the focus has been on folk medical belief *and the religious element was inescapable*" (Snow 1977b:28. Emphasis added). In Chapter 14, in discussing the possible use of indigenous healers in former health services, we will indicate why we believe this trend toward personalistic etiologies is taking place.

NOTES

[1] For a more complete discussion of the personalistic-naturalistic dichotomy, see Foster (1976b).

[2] For India Mandelbaum cuts the etiological pie along the same lines that we do. He recognizes "disharmony in the patient's relations with other people or with supernaturals" as one cause of illness, which stands in contrast to a second cause, "physiological disharmony." The former "is though to result either from aggressive malevolence by a human or a spirit, or from the patient's inadvertent infringement on an irascible supernatural." The latter is a "central tenet of Ayurvedic medicine," which largely explains illness in systemic terms (Mandelbaum 1970:179).

[3] In a complete classification of worldwide medical systems "scientific," or "Western," or "cosmopolitan" medicine (the latter the term used by the contributors to Leslie's recent *Asian Medical Systems* (1976) would constitute a third type. In this system causality is seen as conforming to the basic patterns of cause and effect, as manifest in physics, chemistry, and the sciences of the mind. Pathogens — germs and viruses — and biochemical alterations in the body due to things such as nutritional deficiencies, the aging process, and environmental factors such as cigarette smoke are invoked to explain disease.

[4] Lest we be misjudged by our readers, we hasten to point out that this is the Chinese evaluation, not ours.

[5] These titles are drawn from Pickard and Buley (1945: Chap. 2).

[6] At least among Mexican-Americans "in a large Southwestern city," conscious knowledge of the hot/cold dichotomy is disappearing. Kay found that "No woman under 30 could make such distinctions or seemed to be aware of this system of classification" (Kay 1977:162). Yet a great deal of the health belief and behavior that Kay describes stems directly from humoral assumptions and is identical to what is found in Mexican communities where the hot/cold dichotomy is common knowledge. Thus, "Tonsillitis is prevented by never walking barefoot, especially on cold concrete" (*Ibid.,* 147). In Mexico a cold floor is believed to cause *calor subido* ("risen heat") which results, among other things, in tonsillitis. Again, giving a child with fever an enema with an infusion of *malva* leaves (*Ibid.,* 147) is a classic Mexican humoral treatment: the *malva* is *fresca* ["fresh" (i.e., cold)], and the action of the enema draws out excess heat.

[7] In addition to the citations given in the text for Spanish-American folk medicine, we have drawn from Clark (1959a), Harwood (1971), Kiev (1968), Madsen (1964), Martínez and Martin (1966), and Rubel (1960, 1966).

chapter 5

Ethnopsychiatry

INTRODUCTION

Concepts of disease causation within tribal and peasant societies differ, we have seen, in very basic ways from those that characterize scientific medicine. Thus far we have been looking at manifestations of these belief systems largely in the context of the acute, infectious, debilitating diseases that have taken the greatest toll of the world's populations. Ethnomedicine, however, also includes the study of how traditional societies view and deal with mental illness. In this chapter we turn our attention to this second major area of concern of ethnomedicine, a field usually referred to as "transcultural psychiatry" (e.g., Kiev 1972) or "ethnopsychiatry," the term that we prefer.

The need to articulate a dichotomy of physical and mental illness is more a reflection of Western consensus than of the orientation of societies rooted in naturalistic or personalistic belief systems. In these societies, etiologies of disease encourage the fusion, rather than the separation of physical and emotional states. If we recall traditional explanations of disease causation, this stance is not surprising. Where deities, ancestors, demons, or witches bring on sickness by infiltrating their victims, driving out souls, speaking through them, and commanding their wills, confusion, fever, and emotional and physical distress can be expected to follow. Similarly, where disease is a product of a loss of a natural equilibrium of body, mind, and nature, only the restoration of the harmony that should properly exist among them can constitute a return to health. This is not to say that abnormal behavior goes unrecognized or unlabeled as something qualitatively different from purely physical ailments in the non-Western world (any more than psychosomatic ills are unknown in the West). On the contrary, abnormal behavior seems everywhere to be "labeled," to have a name or names reflecting behavior judgments attached to it. But the contexts in which mental illness is singled out for attention, the seriousness accorded it, and the course of action regarded as appropriate in the face of it — these vary widely cross-culturally, as we will see.

THE BEGINNINGS OF ETHNOPSYCHIATRY

The initial interest of anthropologists in mental illness was far removed from the field of ethnomedicine. It originated in their concern to understand the relationships between personality and the cultural forces that impinge on and shape personality. Particularly important was the concern to test the hypotheses of Freud, to determine whether the Oedipus complex is universal, whether the developmental phases of "oral," "anal," "genital," and "latent" in the individual life-history are universals or are limited to specific societies, and the like. Although Malinowski, in the 1920s, was the first anthropologist to test these hypotheses with voluminous field data, the so-called "culture and personality" school — the first step in the development of what is now known variously as ethno-, cross-cultural, or transcultural psychiatry — took form in the United States. By the early 1930s Margaret Mead, Edward Sapir, and Ruth Benedict were concerned with the relationships between culture and personality, asking questions and testing hypotheses with data from a number of societies. From 1936 to 1940 the psychiatrist Abram Kardiner, in conjunction with a group of anthropologists that included Cora DuBois, Ralph Linton, Edward Sapir, and Ruth Benedict, offered a seminar on culture and personality.

This seminar stimulated the first major study designed specifically to test the theories that were being discussed, but for which existing data were inadequate: Cora DuBois' *The People of Alor*. As DuBois puts it, "We had talked ourselves out, and only field work could test the procedure" (DuBois 1961:viii). Field research on the Indonesian island of Alor was, in her words, designed to find out if there was "a demonstrable relationship between the personalties of adults within a group and the socio-cultural milieu in which they lived. If such a relationship were found to exist, its explanation was presumed to lie in the consistency of life experiences ranging from the earliest child-rearing practices and relationships to the reinforcing effects of adult institutions and social roles" (*Ibid.,* xviii).

Other major studies of similar nature were carried out among a number of North American Indian groups and also among the people of modern nations (Singer 1961:14). In these studies, stretching from the 1930s until well into the 1950s, it is important to remember that the primary interest of researchers was not that of today — the "normal" and the "abnormal," the definitions of illness in various societies, their treatment, the demography of mental illness, and the like — but rather, with the question of "basic personality structure" (to use Kardiner's term) and "modal personality" (to use DuBois' term). The terms "ethnopsychiatry," "cross-cultural psychiatry," and "transcultural psychiatry" were as yet unknown. Yet it is largely from the research that flowed from the immediate pre- and postwar work of Kardiner, Linton, DuBois, and others that our current interest in the relationships between mental illness and culture has come. The history of this period in psychological anthropology and the topics that attracted attention have been well described by Singer, and it is beyond the scope of this chapter to summarize this period (Singer 1961).

As medical anthropologists we are interested in a series of questions that deal with the concepts of "normal" and "abnormal" in cross-cultural settings, with indigenous concepts of psychiatric disturbances, modes of curing, and other related topics. In these concerns we draw heavily on the data and theory of the "culture and personality" school but, with the passage of time, research and interests have, not surprisingly, far transcended this pioneering period. Specifically, some of the kinds of questions that anthropologists have dealt with are as follows:

1. The cultural definitions of "normal" and "abnormal," and how mental illness is recognized and defined in societies other than our own. Anthropologists ask, "What kinds of behavior are considered to constitute mental illness in the world's societies?", and "Are Western terms for the major kinds of mental illness we recognize applicable in all or many societies?" That is, quite apart from culture, do we find the same kinds of syndromes (clinically defined) in all or most parts of the world?

2. Non-Western explanations of mental illness. Just as we can study non-Western etiologies for physical illness, so can we do the same thing for mental illness.

3. The cultural modes of handling deviant behavior defined as abnormal. Anthropologists ask, "Who cures, how, and what are the theories and goals underlying their treatment?" Anthropologists are particularly interested in the question of "harnessing" deviant psychic behavior through socially desired roles as, for example, in the case of the shaman.

4. The incidence of mental illness in societies of differing complexity. Is, for example, mental illness relatively rare in simple, unchanging societies, and more common in urban settings, where stress presumably is heavier? Does rapid acculturation significantly increase the incidence of mental illness among the people undergoing this experience?

5. The demography of mental illness. "Arctic hysteria" and "running amok" are mental aberrations that appear in the earliest ethnological accounts. Other named psychic conditions such as *latah* and *koro* have subsequently been described. These culture-specific illnesses present a series of problems with respect to causes, frequency, and triggering conditions, which have attracted anthropological interest. They have often highlighted significant biocultural dimensions of mental illness.

In the pages that follow we will discuss some of the major findings and points of view on these topics.

CULTURAL DEFINITIONS OF NORMAL AND ABNORMAL

Many kinds of extraordinary behavior recognized by Western psychiatrists as constituting mental illness are widely found in non-western societies. Not *all* kinds known to us are found in every other society, and in some cultures there have been described syndromes (clusters of behavior) strange to our classificatory systems (such as that of the *Diagnostic and Statistical Manual of Mental Disorders* prepared by the American Psychiatric Association). Later in this chapter we will look at some of these syndromes in greater detail. It does seem, however, that within the parameters of cognitive, emotional, and physiological functioning shared by us as a single species we are dealing ultimately with limited possibilities in abnormal behavior, quite apart from cultural variation in its expression.

1. The case for "labeling theory"

Nevertheless, the wide variety of syndrome clusters and names attached to them in the world's societies, Western and non-Western alike, have led some behavioral scientists to declare that mental illness is a "myth," a sociological phenomenon, the product of the "straight" members of the group who feel they need a device to explain, sanction, and control abberant or dangerous behavior on the part of their fellows, behavior sometimes simply "different" from their own. Those who hold to this belief are known as "labeling theorists" (Becker 1963; Lemert 1951, 1967; Scheff 1974; Schur 1971; Szasz 1961). Essentially they argue that once deviant behavior is labeled the deviant, however slight or temporary his symptoms, is stereotyped and stigmatized. His peers, expecting a particular form of behavior from him, treat him in such fashion that he finds the most adaptive behavior on his part to be to conform to these expectations.

The realities of, and the dangers inherent in, this kind of labeling are chillingly described in an experiment carried out by Rosenhan. He and seven other "pseudopatients" presented themselves at different mental hospitals asking for admission. They explained that they "heard voices" that were unclear, but that they seemed to say "empty," "hollow," and "thud." The voices were unfamiliar to, but of the same sex as, the pseudopatients. Beyond these "symptoms," and except for falsifying names, vocations, and employment, no further alterations of person, history, or circumstances were made. Life histories were described as they had occurred, and none of them was seriously pathological. After admission to the ward, the pseudopatients ceased simulation of any symptoms and, apart from a certain nervousnes that they would certainly be discovered, they behaved in completely normal fashions. Except for one, all were admitted as suffering from schizophrenia, and each of these was discharged, after average hospitalization of 19 days, as having schizophrenia "in remission." Apparently no therapists suspected the pseudopatients, but considerable numbers of patients sensed that the volunteers were not what they represented themselves to be.

Rosenhan concludes that "A psychiatric label has a life and an influence of its own. Once the impression has been formed that the patient is schizophrenic, the expectation is that he will continue to be schizophrenic." After a period of time without symptoms, the patient may be considered "in remission" and ready for discharge, "But the label endures beyond discharge, with the unconfirmed expectation that he will behave as a schizophrenic again" (Rosenhan 1973:253). Psychiatric "labeling" thus often becomes a self-fulfilling prophecy for the patient, his family, and his friends. Eventually the patient also accepts the diagnosis, with all of its expectations, and behaves accordingly (*Ibid.*, 254).

2. Arguments against labeling

Intriguing as labeling theory may be as an approach to understanding and dealing with mental illness, it has not been widely accepted by anthropologists working in transcultural settings. Edgerton, for example, is not comfortable with a life-of-its-own psychiatric label to identify illness. It is, he believes, the group and not the tag that imbues abnormality with meaning. The recognition *and* the naming of mental illness, he argues, are the product of a process of "negotiation," a social transaction involving extensive consensus within the community. Edgerton studied the process of negotiation among patient, healer, relatives, and friends in labeling mental illness in four African societies, and concluded that "Because of the force of social negotiation, there can easily be perception of mental illness without consequent labeling, or labeling without consequent action, and there can even be psychosis without perception" (Edgerton 1969:70). The labels that were applied, the actions that followed, and the perceptions that preceded them were all products of a social process that had moral and jural involvements. Labeling, he says, was neither capricious nor unidimensional, as the study by Rosenhan might lead one to believe.

Whether among the Hehe in Tanzania, the Kamba and Pokot of Kenya, or the Sebei of Uganda, informants from all four groups were able to describe the culturally defined behaviors said to characterize a psychotic person, and there was general agreement as to the perceptual and behavioral syndromes involved. "Seen in this fashion," Edgerton concludes, "mental illness does not become merely a 'myth,' nor is it simply another 'social problem.' There are real disturbances in thought, affect, and conduct that require medical management. Neither does it suggest that psychiatric diagnosis is not essentially a sincere, empirical effort to classify symptoms or syndromes into what may some day be a scientific nosology" (*Ibid.,* 70).

This is a widespread anthropological point of view. John Kennedy, citing a number of anthropological studies, finds that "there is agreement among most modern scholars who have looked closely at the subject that though there probably are important variations in frequency and form, the major psychotic patterns known in Western psychiatry are found throughout the world" (J. Kennedy 1973:1139). Similarly, in a major study of the St. Lawrence Island Eskimo, Murphy and Leighton found that in spite of vocabulary differences, "our subjects recognized disabilities that correspond to the whole range of major types of disorder identified in [Western] psychiatry" (Murphy and Leighton 1965:97). Extending these studies to the Yoruba of Nigeria, Murphy concluded that "in widely different cultural and environmental situations sanity appears to be distinguishable from insanity by *cues* that are very similar to those used in the Western world" (Murphy 1976:1019. Emphasis added). Clearly there is no culture in which men and women remain oblivious to erratic, disturbed, threatening, or bizarre behavior in their midst — whatever the culturally defined context of that behavior.

Leighton makes it evident that a great deal of the confusion and disagreement surrounding the question of similarities and differences in mental illness in Western and non-Western societies stems from the fact that we have tended to think in terms of diagnostic categories, as recognized by the members of the societies concerned. Since non-Western etiologies usually are quite different from Western explanations, the diagnostic-labeling process, when studied from within any specific culture, leads the investigator astray. But, says Leighton, "*If attention is limited to the comparison of symptom patterns, rather than diagnostic categories, a great part of the cross-cultural obstacle disappears*" (Leighton 1969:185). Put another way, search for *symptoms* should precede search for duplication or verification of Western *categories* of mental illness. That this is not an easy task Edgerton has documented in his account of the divergent conceptions of psychosis in East Africa, a catalog nevertheless "not markedly at variance with Western symptomatology, especially for schizophrenia" (Edgerton 1966:420). He concurs that efforts to substantiate either the "sovereign force of culture" or common core of mental illnesses are premature. The same data, he believes, can be too easily manipulated to argue either position.

NON-WESTERN MENTAL ILLNESS ETIOLOGIES

Ethnographic accounts are replete with explanations of how the members of the group studied explain physical illness and, during past years, a number of typologies of causality, including that in Chapter IV of this book, have been worked out. In contrast, our knowledge of how non-Western peoples explain mental illness has been much less systematized. In part, at least, this is because many do not make sharp distinctions between physical and mental etiologies of disease: in the small Ladino (i.e., mestizo) town of Tenejapa in southern Mexico, to illustrate, "the causes of . . . [psychotic disturbances] are not judged as different from those of other types of illness" (Fabrega 1974:243). To the extent that we can generalize, it seems that a majority of non-Western mental illness is explained in personalistic rather than naturalistic terms: possession of the patient's body by a ghost, spirit, or deity, punishment for breaking a taboo, or witchcraft. The following examples illustrate a little of the range of etiologies.

According to Leighton, Yoruba explanations for mental illness include superhuman attacks from gods, spirits, and ghosts because of breaking taboos or failing to carry out ceremonial duties; witchcraft; heredity; contagion (i.e., some diseases of mind and emotions can be "caught" by association with a sick person); cosmic forces; physical traumata, such as a blow on the head or loss of blood; and "severely distressing experiences" (Leighton 1969:184-185). Like the Yoruba, the Navaho also attributed mental disorders to violations of taboos and contact with witches, to which they add the suffering of physical trauma, marrying a woman who is not a Navaho, stirring food with an arrow, leaving a poker pointing into the fire, and gambling "too much" (D. A. Kennedy 1961:414). It is also believed that a child will be born mentally deficient if a dog eats the afterbirth, or if during the mother's pregnancy the father sees a bear or completes a buffalo-tail rattle. Particularly dangerous are violations of incest taboos, and insanity is seen as supernatural punishment for incestuous relations (*Ibid.,* 415).

Among the acculturated St. Lawrence Island Eskimo, spirit possession is associated with shamanism, but not with major psychiatric disorders, although this is true among other less acculturated Eskimo. Magic and witchcraft are found as explanations, as are stress factors described as "too much worry," "easy to get afraid," and the like. Hereditary factors are suggested in a "slow to learn" syndrome described by informants as running in families. Taboo violations, including incest, are also frequently cited causes of insanity (Murphy and Leighton 1965).

It should be clear from examples like these that the etiology of much mental illness can be fathomed only when the triggering social context is learned — knowledge often acquired by a process of elimination. Cawte runs over some of the hypotheses tested by Australian aborigines: "Sorcery from introjection of a foreign object 'sung' into the body by the incantation of an ill-wisher? . . . possession by spirits, of whom Aborigines identify a legion, or by devil animals, of which they know a whole menagerie? . . . attention by social avengers, the anonymous and invisible executors of retaliatory sanctions, appointed by the elders? . . . The man's own spirit-counterpart of soul?" (Cawte 1974:37). The latter possibility can be understood only in the context of a belief of the Walbiri tribe. According to this group, every man has an invisible twin brother who watches over him and punishes him if he commits a sacrilege or adultery. A native doctor, sensing the current of events in his people, must be able to diagnose the guilt, remorse, or depression produced by these spirit-counterparts (*millelba*), and treat and generally cure the condition (*Ibid.*, 34).

A synthesis of medical and other belief systems is, as we have already seen, a characteristic of many non-Western cultures, and it presents serious analytical problems for Western observers. The lamination of medicine, cosmology, and law found in aboriginal Australian society, for example, is such that excision of the medical system — and specifically syndromes of mental illness — has proved to be an enormous challenge for investigators. "I doubt if one can study medicine separately, or law separately," says Cawte, "one studies a blend, a category different from familiar modern ones" (Cawte 1974:xxi). As an aid in the study of mental illness, he urges several "thematic" classifications of maladaption, each useful for its particular purpose These include a colloquial scheme that dramatizes acculturation problems, an indigenous classification according to concepts of disease such as sorcery, spirit intrusion, and the like, a refinement of sorcery into smaller categories according to alleged commission, and the use of the modern clinical classification of mental illness based on the *Standard Nomenclature of Disease.* "This classification commonly dismays anthropologists because it mixes etiology with appearances and causes with symptoms but medical workers have gotten used to it; it is the best we have!" (*Ibid.*, 173).

If we are to generalize about differences in Western and non-Western mental etiologies, a significant distinction would be that among the latter, psychological factors, life experiences, and stress are seen as playing a far less important role than among the former. "The people at Kalumburu will not or cannot discuss a sick person's temperament or his mental conflicts" (Cawte 1974:47). Although the Yoruba believe some diseases of the mind and emotions can be "caught" by association with a sick person, cosmic forces, physical traumata (such as a blow on the head or loss of blood), and "severely distressing experiences," on balance psychological explanations play a very minor role in explaining abnormal behavior (Leighton 1969:184-185). The personal, predisposing factors in mental illness, assigned so much significance in Western psychiatric medicine, are for the most part of limited or little interest within traditional systems.

CULTURAL MODES OF HANDLING MENTAL ILLNESS

1. Who cures?

As previously pointed out, while many forms of deviant behavior appear to be universal, the ways in which deviance is handled, the social values sometimes placed on deviant behavior, and the modes of treatment vary widely. Anthropologists have been particularly interested in the psychological and social characteristics of shamans. The term is Siberian, from the Tungus language, but it is used by anthropologists in the generic sense of the curer who has supernatural powers and contact with spirits, usually obtained by "election" by the spirit (i.e., an initial possession causing a serious illness followed by slow recovery). In curing, shamans customarily fall into a trance in which they communicate with their tutelary spirit to diagnose the illness. Extreme cultural relativists use the example of shamanism as a major prop in their argument that what is called mental illness is culture specific. That is, they argue that while in the West a shaman's psychological characteristics would be classed as a threat to the individual, and perhaps to society at large, thus necessitating institutionalization, in many non-Western societies the same behavior is highly valued, and even encouraged. Ackerknecht, for example, argues that the shaman cannot be regarded as abnormal in a psychopathological sense because he is well adapted to his society and serves a useful function (Ackerknecht, 1971:73). Devereux takes issue with this point of view, arguing that "there is no reason and no excuse for not considering the shaman as a severe neurotic and even as a psychotic" (Devereux 1956:28).

Yet the question is not simply is the shaman "normal" (because serving a necessary role) or "abnormal" because so labeled by members of his society. Rather, there is the matter of degree. In a recent article Murphy points out that for the St. Lawrence Island Eskimo the term *nuthkavihak* is translated as "being crazy." The term is applied only to people who *simultaneously manifest* three or four aberrant behavioral forms, such as talking to oneself, screaming at a nonexistent person, believing that a witch has murdered a child or husband when no one else holds this view, believing oneself to be an animal, running away, getting lost, drinking urine, killing dogs, and the like. The term is never used for a single symptom.

On the other hand, the ability to see things that other people do not see and to prophesy is called "thinness." This is a highly valued trait, characterizing minor diviners, and it "is the outstanding characteristic of the shaman." No "thin" person is called *nuthkavihak.* The shaman's behavior in a curing trance, in which (in one example) she imitated the behavior of a dog, would hardly be considered desirable in the West yet, as one informant said, "When the shaman is healing he is out of his mind, but *he is not crazy*" (Murphy 1976:-1022). In other words, Murphy says, when shamanistic behavior is *controlled* and used for curing, it is regarded as normal in the society in which it occurs. But when it takes multiple forms and is uncontrolled, the individual is labeled as crazy.

The shaman, many anthropological accounts suggest, is frequently an unstable person who often suffers delusions and who may be a transvestite or homosexual. Yet when mental instability is culturally channeled into constructive forms, the individual is distinguished from others who may show similar behavior, but who are classed as frankly abnormal by members of their society and subjected to curing rituals. Murphy summarizes the situation succinctly in saying "There is apparently a common range of possible responses to the mentally ill person, and the portion of the range brought to bear regarding a particular person *is determined more by the nature of his behavior than by a preexisting cultural set to respond in a uniform way to whatever is labelled mental illness*" (*Ibid.,* 1025. Emphasis added).

2. Treatment of the mentally ill

In many non-Western societies, the great majority of people who display abnormal behavior, if nonviolent, more often than not are permitted freedom in their communities; their needs are met by members of their families. In African communities, Lambo says, even the severely psychotic and the mentally defective are accommodated as functioning members of the community if they can maintain themselves at some level of sufficiency (Lambo 1962). Osborne is more definitive about the limits of tolerance. "The Yoruba," he writes, "take care of their own and, in keeping with their ideas of predestination and luck, find it difficult to extrude members of their own family" (Osborne 1969:192). Since every adult Yoruba has his own room, "a very sick person . . . may be maintained in the house with very little disruption to the household routine and to the community." An "insane" man is permitted to roam the village; if he becomes too disturbed, he is moved to a bush hamlet for a few days or locked in his room. A rather ingenious door (2 feet by 2 feet) is constructed within the house for the purpose of passing food to him, and an "outside" door allows him to come and go in the community. Nevertheless, the mentally ill who do not respond to reasonable care, although not forced from the village, are left to roam the countryside "working, begging, or stealing to stay alive." If they do not voluntarily leave, houses are sometimes abandoned to them (*Ibid.*).

Particularly where mental illness is clearly viewed as bewitchment or possession, the disturbed person may be seen as a threat to the group; from the beginning he is cruelly dealt with. In Fiji and the New Hebrides, for example, those possessed by evil spirits were often buried alive; in the Congo, Sigerist tells us, victims of witchcraft among the Bengala were routinely put to death (Sigerist 1951:156).

Among folk and peasant groups, the disturbed often evoke empathy and solicitude. For example, at least three persons living in the Taiwanese village of K'un Shen were judged as "seriously enough disturbed that in American society they would be institutionalized" (Diamond 1969:104). Yet, during their calm periods, they are free to participate in daily life as best they can. "They often cause laughter, but rarely fear." One woman has lucid periods of up to 3 months during which time she takes care of herself and chats with neighbors and relatives. At other times she refuses to eat, weeps for long periods, and sometimes throws dirty water at people. Her two married sons care for her, "and the general feeling is that she does not need special care such as hospitalization since she is obviously no danger to anyone" (*Ibid.*).

In villages people know or at least recognize one another, and the confused or sick can roam with greater impunity than in cities. There is almost always someone to lead a disoriented old person back to his family. The situation is sometimes similar in ethnic communities of the United States where sensitivity to their own "differentness" can further serve to discourage discrimination toward even quite aberrant members of the group.

Yet even among traditional peoples, some mental illness, and especially that involving violence or threats of violence, requires more formal modes of treatment. Sometimes treatment is thoroughly professional (viewed within the context of the society in question), and at other times it more nearly partakes of the nature of a "home remedy," as in the case described by Newman for the Gururumba of New Guinea. Among these people, "ghost possession" is a state, dangerous to the individual and the group alike. Newman describes a case of its recognition and treatment. A party of men had gone into a mountain forest to search for wild pandanus nuts. While there, some of them decided to hunt tree-climbing kangeroos. BonGire, one of the hunters, became separated from the others, and burst into camp late at night, bleeding at the nose, his body badly scratched. Rushing to the campfire, he stood for a moment in silence; then suddenly he began shouting wildly and attacking bystanders until he was subdued and tied to a tree at the edge of the clearing. This unusual behavior was interpreted as ghost possession. The campfire was built up and smothered in wet leaves to create smoke; BonGire was suspended, hands and feet bound, from a pole and held in the smoke until he vomited. After 5 minutes or so of this treatment he cried out in his normal voice to be taken out of the smoke, thus indicating that his ghost had been exorcised and that he was again normal (P.L. Newman 1965:84).

Prince has described more elaborate professional treatment among the Yoruba of Nigeria. Psychotic patients "live in" with the healer, for an average of 3 or 4 months, cared for by a family member who remains with them. Generally they are shackled for the first few weeks of their stay, until they can be trusted not to run away. Various herbal medicines are used, and animal sacrifices may be carried out upon admission. When the patient is deemed ready for release, a "discharge ceremony" may be held on the banks of a river, involving blood sacrifice, symbolic cleansing of the patient of his illness, and perhaps symbolic death and rebirth into a new life (Prince 1974).

Just as traditional curers differ greatly from Western physicians in their approach to physical illness, so do we also find striking differences in the treatment of mental illness. John Kennedy recently has outlined the major contrasts often, although not always, found. First, as in the case of major curing ceremonies for physical ills, major treatment of mental illness is also apt to be a public rite in which the curer may have auxiliaries and in which the audience may take a significant part. Perhaps more striking is the usual non-Western emphasis on powerful symbolism, achieved through the dramatic arts (J. Kennedy 1973:1170). This stands in stark contrast to the subdued lighting, the barely audible hiss of circulating air, and the few carefully selected pieces of furniture and art objects in the Western psychoanalyst's office.

The contrast in behavior of Western and traditional therapists also is striking. Whereas the former should not become involved personally with the patient, he (or she) is expected to be empathetic, nonjudgmental, warm, and human, exhibiting behavior that leads to the patient's involvement with the therapist through the phenomenon of transference. The Western therapist is, obviously, quite different in his approach to the patient from the ordinary physician. In contrast, a non-Western mental therapist involved in major curing rites behaves very much as he does when treating physical illness. He "cloaks himself in a powerful impersonal role," exercising authority, charisma, and often feats of legerdemain. "Though he may know the patient well, during treatment he moves into an impersonal role dimension," rarely if ever encountering the "transference" phenomenon (J. Kennedy 1973:1173-1174).

3. Goals of treatment

The goals of treatment in the two systems are also quite distinct. Those of Western therapy range from symptomatic treatment of things such as tics and phobias "to massive personality overhauls" (J. Kennedy 1973:1174). Western therapy is, in a sense, basically reeducation; the patient is encouraged to develop a new view of himself, with greater self-esteem, to be relieved of subjective feelings of pain, anxiety, and stress, perhaps to achieve greater independence, and to function more effectively in society (Ibid.). Non-Western therapies, in contrast, deal little with reeducation, ego-strengthening, and personality modification. Rather, they are pragmatic in approach, aiming at quick results, which means reduction or elimination of the abnormal symptoms that have brought the patient to the therapist. Although rituals may continue for several days and patients may occasionally spend weeks or even months in some societies with noted curers, treatment is generally short term, little if any longer than that for treatment of physical ills. Again, whereas verbal interchanges between therapist and patient are basic to Western treatment, in most non-Western societies many verbal exchanges are between the therapist and the spirits and, when involving the patient directly, they are directed toward him and do not necessarily require a reply. There are verbal similarities, of course, particularly in regard to confession, a major element in some non-Western societies, which can be compared to the need for the Western patient to bring up and discuss with the therapist painful, often shameful experiences in his past. In general, however, the striking thing is how different non-Western curing is from Western therapy. Yet in spite of these differences and the fallacies that many Western therapists believe underlie non-Western psychotherapy, many anthropologists and Western therapists have found that shamans and other traditional curers often achieve remarkable results in treating mental illness.

THE COMPARATIVE INCIDENCE OF MENTAL ILLNESS IN DIFFERENT SOCIETIES

In these paragraphs we direct our attention to two related questions: (1) Are technologically simple societies, as is often popularly believed, inherently less stressful than complex societies, and hence marked by lower incidences of mental illness? And (2) Are the major patterns of abnormal behavior recognized by Western psychiatrists found throughout the world and, if so, to what extent do they vary in form and frequency?

1. The myth of a stress-free "primitive" existence

Western man has long believed — and wanted to believe — that in simple societies, uncorrupted by civilization, human beings live in a "natural" relationship with each other, a relationship marked by love, cooperation, and mutual support. Since stress levels, logically, must be low in such a society, mental illness derived from stressful living must also be rare. This "noble savage" stereotype of primitive life has long since been destroyed by ethnographical fact, yet the image lingers on to color our views about mental illness. Although it is true that simple societies historically have lacked the stresses of civilization, a world peopled by vengeful deities and ghosts, witches and sorcerers, and angry neighbors and envious relatives, is not less stressful than is our own. Fear, which is certainly stress, is probably a more common experience in these societies than in modern life.

Anthropologists and psychiatrists who have studied traditional peoples agree that the ways in which the mentally ill are cared for seem to reduce the magnitude of the problem; they also agree that, quite apart from the stress of rapid sociocultural change, these societies are by no means strangers to abnormal behavior. They feel we should not assume that mental illness is one price we pay for civilization. As Field says, "There still lingers the idea that mental stress and mental illness are the prerogative of 'over-civilized' societies: that the simple savage may have Ancylostomiasis but cannot have Anxiety: that he may, in his innocence, believe his neighbour to be making bad magic against him, but he still sleeps like a top" (Field 1960:13). Nothing, she insists, could be further from the truth. "Whether the rural African has more mental illness than in the past — as he has, in the physical sphere, more venereal disease and more influenza — is another question. But mental illness, and plenty of it, is rooted in ancient tradition" (*Ibid.*). Similarly, Levy and Kunitz found many of the maladaptive patterns of reservation Navaho and Hopi rooted in their own precontact profiles of deviance. "The style of Hopi drinking and the very high mortality rates may best be explained as the response of repressed and covertly aggressive people to the opportunity to drink rather than as the result of moral confusion or conflict" (Levy and Kunitz 1971:117). In American Samoa evidence also suggests that stress is inherent in traditional life, because some stress diseases appear to be more common than among white, middle-class North Americans (Mackenzie 1978). And apparently contemporary farm life constitutes a less than optimal alternative to the frenetic pace of cities. In an analysis of mental illness and Irish culture, Scheper-Hughes hypothesizes that schizophrenia seems to be particularly associated with the stoical demands of rural Irish living: celibacy, social isolation, and relative economic deprivation (Scheper-Hughes 1978).

2. Variations in major patterns of abnormal behavior

We agree (within the context already defined) with the psychiatrists and anthropologists who believe that the major patterns of abnormal behavior recognized by Western psychiatrists are found throughout the world. We also agree that there are important variations in the form, frequency, distribution, and social implications of this behavior. Leighton, for example, found that a great many of the symptom patterns displayed by Yoruba patients were those recognized in psychiatry. But he also found important gaps, especially the near-absence of obsessive-compulsive and phobic symptoms. Depressive symptoms were not found as such, although components of the syndrome, such as loss of interest in life, extreme worry, sapped vitality, and the like came up in other contexts. Psychophysiologic, psychoneurotic, personality, sociopathic disorder symptoms, and senility changes were not mentioned but, when described, informants agreed that they were present, but not generally considered to be serious enough to warrant the label "illness" (Leighton 1969:184-185).

Similarly, the Tahitians studied by Levy "fit easily into western diagnostic categories." The behavior of a native considered "to have a bad head" closely resembled that of Western hospitalized schizophrenics (Levy 1973:407). On the other hand, "hysterialike" states are reported as seeming quite rare in comparison with hallucinations (*Ibid.,* 398).

Attempts to compare types of mental disorders cross-culturally have generally not been successful, partly because of difficulties at this stage of research in unraveling what may be thought of as "primary symptoms" from "secondary symptoms." For example, primary symptoms — those that may be basic to depression — occur early and constitute the essence of the disorder. Secondary symptoms are regarded as part of the individual's reaction to his illness; they develop because he attempts to come to terms with his changed behavior (Murphy, Wittkower, and Chance 1970:476). Since the latter are thought to be particularly dependent on the social and cultural background of the patient, Western-trained psychiatrists lacking familiarity with the world of the patient may find it difficult to distinguish priority of symptoms. Cawte, for example, believes that Western specialists caring for Kaiadilt patients in Australia have sometimes erred in diagnosing depressive symptoms such as suicidal tendencies and profound sadness, stemming from fear of sorcery, as schizophrenia. Instead, he argues, in the light of Kaiadilt beliefs about malign magical influences, it is more accurate to depict sorcery complaints (common in this culture) as a chronic depressive state arising in response to gross stress of forced emigration, loss of social role, and domestic disharmony (Cawte 1974:97).

Evidence of frequencies of mental disorder in non-Western societies have been impeded largely because there is no feasible method to obtain reliable data (Dohrenwend and Dohrenwend 1965). Many studies have been based on hospital statistics, yet in Third World countries with poorly developed mental health services, admissions can hardly be taken as representative of prevalence. For example, Field believes that depression is common in Africa, but that African women suffering from depression would not be apt to go to a European hospital; hence the rarity of reported cases (Field 1960:149). Studies based on sample interviews likewise seem of doubtful value where the possible variables, including undetected disease, are so great as to cast doubt on such findings.

MENTAL ILLNESS AND CHANGE

If the evidence is not good on comparative frequencies of different types of mental illness in societies of differing complexities, anthropologists and some psychiatrists agree that it *is* good with respect to the consequences of rapid sociocultural change: such change is productive of high average incidences. Okinawans, for example, known for the relatively low incidence of mental illness on their home island, apparently found migration to Hawaii enormously stressful; in their new home they developed rates of psychoses significantly higher than any other major group in the islands (Moloney 1945:391-399; Wedge 1952:255-258). The same appears to be true in indigenous Australia, where Cawte has borrowed the song title "The Birth of the Blues" to dramatize his observation that "the blues" — intrapunitiveness leading to depression — emerges more prominently in transitional than in stable societies. The full syndrome, he finds, is a product of forced replacement of the extended family by the Western conjugal one, the loss of objects that sustain the patient's self-esteem and identity, repression of familiar moral codes and, in the crisis of stress, a general affect of guilt (Cawte 1973:11). Similarly, working with migrants from India in Trinidad and Surinam, Angrosino found disabling conflicts between the ties of family and ethnic community and the desire to play a part in the "outside" modern community. A flamboyant alcoholism, together with periods of depression and suicidal tendencies, came to be associated with rebellion against the complex of family-religious duty (Angrosino 1974:129-131).

In recording increased incidences of mental illness in populations that are undergoing rapid sociocultural change, it is well to remember, as pointed out a few pages earlier, that we are not measuring from a zero-baseline of no mental illness whatsoever. Hence, the "evidence" for increased mental disorder under the stress of acculturation must be compared with that prevailing in the preacculturative setting if a true measure of change in rates is to be determined. Some traditional and folk cultures provide individuals with little psychological armature in the face of seemingly minimal change demands. David Looff has shed light on the interrelationship between mental illness and socialization practices in Appalachia. He has demonstrated how overreliance on restricted sources of security fosters a stultifying closeness, how the closed, tradition-bound family system molds the child into pathological fearfulness of anything unfamiliar. As a consequence, severe "school phobia" and fear of leaving the valleys become commonplace in a process that ends with "the pride and privatism of people unable to compete outside the ancient kinships of the Hollow," even in the face of pervasive and grinding poverty (Looff 1971:x). In adulthood as well exposure to procedures beyond their very limited experience can create overwhelming and persistent terrors (*Ibid.,* 18).

In contrast to this depressing example, there are other societies that have shown a remarkable capacity to absorb stress and provide alternative opportunities in the face of extreme adversity in change situations. For example, among California Japanese relocatees in World War II "The ethnic community and family — their structure, their function, their values, and their 'culture' " were sources of strength that enabled them to endure camp life with a minimum of mental breakdown (Kitano 1969:269). However, as the Japanese have become more acculturated and like other Americans, there is evidence of rising pathology of many kinds (*Ibid.,* 260-261).

CULTURE-SPECIFIC DISORDERS

In the field of mental illness no topic has intrigued anthropologists more than the so-called culture-specific illnesses (i.e., syndromes that, from the accounts of early travelers and missionaries, have come to be associated with specific racial and ethnic groups). Among the best known of these "diseases" are "arctic hysteria," (known as *pibloktoq* among the Eskimo); *windigo,* a cannibalistic obsession described for the Indians of northeastern North America; "running amok," a frenzied killing spree of Malaysian males; *latah,* an hysterical imitative reaction similar to the Siberian form of arctic hysteria; *koro,* a fear among Chinese males that the penis will withdraw into the body; and *susto,* a depressive-anxiety condition described for many parts of Latin America. We doubt that the last-named condition should be considered in this list since *susto* (Spanish for "fright") is more properly a cause of a variety of physical and mental illnesses, particularly of the widespread Latin American folk illness known as *bilis,* an upset liver. Recently *malgri,* an incapacitating anxiety syndrome characterized by drowsiness and abdominal pain, has been described as exclusive to the Wellesley Islands. This disorder has as its central theme a phobic concern with violation of specific food taboos (Cawte 1974:-106-119). As with *susto,* however, a psychogenic syndrome appears linked to a psysiological disorder, here gastrointestinal disturbances.

The literature on culture-specific illnesses and the varied explanations that have been advanced to explain them have been admirably summarized by John Kennedy (J. Kennedy 1973:1152-1169); space limitations preclude even brief discussion here of most of these conditions. The principal question that arises from a consideration of culture-specific illnesses is whether named conditions in fact represent clinically distinct syndromes or are variations on, or combinations of, the common psychiatric syndromes recognized by psychiatrists. The latter view predominates among modern scholars, yet there is sufficient evidence that dietary deficiencies, (often) harsh environmental conditions, and extreme social and psychological pressures that may play precipitating roles in episodes of illness justify more detailed research into the nature and causes of these illnesses. We propose to take the case of *pibloktoq,* the Eskimo version of arctic hysteria, to show how biological and cultural research lead us to a clearer understanding of this dramatic condition. In so doing we draw largely on the model study of the physician-anthropologist Foulks (Foulks 1972).

Arctic hysteria is found among the circumpolar peoples, from the Lapps in the west to the Greenland Eskimo in the east. Foulks recognizes two main syndromes: one marked by a mindless, imitative mania, found only in Siberia, and the other, a frenzied dissociative state found among all circumpolar groups. Both forms are marked by a (usually) sudden onset of a short-lived period of bizarre behavior, followed by cessation of acute symptoms and a return to normalcy. *Pibloktoq* sufferers tear off their clothing, often struggle with others with superhuman strength, throw themselves into snowbanks, or imitate the sounds of birds and animals. Western observers have most commonly compared the symptoms to those of hysteria; explanations range from traditional psychoanalytic interpretations to environmental conditions that cause intense food anxiety during the winter months. Several investigators, however, have suggested dietary deficiencies, and particularly reduced levels of serum calcium, as possible explanations for *pibloktoq.* Some years ago Wallace stated this hypothesis in its clearest form; he argued that *pibloktoq* results from hypocalcemia, a calcium deficiency resulting from inadequate calcium sources in the Eskimo diet, and low vitamin D synthesis during the sunless winter months, a biochemical process necessary to maintain normal calcium levels (Wallace 1961b:266-270). The calcium hypothesis is intriguing, because calcium is an essential element in the chemical transmission of the neural impulses, and abnormalities in the physiological functioning of calcium have been demonstrated to be capable of producing various forms of abnormal behavior, including the hysterialike manifestations found in arctic hysteria.

Foulks, a student of Wallace, recently has tested this hypothesis. As consulting psychiatrist for the Northern Regional Clinic of the State Division of Mental Health in Fairbanks from 1969 to 1970, he administered psychiatric care to a great many Eskimos, including ten cases of patients who had exhibited *pibloktoq* behavior. Using this sample and drawing on a number of highly technical nutritional and serological studies of other researchers, he concluded that the symptoms of *pibloktoq* are compatible with a diagnosis of hypocalcemia (Foulks 1972:70). Moreover, it appeared that the diet of many Eskimo is, in fact, deficient in calcium. Nonetheless, studies of large samples indicated that in spite of apparent low availability of calcium in food sources, most Eskimo maintain normal serum calcium levels. Repeated blood samples from the ten cases likewise indicated that, with the exception of a single test, they also appeared to maintain adequate serum calcium levels throughout the year, although several were on the low side of the normal range. The original hypothesis, obviously, did not stand up.

Foulks then turned to another lead, the possibility of "circadian," or daily rhythms, in the body's biochemical processes. In the temperate zones of the earth, human physiology has adjusted to diurnal cycles of rest and activity based on night and day. Many human physiological functions vary significantly according to the 24-hour day: blood pressure, body temperature, pulse, respiration, blood sugar, hemoglobin levels, and amino acids. But, in the Arctic, light-dark synchronization regularized in the tropics and temperate zones by roughly equal periods of day and night is possible neither in winter nor summer. Foulks, quoting a number of researchers, suggests that certain of these diurnal rhythms begin to "free run" out of phase with the normal 24-hour sleep-work cycle, and that these losses of synchronization may affect the central nervous system, predisposing the individual to irritability and excitation. Calcium rhythms are among those that may be desynchronized. In the one case (out of the ten) tested, Foulks found this loss of synchronization in calcium metabolism. He does not believe that this alone produces *pibloktoq*, but he does suggest that individuals predisposed by other factors to anxiety attacks, or individuals with cerebral pathology, might well be pushed over the brink by this desynchronization (*Ibid.,* 86).

To test this hypothesis, Foulks says, it is necessary to demonstrate that his ten subjects exhibiting *pibloktoq* behavior symptoms also manifest cerebral pathology compatible with the seizures characterizing the condition. Careful reviews of their case records revealed that only three demonstrated evidence of cerebral pathology that might contribute to seizures. Foulks then turns to the psychosocial factors that characterize his ten subjects. The common element here is that all "were threatened or were actually unable to maintain a way of life that was gratifying socially" (*Ibid.,* 108). At some point all had experienced the anxiety of being unable to maintain a way of life that others in their villages would find acceptable. They were insecure as to their identity and place in society. "They felt their inadequacies intensely, and feared others would also see their weaknesses. They were shameful at not being able to live up to a 'meaningful' way of life" (*Ibid.,* 109). In other words, they were likely candidates for psychological problems, even under the best of circumstances.

The main lessons we learn from Foulks' careful study is the danger of trying to interpret complex phenomena is unicausal terms. In the case at hand harsh environmental and climatic conditions, nutritional problems, special disease dangers that affect the brain, and social conditions and pressures combine to predispose certain individuals to exhibit from time to time the symptoms that long ago were labeled arctic hysteria. "The fundamental proposition of this study," he concludes, "has been that human behavior is multiply determined and that single, linear, causal theories lack comprehensive and predictive value" (*Ibid.,* 113).

CONCLUSIONS

Foulks' conclusions represent a major step forward because, as Wallace charges, most anthropologists have been guilty of uncritically following the early culture-and-personality model as the way to explain mental illness, failing to acknowledge that many known organic impairments produce symptomatologies essentially indistinguishable from those that may also be produced by psychosocial mechanisms. A psychosocial rather than a physiological frame of reference for the study of mental illness is, of course, congenial to anthropologists, since the research methods — above all observation — and the data themselves that "explain" behavior are those most familiar to them. Wallace explains this apparent blindness in historical terms; when anthropologists, beginning with Sapir's 1927 paper, "The Unconscious Patterning of Behavior in Society" (Mandelbaum 1949) first began seriously to explore behavior and the individual, psychiatric theory, and especially Freudian theory, was well developed, but our knowledge of genetic and biochemical structures in their relationship to behavior was so little developed as not seriously to influence theory development (Wallace 1961b:258).

Since that time, enormous strides have been made in unlocking the secrets of brain chemistry. Much of the recent research centers on neurotransmitters, substances with names such as acetylcholine, dopamine, and norepinephrine, which are "chemical messengers" that the brain's billions of brain cells, or neurons, use to communicate with each other. Some types of severe mental illness are now being blamed on malfunctions in the transmission process. For example, too little norepinephrine may precipitate some forms of depression. For some years the evidence has grown that schizophrenia is precipitated and maintained by a biochemical disorder or disorders (e.g., Wallace 1969:76). Recent research is beginning to explain the precise nature of these disorders. Protein fragments known as "endorphins" (meaning the body's own morphine), discovered in 1973, produce body rigidity that resembles catatonic schizophrenia when injected into rat brains. "The rats can be stood on their noses for hours or propped between bookends, neck ón one and tail on the other, without moving a whisker. All of this implies that schizophrenia may be due to an endorphin imbalance" (Shaffer 1977).

Clearly, physiological factors play a far greater role in mental illness than was formerly believed. At the same time, culture certainly plays a major role in precipitating much mental illness, given the hereditary-physiological tendency as well as the responses to it. The kinds of stress that living creates vary with different cultural pressures, but stress is a fact of life in all societies, and just as it may precipitate organic illness, so may it produce mental illness. Hereditary, physiological, and psychocultural factors all play roles in explaining mental illness. The goal of research is not to assign dominance to any one, but to fathom their interlocking relationships.

chapter 6

Shamans, Witch Doctors, and Other Curers

THE THERAPEUTIC INTERVIEW

In this chapter we are concerned particularly with the roles, behavior, and personality characteristics of non-Western curers. In the ethnographical literature non-Western curers can be, and usually are, described in the context of the cultures and the medical systems of which they are a part. In a structural-functional analysis of a specific society, this is the appropriate presentation. At the same time, such an approach inescapably obscures the generic characteristics of curers *as a professional type* found in one form or another in every society. Since our design in *Medical Anthropology* is cross-cultural and our intent is to illustrate general patterns, we propose to examine the topic of non-Western curers by focusing on what is usually called the "therapeutic interview" (i.e., the formal interaction occurring between a person who suspects or knows he is ill and an individual designated by his culture as qualified to aid the sick). We believe, with Wilson, that this interaction is "the crux of medicine" (R. Wilson 1963:273) and, by virtue of this, the constant that links all medical systems. As such, it has proven to be an enormously productive research focus, of intrinsic interest both for its frequent high drama and for what it tells us about the quality of health care delivery. At first glance therapeutic interviews in different societies appear to have very little in common, as the following vignettes from the Eskimo, a Colombian village, and the United States suggest.

In aboriginal times an Eskimo man who continued to feel unwell consulted a shaman who "walked about the patient, examining him from all angles. Then he might touch the patient about the spot where the 'pain' lay. He licked his hands, then rubbed them over the painful area. Some shamans blew on the affected part, occasionally sucking at it tentatively at first if the case was diagnosed as one of [object] intrusion . . . When these preparations were completed, the shaman began to sing" (Spencer 1959:306).

In Aritama, a Spanish-speaking mestizo village in Colombia, a curer, a *curioso*, is called in when illness persists. "After a few searching questions concerning the patient's enemies who might have caused the disease, the practitioner goes to great length in asking in detail about the food consumed during recent days or weeks, about any hallucinations, heavy physical efforts, or exposure to sun, rain, wind, or water. The pulse is taken and if it beats rapidly then a 'hot' disease is diagnosed or, vice versa, a 'cold' disease. Facial expression is studied carefully . . . Some specialists examine the urine . . . The pupils of the eyes are examined . . . Fecal matter, sputum, and vomit are occasionally examined." Only then does the curer prescribe (Reichel-Dolmatoff, G. & A. 1961:289).

In the United States a middle-class man asks for an appointment with his physician after several days of nagging abdominal pain that he suspects is something more than indigestion. The doctor "fits him into" a busy schedule, examines him, presses his stomach, localizes the pain, and orders a blood count. If the results are positive, an appendectomy will follow.

Although the behavior of the Eskimo shaman, the Colombian *curioso*, and the American doctor may seem very different in their views of themselves and of their status in their societies and in the performance of their professional roles, they in fact reveal more similarities than differences. In order to elucidate these similarities (and differences) as clearly as possible, we have found it expedient in our cross-cultural exploration to include the therapeutic interview as it is carried out in the United States and the West, even though our primary concern is with non-Western curers.

The therapeutic interview, it is generally agreed, is best analyzed in terms of role relationships, the norms of behavior, of recognized expectations that characterize both actors in the drama. It is not enough, however, to consider these role relationships in the limited context of medical treatment alone since, as Wilson points out, "The welter of behaviors and expectancies subsumed under 'the physician's role' or 'the patient's role' does not . . . transpire in a vacuum. Rather, these roles are exquisitely sensitive to the environing frame of cultural values, of nonmedical activities, of the tempo and tenor of the community around them. Just because health and illness are such salient human problems, the effort to cope with them through doctor-patient interaction is especially exposed to the influences of the time and place in which the effort occurs" (R. Wilson 1963:274). Full appreciation of any therapeutic interview requires knowledge of the cultural background in which it is imbedded and of the expectations that each actor brings to it.

SOME CHARACTERISTICS OF DOCTOR AND PATIENT ROLES

The roles of doctor and patient are, like all roles, complementary and interdependent; each requires the other. Without patients there would be no doctor's role, and without doctors, no patient's role. But beyond this interdependence the two roles are marked by quite distinct characteristics that can be analyzed in terms of four basic paired dimensions: *restricted-universal, permanent-temporary, superordinate-subordinate,* and *voluntary-involuntary.* By restricted-universal we mean that in every society the number of people recognized as able to cure is very limited while, in contrast, everyone can reasonably expect at some time during his life to fall ill, to be a patient. It is in this sense that the role of patient is a universal while that of the curer is severely restricted. Permanent-temporary refers to the fact that for most curers, the role is lifelong, whereas for most patients, the condition is temporary. The superordinate-subordinate dimension describes the hierarchy of dominance-submission that in every society marks the doctor-patient relationship. The curer is in charge; it is his responsibility to make decisions, to take action. The patient is in a subordinate, largely passive position; it is his obligation to follow the instructions of the curer if he wishes that particular curer to continue to attend to him.

With respect to the voluntary-involuntary dimension, the contrast is not quite so clearly marked as with the other dimensions. As far as the role of patient is concerned, it is usually seen as involuntary. Although some people are accident- or sickness-prone and the role of patient sometimes has attractions, most illness is seen as involuntary and unwanted. In many non-Western societies the role of curer is also involuntary, something that is forced on a reluctant individual by the spirits who confer on him the powers the curer will use. The story of Gabriel Mir (p. 107) illustrates this pattern of "election" by spirits, a pattern that usually characterizes shamans and all forms of spirit and faith healers. In many other situations the role of curer is voluntary, something actively sought by people who consciously choose it from among the life options offered by their societies. Physicians in the West, of course, fall in this category. But the pattern is equally true of African witch doctors, who train and study with older professionals who have accepted them as paying students, and by most midwives, masseurs, bonesetters, and herbalists in non-Western societies whose skills are learned rather than miraculously conferred on them.

As is almost always the case with cultural generalizations, exceptions can be found. Thus, although historically illness usually has been regarded as a temporary state — the patient either recovered or died — control and elimination of infectious disease in recent years has saved increasing numbers of people to become victims of chronic illness in their later years. Permanency thus characterizes the role of many patients. And, although dominance-subordination marks any continuing doctor-patient relationship, the degree of authority may be far from absolute. Thus, among the Spanish-speaking people of Sal si Puedes, a California urban barrio, the curer's role is not authoritarian. "Curers may advise, but they may not dictate. Medical advice may be followed only if it is sanctioned by the powerful members of the patient's social group" (Clark 1959a:213).

UNIVERSALS IN CURING ROLES

The differences between disease theory systems are qualitative; personalistic and naturalistic causative concepts, not to mention scientific concepts, can hardly be compared. This is not true of health care delivery systems, where we find marked similarities in professional premises, self-images, and modes of relationships with the public, regardless of the causative assumptions that may underlie the system. The remarkable thing is that in most societies a doctor clearly is a doctor, rarely to be confused with other people in his group. The important ways in which doctors, viewed in cross-cultural perspective, display common traits include things such as specialization, selection and training, sense of a professional image, expectation of payment, and belief in their powers. In most societies, too, they are viewed more or less with ambivalence by the public. We will consider these common characteristics in turn.

1. Specialization

In Western societies medical specialization is increasingly the rule: internal medicine, surgery (itself with many specialties), cardiology, neurology, optometry, pediatrics — the list grows with each passing year. And not only is there specialization within establishment medicine, there are alternative forms such as spiritualism, faith healing, and ethnic folk medicines such as those described in Chapter 4. In traditional societies the degree of specialization is less marked, but it is a poor community indeed that does not recognize distinct curing roles. In a rural Philippine peasant area, for example, there is the midwife (*mananabang*), the masseur or bonesetter (*manghihilot*), and the general practitioner (*mananambal*) (Lieban 1962b:512). The logic underlying these specialties seems essentially the same as that underlying modern medicine.

In other societies the basic dichotomy is between the shaman or witch doctor — highly trained, usually supernaturally endowed curers — and the herbalist — wise in nature's ways, but less professional in status and behavior. Thus, among the Yoruba of Nigeria we find both the priests of the Ifa cult, the *babalawo,* who specialize in divination and psychotherapy, and the herbalists, the *onishegun.* Although there is a good deal of overlap in practice, "On the whole it would be true to say that the *onishegun* are less highly regarded than the *babalawo,* the former dealing with the commoner, more easily recognized disorders whilst the latter take on more of the difficult diagnostic problems and prescribe more radical regimens for a patient to follow" (Maclean 1971:75). Similarly, among the Bomvana (a Xhosa subgroup in the Transkei of South Africa) there are two main types of healers: the diviner and the herbalist. The former, a medium with supernatural powers, serves primarily as a diagnostician and is visited only once by the same patient. The herbalist, in contrast, who has no spiritual contacts, is the primary curer and may admit patients to his kraal for treatment for up to 3 months (Jansen 1973:35).

This basic dichotomy is made particularly clear by Thomas in writing about the Kamba of Kenya: "The characteristic which differentiates the diviner, or religious-medical specialist (*mundumue*) from the other specialists, i.e. the herbalist and the midwife, is the *mundume's* privileged use of *ue* [supernatural power] for solving problems of sickness or other misfortune. In contrast, the role of the herbalist (*mukimi wa miti*) is more narrowly limited to that of a traditional pharmacist who administers individual herbs and mixtures of herbs for specific illnesses such as stomach-ache or rheumatism. In the process of diagnosis and treatment, he does not claim to utilize supernatural power." Unlike the *mudumue,* the herbalist does not transform *miti* (herbs) into a magical substance: "Rather, his expertise is considered to lie in the administration of herbs as medicines in their natural state" (Thomas 1975: 270).

These categories — shaman or witch doctor with supernatural powers, herbalists, bonesetters, and midwives — are the specialties most commonly observed in non-Western societies. And, just as medical specialties are graded in prestige in the West, so in other societies is there a hierarchy of status, with the supernaturally endowed curer outranking the others.

2. Selection and training

In every society only a few people have, or are believed to have, the skills necessary to cure. These skills (powers is sometimes a better word) must be acquired, and the ways in which they are acquired vary widely from one society to the next. In Western societies the decision to study medicine, to become a doctor, usually reflects personal choice. Although the decision may reflect parental as well as personal choices, a "call" from a higher power is not often a factor in the decision. After a long period of training and final certification that he has mastered the details of the profession, the new doctor is considered qualified to treat patients. Some physicians are recognized as more skillful than others, but these differences are not thought to stem from differential access to supernatural or magical powers. Curing competence is achieved in the same way that it is acquired in other professions; intelligence and willingness to work hard are the necessary qualifications that one brings to the task.

In traditional societies similar personal decisions, as we have seen, often underlie medical careers. Herbalists and midwives, for example, frequently acquire their skills from their mothers or other close relatives. Through interest and observation herbalists may learn about the different plants that grow nearby or that can be obtained in the sidewalk pharmacies of market towns. They may note the effects of food and herbs on patients and exchange information with other people similarly skilled; in this way they build reputations as home curers, to be turned to for common childhood illnesses and for diarrhea, colds, rheumatism, and the like.

More highly trained specialists may also make initial rational decisions. Among the Azande of the Sudan, a young man may express his desire to become a witch doctor to an older, established curer. If accepted, he studies with him over a long period of time, making frequent and substantial gifts to him as payment. Magic, like all other property, must be bought and sold; in learning to become a witch doctor, the significant part of the initiation is the transference of magical plant lore and other cures from teacher to pupil in return for payment. Knowledge and power also are acquired by the novice when he eats magical meals containing herbs and other charms, served him by the master (Evans-Pritchard 1937:202-215).

Among both Western and non-Western peoples supernatural elements often play a role in determining who will become a curer. In Spain the most important folk curer, the *saludador* ("the one who makes well," from *salud* = "health") enjoys the *gracia,* the special grace of God, manifest in the circumstances of birth. Persons with "grace" are those who cried while yet in their mother's womb (and provided she told no one at the time), those born on lucky days, especially Maundy Thursday and Good Friday, and the seventh consecutive son born to the same woman. Persons falling into these categories are believed to show a cross or a St. Catherine's wheel clearly marked on their hard palate. Twins, too, are thought to have grace, with special powers to cure by the laying on of hands (Foster 1953a:213).

In Catholic countries Christ and the saints are believed to have special powers to cure or to enable living men to cure. In traditional societies in these countries the conditions surrounding supernatural "election" to the curing role and the personal qualities of human curers often partake of the nature of shamans. One of the most famous of Mexican curers, known as *El Niño Fidencio* ("Fidencio the Child"), lived in the northern state of Nuevo León. Like many Spanish curers, he was reputed to have had a cross on his hard palate; like many Siberian shamans, he appears to have been a transvestite who often disguised himself as a woman to escape crowds, dressed in a loose gown, cooked, and cleaned house. As a boy he had complete responsibility for a younger brother. Once when the latter was ill and Fidencio was at his wit's end, a man appeared at the door and said that the book he held in his hands told how to cure with herbs and that with it Fidencio could cure his brother. He searched out the herbs, cured his brother, and only then realized that the man at the door looked like the Sacred Heart of Jesus, and that undoubtedly it was Christ himself (Macklin 1967:532). With time his fame as a curer grew, until he attained popular "sainthood"; today, long after his death, his shrine is a place of veneration for pilgrims who go there seeking cures (Macklin 1974b).

More dramatic is the story of how Gabriel Mir, the leading Indian curer of *espanto* (fright) in a Guatemalan town, acquired his power. Although miraculous circumstances attended his birth — a ball of fire appeared in the sky while his mother was in labor — there was nothing unusual about his life until the age of 32. Then a series of catastrophies struck: his wife and all five children died in a plague, and he himself was critically ill for many months, barely escaping with his life. With no woman to care for him and unable to work, he lived in squalor and on the slim charity of neighbors in a shack on the outskirts of town, too weak even to go to the public fountain for water. One dark night, lying on his platform bed, he noticed a faint brilliance at his door, and out of it appeared a human figure about 4 feet tall, wearing a flowing blue robe and a small crown.

"Ave Maria" said San Antonio (Gabriel recognized him from a postcard on his home altar). "You have been ill, my son, close to *La Gloria.* I have come to impose on you. I have a sick person, and I want you to tell me what his sickness is." Gabriel denied that he could cure. "Indeed you do. Do not deny it," and now San Antonio was speaking, not in Spanish, but in the Indian tongue. Gabriel felt, but could not see, the emaciated arm of a child. Feeling his pulse he said, "This child has *espanto* . . . he has fallen into the river." San Antonio patted Gabriel on the shoulder: "With this, my son, you begin curing." Gabriel, however, did not want to cure. "Wait, wait, San Antonio, holy padre. I do not want to cure — relieve me of this burden. Take it with you." But San Antonio and the disembodied arms of the child floated to the door and disappeared. "Holy Mother of God. I don't want the power," shrieked Gabriel. There was a blinding flash, and Gabriel found himself sitting on the edge of his bed, soaked in sweat, his heart beating, the early morning sun pouring in.

From that time his strength began to return. Each night for a week or more, San Antonio returned, teaching him the basic techniques of his calling; Gabriel's protests grew weaker as his confidence grew stronger. Then intervals occurred between visits, and they grew longer and longer. But San Antonio was never far away, Gabriel knew, from time to time returning to teach still a new technique. After this Gabriel became a great curer of *espanto* (Gillin 1956).

Although cloaked in Christian imagery, Gabriel's experience (and the Indian lineage of the experience) conforms to widespread primitive patterns of the acquisition of curing power in native America and Siberia. This is the forcible "election" by a powerful spirit which, over protests of the human, insists that he must become a curer. Election almost always is marked by a serious illness that carries the future curer to the edge of the grave, and only after a long and slow cure, during which the secrets of curing are revealed, is the training completed. The term shaman, Siberian in origin, is widely used to describe the type of curer who is "elected," who suffers serious illness, and who (usually) maintains close contact with his spirit familiar, in the Siberian variant being possessed by the spirit as he cures.

Among the Indians of northern California, where most shamans were women, curing power resided in a "pain," a small inanimate object shot into a person's body by the sprit that had elected her to be a curer. Among the Shasta, election was signaled by dreams in which an ancestor, herself a shaman, appeared. The novice avoided the sight and smell of meat during the period of these dreams; to eat meat or to refuse to recognize the meaning of the dreams was believed to result in death. The next step in the supernatural sequence was the appearance of a spirit during the woman's waking life who aimed an arrow at her heart and commanded her to sing. The novice fell to the ground in a seizure, during which time the spirit taught her her song. Reviving in the evening, she would sing her song loudly, dance, ooze blood from her mouth, and be told the spirit's name and abode. Only after three more days of dancing was the pain shot into the novice who, after again falling in a cataleptic fit, would revive, draw the pain from her body, and show it to those present as proof of of her power. On subsequent nights other spirits shot her with additional pains until she had four or five, which she stored in her body but could remove at will. Still a novice, she spent a year or more in accumulating her curing paraphernalia, after which she again danced in the presence of older shamans. She then became a fully qualified shaman herself (Kroeber 1925:301-302).

In the Christian peasant area of Sibulan, Negros Oriental, in the Philippines, much of the curer's art is learned through observation or instruction from other curers but, in the case of the most powerful, the *mananambal,* it is the "special connection with the supernatural" that validates power. The call to be a *mananambal* usually comes from someone from the spirit world who appears in dreams. Some novices wish to resist, but pressure mounts. Lieban tells how one man had practiced simple medicine, but had no desire to be a full-fledged *mananambal.* Then, on one occasion, he refused to treat the illness of a friend, feeling he was not qualified. That night a voice in a dream ordered him to do so, under pain of having the illness turned on him. He refused. Three nights later he had a similar dream. Still he refused. Then he dreamed that the Virgin Mary floated by on a river. The voice of the first dreams told him that if he did not visit the river bank in the morning, he would fall ill. He followed instructions, and saw the Virgin floating by, just as in the dream; she smiled at him and then disappeared. This convinced him he should be a *mananambal*, so he treated his friend, who recovered (Lieban 1962b:512-513).

However the decision is made to become a curer, indigenous doctors, like their Western counterparts, usually undergo a long period of training. Among the Iban of Sarawak (Borneo), "Training to become a *manang* may take as long as eight years of part-time study. He must learn a vast volume of lore, songs, and incantations. And, even more important, he must come to understand and be able to control his own guardian spirit" (Torrey 1972:95). In a study of 100 Yoruba curers in Ibadan, it was found that only six were under 40 years of age, and "all had undergone a prolonged period of apprenticeship or training before feeling qualified to set up in practice on their own" (Maclean 1971:76). Other training periods include 2 years for a Yoruk Indian shaman and up to 7 years among the Blackfoot Indians and for the Nigerian *babalawo* doctors (Torrey 1972:52).

As in Western society, in those non-Western societies where curing is a highly developed art, apprentices or student healers are expected to pay for the part of their training that comes from older professionals. Sometimes this is seen as payment for the training itself and, at other times, as among the North Alaskan Eskimo, payment was for the possession of the necessary songs and charms the shaman would use (Spencer 1959:302). The power inherent in songs and other charms was a salable commodity that could be acquired by inheritance or purchase. Among the Azande of Africa, magical powers are transmitted from the teacher to younger apprentices, normally in return for payment. Evans-Pritchard reports having seen as many as seven or eight students gathered in the homestead of an experienced colleague undergoing training (1937:206).

3. Certification

In contemporary Western society scientifically trained physicians must be certified before they can practice. Although legal certification comes from the state, this authority ultimately is based on the evaluation of members of the medical profession, who vouch for the competence of the new doctor. It is well to remember, however, that legal certification is a relatively recent concept. In many American states, until well after the Civil War, a "doctor" was anyone who wished to call himself a doctor!

Often, although by no means always, novice curers in non-Western societies are ritually certified by older shamans after they have completed their training period. Such an "initiation," which involves dancing and ritual burial, has been described for the Azande (Evans-Pritchard 1937:239-242). Among the Shasta Indians of California, whose female shaman's mode of election and training has been summarized above, full professional competence was announced at the end of the training period, when she invited her friends to a dance. "During the dance her spirits reappeared to her and inspected the paraphernalia which she had prepared. After three days of dancing the novice was a fully qualified shaman" (Kroeber 1925:302).

4. Professional image

In all societies curers have a strong sense of their professional image, of their role, and of their place in society. Through behavior, dress, and other accoutrements, they usually seek to enhance this professional image. The Western doctor feels unprofessional without white coat and stethoscope, just as the Siberian shaman feels lost without his spirit-calling tambourine. Even among Western doctors there are differences of image, based on specialties. Psychiatrists, for example, "stand apart from their healing brethren in other medical specialties. They dress differently, have beards, and are rarely in danger of being confused with surgeons or pediatricians" (Torrey 1972:51). Among non-Western peoples, the cartoon stereotype of the witch doctor in an elaborate, masked disguise, dancing away evil spirits, is overdrawn. Yet almost always professional curers with supernatural powers (as contrasted to midwives and herbalists) have ritual objects such as feathers, rattles, drums, corn pollen, and the like that clearly set them off from other members of their communities.

Curers are set off from their nonprofessional friends by costume and behavior, and are often marked by distinctive psychological characteristics as well. Ethnologists who have worked with Siberian and Alaskan shamans agree that individuals marked by neurotic, even psychotic, personalities were the most likely candidates for election to the role of curer. Often, indeed, personality characteristics that in Western society would be branded as dangerously deviant are recognized in non-Western societies as prerequisites for successful curing careers, and when these characteristics begin to manifest themselves at an early age in children, members of the group feel most fortunate.

Although neurotic and psychotic temperament hardly give special qualification for medical careers in the United States, it is recognized that doctors live under enormous stress, greater than that of members of most other professions. Working hours are long and often irregular, and there is the constant strain of knowing that many decisions literally are life and death matters. Perhaps because of these circumstances the suicide rate of physicians in the United States is higher than that of laymen, and alcohol and drugs are constant threats to some. Psychiatrists, too, work under conditions of great stress. Not only do they live their professional lives in settings of (patient) depression and anxiety, but often after months or years of treatment of the same patient, the evidence of a "cure" is less convincing than, say, recovery following an appendectomy. Whatever the cause, the suicide rate of psychiatrists is twice that of other doctors, and they have a comparatively high rate of drug addiction (Torrey 1972:40).

5. Expectation of payment

The belief is widespread among many Americans, and particularly among those who turn to "alternate" systems of curing in preference to "establishment" medicine, that non-Western curers are little interested in money. Physicians are characterized as moneygrubbers and are compared unfavorably to their primitive counterparts who, it is assumed, have greater concern for the welfare of humanity. Like most stereotypes, this one is far from true. In all societies curers receive compensation in some form; tribal and peasant peoples are too realistic to expect them to perform solely for the good of their fellow men. The kinds and amounts of payment vary greatly, of course, depending on factors such as the time and cost of professional training, the extent to which power stems from the "grace" of a deity, and what the market will bear.

Among herbalists, some Mexican *curanderos,* and often among more specialized curers such as Zar cult priests in Ethiopia (Torrey 1972:94), the cost of treatment is whatever the patient wishes to leave. Particularly in Christian societies there is a strong belief that God gives special powers to a few select people for the good of mankind, and should a person so-favored try to enrich himself with this talent by charging for his help, his talents would be taken away by God. Yet it is a rare patient who abuses this relationship, since the curer is under no obligation to accept him a second time if he fails to reciprocate in some fashion. Perhaps more often a small fee is the rule. In Tzintzuntzan Doña Natividad Peña is locally known for her skills in curing childhood *empacho,* constipation attributed, among other things, to the eating of green peaches, which abound in June. Frequently during this month, half a dozen or more mothers will be seen on her porch, waiting their turn for treatment. "It's just like a doctor's office," she says, laughing. During 1974 her standard fee was 5 pesos ($.40 U.S.).

A picture of the folk medical curer that conforms to the common stereotype is given to us by Margaret Clark, who tells of Paula, a *curandera* in a Mexican-American enclave in California, and her patients. "When Paula is asked to examine a sick person . . . she is called upon both as a curandera and as a friend. People know that she is one of them and that she really cares what happens to them and has their welfare at heart . . . Patients are brought to her house, and she greets them in her kitchen, which smells faintly of the tools of her trade — mint, rosemary, cinnamon and coriander. Paula's manner is as warm and friendly as her kitchen-dispensary. She observes the requisite social amenities and always behaves in a manner which her clients regard as courteous . . . [When she makes a house call] she knows that she is expected to sit down with the family, drink a cup of coffee, and make small talk before getting down to the business at hand . . . A courteous and well-bred person does not rush into the middle of things . . . After a 'decent' interval, the illness can be mentioned and the patient seen" (Clark 1959a:208).

Paula makes her diagnosis on the basis of previous knowledge of the patient, neighborhood gossip, looking at the patient's eyes, taking his pulse, and palpating his abdomen or the calves of his legs. "The diagnosis is usually one that is familiar to the patient and his faimily — he is suffering from susto or empacho or bilis, or he has been afflicted with aire or mal ojo" (*Ibid.*).

Therapy is uncomplicated: topical treatment or instructions for home care. Relatives are welcome to make suggestions, and Paula never dictates what must be done. She charges little or nothing for her services; if she believes the disorder is serious, she recommends a medical doctor who is friendly and not too expensive. Perhaps, says Clark, because patients recover from a majority of their illness, regardless of treatment, "Paula's remedies often work well and she has a grateful and devoted clientele" (*Ibid.,* 209).

There is perhaps a tendency among anthropologists and laymen alike to sentimentalize the non-Western curer's approach to the patient, to assume that — as with Paula — the curer is always warm, friendly, and supportive. Yet it is a mistake to believe that Paula illustrates all or most traditional curers. In fact, the range of personality, attitudes toward the patient, and professional manner found among non-Western curers is at least as great as that found among American doctors, who range from those with a warm bedside manner to highly paid specialists who seem interested only in the clinical symptoms of the case. Non-Western curers can on occasion be just as formidable as the most aloof American doctor. How many people in the United States, for example, would seek out a physician whose terms were those of the Apache curer, described in the following lines? "An Apache who seeks shamanistic help has to humble himself to a point which would be unacceptable unless he were prepared to put himself unreservedly in the hands of the practitioner. The sufferer or a relative who speaks for him must approach the shaman in the most obsequious fashion. He must call him by a relationship term, whether or not the shaman is a relative, lay a ceremonial cigarette at his foot, tell of his great need and of his absolute dependence upon the particular shaman's ceremony. 'Only you can help me. Do not fail me now' is the closing plea. The shaman ponders the matter. He mutters something about the ingratitude of a former patient or the pressure of duties. After a sufficiently significant pause he stoops with fine condescension, picks up and smokes the cigarette, and so indicates that he will take the case" (Opler 1936:1375).

In contrast to Paula's easygoing and supportive manner and her minimal fees, among shamans and witch doctors (the real professionals of the traditional world), not only is treatment often cold and aloof, but fees are remarkably high, even by contemporary American standards. Among the North Alaskan Eskimo "an acceptable payment was the offering of a wife or daughter as a sexual partner . . . An average payment for a successful cure was an umiak (women's boat), which, in terms of aboriginal culture, represented a handsome fee" (Spencer 1959:308). In some societies curers ask to see the actual payment prior to accepting the patient, an act remarkably similar to the admittance procedures in many American hospitals. When, in aboriginal California, a Yuki Indian doctor was called, a rope was stretched in the house and on it were hung beads, blankets, baskets, and other objects of value, all to be given to him if a successful cure ensued. Dissatisfaction with the offered goods provided grounds for refusing the case (Foster 1944: 214). The Apache shaman, before fully committing himself to a patient, demands four ceremonial gifts as payment to his "power." Representative "gifts" may include a pouch of pollen, an unblemished buckskin, a downy eagle feather, and a piece of turquoise (Opler 1936:1375).

6. Belief in powers

In every society great prestige is given to curers of recognized ability; the practice of medicine (although historically not of surgery) almost always is associated with high status. In every society, too, most curers believe in their powers. The honesty of shamans has often been questioned by Western critics, since sleight of hand and other forms of legerdemain — important adjuncts in their art — are regarded in Western society as unprofessional conduct when engaged in by physicians. The California shaman who diagnosed an intruded disease object, a "pain," produced a bloody quartz crystal as evidence of correct diagnosis and successful treatment. He hid the crystal in his mouth and bit his cheek to produce the blood. Was he a mountebank? A charlatan? The consensus is that he was not. After all, physicians do not hesitate to use a placebo when they feel it contributes to the patient's ease of mind.

In evaluating the Iban *manang* of Sarawak, Torrey comes to the conclusion that probably is correct in other similar cases: "My conversations with three of them convinced me that while they are not above trickery, they use it in the belief that they are helping the patient. They have absolutely no doubt that the patient's soul is lost, and they believe that anything which will assist in its retrieval is not dishonest" (Torrey 1972:97). Although there are certainly frauds in primitive and peasant societies (just as in Western society), unscrupulous indigenous curers who manipulate the credulity of their fellows for profit, most curers appear to believe fully in their ability. Where people can enter a trance state almost at will, there seems nothing deceptive about believing that one's soul is travelling to distant places, searching out the place of captivity of a stolen soul so as to return it to its owner, the patient. In societies where everyone believes in spirits of many kinds, to be able to communicate with them, in dreams or in trances or seizures, requires no self-deceit. Just as scientifically trained physicians know they are masters of the science of curing beyond the abilities of their untrained fellows, so do most indigenous curers have unquestioned faith in their ability.

7. Attitudes of the public

In still another way powerful shamans and witch doctors resemble physicians in Western society: they are frequently viewed with ambivalent feelings by their clients. In all societies we turn to our curers in time of need; they are our last hope. We want them to be above other men, more capable, more skilled. In the United States we criticize physicians for sometimes seeming to confuse themselves with the deity, yet in times of crisis we insist that they play God. We force the role on them. Yet simultaneously we may criticize these "gods," perhaps even taking wry satisfaction from hearing how they have bungled the treatment — of others! If we can judge from the comments of students in classes over many years, the American physician's image of himself as a paternalistic, kindly, family physician always willing to help someone in need and genuinely believing that good care is available for everyone who needs it, is far from true. "It seems quite possible, even likely, that as the doctor appears in an increasingly prosaic light, he will lose his power to claim the patient's absolute confidence and in so doing will lose an essential ingredient of his success" (Myerhoff and Larson 1965:191).

Why is it that in societies as different as contemporary America, native California, and the North Alaskan Eskimo ambivalent feelings characterize attitudes toward doctors? The answer appears to lie in the control and exercise of power. In all societies people fear, and hence dislike and distrust, their fellows who exercise power, potential or real, over them. This is particularly true when the average man has only an imperfect understanding of the nature of this power.

In many non-Western societies the reason that shamans and witchdoctors are feared is that the role of evil sorcerer and ethical curer are not distinguished. Thus, among the North Alaskan Eskimo, the shaman fulfilled the role of healer and physician but, at the same time, his presence was "productive of fear and anxiety" because he could — and also did — bring illness. "One never knew at which point his personage might be offended so as to call forth his vengeance. He could, moreover, bring illness so as to cure and profit from it" (Spencer 1959:299). The shaman of the Yokuts and Western Mono in aboriginal California was viewed in similar fashion. "His supposed ability to manipulate supernatural elements for both good and evil purposes left him in an equivocal position. A doctor was both feared and respected; but whether he was more respected than feared or vice versa depended entirely upon his personal character" (Gayton 1930:388).

Central and Southern California tribes regarded shamanistic power as indifferently beneficent or malevolent. "Whether a given shaman causes death or prevents it is merely a matter of inclination. His power is equal in both directions. Much disease, if not the greater part, is caused by hostile or spiteful shamans. Witchcraft and the power of the doctor are therefore indissolubly bound up together" (Kroeber 1925:303). Common people are not absolutely defenseless in the face of witchcraft, and curers whose failures seem too numerous may be targets of vengeance. Kluckhohn describes a Navaho situation that applies to many other peoples, as well: "Feeling toward singers (native curers) always tends to be somewhat ambivalent. On the one hand they have great prestige, are much in demand and may obtain large fees. On the other hand, they are feared, and the border of active distrust is always close. *A singer must not lose too many patients*" (Kluckohn 1944:120. Emphasis added). Similarly, among the Shasta Indians of California, "The repeatedly unsuccessful shaman met the usual fate: a justified violent death" (Kroeber 1925:303).

Not surprisingly, where native doctors are also viewed as possible witches, they are careful in the selection of their cases. Among the Apache, for example, the "shaman is not a credulous dupe of his own supernaturalistic claims and boastings, who undertakes to cure any ailment, no matter how hopeless. Such an indiscriminate practitioner soon finds himself without honor or clients. The seasoned shaman is a shrewd and wary person who has witnessed enough of suffering and death to recognize serious organic disturbances when he sees them, and he is often very reluctant to accept responsibility for the cure of these. In many cases the shaman will simply tell the patient, 'You waited too long to call me,' or 'The good in you is mostly dead already; I can't help you' " (Opler 1936:1372-1373).

In a Mayan village in Chiapas, *curanderos* are similarly cautious. The patient, accompanied by members of his family, bears liquor, chocolate, and bread to the house of the curer who, before accepting the case, takes the patient's pulse and assesses the seriousness of the illness. If he feels he cannot treat him because the illness is too far progressed, he refuses it. Cases of measles, for example, often are refused, since the bathing technique that is a part of most cures often seems to cause death (Nash 1967:132-133).

In societies in which most illness is attributed to witchcraft, it is not unreasonable for people to believe that the specialist who can control and fight sorcery also has the requisite knowlede to practice it himself when it suits his needs. And, by the same token, it is reasonable to assume that when disease is believed to be the result of natural causes, the role of the curer is seen as more nearly beneficent. It is no accident that the Hippocratic Oath, by which the new doctor swears never to harm his patient and to work only with his best interest in mind, was the product of an intellectual world that, for the first time in history, could recognize that disease is the product of natural causes and not of evil men and spirits.

CURING, PUBLIC AND PRIVATE

Thus far we have emphasized the common elements we believe characterize curers and the practice of medicine in Western and traditional societies. But there are also significant differences, and none is so striking as the differences in social ambience in which patients are treated. In the West, "everyday medicine is practiced in privacy. In the other established professions, work goes on in the publicity of the court, the church, and the lecture hall as often as in the office. The work of the doctor is characteristically conducted in the closed consulting room or the bedroom. Furthermore, the physician usually renders personal services to individuals rather than to congregations or classes" (Freidson 1972:91). Wilson, in comparing the doctor-patient relationship to the priest-parishoner relationship, echoes the same sentiment with respect to "the privacy of the two relationships. . . . It is assumed that in dealing with salvation or healing an intimate compact is required. The self-revelation so vital to any exploration of the soul or the self necessarily demands a protected situation; the physician's consulting room may well be the appropriate modern analogue of the inviolable sanctuary of the medieval cathedral" (R. Wilson 1963:289). Patients of scientifically trained physicians desire and expect privacy in the treatment of their ills; although in a teaching hospital this right to privacy sometimes seems open to question, no one — medical professors or patients — expects treatment to be a public show.

In non-Western societies privacy also may prevail. But perhaps more often than not there are public aspects to diagnosis and treatment that seem quite foreign to the Western way. Harper, for example, gives a full description of a shamanistic seance in Mysore state in south India, attended by about 35 people assembled by the ringing of temple bells and gongs. Nineteen cases, most of them dealing with health problems, were presented to the shaman who, in full view of the assembled group, prescribed treatment (Harper 1957). A greater contrast to the usual Western pattern can hardly be imagined. The picture is similar among the Azande, where witch doctors diagnose in seances "held in public and heralded and accompanied by drums. These public performances are local events of some importance, and those who live in the neighborhood regard them as interesting spectacles well worth a short walk" (Evans-Pritchard 1937:154). Similarly, among the Navaho, favorite chants attract large crowds. Since these chants are held in the winter and last two or three nights, visitors bring their own bedding (Reichard 1963:120).

Public curing rituals like those in south India and those among the Azande and the Navaho reflect much more than mere cultural tradition. In many non-Western societies, as we have seen, illness is marked by social dimensions not normally felt to be a part of scientific etiologies. Patients may have fallen out of harmony with their natural and social environments, and their illnesses are often interpreted as reflecting stress or tears in the social fabric. The purpose of curing therefore goes well beyond the limited goal of restoring the sick person to health; it constitutes social therapy for the entire group, reassuring all onlookers that the interpersonal stresses that have led to illness are being healed. In societies, too, where illness is explained in personalist terms, as due to the anger of deities, ghosts, spirits, and witches, public demonstration of the curer's powers reassures the spectators that man is not without means to defend himself against earthly and supernatural forces for evil.

In other situations public or semipublic therapy may reflect other purposes, or perhaps no purpose at all beyond the convenience of doctor and patient. This would seem to be the case in Ibadan, Nigeria, where "Hausa barber-surgeons ply their ancient trade in the open air in full view of passers-by," their operating table a rush mat beneath a tree and their surgical instruments a set of razors in a pouch and rows of horns for cupping (Maclean 1971:65). In rural and small town Mexico, surgery, while not as public as in Nigeria, also has its open aspects: friends and relatives of the patient routinely are admitted to the operating room. But the rationale for this practice is quite different from the public spectacles of India, the Navaho, and the Azande, where the sha-man's or singer's powers and dedication are rarely in question. In rural Mex-ico, where it is considered only prudent to withhold a favorable evaluation of the skills and motivations of others — especially strangers — until the evidence is incontrovertible, as advocates of the patient nonmedical visitors can testify that the surgeon and his team worked thoroughly and efficiently, taking no shortcuts, and doing all in their power to save the life of the patient. And, when recovery is complete, they are walking advertisements for the surgeon. In this same cultural setting a patient, at home or in a hospital, is never left alone. The number of well-wishers pressing into the room varies directly with the gravity of the patient's condition to the point where, to an outsider, it seems a miracle that a dying man's departing soul can fight its way clear of the press of humanity.

ROLE BEHAVIOR IN THE THERAPEUTIC INTERVIEW

King has caught the essence of the doctor-patient nexus in the therapeutic interview by pointing out that a patient is not a passive being that the doctor examines, not an inert host in which microorganisms grow, not a machine whose parts fail to function or wear out. Rather, the patient is an active being, with and through whom the physician works in treating disease. "Intertwined with biological dysfunction are emotional reactions of the patient to his disease or injury, overlaid with all manner of social norms, values, and expectations. Treatment of disease . . . is *a process of social interaction*" (King 1962:207. Emphasis added).

Therapeutic interviews have been observed in many different societies, and the patterns that have been found prove to be remarkably similar. That is, the kinds of interaction noted seem inherent in the relationship itself instead of being rooted exclusively in a cultural matrix. As in all culturally molded social interactions, both patient and physician have clear ideas as to how they should behave in this setting, and they have equally clear ideas as to how the other person should behave. When these role expectations are essentially congruent, as among upper-middle-class American patients and their doctors, the doctor-patient interview is much more apt to be mutually rewarding and therapeutically successful than when mutual expectations are quite different. When role expectations are less congruent, as when patients differ from their physicians in social class, ethnic affiliation, or cultural identification, the doctor-patient relationship has been found to be less satisfying and successful.

The problem can be explored by asking, "What are the mutual expectations of physician and patient in the United States? In non-Western societies? What happens when these differential expectations are brought together in a therapeutic setting involving a scientifically trained doctor and an unsophisticated (in the ways of science) patient?" At the risk of oversimplification, we can say that the American doctor, in dealing with patients from the upper end of the socioeconomic spectrum, expects a continuing relationship in which he holds the trust of the patient, who will carefully follow his instructions. He also expects to be paid without complaint, and perhaps to receive a degree of gratitude for his work. The physician expects to maintain records on the patient, to ask a multitude of questions that aid in diagnosis, to examine the patient as needed, and to send him for laboratory tests and X rays as indicated. The patient's expections are the same; he considers that all of these actions are reasonable.

This model is, of course, vastly oversimplified; it conforms more nearly to that of the internist (the contemporary analog of the old-time family physician) than to that of the surgeon, the orthopedic doctor, or other specialists to whom the patient may be referred as needed by his internist. In non-Western societies, too, any model of doctor-patient expectations must be vastly oversimplified. Still, there are basic contrasts as compared to Western practice. The expectations of the shaman or witch doctor (in contrast to the herbalist) are not, as we have seen, very different from those of the scientific physician in many ways. But the differences are critical insofar as they fail to prepare a patient for subsequent therapy with a western physician. The shaman expects submission from his patient, compliance with his instructions, and payment for his services. He also may reasonably assume, at least in many societies, that the patient will return to him from time to time. It is in the realm of diagnosis rather than the intrinsic relationship that the differences are critical: shamans and witch doctors rarely ask patients for detailed explanations of their symptoms, the length of time they have had them, or any other information that may be pertinent to determining the cause and nature of the illness. Through divination, such as casting lots, or through communicating with the supernatural while in a trance, the shaman is expected to find out himself what the problem is or, more properly, as we have seen, *who* or *what* has caused the illness, since therapy will be directed at the cause more than toward the symptoms. That is the kind of skill, after all, for which he is being paid.

Therefore, when a patient whose expectations are those just described finds himself consulting a physician whose expectations are quite different, confusion at the least and total lack of confidence at the most may ensue. Jansen graphically describes the problems of medical practice among the Bomvana Xhosa as they relate to the therapeutic interview. Following the indigenous pattern, the sick person and his company walk single file to the home of the diviner, long sticks in their hands and a bundle of clothes on their heads, thus indicating their mission. "When the diviner starts the consultation, he begins by guessing. He is not supposed to take 'the medical history' by interviewing the patient and/or his relatives. On the contrary, he is the one who has to give answers to all the questions about the patient and the causes of his disease" (Jansen 1973:43). "The tribesmen are not trained by their own practitioners to give full account of their complaints. On the contrary, the Xhosa diviners describe the concealed complaints to the patient in the process of *uku-vumisa* [divination] and then jump to the diagnosis and interpretation" (*Ibid.,* 84).

For patients with these expectations about the curer's role, the physician's questions are puzzling and disturbing. "Interviewing is unknown in tribal medicine," says Jansen; interviews such as people have deal with court matters, registration of cattle, taxes, and other topics that, in their position of political subordination, they view with suspicion. In Western medicine, adds Jansen, history is a fundamental concept in our thinking, a reflection of our historically structured thinking. Illness, at least subconsciously, is thus viewed as a "historical" event in part requiring historical treatment. In contrast, "The mythological approach of (Xhosa) diviners presumes life as part of a cyclical time experience opposite to the western linear conception of time, and does not recognize sickness as a historical event in human life" (*Ibid.,* 73).

For all these reasons, the physician who has to ask so many questions before he can help is viewed with grave suspicion. Even the simple question "What is your name?" often causes distress; it is an "unusual" question in the daily life of the tribesmen, and some elderly patients shrink from revealing this information. Jansen found that when he introduced consultation with "What is wrong with you?", more often than not he received the reply, "Must not the doctor answer this question instead of me?" (*Ibid.,* 81).

Jansen also points out the problem inherent in differing doctor-patient views about how long the curer should spend with the patient. Lacking a Western time sense, the Bomvana patient expects a leisurely consultation; efficiency is not an element in the treatment process. The doctor, in contrast, has been trained to make efficient use of his time, and this expectation is reaffirmed as a basic desideratum by the long lines in the waiting room. "Probably we have often erred in talking with our Bomvana patients in that we drove our communication with them in a too high gear." But, he adds, and one can only sympathize with him, "Busy clinic days were not the ideal moments to make our western pace more suited to the slow tempo of Bomvana life. Unfortunately it is nearly inevitable to 'hurry up' when a crowd of approximately [one] hundred patients were waiting to see the doctor at one of the outstations" (*Ibid.,* 77).

COMMUNICATION

Of all the difficulties encountered in the therapeutic interview, in Western and non-Western settings, and in the cross-cultural practice of medicine, those associated with doctor-patient communication are probably the most common. The essence of the problem is captured in a simple vignette, almost a burlesque if it were not deadly serious. An Anglo public health physician in California advises a Mexican mother in words that would tax the understanding of the most sophisticated patient how to wean her infant. "Apply a tight pectoral binding and restrict your fluid intake" (Clark 1959a:220). Although the woman understood a little English, these words were beyond her comprehension, and pride and shyness prevented her from asking for an explanation.

Evidence from the United States and abroad suggests that physicians (1) frequently assume that their patients have a much clearer understanding than is the case of what they are being told and what the implications for treatment and follow-up care are, and (2) sometimes have a stereotyped view of their personal behavior in the interview that is quite inaccurate. Illustrative of the first point is a study of 214 medical clinical patients and their physicians; the study found that the physicians believed that 82 percent of the information on a medical questionnaire for patients should be understood by them. In fact, patients understood only 55 percent of the information, and even high school graduates understood only two-thirds of the information (Pratt et al. 1958:-225).

Comparable finds come from a study from India, where 50 female patients were asked to define 25 common words used by doctors. Slightly less than three-fifths of the answers could be considered to indicate patient understanding of meaning. Injection, itch, menstruation, and swelling were the most commonly understood words, while blood, glands, and operation were the least commonly understood. The list consisted of two groups of words: one picked up from the patients' vocabulary by the doctor, the other comprising technical words commonly used by doctors and absorbed by patients. "Words in the former group appear to provide maximum understanding" (Anand and Rao 1963:153). The authors conclude that doctors should be sensitized to the importance of learning patients' words and their meanings and, to the extent possible, to using these words in treatment.

In other situations the patient may understand perfectly well the word, but its connotations may influence his behavior. The small child of a Southern migrant couple to Detroit was taken to the emergency room of a large hospital where a head gash was sewn up. The father, who had been told to return in a week for the removal of the stitches, did the job himself with nail clippers. In part, the father was rebelling against the $22 fee for emergency help. Perhaps even more important was the fact that he had been instructed to go to "surgery" for removal of the stitches. This was a horrifying prospect. "Traditionally the person from the Southern Appalachians cites as one of his basic distrusts of doctors the idea that they will 'cut on him' or perform surgery" (Stekert 1970:130).

Fortunately, clear verbal communication is not always essential to a successful therapeutic encounter, as evidenced by the American child who, in response to an English-speaking Danish physician's request that she "respire profoundly," took her cue from the stethoscope and drew a deep breath at each repetition of the incomprehensible command. While patient knowledge of what is expected of them in the doctor's office undoubtedly smooths many comparable situations, it sometimes produces curious results, as in the case of the Bomvana Xhosa 4-year-old boy who visited a mission doctor with his mother. Finally he could contain his curiosity no longer: "When is this doctor going to start dancing?" he asked (Jansen 1973:142-143). One does not have to go to Africa to encounter dramatically different interpretations of medical acts. When a Texas physician lit a burner and passed a throat-smear slide back and forth over it in the ritual fashion appropriate to the laboratory, the patient, a Kickapoo Indian grandmother, started to chant and dance in a bent position of humility (communicated by Rafael Toledo, M.D.).

A recent study in the pediatric clinic of Children's Hospital in Los Angeles illustrates how wrong physicians may sometimes be in their assumptions about how they are viewed by patients. In this study it was found that what mothers liked least about the care their children received was the efficient, impersonal, seemingly disinterested behavior of the physicians. Yet in a sample of 800 interviews it was found that while most of the physicians believed they had been friendly in manner, fewer than half of the "patients" (i.e., the mothers) had this impression (Korch and Negrete 1972:72). Participating physicians, after listening to their taped interviews, were surprised to find that they did more talking than the mothers, an important discovery in view of the fact that "The session tended to have a more successful outcome when the patient had an active interchange with the doctor than it did when she remained passive and asked few questions" (*Ibid.,* 73).

Although it was reassuring to find that 76 percent of the mothers were "highly" or "reasonably" satisfied with the doctor's performance and only 24 percent were dissatisfied, nearly half of the mothers nevertheless left the doctor's office still wondering what had caused their child's illness (*Ibid.,* 69). One of the most interesting findings was that contrary to popular belief, the length of the consultation had very little to do with patient satisfaction. "The 800 visits we examined varied in length from two minutes to 45 minutes, and we could find no significant correlation between the length of the session and (1) the patient's satisfaction or (2) the clarity of the diagnosis of the child's illness" (*Ibid.,* 71). Friendly doctors who used terms that the mothers understood carried out effective consultations in short periods of time. "The severest and most common complaint of the dissatisfied mothers was that the physician had shown too little interest in their great concern about their child. High among the expectations of mothers in coming to the clinic was that the doctor would be friendly and sympathetic not only to the child but also to the worried parent. The recordings show, however, that less than 5 percent of the physician's conversation was personal or friendly in nature" (*Ibid.,* 72).

CONCLUSION

In sketching a cross-cultural comparative picture of the therapeutic interview, we are on fairly solid ground. Data are good for doctor-patient interaction in the United States, and we have many accounts of the problems that have arisen when Western physicians or physicians trained in scientific medicine attend patients from traditional communities, patients whose expectations of the physician's role behavior may be quite different from his. The ethnographic record is also good insofar as shamanistic seances and other doctor-patient relationships within a single traditional society are concerned.

When, however, we turn specifically to the matter of communication — How well does the patient understand what the doctor wishes to communicate? — the record is less good. The use of questionnaires asking that specific medical terms be defined or simply asking whether the patient understood the doctor's instructions are largely limited to the West, or to the context of scientific medicine in non-Western countries, as in the example of Anand and Rao. But we have no comparable data from traditional societies. No anthropologist seems to have systematically asked patients, Did you understand the shaman? Did the herbalist make herself clear? Did you come away with unanswered questions? What did you like about your visit to the curer, and what did you not like? Noting the frequent misunderstandings that characterizes the therapeutic interview when it involves a physician and a patient from another culture or social stratum, we have *assumed* that that same patient will fully understand the shaman, witch doctor, or herbalist of his or her society when selected instead of the physician. But we do not know for sure. This is a topic that calls for much more ethnomedical research.

chapter 7

Non-Western Medical Systems: Strengths and Weaknesses

THE PROBLEM

In the preceding three chapters we have described the principal characteristics of non-Western medical systems. We have dealt with etiologies, and with the therapies and therapists associated with different types of societies and different illnesses within a given society. We have found that the frequent Western dichotomy of diseases of the body and diseases of the mind, each with its distinctive doctors, therapeutic approaches, and even hospitals, is largely lacking in non-Western societies, a fact emphasized by the combining in a single shaman or witch doctor the skills deemed essential to either kind of problem.

In this chapter we turn to a question that intrigues anthropologists, psychiatrists and other medical doctors and laymen alike: How sound a base for effective therapy do non-Western causation theories provide, and how well do the therapies themselves work in relieving pain, reducing abnormal behavior, sustaining a patient during illness, and restoring his physical and mental health? Opinions differ vastly; depending on the writer, evaluations range all the way from out-and-out quackery to highly effective, protoscientific, rational, trial-and-error-based medicine.

Evidence can be adduced to support either point of view. For the skeptic, the sleight-of-hand deceptions of the shaman and the trickery involved in sucking a bloody quartz crystal — the disease object — from the body of the patient, not to mention low longevity and high mortality and morbidity figures in the shaman's society, is sufficient proof of the inadequacies of non-Western medicine. For the enthusiast the herbal contributions of primitive medicines to the Western pharmacopoeia and the psychosocial support that curing rites frequently lend to the patient and the members of his society who attend him are adequate evidence that non-Western medicine has much to offer the Western world, and that it should continue to play a major role in meeting the health care needs of the people who believe in it.

The arguments about the effectiveness of non-Western medicine are far from academic; today, in the World Health Organization and in the Agency for International Development, serious thought is being given to incorporating non-Western curers and parts of non-Western therapies into national health plans. If the skeptics are correct in their views, such action will squander money and cost lives. If the enthusiasts are correct, it is a logical step in extending primary health care to areas where cost will prevent the development of fully adequate health services for many decades. This problem is more fully discussed in Chapter 14. Here we are concerned with dissecting non-Western medical systems in order to determine, if possible, their strengths and weaknesses, their dangerous practices, and their positive aspects.

DIFFICULTIES IN MEASUREMENT

The efficacy of a medical system is not easily evaluated; there are no universally agreed on units to be measured, and the personal biases and expectations of those who evaluate may differ greatly. There is not even agreement as to what is being judged. In the United States we see our medical system as relatively discrete from law, religion, and society. Our evaluations of the success of our system, therefore, have little to do with these institutions. We are concerned with things such as accurate diagnostic techniques, therapeutic efficacy, immunization, skilled surgery, and chronic illness relief. More broadly we are interested in the scientific base of medical practice and what it teaches us about proper diet, exercise, and the dangers of obesity and cigarette smoking. In other words, we tend to judge our system in fairly narrow pathological terms: we cite favorable longevity, mortality, and morbidity figures and rising survival rates after cancer and heart surgery in measuring progress. Judged by these criteria, our system is impressive.

Yet, paradoxically, when judged by the ultimate criterion toward which all of the above is directed — consumer satisfaction — our system is much less impressive. Medical doctors are far from the beloved family counselors that, at least in an earlier generation, they have imagined themselves to be. Medical malpractice suits are mushrooming, and increasing numbers of people are turning to alternate systems such as faith healing, organic foods, and natural childbirth. In the wider psychosocial context of life, we obviously have much to learn.

In many non-Western societies, in contrast, the dividing lines between medicine on the one hand and religion, law, and society on the other hand are much less distinct. In these societies religion and medicine, or etiological beliefs and social control, may be inextricably intertwined in the same institutional context. The efficacy of medical systems in these societies must therefore be measured by their ability to successfully play roles that lie far beyond the cure of illness and the maintenance of health. Maretzki states the general principle when he writes, "Whatever the label health denotes, it is as much a condition of the community and the social system as it is of an individual who is part of it" (Maretzki 1973:135). Thus, for the Navaho, it can be argued that the belief that a patient has been brought back into harmony with nature and society is a more convincing "proof" of efficacy than the alleviation of a clinical symptom. Similarly, among the Ojibwa as described by Hallowell, successful conflict resolution and the maintenance of viable social relations between members of these widely dispersed people must be one measure of the value of their etiological beliefs. These differences in what must be evaluated in Western and non-Western medical systems is further emphasized by the differing roles of healers. As Alland has said, "Non-Western medical specialists generally practice within a social context which makes nonmedical demands upon them. They are social adjudicators as well as religious functionaries whose duty it is to restore relationships between men, or between men and the supernatural. As such they treat social cause rather than disease" (Alland 1970:128).[1]

We see from this contrast between the roles of Western and non-Western medical systems that one measure of efficacy must be ability to satisfy the expectations of the people served. But, since expectations vary so greatly, comparative ratings of the effectiveness of different systems cannot be achieved in absolute terms. It is a little like the problem of how to add apples and oranges.

The task of anthropologists in attempting even a superficial evaluation of non-Western medical systems is further complicated by our data which, although extensive, are not always pertinent to the questions that must be answered. We have, for example, many accounts of how disease etiologies and shaman's roles serve as modes of social control. But these are models constructed by anthropologists, and we are not even sure to what extent, at a conscious or unconscious level, these models are shared by the people whose behavior they are intended to explain. In other words, we hypothesize these functions for non-Western medical systems, and we believe they are true, but we have no clinical proof that they are, indeed, valid.

A second complication in evaluating non-Western systems is that insofar as the effectiveness of specific therapies is concerned, we also have very poor data. Most of our judgments are based on a single or a few observations; we lack the statistical base, the double blind experiments, the cumulative records of success or failure, that in scientific medicine is judged essential to prove effectiveness.

Anecdotes often substitute for hard data. On one occasion one of us (Foster) was suffering from a bad chest cold in Tzintzuntzan, Mexico. The members of the family with whom he lives when in the village diagnosed his condition as due to "risen heat," adjudged to have resulted from his careless habit of stepping on the cold concrete floor in his bedroom in his bare feet. They urged that medicinal *tepusa* leaves and oil be applied to the soles of his feet to draw out the cold that had forced his body heat to his chest. He retired to his bed (with a hot toddy), the treatment was applied, he slept soundly, and the next morning he felt vastly improved.

Many of the "proofs" of the effectiveness of popular treatments are of this order of validity. Before convincing answers can be given, we need much more complete data and, especially, good case examples in which the level of sophistication in analysis and conclusion drawing is superior to the above. For many major topics in non-Western cultures we have excellent data that we can reasonably call "facts" that enable us to talk about marriage norms, political organization, fictive kinship, agricultural productivity and the like with considerable scientific accuracy. But most of what we know about medicine is what our informants have told us, or casual observations such as the example just given.[2]

Recognizing the evidential problems that face us, we will nevertheless attempt to evaluate, positively and negatively, non-Western medical systems.

POSITIVE ASPECTS OF NON-WESTERN THERAPIES

The strengths of non-Western medical systems can conveniently be considered under the categories of psychosocial support therapies, and clinical or therapeutic acts, especially indigenous pharmacopoeias. Anthropologists who have been concerned with these questions and a growing number of psychiatrists who have worked with non-Western peoples generally feel that it is in the former and not the latter category that non-Western medicine has proven most effective. This is probably due to the fact that to a far greater extent than in the West, as we have seen, illness in traditional societies (serious illness, at least) represents dysfunction not only within the patient's body, but also in his relationships with his society and, perhaps, dysfunction as well within the society itself.

This view is nowhere more clearly seen than among the Navaho. "The Navaho conception of health is very different from ours. For him, health is symptomatic of a correct relationship between man and his environment: his supernatural 'environment,' the world around him, and his fellow man. Health is associated with good, blessing, and beauty — all that is positively valued in life. Illness, on the other hand, bears evidence that one has fallen out of this delicate balance" (Adair et al. 1969:94).

It is this comprehensive man-environment setting in which so many non-Western peoples view illness that explains why the role of the powerful curer (the shaman or the witch doctor) is conceived to be far broader than that of his Western counterpart. The curer usually is not a simple therapist, one skilled in the ways of treating symptoms; indeed, he works to maintain harmony between man, his society, and his environment. We have seen, for example, how in Colombia the Tukano shaman, through his supernatural contacts with the "master" of game animals, works to prevent illness by controlling and limiting the places and times where men can hunt, thus avoiding undue stress on a delicately balanced ecological system. We have seen, too, how in aboriginal Australia the native curer is a social and legal arbiter who, reminding his fellows of the risk of illness from social nonconformity, is able to mediate and compromise social strains that might otherwise produce major community dislocations.

This fundamental contrast in views about the context of illness between the West and the non-West helps to explain the frequent importance of public curing ceremonies found, at least insofar as "establishment" medicine is concerned, only among traditional peoples. Sometimes the role of the public is simply that of interested or amused spectators who enjoy a good show. Perhaps more often relatives and friends play active parts in rituals. For example, among the Navaho the members of a family who have brought a "singer" to conduct a curing rite for an ill member of the group all remain during the entire ceremony, which may last up to nine nights. "Relatives and friends come to the ceremony and take part in the chants and prayers directed by the medicine man and his assistant. By association they too receive positive benefits from the cure, and in turn the presence of the family and friends is assuring to the patient who feels they are all working to restore his health" (Adair et al. 1969:95-96). The extent of community commitment to therapy is indicated by the late Clyde Kluckhohn's 1938 estimate that "Navaho men devoted from one-quarter to one-third of their time to such ceremonials, and the women only slightly less" (*Ibid.,* 94).

Occasionally, as in the case of the Huron Indians' *andacwander* ceremony, a ritual mating of men and women, public participation went much further. The need for the ceremony might be revealed in a dream to a troubled postmenopausal widow and certified by a shaman sophisticated in the hidden meanings of dreams. In a culture where any exhibition of sexual interest was almost prudishly disapproved, the *andacwander* was not uncommon and apparently allowed villagers of all ages and statuses to transgress the restrictive norms of their society. The context, although permissive, was not orgiastic; it channeled social empathy in a manner which suggested that the individual was not alone in his frustrations and that their expression should not be shameful to a particular man or woman (Trigger 1969:114-119).

Speaking specifically of mental illness, Carstairs takes the position that "spiritual healing . . . may be based on quite ill-founded theories of the causation of disease, but it has two striking advantages over supposedly scientific reliance upon physical treatments: first, the patient is not exposed to the undesirable side effects of many of the newest psychotropic drugs; and second, spiritual healing requires the participation of other persons in addition to the patient and thus helps to reintegrate the mentally ill patient with the rest of the community from whom he has become estranged" (Carstairs 1969:409).

Another nonestablishment therapeutic technique, public confession, reflects the extent to which the actions of a patient are believed to have endangered not only the patient but also society. In addition to providing emotional catharsis and a sharing of guilt, confession often induces a reliving of painful experience (abreaction), which may in itself be therapeutic (Torrey 1972:64-66).[3]

There is a virtual consensus among anthropologists that in its psychosocial supportive dimension, non-Western medicine is often remarkably effective. Adair et al. write of the Navaho sings that "There is no doubt that these curing ceremonies, in which the Navaho people have so much faith, have a psychotherapeutic effect on the patient. There is also good evidence that the sweat bath sedative and the body massage that is used in some ceremonies may act as beneficial physiotherapy" (Adair et al. 1969:96).

Speaking of the Amhara of Ethiopia, Young states: "From a practical or instrumental point of view, people find that they [i.e., their traditional medical beliefs and practices] are useful, since they do what they are expected to do. From a social point of view, they are necessary and morally imperative because they are socially approved ways of dealing with disruptive and anomalous events that cannot be allowed to persist. From a cognitive point of view, they are meaningful since they communicate important ideas about the real world and through medical praxis they provide the means for confirming and preserving this sense of reality" (Young 1974-1975:88).

That the value of community-oriented therapy may go beyond the purely psychological is indicated by Horton, who sets therapy in Africa in an ecological-evolutionary context. "A given population and a given set of diseases," he writes, "have been co-existing over many generations. Natural selection has played a considerable part in developing human resistance to diseases such as malaria, typhoid, small-pox, dysentery, etc." Moreover, individuals who survive childhood probably have acquired additional resistance from exposure to these illnesses, so that they have a good chance of surviving in a situation that would mean sure death for a European without Western medicine. "In these circumstances the traditional healer's efforts to cope with the situation by ferreting out and attempting to remedy stress-producing disturbances in the patient's social field is probably very relevant. Such efforts may seem to have a ludicrously marginal importance to a hospital doctor wielding a nivaquine bottle and treating a non-resident European malaria patient. But they may be crucial where there is no nivaquine bottle and a considerable natural resistance to malaria" (Horton 1967:56-57).

Since so much illness in traditional societies — and especially in those where personalistic etiologies predominate — is viewed by patient and curer alike in a broad psychosocial-religious context in which the line between physical and mental symptoms is often hard to draw, it is not surprising that indigenous psychiatric therapies often seem remarkably successful. Illustrative of such practices is the case of a Tanzanian Hehe curer named Abedi. Like many non-Western curers, Abedi's powers came partly from hallucinations ("hearing voices I could not see") followed by 2 weeks of being "completely out of my senses" before being cured (Edgerton 1971:261). Abedi deals with the entire social context of the patient and his illness. Although he lays great stress on herbal treatment, he is astute enough to realize social pressures; in extreme cases he recommends that patients move away from their neighborhood for a prolonged stay with distant kinsmen. Edgerton feels that Abedi's therapeutic techniques "often, perhaps even usually, [are] rewarded by the remission of symptoms" (*Ibid.,* 269).

Crapanzano likewise is impressed with the successes of the Hamadsha curers, members of a loosely organized religious brotherhood in Morocco, who are concerned with the cure of victims possessed by the devil. "The Hamadsha are not just curers but successful curers at that, in terms of the standards their society sets and, in some instances, in terms of the standards set by modern medicine" (Crapanzano 1973:4). They effect, often dramatically, remission of common anxiety reaction symptoms such as paralysis, mutism, sudden blindness, and severe depression. "The Hamadsha are, in their own fashion, superb diagnosticians" who wisely usually avoid treating illnesses that Western medicine regards as organic in origin, such as epilepsy (*Ibid.,* 5).

One of the most unusual, and apparently effective, of non-Western therapeutic practices has been described by Messing for the Amhara of Ethiopia. Here patients who are possessed by Zar spirits (as evidenced by extreme apathy, convulsive seizures, sterility, and proneness to accidents) are treated by Zar cult healers who are former patients who have come to terms with the spirits that possess them and, through them, are able to cure others. Zar spirit victims are predominantly lower-class, rural, married women, neglected in a man's world, discriminated against by the Coptic church, and lonely for the warmth of kinship relations. Following initial treatment the patient is "enrolled" for life in the Zar cult, where she enjoys the sympathy and support of fellow sufferers. Zar spirits usually are not exorcised, so the patient lives with them for life. But group membership, Messing believes, mitigates symptoms and prevents relapses (Messing 1958). The Zar cult is also known in Egypt, where it plays a therapeutic role very similar to that in Ethiopia (Nelson 1971).

In a similar vein Torrey believes that, in spite of the anecdotal nature of the evidence on the efficacy of therapists in non-Western societies, "It is almost unanimous in suggesting that witch-doctors get about the same therapeutic results as psychiatrists do" (Torrey 1972:102).

On balance, when judged not alone in terms of therapeutic ends but also against all religious, legal, social, and psychological functions they may be expected to fulfill, in the estimation of most anthropologists non-Western medical systems come out remarkably well as adaptive cultural institutions that promote the well-being of the societies concerned.

NEGATIVE ASPECTS OF NON-WESTERN THERAPIES

When we turn to the specifically clinical aspects of non-Western medicine (therapeutic acts and drugs), we find a wide range of opinion among anthropologists (and others) as to effectiveness. A strong case for those who believe that non-Western medicine is also effective therapy in its clinical aspects is made by the ethnologist-physician Ackerknecht, who has written that "an amazing percentage of the herbs, barks and roots used by the natives — a percentage which is far above the mathematical probability of random sampling — is of objective medicinal value . . . Even today," he says, "our own pharmacopoeia is heavily indebted to primitives" (Ackerknecht 1971:17). He lists quinine (which contrary to popular view was *not* used as a specific against malaria by South American Indians),[4] picrotoxine (a powerful stimulant of the respiratory center), strophantine (for heart disease), emetine (a specific for amoebic dysentery), coca (all of American Indian origin), salicylic preparations for rheumatism (from the Hottentots), and opium, hashish, hemp, and a number of others (*Ibid.*, 17, 128.) To this list, Huard adds ephedrine, strichnine, curare, chaulmoogra oil (formerly used to treat leprosy), and *Rauwolfia serpentina*, which is both a hypotensive and a tranquilizer (Huard 1969:216).

Laughlin comes to similar conclusions. "Primitive medicine," he writes, "contains a storehouse of empirical knowledge. Embedded in its variegated corpus of techniques, procedures and beliefs are many strands of pragmatic approaches, comparative tests and effective treatments for the restoration and maintenance of well-being in the human organism. The remarkable success of our species is due in no small part to the local solution of medical problems. . . ." (Laughlin 1963:116).

Against these strongly positive evaluations, we note the cautionary view of the epidemiologist Ivan Polunin. "I am skeptical of the idea that there must be something valid in all traditional practices, which we might call the 'moldy-bread-on-wounds-means-they-had-antibiotics' theory. By a valid medical practice, I mean one where the effects claimed for it are exerted by means of its intrinsic properties, though I do not deny psychological and social benefit of a practice which can exist independent of this kind of validity" (Polunin 1976:120).

Loudon is similarly cautionary: " . . . there is often a marked contrast between the scepticism of some observers concerning categories employed in scientific medicine and their insistence on the indigenous wisdom distilled in pre-scientific herbal remedies or encapsulated in primitive healing techniques. The time is long past when naive advocacy, however well-intentioned, helps to gain due recognition for the undoubted skills of healers operating in cultures other than our own" (Loudon 1976:39).

Hippler and Stein are even more emphatic. Hippler writes, "I have noted . . . a peculiar habit in the work of medical (and other) anthropologists to carry the concept of cultural relativism to extraordinary and unwarranted lengths. Specifically, one such implicit assumption that non-Western, or 'primitive,' or 'client' populations are always the 'good guys' and the medical establishment always 'unfeeling,' is no more adequate a way of developing theory or indeed practical assistance than the use of the 'disease-oriented Western medical model' in its most simplistic form" (Hippler 1977:18). Hippler also reminds us of an important fact that sometimes tends to be overlooked in evaluating indigenous medical systems: "We must not forget that patho-organisms and anti-agents, chemo-therapeutic or organic, are *real*. To reject their significance or underrate them is simply a form of adolescent rebelliousness. . . . " (*Ibid.*).

Stein simply says: "Anthropologists have been absolutely phobic in their contempt for Western (read: dehumanizing) medicine. Through our contempt of Western civilization, our patient bias, and our transference to our favorite primitives (patients, ethnic groups, traditional healers), we seem unable to identify with the vilified Western medical professionals and their institutions. . . . I am afraid it will take some working-through before we are able to be skeptical about shamanic-native cures, or to consider the possibility that the Western health care delivery system is anything but an Ivan Illichian 'medical nemesis' " (H. Stein 1977:16).

Most anthropologists — even Hippler and Stein, we suspect — recognize that numerous items in indigenous pharmacopoeias have specific therapeutic value and that the skills of many native healers cannot be doubted. At the same time, the evidence seems to us to indicate that non-Western pharmacopoeias as systems are relatively ineffective when compared to antibiotics and other drugs available to physicians trained in scientific medicine, and that not all indigenous curing techniques have positive value. Gonzalez writes as follows about Guatemala. "We know that many native medicines do have some effect in relieving such symptoms as diarrhea, constipation, pain, fever, etc. But *Western medicines are better for the most part. This is a fact well recognized by almost anyone who has tried them*" (Gonzalez 1966:124. Emphasis added). Opler, speaking of traditional Apache curing, is more emphatic. "It is apparent that *so far as organic pathology is concerned,* the shaman's contribution is largely a negative one; the less he does, the better for the patient" (Opler 1936:1374. Emphasis added).

While we tend to agree with those who, like the above, are skeptical of the excessive claims sometimes made for indigenous pharmacopoeias, we note the contrasting opinions of others who are qualified to speak authoritatively. For example, the physician-anthropologist-epidemiologist Frederick Dunn draws on broad professional training and wide field experience in tropical areas in concluding that many medicinal plants from primitive societies appear to have beneficial effects. He goes even further and hypothesizes how beneficial discoveries were made. "Traditional use of such remedies evolved through countless trials and errors — in short, through human experimentation. The methods of investigation employed by traditional herbalists are not qualitatively different from those employed in modern clinical chemo-therapeutic investigations. The difference lies principally in time," primitive herbalists requiring decades or generations of testing (Dunn 1976:136). Dunn feels that the traditional herbalist, or a line of herbalists through several generations, "reaches a decision about a remedy through decades of experience in treating his fellow men with it, and his 'controls' are others of his fellows with similar disorders who are treated with other remedies or not treated at all" (*Ibid.*, 136).

For medical practitioners in what we have called "naturalistic" systems, this is possible. After all, classical humoral pathology, Ayurvedic medicine, and traditional Chinese medicine represent a literate tradition, and at least some practitioners could read and write and so keep records. But we feel that this is not a valid assumption as far as practitioners of "personalistic" medicine are concerned, and this category includes the bulk of the ethnographic record. Dunn's point of view attributes an excessive degree of scientific rationalism to these traditional herbalists that is simply not congruent with their basically magical, ritualistic, and personalistic approach to illness. They lack the means of keeping records, and they lack comprehension of "controls" and of statistical inference, which are essential to such an empirical approach.

Alland speaks to what we believe is a fundamental dichotomy in the non-Western and scientific approaches to medical investigation. "A specific feature of Western culture has been externally oriented and empirically based technology and science. The major aspect of its success has been the development of a consistent set of methodological rules codified in the scientific method. Applied to disease and medicine, this orientation, particularly when combined with a highly involved technology, must inevitably lead to the development of a rational and effective medicine. Without such a methodology the cues available in the external world for the delineation of cause and the discovery of effective treatment are obscured by a high noise level. This noise level is due to difficulties of diagnosis where internal conditions produce only vague somatic symptoms, and where it is extremely difficult to distinguish one set of symptoms from another. The noise level is increased to crescendo by the fact that most patients get well regardless of therapy. . . . Of course the noise level can be reduced through carefully structured and controlled experiments, but this is precisely the point where non-Western medicine in most cases falls below the mark of the required objectivism and empirical orientation" (Alland 1970:127-128).

Even in naturalistic medical systems there is evidence contrary to Dunn's hypothesis that Western and non-Western medical investigative methods are not qualitatively different. Carl Taylor, who feels that a synthesis between modern and Ayurvedic medicine is desirable, points out the problem in the context of the hot-cold dichotomy. "Beliefs about hot and cold foods are so widespread in India that it seemed reasonable to think that there might be some uniformity in these patterns . . . Eating patterns seem to be related to ideas about hazards of eating hot foods in summer or cold foods in winter, or in association with fevers, diarrheas, or rheumatism." Nevertheless, "Dramatic geographical differences became apparent. Many foods that were considered hot in the North were thought to be cold in the South. *It seemed apparent that any possible empiric validity underlying the concept of hot and cold foods could not be substantiated*" (C. E. Taylor 1976:293. Emphasis added).

The assumption that the methods of investigation employed by traditional herbalists are not qualitatively different from those used in contemporary medical research is, we feel, unsatisfactory for still another reason; it presupposes an equal degree of cooperation and sharing of medical knowledge. Yet when, as among the Azande, medical knowledge and magical spells are viewed as property to be transmitted to others by means of commercial transactions, easy "sharing" of accumulated knowledge is not the rule. In England as late as the seventeenth century the Chamberlen family of physicians was strongly condemned because of the secrecy with which it guarded its vastly improved obstetrical forceps. Finally, history shows that busy practitioners rarely have had time for systematic research, and many of the men of the past three centuries whom we now admire for their discoveries almost literally stole time from practice for research. Not only was it difficult to find time for research, but such investigators were frequently criticized by laymen and by their peers for neglecting their patients (Shryock 1969:47). For such reasons we believe it misleading to compare the "research" of nonliterate herbalists with that of contemporary medicine.

We recognize that considerable numbers of native remedies have been incorporated into the Western pharmacopoeia; about this there can be no disagreement. But the number and characteristics of such remedies is not the right question. The right question is, how many of these specifics are used in a single indigenous medical system, and to what extent are those used applied in those cases where they are specifics? To take examples of pharmacologically active remedies from all of the world's people as evidence of the effectiveness of specific medical systems is akin to making a list of all of the words in native American Indian languages that bear a resemblance to words found in Asian languages as proof of trans-Pacific contact.

NON-WESTERN THERAPIES: EXAMPLES AND DANGERS

Some observers argue that non-Western remedies, if not all effective, at least are harmless and, if they satisfy psychological needs, their use should be encouraged. Yet there are enough examples of dangerous practices to show that this philosophy is untenable. Carl Taylor, in warning against the slogan "frequently heard in Indian and other Asian countries . . . that indigenous drugs are innocuous," writes that "Many mistakes are being made because of the improper use of some of these drugs. For example, mercurials and other heavy metals that are extensively used in Ayurvedic and Islamic medicine are extremely dangerous" (C. E. Taylor et al. 1973:308). In the same article Leslie gives the example of "glaucoma caused by a poppy that got into indigenous medicine in India and Pakistan" after it was introduced from Mexico, because it was erroneously identified with a plant listed in Ayurvedic texts (*Ibid.,* 312).

Similar dangerous practices are reported from Africa. In Ibadan, Nigeria *Agbo tutu* is a widely known tonic thought to be the best remedy for convulsions in small children and also used as a prophylactic. Green tobacco leaves are marinated in human or cow's urine to which other herbs have been added, while "there is controversy over whether the addition of Gordon's Gin is a necessity or an extravagance." The end product is a strong solution of nicotine which, in large amounts, depresses the activity of the brain. "Children brought to hospital after having received excessive doses of this medicine are often deeply unconscious" (Maclean 1971:84).

Other traditional treatments, like the following three from Peru, appear less threatening, but probably would not be the first choice of patients accustomed to scientific medicine.

For jaundice, mix powdered frozen potatoes with three lice and the urine of a black cow, and drink the potion on Tuesdays and Fridays (Valdizán and Maldonado 1922:II:322).

For erisypelas, cut off the crest of a cock and apply the blood to the afflicted parts (*Ibid.,* 475).

For typhus and typhoid fever, split a black dog open along the ventral line and place the warm and bloody side of the body on the patient's stomach (*Ibid.,* 515).

A more complicated treatment is reported for the Indian village of Chinaura, in the Lucknow district, where a dogbite victim bathes on a Sunday and the following Tuesday in a river 15 miles distant from his home. He then gives parched grain flour and jaggery (palm sugar) to the dogs living on the riverbank. Clay is plastered on the wound, and the patient crosses and re-crosses the river seven times on each day. Then an exorcist removes the poison of the dogbite by passing an iron rod seven times around the wound, reciting the appropriate mantras (Hasan 1967:160). If the offending dog is not rabid, the patient probably recovers. Still, in case of rabies, the Pasteur treatment would seem preferable.

George Way Harley, the American physician cited earlier who practiced for 15 years among the Mano of Liberia and who found a number of "rational" indigenous treatments such as enemas, poultices, and splints for fractures, nonetheless found his patience tried at times. "A half-Mano baby in an official's house, suffering from an attack of fever with convulsions, was treated as follows: First it was given a bath in swamp mud, washed off with water from a basin, some of which it was forced to drink. Asafoetida was then rubbed on its head, and tobacco smoke blown into its mouth. Aromatic herbs were rubbed on its face. Then a Mandingo leech was called, who administered a solution of ink made by washing off from a wooden tablet the sacred verses from the Koran which had been written on it . . . After this, a sneezing powder was blown up the child's nose. It was fed a mush of certain green leaves. Subsequently its clothes were burnt at the crossroads. Finally, the white doctor was allowed to administer a hypodermic of quinine" (Harley 1941:44). Faintly awed, Harley adds laconically, "The patient recovered."

Our intention in these pages is not to hold up to ridicule the curing techniques of non-Western peoples but rather to remind ourselves that the Western "scientific" tradition was, until late in time, remarkably similar in its approach to healing. Anglo-Saxon medicine, for example, was little if any advanced beyond that of contemporary primitives and peasants. Bonser concedes that the numerous green herbs used may have been beneficial for their antiscorbutic properties when used in the spring by people who had gone through the winter on a diet consisting largely of salt meat and dried peas. But the overwhelming majority of remedies used, he believes, would have benefited only the mind of the sufferer. That skepticism about efficacy was not entirely absent from physicians and patients themselves is indicated by one prescription which ends with the words, "With God's help no harm will come to him" (Bonser 1963:9).

Bonser also notes the large number of drugs in each prescription, a feature in striking contrast to the practice of the Hippocratic authors. A good many classical drugs are found in Anglo-Saxon pharmacopoeias; their presence is due more to the glamor of their origin than to experience in their efficacy. In some cases, it is undoubtedly the *name* and not the drug itself that has endured. One prescription, an antidote against snakebite, is to eat the bark of a tree "which comes out of paradise." With straight face the Anglo-Saxon recorder remarks that "this would be obtained with difficulty" (*Ibid.,* 9). One prescription of the good King Arestolobius, "wise and skilled in leechcraft," contained the seeds of 29 plants, equal amounts of each to be ground to a fine dust and drunk in cold wine upon arising. This conferred protection against, among other things, headache, lung disease, jaundice, dimness of the eyes, heaviness of the chest, swelling of the belly, pain in the small gut, itching, poison, and "for every infirmity and every temptation of the fiend" (*Ibid.,* 307). Still another prescription contained 37 named herbs, and a third, no less than 58.

On one occasion Doña Andrea Medina of Tzintzuntzan, wise in the ways of herbs, spoke of that ubiquitous Mexican ailment, *bilis.* "It comes from anger," she said, "a bad experience, a fright, a surprise — but it can also come from pleasure. The gall bladder becomes bilious and the yellow liquid overflows, entering the blood-stream and yellowing the body. This is a hot illness." Then, scarcely pausing for breath, she continued, "To cure it, drink a bilious tonic made of three bitter oranges, some leaves of the same tree, three small green limes cut in a cross, cinnamon, a lime root, root of wild mallow, root of *manrubio,* a handfull of the tips of the same plant, three 'palms' of bitter Spanish broom, a handful of *prodijioso* tips, a fistful of tomato skin, of *betulia* flowers, of lime blossoms, of basil leaves, of *toronjil* leaves, and three leaves of thyme. Boil well in enough water to have a couple of liters of the liquid. In a new pot place half a kilo of refined sugar, half a kilo of crude brown sugar, a small cup of honey, twenty centavo's worth of cinnamon, and a quarter of a liter of alcohol. Then stand back, ignite the alcohol with a long burning stick, and slosh it around until it has burned out. Mix this with the first batch, stir, strain, add another quarter of a liter of alcohol, bottle, and keep by the bedside. Drink before arising, and also take a shot before meals, and before going to bed. Since the *bilis* concentrates in the stomach at night, the morning draught goes right to the seat of the trouble." Doña Andrea also gave the hot-cold qualities of all of the ingredients.

Doña Andrea was a very successful herbalist, famous for her cures, and much loved and admired as a person. When she took charge, one felt sure that recovery was imminent. Yet neither her remedies nor those described by Bonser for Anglo-Saxon England can be described as the product of a semi-scientific trial-and-error method, the distillation of the experiences of generations, of adding and discarding ingredients as observation indicated. Rather, we are dealing with a process of accretion. Few items disappear from standard remedies but, over time, many things are added, perhaps as substitution for something not immediately available, perhaps because other items are remembered to be efficacious for similar ailments. In this fashion, native potions tend to grow in complexity until only the limits of the memory of the curer and access to desired ingredients call a halt.

SHORTCOMINGS IN CONTEMPORARY AMERICAN MEDICINE

In arguing that scientific medicine is significantly superior to non-Western medicine in its clinical dimensions, we recognize that this superiority is of recent date — a century or a bit more. We also note that as clinical skills and competence have developed, other aspects of American medicine have suffered. When we consider the inadequate availability of medical care to the nation's poor, the problems inherent in the doctor-patient relationship, and the relative loss of the "human touch" during recent decades, we find scientific medicine wanting. Is it because the clinical achievements of modern medicine have been so dramatic and because a patient can often be restored to health by a single injection or a handful of pills that we tend to forget that the patient also needs psychological support and the reassurance that "everything is going to be all right."

In the recent past American medicine offered these reassurances. Fifty years ago the family physician was judged by his "bedside manner," the empathy, the concern, the sense of psychological support he conveyed to the patient and family members. The time taken on home visits by the family doctor, his words of hope and encouragement, and his obvious personal interest, certainly contributed to the patient's recovery. In a preantibiotic era a good bedside manner was often the most powerful weapon at the disposal of the physician. Today, in contrast, the expression has almost disappeared from our vocabulary. It has been said that contemporary medicine has made great progress in the science of curing but, in so doing, it has lost the art of healing.

Today, doctors and nurses sometimes do not seem to appreciate fully how greatly this earlier image of the relationship between the sufferer and those who hoped to cure him has changed. Carol Taylor suggests that a "cult of efficiency" within contemporary medicine, a cult that has created a serious slippage between what physicians and nurses want to do — and sometimes *think* they are doing in caring for patients, is in considerable part responsible for this misconception. "The most important thing to remember is that the patient is a person," Taylor was told by a nurse supervisor in charge of a hospital unit. "My aim is to get rid of . . . the how-are-we-this-morning approach, and see to it that the care of each patient on my unit is personalized." But when a floor nurse knocked on her door immediately after she expressed these sentiments, the following exchange took place.

Floor nurse: "Mrs. D. in 604 keeps insisting that she needs a painkiller, and I can't do anything with her."

Supervising nurse: "Give her a placebo. When you've settled 604, give the colostomy in 615 a sitz bath" (C. Taylor 1970:12).

In reviewing the history of medical practice in the West, we are reminded that in the eighteenth and nineteenth centuries it was virtually a sentence of death to be admitted to a European hospital, notorious for septic infections and "hospital fevers" (Burnet and White 1972:186). An American or European patient was probably at least as well off, and perhaps more so, if he escaped the attentions of trained physicians. The heroic bleeding, the purging, and the massive use of arsenic, mercury, antimony, and other poisons seem, in retrospect, quite as hair-raising as the Liberian treatment of the Mano baby and infinitely worse than Doña Andrea Medina's cure for *bilis*.

Nor is it realistic, even today, to suggest that dangerous medical practices lie exclusively in the historic past or within the province of non-Western medical systems. The traditional practitioner's misuse or abuse of drugs certainly has counterparts in contemporary Western medicine. These would have to include failure to assess adequately drug side effects, as in the case of thalidomide, the sedative prescribed for pregnant women, which deformed thousands of infants, and the prescription of drugs that produce toxic effects in combination with each other. Some antiabortion drugs given to women in danger of miscarriage, in use for more than two decades, have shown evidence of increased uterine cancer in those salvaged baby girls who are now of childbearing age.

Other medical practices, belatedly recognized as dangerous, include the indiscriminate use of radiation, penicillin, vitamins, hormones, and diet supplements before the full consequences of treatment were known, unnecessary surgery (with anesthesiological and other risks involved), and the removal of organs prematurely assumed to have no physiological "use." For many decades, for example, tonsillectomies and adenoidectomies were routine for many patients under the care of Western physicians, based on unsubstantiated ideas about the role of these organs in the frequency of colds produced. A current trend (related to the population increase afforded by Western medicine) is the use and exportation of intrauterine devices and oral contraceptives whose long-term effects are not known. Unanticipated short-term effects recently brought to light include increased frequency of thromboembolism and migraine headache associated with the use of oral contraceptives.

There seems to us, however, to be a significant difference between the medical thresholds from which the limitations and excesses of non-Western and Western medical systems emanate. The shortcomings of traditional medical systems are linked to *ignorance* of physiology and of the etiology of disease (in the view of Westerners); those of scientific medicine appear largely related to *overextension* in the control of physiological processes and in the consequences of disease eradication. In personalistic systems, particularly, confidence in what amounts to a magical orientation to the etiology of disease has, we have seen, limited effective therapy in the treatment of infectious and chronic physical disease; in scientific systems the absorption with clinical or surgical answers has sometimes led to a kind of "therapeutic overkill" as a result of unforeseen (or foreseeable) biochemical or ecological factors.

It is ironic that scientific advance has brought, as a product of many impressive breakthroughs, medical problems that exist only by virtue of these advances. "With hardly an exception," Burnet and White tell us, "we fail to anticipate some longer-term implication of such action and the repercussions are often unhappy ones. Not a few of the advances of medicine in relation to infectious disease have had to qualify success with some long-term difficulty or accidental disaster" (Burnet and White 1972:186). In the most recent edition of their history of infectious disease, a new chapter has been devoted exclusively to the subject of hospital infections and iatrogenic diseases (those accidentally induced by a physician in the course of treatment for another disease or condition). Most are regarded as "the inevitable result" of the organization of treatment within the standard hospital framework, of the establishment of hospital strains of antibiotic-resistant bacteria, of transmission of disease by transfusion (most notably in serum hepatitis), and of the use of high-risk techniques such as chemotherapy for cancer and immunosuppressive drugs in surgical transplantation. These problems, it is well to remember, can exist even where there is no evidence of human error. In fact, the opposite is true; they are pernicious products of medical progress. In a fascinating account, these same authors point out, for example, that if cancer has — as many believe — a viral base (at least in part), it owes its etiology to scientific medicine's success in facilitating long-term "quality housing" within the human body for singularly lethal, slow-growing viruses.

"Blame" for the complex reverberations of medical advances is perhaps more properly relegated to the character of Western progress itself. More particularly, it relates to the growing articulation of the biotechnical sciences as fields apart from, or only tangential to, the science (and art) of medicine itself. The consequences have been complex with criticisms, we have seen, leveled most often at the dehumanization of medicine, its Cartesian division of mind from body, and its failure to consider the cultural-ecological complexity of man. The point to be emphasized is that the trend to relate to "the colostomy in 615" instead of to the patient as a whole, a human being with family, friends, obligations, and fears, has serious health consequences because *it affects the efficacy of medical treatment.* A postoperative mastectomy patient with whom one of our students spoke expressed resentment toward her doctor, saying that he viewed her merely as a beautiful piece of surgery. In this case the doctor felt obligated to treat only the physical dimensions of the mastectomy. By ignoring the emotional aspects, he created resentment for himself as a doctor and jeopardized his patient's rapid return to a normal, healthy life. Problems such as failure to follow a doctor's orders, reluctance to keep follow-up appointments, disabling fear and anxiety regarding the implications of disease and its treatment, and frustration on the part of patients with psychosomatic illness all negatively affect the treatment of disease and are related to what some people feel is a dehumanization of the doctor-patient relationship.

And how does one evaluate relative efficacy when medical technology has confronted the entire modern world with profound human dilemmas that increase medical costs and raise serious ethical and legal issues? For example, in the United States today, the cost of one patient on renal dialysis can be up to $30,000 per year. What factors should operate in assessing the most efficacious use of this resource? Age? Remaining productivity? Contribution to medical knowledge? Is money better spent in terms of life for one person or for life for an entire village if these monies were spent for better nutrition and pre- and postnatal clinics? In raising these questions we must not forget that it is a testimony to Western scientific medicine that many of these options, however difficult, exist at all.

SUMMARY

To summarize our views about the efficacy of non-Western medicine, we believe that when judged against the many functions it is expected to fulfill in the societies of which it is a part, and considering the inherent limitations to systematic medical investigations in these societies, traditional medical systems seen as adaptive devices have been remarkably successful. They have existed for thousands of years, they have brought hope and relief to the ill, they have dealt with social ills as well, and they have contributed to a slow increase in the world's population. We also believe that in contrast to scientific medicine in both its preventive and clinical aspects and for all its health care delivery defects, non-Western medicine is a less satisfactory way of meeting the health needs of contemporary peoples. This is not our judgment alone; it is the verdict of the ultimate judges, the traditional consumers who increasingly may choose between their own and scientific medicine. As will be seen in Chapter 14, their verdict more and more favors the latter instead of the former.

NOTES

[1] The nonmedical functions of a Puerto Rican spiritist *centro* in New York City are described by Harwood: " . . . the *centro* becomes an important primary group outside the family and assumes many of the functions voluntary organizations perform for urban migrants the world over . . . it operates as a job-referral network and offers assistance to members during life crises. It also serves as an agent of social control through informal gossip among its members, through the more formal rules of the organization, and during seances, through the ritual authority of mediums" (Harwood 1977:179). Most important of all, the *centro* and its chief medium function to socialize members to urban ways. Clearly, the efficacy of an alternate medical system such as spiritism cannot be judged in the same narrow terms that are used in evaluating the physician's therapies.

[2] Kleinman recently has called for more precise methods of evaluation of the efficacy of indigenous therapies. "Up to now, medical anthropological studies have assumed that indigenous healing systems were effective without systematically examining this question. Clinically-oriented studies suggest that

little is gained by further speculation on questions like 'how symbols heal,' and that it is essential to conduct studies which test specific psycho- and socio-somatic mechanisms of therapeutic action and which use appropriate controls (Kleinman 1977:13).

[3] Public confession is, of course, a part of many faith healing rituals in the United States. "Private" confession, in the confessional or psychiatrist's office, is regarded by many as having powerful therapeutic value.

[4] In a tightly reasoned article Dunn persuasively argues that malaria was unknown in Pre-Colombian times in the Western Hemisphere. The value of cinchona bark, from which quinine is derived, as a specific for malaria was discovered accidentally by Europeans in the seventeenth century (Dunn 1965).

part 3

THE WESTERN WORLD

chapter 8

Illness Behavior

INTRODUCTION

In the preceding four chapters we have dealt with a variety of medical and health themes particularly but not exclusively as they have been portrayed in ethnographic accounts from the non-Western world. The principal disease etiologies found in traditional societies have been summarized, and these have been correlated with other aspects of medical systems. We have considered the nature of mental illness in societies around the world and have examined some of the problems associated with its occurrence that have interested anthropologists. The characteristics and roles of shamans and witch doctors have been explored, and we have noted the ways in which their behavior resembles, and differs from, that of their Western counterparts. Finally, we have examined the evidence that bears on the strengths and weaknesses of traditional modes of diagnosis, and the therapy that follows.

In this and the next three chapters we shift our primary focus from the non-Western world to the United States. We do not, however, alter our course by 180 degrees. Just as in the earlier chapters we sometimes found it expedient to draw in data from the West to provide comparative perspective, so too in this section we consider data from the ethnographic record when we feel that it illuminates patterns characterizing the contemporary world. This comparative stance has proven particularly valuable in this chapter, which is about illness behavior.

ILLNESS BEHAVIOR, THE SICK ROLE, AND THE PATIENT ROLE

In studying illness behavior it is important to remember, as von Mering reminds us, that "the proper study of the ill human being assumes that each individual lives with both the symptoms and consequences of disease in its physical and mental, medical and social aspects. While attempting to alleviate disease, the ill become involved in a variety of specific or non-specific internal and external problem-solving processes" (Von Mering 1970:272-273). Not surprisingly, behavioral scientists have concerned themselves especially with the social and mental aspects of these problem-solving processes, and particularly with the social roles of illness.

The social aspect (or state) of illness, like the physical, mental, and medical aspects, represents a time sequence. There is a beginning, an awareness of the first faint symptoms; there is progression, the social and physiological processes that occur; and there is a termination, through recovery or death. At many points during "the course of the illness," medical and social decisions must be made, roles readjusted, and attitudes changed to conform to the reality of the situation. Medical sociologists have coined the term *illness behavior* to describe these sequential actions, and they have developed role models — the *sick role* and the *patient role* — to aid them in their analyses.

Illness behavior, the most general of these terms, has been defined as "the way in which symptoms are perceived, evaluated, and acted upon by a person who recognizes some pain, discomfort, or other sign of malfunction" (Mechanic and Volkhart 1961:52). Illness behavior may occur in the absence of sick roles and patient roles. An adult who awakens with a sore throat engages in illness behavior; he must decide whether to take an aspirin and hope for the best, or call the doctor. But this is not sick role behavior; it is only when illness is defined as sufficiently serious to remove a person from some or all of his normal roles, thus altering and placing extra demands on the role behavior of those around him, that a person assumes the sick role. As Jaco says, "When behavior related to illness is organized into a social role, the sick role becomes a meaningful mode of reacting to and coping with the existence and potential hazards of sickness by a society" (Jaco 1972:93).

The concept of patient role is more restricted than that of sick role. If the adult with the sore throat decides to spend the day resting in bed, with the expectation that other family members will bring food, the sick role has been assumed. But only if a physician is consulted and the individual acts on his instructions does the patient role come into being. The patient role is thus a special case of (an extension of) the sick role. "The larger society defines the legitimate criteria for sickness for its members (i.e., it can validate the sick role), whereas the therapeutic and organizational setting in which the sick person obtains care and treatment sets up the criteria for his role as patient in that social system" (Jaco 1972:94). In other words, the patient role requires formal medical validation, the submission by the sick person to the ministrations of the physician with his supportive resources. Carol Taylor succinctly sums up the difference between the two roles. "When a sick person enters the hospital, he must be turned into a patient"(C. Taylor 1970:76). The concepts of sick role and patient role are, of course, ideal types, and it is unproductive to draw an absolute distinction between them. They are useful analytical devices but, in the study of the behavior of sick people, a good deal of overlap will be inevitable.

Illness behavior and the sick and patient roles are strongly influenced by factors such as social class and ethnic and cultural differences. Consequently, the same health threat (clinically defined) may, depending on these variables, produce widely differing reactions among patients. Koos, for example, has demonstrated how illness behavior differs significantly according to social and economic class within an otherwise homogeneous population. He found that members of the upper class of the small upstate New York community he studied were more likely to interpret particular symptoms as indicative of illness than members of the lower class; consequently, they were more apt to seek the physician's attention (Koos 1954:32-33).

Cultural differences in illness behavior are perhaps more marked than socio-economic differences. In a study carried out in a veterans' hospital in New York City, Zborowski found that Jews and Italians were much more emotional in their responses to pain than north Europeans (Zborowski 1952:21-22). Although some doctors felt that the members of these groups must have a lower threshold of pain than members of other groups, the differences, beyond reasonable doubt, are cultural. Since Jewish and Italian cultures "allow for free expression of feelings and emotions by words, sounds and gestures, both the Italians and Jews feel free to talk about their pain, complain about it and manifest their sufferings by groaning, moaning, crying, etc. They are not ashamed of this expression. They admit willingly that when they are in pain they do complain a great deal, call for help and expect sympathy and assistance from other members of their immediate social environment" (*Ibid.,* 262).

In contrast, "Old Americans" tend to "report" on pain, trying as dispassionately as possible to find "the most appropriate ways of defining the quality of pain, its localization, duration, etc . . . The interviewees repeatedly state that there is no point in complaining and groaning and moaning, etc., because 'it won't help anybody.' However, they readily admit that when pain is unbearable they may react strongly, even to the point of crying, but they tend to do it when they are alone. Withdrawal from society seems to be a frequent reaction to strong pain" (*Ibid.,* 24-25).

Anthropologists are beginning to make use of the concepts of illness behavior, the sick role, and the patient role; the terms, certainly, are as applicable to one society as to another. In examining the topic of the "social roles" of illness, for example, we find that some of the most illuminating examples come from the ethnographic record. At the same time, it must be confessed that explicit accounts of illness behavior in societies other than our own are fairly rare. Like curer-patient communication in non-Western societies, this is a neglected theme, a research lode begging to be opened up.

In one of the few really good accounts of illness behavior in a culture that is significantly different from that of the United States, Kenny tells us how in

Spain, "Being ill calls for loud complaint — an exercise of Latin spontaneity rather than Anglo-Saxon self control — and this evidently alleviates his condition in his own mind. The sick person needs an audience either of his fellow men or of God whom (plus his mother) he frequently invokes. He puts his heart and soul into his illness as he does into other experiences of life. Rarely does he console himself with the thought that he is perhaps only one of thirty thousand others in a similar plight" (Kenny 1962-63:284). In contrast, observations of pain response at the Papago Indian Hospital at Sells, Arizona prompted one of the nurses to comment, "We have learned from experience that when a Papago complains of pain or requests medication, such requests should receive prompt attention, for he is usually in serious trouble" (Christopherson 1971:36).

THE SOCIAL ROLES OF ILLNESS

The behavioral scientist studying illness must, obviously, be aware of the role of culture in shaping the behavior he observes. He must also bear in mind the role of individual psychologies and the conscious and subconscious goals of the sick. Most people prefer, or believe they prefer, health to illness. "Everybody wants to be healthy" has for decades been a commonly voiced justification for public health programs. Most sociological analysis is based on the same assumption; as we will see shortly, the "Parsonian" sick role model has as a major premise the desire of the patient to get well.

In a sense this premise is correct; most of us do prefer health over illness. Yet uncritical acceptance of this assumption blinds us to some of the most important aspects of health behavior. Good health, like other desired things in life, takes it place in everyone's personal priority scale. For some, it is near the top; for others, it is further down. That is, few if any people want good health at all costs, and particularly if the enjoyment of good health may seriously curtail pleasures. The evidence that cigarette smoking greatly increases the likelihood of lung cancer, emphysema, and heart disease seems overwhelming. Yet tens of millions of Americans risk future ill health for the present satisfaction of smoking; for them, good health is not an absolute priority. Other Americans postpone or ignore regular physical examinations because they are "too busy" with other things that seem to have a higher priority. Good health, it must be remembered, competes as a priority with all nonhealth priorities, so that individual health behavior can be understood only in this wider context of life goals.

Quite apart from personal priorities, illness often has positive adaptive functions. Almost everyone, at some point, welcomes illness as a temporary release from stressful situations. The sick role can thus be seen as a coping mechanism, as a useful element in the total life strategy of the individual. Early in life people learn that to be ill brings special privileges. Young children soon discover the manipulative possibilities of colds and sore throats ̱vis-à-vis school, and not infrequently throughout adult life everyone welcomes a day or two in bed with a mild cold or "a touch of the flu," either of which provides a socially sanctioned break from normal routines.

While the "sick-role-as-temporary-release" represents a reasonable form of adaptive behavior for most people, for a few the role of patient is actively sought, and it may become a satisfying way of life. The surgeon-author Nolen describes these people, who are known to all doctors. "Enjoying poor health is their hobby, their business, their only interest. They build their entire lives around their symptoms, their trips to the doctor, their stays in the hospital" (Nolen 1974:294). In other words, illness may fulfill social roles, as the following examples show.

1. Illness provides release from unbearable pressure

A Mexican-American couple with six children living in California faced acute financial problems because of a prolonged visit by the husband's brother, wife, and five children, a visit that threatened to last until the brother found employment. Fifteen people lived in a three-room house, meeting all expenses from the wages of one common laborer. The grocery bill mounted, and the grocer finally cut off credit. Mexican social norms include extremely long (by Anglo standards) visits, and the wife felt obliged to provide food and shelter to her husband's relatives. At the same time, she feared her own children would go hungry. Presently she began to suffer from shortness of breath, sweating, and rapid pulse. A conference with her sister and two *comadres* resulted in a diagnosis of *susto* (fright), a common Mexican folk illness. A local *curandera* confirmed the diagnosis. The patient's relatives and *comadres* then asked the brother-in-law and his family to move out, since a woman suffering from fright obviously could not take care of the extra people, an action fully justified in the eyes of the local community. "As soon as the visiting relatives left, the patient's anxiety was relieved and her symptoms disappeared. Her rapid recovery was attributed to the excellence of the cure performed by the local *curandera*" (Clark 1959b:154-155).

At least subconsciously, the *curandera* and the members of the Mexican-American community recognized that "if a person is defined as sick, his failure to perform his normal functions is 'not his fault,' and he is accorded the right to exemption and care" (Parsons and Fox 1952:32-33). Consequently, in the face of heavy social pressures, illness provides "a tantalizingly attractive 'solution,' " since the sick role is a "semi-legitimate channel of withdrawal — exempting the social actor from adult responsibilities and enjoining him to allow himself to be taken care of by others" (*Ibid.,* 34).

2. Illness helps to account for personal failure

The use of illness to provide a temporary respite from overwhelming pressure is probably a healthy safety valve, a fortunate provision made by all societies to permit a person to buy time to attack anew difficult problems. But for some the strategem becomes a permanent way of life that is used on the slightest pretext and ultimately develops into a person's self-justification and justification to others of failure. "Illness represents one way of coping with failure in Western society. To be sick implies an inability to fulfill tasks and an acceptable avoidance of responsibilities. Sensing failure, one can justify this failure, to oneself or to significant reference groups, in terms of one's inability to perform as a result of illness" (Shuval et al. 1973:260). All of us probably have known people who "enjoy poor health," figuratively and literally. Whether it is bad luck, a "trick" knee, or migraine headaches, there are countless people who obviously cannot be expected to lead a normal life, to do the same things that other people with these conditions manage to do, despite the handicap involved.

3. Illness may be used to gain attention

Cultural conventions dictate that the sick receive special attention: solicitous and hopeful enquiries about how the patient feels, special foods, hot water bottles, pillows fluffed, and backs rubbed. For people who are lonely, who are unsure of their acceptance by others, who feel on the fringe, illness is an attractive device to gain attention. Balint notes this in London where, particularly as a result of urbanization, many people have lost their traditional roots, and life is solitary and lonely. If trouble comes, these people have few resources for advice and consolation or simply for unburdening themselves to a sympathetic listener. Since mental and emotional strains stemming from these causes often produce physical symptoms, "in such troubled states . . . a . . . frequently used outlet is to drop in to one's doctor and complain"(Balint 1966:-282). Balint gives several case histories describing behavior that very clearly portrays the patient's obvious need for attention and affection.

Such behavior is not limited to Western societies. Among the Navaho, for example, to exhibit the symptoms of bewitchment (hence illness) is one way to gain attention. "A high proportion of those who have suddenly 'fainted' or gone into a semi-trance at 'squaw dances' or other large gatherings are women or men who are somewhat neglected or occupy low status" (Kluckhohn 1944:-83-84). In a sample of 17 such cases, 13 were people of minimum prestige. The wealthy, in contrast, "tend to announce or to have it discovered by a diagnostician in the privacy of their homes that they are victims of witchcraft" (*Ibid.,* 84).

4. Hospitalization may be a vacation

Not infrequently, and perhaps surprisingly in view of frequent attitudes toward hospitals, women in traditional societies, when first introduced to maternal and child health care, including delivery in a clinic or hospital, happily accept the latter, even in the face of possible violations of traditional birth practices and taboos; the four or five days of bed rest and good food, and freedom from worry about other children and home care, are viewed as relaxation, in a sense, a vacation.

In a like vein, Nolen tells of George, a frequent repeater at New York City's immense public hospital, Bellevue. "The rich man goes to Miami for a few weeks every February; George came to Bellevue and had an operation. It wasn't difficult to arrange, if you knew the ropes. One year George complained of severe pain and a 'lump' in the groin. He convinced an intern that he had a hernia and was admitted to have it repaired." The following winter it was a hemorrhoidectomy, which gave him three weeks of hospitalization. A year later it was still another hernia, this time on the other side. "By then I was on to his game and thought I'd see if he'd admit it. But George was no dope. When his hernia was healed and he was ready to be discharged, I made a big point of examining George's legs.

" 'George,' I said, 'you've got a few varicose veins here. Maybe we ought to fix them. What do you say?'

" 'No thanks, Doc,' he answered.

" 'Sure, George? It'll mean another couple of weeks in the hospital.'

"George smiled. 'I'll tell you, Doc, I've had a pretty good rest for the last two weeks. Three meals a day and a warm bed. It's almost spring now and I can manage till next winter. Thanks anyway, but I'm saving those veins for next February.'

"Sure enough, the next February George came back in and we operated on his veins" (Nolen 1972:52).

Most private patients, says Nolen, prefer home treatment, with comfortable beds, steak dinners, and martinis. But what if you have no home? What if you sleep in doorways in the warm weather and in a flophouse in the cold? What if you never know where your next meal is coming from and have no family to solace you? Under such circumstances, George's behavior is entirely rational.

5. Illness may be used as a social control device

In American society the stereotype of manipulation through illness is the widowed mother, the chronic sufferer, who plays on her children's feelings of guilt to ensure that they do what she wants. The extreme case is the daughter who remains single all of her life, "devotedly" caring for (and simultaneously hating) her mother and drifting into a lonely old age herself. Sons, too, find themselves in the role of "mamma's boy," respecting her wishes that they not marry "because she's not good enough for you" and then rushing out to marry in indecent haste as soon as the old woman is gone. In Tzintzuntzan, Mexico, numbers of early migrants to the United States were drawn home by the pleas of elderly and ill mothers; once in the village most of them found it impossible to escape.

Clark gives a classic example of how illness can be used as a device to control the behavior of others. In a Mexican-American community "A young woman expecting her first child became angry with her husband one night when he came home drunk. She scolded him thoroughly for this, whereupon he beat her and put her out of the house in the rain. She walked to her mother's house, some blocks away, where she related her trying experience. Her relatives immediately took her to a curandera, a curing-woman, for treatment; it was feared that her unborn child would, as a result of prenatal influence, later suffer from *susto* or fright.

"This young wife felt that she had been badly abused by her husband. Ordinarily she would not have been thought justified in openly condemning her husband for beating her. After all, she had scolded him and insulted him for getting drunk with his friends — a type of entertainment regarded by most men of the community as their prerogative. Because his wife was pregnant, however, she had recourse to a folk-defined disease, *susto,* and she thus gained the sympathy and support of her entire social circle. Soon the news of her unfortunate experience spread through the neighborhood and open criticism was directed against the unfeeling husband who had threatened the life of his unborn child. Through group pressure he was finally persuaded of the error of his ways, he made the necessary apologies and promises and the couple was happily reunited" (Clark 1959b:154).

Illness can also be used as a control device to obtain desired but scarce rewards. When good housing, desirable work, social welfare benefits, and other similar things are in short supply, some mechanism must be devised to determine the basis of their allocation. In Israel some people have found illness to be such an allocative tool, and Israeli physicians are often badgered for "certificates" testifying to the genuine illness of the seeker and his right to acquire the coveted object (Shuval et al. 1973:260).

6. Illness may be a device to expiate sinful feelings

As we saw in Chapter 3 many Western and non-Western people view illness as a product of their having sinned or in some way offended their deities. Speaking specifically of the Judeo-Christian tradition, Sigerist states: "God has revealed his law. Whoever follows it piously will be blessed in this world. Whoever breaks the law will be punished. Every disease is a punishment. Every suffering is a suffering for sin — for the sins of the individual himself, for those of his parents, or for those of his relatives. . . . As a consequence of this view of disease as punishment, the sick man was marked with certain stigma. He was not a guiltless victim. To be sure he suffers, but he has deserved his suffering because he has sinned. Through his sickness his sins become a matter of public knowledge" (Roemer 1960:14).

For people who, consciously and subconsciously, hold these views, illness permits one to atone for wrongdoing. The moral slate is wiped clean, and the sufferer again has a valid claim on good health. We have all known people with chronic complaints who, almost self-righteously, proclaim "I have my cross to bear." In this context of expiation, one wonders if the feeling — still prevalent among some Americans — that if an antiseptic does not sting, if a medicine does not taste bad, and if a hypodermic injection does not give pain, then it is valueless, is a reflection of the conviction that man must pay with suffering for his sins.

THE EVOLUTION OF PARTICULAR ILLNESS STRATEGEMS

Balint has provided a useful model to show how a person works out a particular "strategem" when, with or without specific intent, he seeks to use illness to justify personal goals. The patient "offers" or "proposes" various illnesses to legitimize his claim on the physician's time and, he hopes, to find a sympathetic ear into which he can pour his troubles. The unsuspecting physician — or the physician unaware of the psychic dimensions of many illnesses — accepts the "proposal" at face value and diligently searches for organic causes to explain the symptoms, probably ultimately sending the insistent patient to a series of specialists. Little by little the patient's "offers" are shot down or rendered nonfunctional by a continuing stream of negative reports, or are countered by alternative offers by the physician. With each such report or unsatisfactory counteroffer, the patient must propose a new or revised set of symptoms "until between doctor and patient an agreement can be reached, resulting in the acceptance by both of them of one of the illnesses as justified" (Balint 1966:286). Balint describes the process of searching for a mutually agreeable definition of illness as "organizing the illness" on the part of the patient. Both doctor and patient are engaged in a deadly serious game, although frequently neither one fully appreciates what is happening.

To summarize to this point, the behavioral scientist studying illness behavior and the sick and patient roles must be aware not only of social, ethnic, and cultural factors, but must also remember that however subconsciously, patients may be using their condition as a manipulative device, that illness has positive as well as negative value to them. With these points in mind, we can return to a more detailed examination of the concepts of the sick role and of illness behavior.

THE PARSONIAN MODEL OF THE SICK ROLE

The sociologist Talcott Parsons has provided the sick role model that has been most widely used by behavioral scientists.[1] Although he correctly recognizes illness as a disturbance in the normal functioning of the individual, "including both the state of the organism as a biological system and of his personal and social adjustments," the model deals only with the social and cultural aspects of the conditions. Illness, says Parsons, is a form of deviant behavior that provides a socially sanctioned and institutionalized way to withdraw from the demands and stresses of everyday life. Following legitimization of his claim to occupy the sick role (in Western society normally by the physician accepting him as patient), the patient has two principal *rights* (or expectations).

1. Exemption from his normal social role responsibilities.

2. Care until he recovers. He is not expected, by an act of decision or will, to "pull himself together" without help. Furthermore, he is not held responsible for his condition.

The patient also has two principal *duties* (or responsibilities).

1. To acknowledge the sick role as undesirable and feel obligated to get well as soon as possible.

2. To seek technically competent help (i.e., the doctor) and cooperate with this help in getting well (Parsons 1951:428-479).

This model has been found most useful when applied to people who are suffering acute, self-limiting diseases in which full recovery is the normal expectation. It is based on the assumption that illness normally is a *temporary* state. But, when applied to chronic, degenerative diseases, which are *not* temporary conditions and in which full recovery is not possible, the model has been less useful (cf. Kassebaum and Baumann 1965; McKinlay 1972). In these cases the sick role may never be abandoned, and it is unreasonable to exhort patients to attempt recovery when recovery is impossible. Furthermore, much chronic illness does not completely disrupt normal role performance. Heart disease may restrict a person's strenuous physical activities yet still permit normal or nearly normal social and business roles. Again, chronic illness is not randomly distributed in the population; it correlates with advancing age. Old age in itself is marked by some of the role expectations of Parson's model. "Hence, failure to distinguish between illness and old age as bases for role-expectations may have dysfunctional consequences both for the patient's therapy, and for the doctor-patient relationship" (Kassebaum and Bauman 1965:19).

The Parsonian model has also proved to be deficient with respect to mental illness. Segall recently has summarized the findings of a number of researchers who have been concerned with this problem. A person who seeks psychiatric help for a mental condition is, like a physically ill person who goes to a physician, committed to recovery. Yet the person who is physically ill normally is not stigmatized by virtue of illness and, as we have seen, is expected to lay aside his normal role obligations. The mental patient, on the other hand, must be prepared to face stigma and perhaps rejection because of his illness. Moreover, in many therapies it is felt best that a mental patient *not* be exempt from all of his social responsibilities. Whereas the behavior of the physically ill patient is expected to be marked by passivity, submission, and dependency, that of the mentally ill patient is expected to be marked by action, independence, and self-direction in relation to the therapist. "The medical and psychiatric sick role models, then, entail rather different types of reciprocal relationships between doctors and patients" (Segall 1976:164).

Finally, although the matter has been little discussed by sociologists, we feel Parson's model is overly simplistic in its insistence that the patient is not viewed as responsible for his condition. Americans, in fact, place a remarkable degree of responsibility for health on the individual himself. It is assumed that he has the knowledge, if not the moral strength, to avoid illness and, if he succumbs, he is responsible. If there were no feeling of responsibility there would be no such thing as a "shameful disease" of which, in earlier years, tuberculosis, cancer, and epilepsy were the most common. Today these attitudes have largely disappeared, and one talks openly about almost all illness. Nevertheless, residual feelings of shame or, minimally, pity, are still found, as in the use of euphemisms in some illness contexts. When, for example, we read that a well-known person has died "after a long illness," we can be reasonably sure it was from cancer.

There still lingers in American society the feeling that alcoholics and sufferers from venereal disease have only themselves to blame for their condition. The former is thought by some to reflect moral weakness, to be cured by willpower rather than medical attention, while the latter is seen as punishment for transgression of a strict moral code.

Residually, and largely subconsciously, acceptance of moral responsibility for illness is seen in linguistic usages. We still "come down with" or "fall ill," just as a sinner falls from divine grace or, in an earlier and simpler time, a wayward girl becomes a "fallen woman." The equation of loss of health with loss of grace is also suggested when we say of an alcoholic who struggles unsuccessfully to abstain that "he fell off the (water) wagon." The admonitions of mothers to their children likewise reflect responsibility. Children are told to "Bundle up!", "Wear your rubbers!", and "Take good care of yourself!", with the implicit reminder that failure to do so will result in illness, just retribution for the careless student. And when we say to a friend with an arm or leg in a cast, "What did you do to yourself?" instead of "What happened to you?" we imply that he, not fate, is the active agent. To say "I caught cold" is (subconsciously) to confess responsibility for one's discomfort, just as the expressions "*He* sprained *his* ankle," "*He* cut *himself*," "*He* broke *his* leg," or "*He* picked up" an infectious disease make clear the locus of responsibility.

These common American expressions stand in interesting contrast with Mexican village Spanish usages. In Tzintzuntzan one "becomes" ill but does not "fall" ill. *Que te pasó* ("What happened to you?") is appropriate, but not "What did you do to yourself?" One is "struck" by a cold, but one does not "catch" or "pick up" a cold. My leg can be broken, but I do not break my leg. In illness, as in many other situations, linguistic forms clearly place the locus of responsibility "out there," away from the victim.

STAGES OF ILLNESS

Both anthropologists and sociologists view the course of illness as marked by analytically distinguishable stages. Perhaps the most widely used sociological schema is that of Suchman, who sees "the sequence of medical events . . . representing major transition points involving new decisions about the future course of medical care" as divided into five stages (Suchman 1965). Anthropologists recognize similar stages. At the same time, their emphases are rather different; the sociologist never seems far removed from roles and decisions, but the anthropologist seems more descriptive, more universal (i.e., cross-cultural and comparative), but less rigorously analytical. In the following pages Suchman's five stages and the names he gives them are used as a basis for illustrating the way in which anthropologists and sociologists view the sequence of illness.

1. The symptoms experience stage *("the decision that something is wrong")*

The first step in the medical drama occurs when physical discomfort, pain, change of appearance, or debility suggests to a person that something is wrong with his physiological state. "These symptoms," says Suchman, "will be recognized and defined not in medically diagnostic categories, but in terms of their interference with normal social functioning" (Suchman 1965:115). After symptoms are recognized, they must be interpreted, their meaning sought. Both recognition and interpretation arouse emotional responses of fear and anxiety, because one knows that mild symptoms *may* be the precursor of something far more grave.

Anthropologists agree with these points. Most would go on, however, to ask how people recognize and accept the presence of illness. Here we find a qualitative difference between many Western and non-Western peoples. Although members of both groups assign priority to physical symptoms as evidence of illness, Western patients can also believe that in the absence of overt indicators, laboratory tests and the physician's physical examination may reveal pathological evidence that treatment is required. The relative docility with which some of us submit to "the annual physical" indicates our assumption that the onset of disease precedes our awareness of its symptoms; we take on faith the physician's interpretation of the evidence and begin treatment in the absence of symptoms. In contrast, non-Western peoples tend to believe that unless pain and real discomfort are present, there can be no illness. They define health as "feeling good," or as "the absence of symptoms." Thus, among Egyptian peasants, who share this view, bilharziasis and other parasitic infections that weaken an individual but do not cause overt pain are not attended (Read 1966:26). And in Pachmarhi, a hill station in central India, a comparatively large number of people show evidence of goiter. But, since this condition is not incapacitating, it is not classed as illness, and nothing is done about it (J. Ramakrishna, communicated).

From the standpoint of introducing scientific medical care into the traditional world, the definition of health as "feeling good" has important negative consequences. Not only are such people reluctant to accept laboratory diagnosis as evidence of disease in the absence of overt symptoms but, when treatment reaches the point where symptoms have disappeared, patients often are little motivated to continue with the indicated medical regimen. For example, it is difficult to convince the parents of Mexican-American children who have had heart surgery at the Driscoll Foundation Children's Hospital in Corpus Christi of the need for periodic postoperative checkups so that medication and exercise programs can be properly monitored. In the parents' eyes discharge from the hospital is equated with full recovery. Very often only serious relapses or actual heart failure will convince them — sometimes too late — of the need for sustained medical attention for a "well" child.

2. Assumption of the sick role state (*"the decision that one is sick and needs professional care"*)

If the sufferer interprets the symptoms of stage one as indicating illness, he enters the second stage, in which he seeks advice and care. Initially care is limited to home remedies and self-doctoring, and advice is sought within the "lay referral system" (i.e., through discussion of symptoms with relatives and friends). Highly important at this stage is the "provisional validation" of friends and relatives to the claim of illness, temporarily excusing the person from his usual obligations to others. "How the individual's lay consultants react to his symptoms and their acceptance of any interference with his social functioning will do much to determine the individual's ability to enter the sick role" (Suchman 1965:115). If family and friends generally are supportive of the sufferer's claims, he is more apt to go on to the third stage than if they express skepticism.

Anthropologists tend to see stage two among the peoples they study as one in which stress is placed on naming the illness. To name an illness is important for two reasons. First, since the known is less threatening than the unknown, it is easier to live with a named than an unnamed illness. And second, naming an illness determines its etiology, its cause, which in turn provides the doctor with the information he needs to carry out treatment. Shiloh describes how in the Middle East the curer, when summoned to the bedside of the patient, identifies the illness. "To do this is to immediately define it, circumscribe it, tame it, weaken it. The diagnosis provides the patient with a sense of relief that the unknown pain has been mastered and it provides the practitioner with a medical treatment" (Shiloh 1961:285). Even when a diagnosis indicates a very serious health threat, most people feel relief when the doctor decides what is wrong, because the probable course of most illnesses has been charted, and doctor and patient now know what they reasonably can expect.

3. The medical care contact stage (*"the decision to seek professional medical care"*)

At this stage, the person who suspects that he is ill is well on the road to becoming a patient. He is seeking two things: authoritative confirmation of the "provisional validation" of his sick role, previously granted him by his lay consultants and, if such confirmation is forthcoming, he expects a medical diagnosis and a proposed course of treatment designed to restore him to health. If the doctor denies his claim to the sick role by insisting that nothing is seriously wrong, the claimant may return, reassured, to his normal activities. Not infrequently, however, he will simply turn to another physician, continuing the process of "shopping around" until he finds one who is willing to accept his claim to illness (e.g., Balint 1957).

The ways in which the decisions of stage three are made vary significantly from one society to another. Those Americans with access to good medical facilities usually make decisions about medical treatment in consultation with the physician, perhaps with the participation of the husband or wife. That is, basic medical decisions, even grave ones, usually are made by a very small group of people; the decision is not primarily a social one.

In contrast, in traditional and tribal societies medical decisions are reached much more slowly, and only after deliberations that involve a larger number of people. Clark has described how, in a Mexican-American enclave in California, people do not act as isolated individuals in medical situations. "In illness as well as in other aspects of life, they are members of a group of relatives and compadres. Individuals are responsible to their group for their behavior and dependent on them for support and social sanction. Medical care involves expenditure of time and energy by the patient's relatives and friends. Money for doctors and medicines comes from the common family purse; many of a sick person's duties are performed during the period of illness by other members of his social group. Illness is not merely a biological disorder of the individual organism — it is a social crisis and period of readjustment for an entire group of people.

"It is customary, therefore, for an individual to present his symptoms to his relatives and friends for their appraisal before he takes steps to obtain medical treatment. The patient alone is not authorized to decide whether or not he is ill; even though he himself may be convinced that he is sick enough to warrant special attention, his intimates must still be persuaded of the seriousness of his complaints. In other words, an individual is not socially defined as a sick person until his claim is 'validated' by his associates. Only when relatives and friends accept his condition as an illness can he claim exemption from the performance of his normal daily tasks.

"In relations with medical personnel, then, a patient is not free to make immediate and conclusive decisions concerning his own health. He is acting not as an individual but as a family member" (Clark 1959a:203-204).

Marta, a married woman, was advised by a school physician to begin prenatal care at a local public health clinic. But the decision was not basically Marta's. First she had to make sure her *comadre* would care for her other children if she required hospitalization. Then she had to have the approval of her husband, who would provide money, medicine, and transportation. "Only after her husband and her comadre had said, 'Yes, Marta, you are sick and should go to the clinic,' — only then could she speak with authority about her medical plans" (*Ibid.,* 204).

4. The dependent-patient role stage (*"the decision to transfer control to the physician and to accept and follow prescribed treatment"*)

Through the first three stages, the *nature* of the illness has little bearing on what is done. But when we reach stage four, this becomes an important matter. A patient who can reasonably expect to recover will be treated, and will react, in a way quite distinct from that of a patient suffering from a chronic illness from which recovery is impossible. Patients in the first category often view their role with ambivalence: relief that the condition is recognized by the physician, and that a particular course of treatment should result in recovery, coupled with reluctance to accept a dependency relationship that by definition deprives them of many of their usual decision-making rights.

When patients in the second category recognize the full implications of their diagnosis — that recovery is impossible and that rehabilitation or a slowing of the chronic condition is the best they can hope for — their reactions may be very different. To a greater or lesser degree, they are forced to adopt a perpetual "patient role," with frequent visits to the physician, perhaps periodic hospitalization, and an inevitable loss of physical competence. A dependency relation with the physician is thus inevitable. And, far from resenting the relationship, many chronic patients find comfort in it; their worries are shared with another person who, it is always felt, may learn of the miracle that will restore the patient to his former state of health.

The contrast between the two situations has been well presented by Gussow. Whereas the sufferer from an acute, short-term illness anticipates either death-in-the-not-too-distant-future, or more likely, a return-to-things-as-they-were, "chronic disease involves persons in a long-term commitment to the meaning and implication of disability, requiring adjustments, adaptations, and transformations on a number of social, interpersonal, and psychic levels of functioning. Changes and alterations assume a more permanent character with more or less lasting re-arrangements in the organization of the life program" (Gussow 1964:179). Whereas the role alterations occasioned by short-term illness are usually seen as minor, those occasioned by chronic conditions mean major reorganization of previous life ways, both for the patient and for those around him who are most affected by his illness.

The problems of sufferers from chronic illnesses are exacerbated when these conditions stigmatize them in the eyes of others: that is, people with some chronic illnesses such as tuberculosis, cancer, or leprosy, or who are seriously disfigured because of an accident or congenital factors, may arouse emotions of excessive fear, abhorrence, or psychological discomfort in others. Mental illness also has long stigmatized sufferers, and many people believe that a person once hospitalized or intensively treated for severe psychological problems can never return to full normalcy. Of all such illnesses the stigmata of leprosy is probably the greatest since, in spite of the fact that it is not highly contagious nor seriously disfiguring if treated early, it arouses a revulsion unparalleled by other diseases. Gussow and Tracy interviewed patients at the Public Health Service leprosarium at Carville, Louisiana, to discover the coping mechanisms that are used in facing life. They suggest the concept of *career patient status* as one mode of adaptation to stigmatization. Incumbents in effect become health educators of a rather special type.

"In the interest of altering the public image of leprosy, which they hold as bearing the major responsibility for their discredited status and predicament in life, these patients assume the stance of educators bringing specialized information about leprosy to the public" (Gussow and Tracy 1968:322). This role, of course, is open only to sufferers from leprosy who are not seriously disfigured and who are medically certified as not contagious. Moreover, a relatively limited "demand" for this kind of education limits the opportunity to assume this particular career patient status. We believe career patient status is a concept that can be extended profitably to other stigmatizing diseases and to some of the coping mechanisms used by people who are suffering from chronic and degenerative diseases.

Most research on chronic illness has been carried out in technologically complex societies where effective clinical and preventive care has greatly lengthened the life span. In traditional societies chronic illness was relatively rare, since few people survived the hazards of childhood and adult life to live on into the age brackets where degenerative afflictions become common. Consequently, anthropologists have paid little attention to this problem in the societies they have studied. Now that modern medicine has vastly extended life in many developing countries, it will be interesting to see what new ways are found to cope with chronic illness.

5. The recovery or rehabilitation state (*"the decision to relinquish the patient role"*)

For reasons we have just considered, the applicability of stage five to chronic illness is strictly limited. Rehabilitation may aid the victim of accident and stroke to cope better with life than if nothing is done and, to some extent, the patient role may be relinquished. But this is relative, at best; sufferers from chronic conditions know that the patient role always lurks around the next corner. For other patients, stage five is realistic; in all societies we find rituals and symbolic actions that certify that a recent patient has now resumed, or is about to resume, his normal roles. In the United States certification of recovery is based largely on the attending physician's word. To be able to say "My doctor told me I can now do anything I want" is the patient's usual way of assuring his friends that all is well. In Tzintzuntzan, Mexico, a recently ill person achieves the same end by saying "I have already bathed." Bathing is believed to be highly dangerous for the sick; it is immediately proscribed when the first symptoms appear and permitted again only when all evidence of indisposition has disappeared. To state publicly "I have bathed" is the definitive way to express complete recovery.

In other societies the rites are more elaborate. From Nigeria comes a description of a ritual enacted to symbolize recovery from mental illness. Dressed in the clothing worn during his illness, the patient is taken to a river where a dove is sacrificed over his head, and he is washed in its blood. Then his old clothing and the carcass of the bird are thrown in the stream and carried away, while the priest chants:

As the river can never flow backwards,
So may this illness never return.

The former patient, now dressed in his best clothes, meets his relatives, who have assembled for a feast in honor of his newly recovered health (Maclean 1971:79-80). Both patient and family presumably benefit from this ritual; the patient is reassured that his relatives welcome him back to his usual role, and the family has the priest's assurance that he can be counted on to carry on with his normal activities. This is in striking contrast, says the author, to Western society, where a former mental patient leaves the hospital "with the traces of his illness still clinging about him, constituting a stigma which he may never succeed in shaking off" (*Ibid.,* 79).

As pointed out near the beginning of this chapter, and as has been apparent from the examples we have given, illness behavior has not been adequately described in studies of non-Western peoples. We suspect that to a considerable extent, research conditions explain this apparent lack of anthropological interest. A behavioral scientist working in an American hospital can devote large blocks of time to illness behavior when there is a handy sample of 10 or 100 patients available. But a lone anthropologist can hardly set aside all other research to sit beside a sick person in his hut, night and day, observing what is done for him and how he reacts, until he recovers or dies. As anthropologists begin to study hospitals in non-Western societies (in India and Indonesia, for example), we can expect accounts of illness behavior comparable to those from U.S. hospitals. These will not be the same as detailed observations of sick people in remote tribal societies; it is asking too much, probably, ever to expect comprehensive data from such groups. At the same time, hospital studies of patient behavior in cultures drastically different from our own will vastly increase the validity of generalizations made about illness behavior and the sick and patient roles.

NOTES

[1] In the sense in which the terms have been defined at the beginning of this chapter, Parsons is describing the patient role, not the sick role. But, since Parsons himself uses the expression "sick role," we conform to this terminology in examining his model.

chapter 9

Hospitals: Behavioral Science Views

SOME WESTERN-NON-WESTERN CONTRASTS

In contrast to the traditional world, in the contemporary Western world a great deal of illness is played out in the hospital where the patient is under the care (and control) of physicians, who are aided by nurses and many other supporting personnel. Nonmedical people — friends and family members — play relatively few roles in attempting to restore a patient to health, at least as long as the acute stage of illness requires hospitalization. Health care delivery in the West thus differs greatly from that of the traditional world, where family and friends may play major supportive therapeutic roles, but where the curer is largely unsupported by other medical personnel.

When, as sometimes happens, assistants are included in the therapeutic situation, their roles are, for the most part, peripheral or ceremonial and contribute little if anything to the cure. Thus, the *manang* of Borneo employs an assistant to stand by, ready to cover him with a special blanket when, in a trance, he falls to the floor to depart — unseen — to retrieve the lost soul of his patient (Torrey 1972:96). And in parts of New Guinea the shaman may use a medium who has proved particularly attractive to spirits (or to *a* spirit) to lure them to the curer's presence. Occasionally an apprentice may relieve the therapist of routine aspects of curing, for example, repeating many of the incantations. In these cultures, however, we cannot speak of a "team" approach to patient care. The curer has no pharmacist to call on, no pathologist to aid in his diagnosis, and routinely no paramedical assistants to support him in the curing process. Where a range of specialized skills is involved in effecting a cure, those who possess them function within a prescribed hierarchy as independent specialists. "The herbalist prepares and dispenses medicines. The diviner makes diagnoses (as well as often finding lost objects and predicting the future), and the healer treats people. . . . Often people will begin with the herbalist and work up, depending on how difficult a case is" (Torrey 1972:5). Nursing, to the extent the term is applicable, is done by members of the family.

Thus, to understand the therapeutic process in complex societies, we must consider roles and institutions that are little, if at all, developed in simpler communities. Specifically to be noted in Western Europe and the United States is that most treatment of serious illness takes place not in the home, but in the hospital. There the physician does not work alone; rather, he is the captain of a team, who makes primary decisions, and directs the activities of a wide variety of supportive professional aids. Of these, the nurse is the most important; it is she (or they) whom the patient sees many times a day and to whom the patient looks for comfort and relief.

In their attempts to understand contemporary medical care in the United States, behavioral scientists have concentrated their studies on three major topics: *hospitals, doctors,* and *nurses.* The American hospital has come to be the primary care setting for the practice of medicine. Most physicians spend a significant part of their days in hospitals, where they see their most seriously ill patients. Two-thirds of all registered nurses are employed in hospitals, within which their role as mediator between physician and patient is most clearly seen. So it is to these three topics that we turn our attention in this and the following two chapters. Each topic is marked by such a vast literature that we can do no more than touch on the principal theoretical and practical points that have emerged from studies during the past generation.

The role — or rather, the relative absence of the role — of anthropologists in these studies will be noted, for we can claim credit for only a small part of the research that has been done. While anthropologists have been busy studying shamans and witch doctors and unravelling the mysteries of non-Western disease etiologies, sociologists and psychologists have been primarily concerned with the training and practice of physicians, the status of nursing, and the structure of hospitals. This neglect is far from absolute, however; some of the most important studies of hospitals have been done by anthropologists, and one of the earliest behavioral scientists to be concerned with nursing is an anthropologist (Brown 1936). Moreover, in recent years, anthropology has acquired great significance to nursing; in their quest for higher professional status, considerable numbers of nurses turn to doctoral programs in anthropology. Nevertheless, the bulk of the studies to which we refer in this chapter represents the work of nonanthropologists.

THE CHANGING ROLES OF HOSPITALS

Hospitals, as we have just pointed out, have become the primary health care centers in the United States. Patients routinely make use of outpatient departments for care that, in an earlier period, they would have received at home or in their physician's office. Laboratory, X ray, physical therapy, and other services are widely used for outpatient care and diagnosis and to meet the needs of hospitalized patients. No longer is the hospital feared, at least to the extent of earlier years.

This has not always been the case. Throughout most of history the hospital has functioned as a charitable institution, as an almshouse and as a last resort for the critically ill poor. It has been viewed quite realistically as a place where people have gone to die. Hospital attendants were untrained, drawn from the lowest social classes, and few physicians, other than those hired by the government or a religious order, passed through their doors. Well into the twentieth century well-to-do patients were cared for at home, the house-calling physician aided by a full-time private duty nurse. Only with the great strides made by scientific medicine during the present century has the function of the hospital been revolutionized. Particularly important in sparking this change was the relatively early and rapid development of surgery. Tonsils and adenoids might be removed on the dining table by the general practitioner, but appendectomies and mastectomies clearly required complex procedures that could only be carried out in a hospital. Complex diagnostic tasks, too, were recognized as more effectively achieved in a controlled setting with laboratory, X rays, and other resources under the same roof. And not the least of the factors in changing the function of the hospital has been conservation of the physician's time: a dozen patients can be visited, and their needs better met, in the same time that a physician formerly made a single house call. So today it is to the hospital that we turn to study, and comprehend, contemporary medical care.

HOSPITALS AS SMALL SOCIETIES

We have hinted at the multiplicity of functions found in the modern hospital. It is, in fact, one of the most complex of all institutions in our society. Its manifest function — the best possible care of the sick — is fairly obvious. Its product — patient care — is achieved only by coordination of the work of many people of both sexes and of a wide range of ages, arranged in rigid hierarchies of responsibility and authority. Most behavioral scientists view the hospital as a small society with its own culture, in much the same way a peasant village or a small tribe is seen as a society with a culture; most behavioral science research in hospitals is based on this conceptualization of the unit of study. Freidson, who questions this model, is the exception to the rule. He feels that since hospitals are not true, self-sufficient communities, they can only very loosely be called small societies. Lack of autonomy is the key to his reservation: " . . . the hospital is neither self-sufficient nor sovereign and so cannot make its own rules for the exercise of power by 'citizens,' including patients" (Freidson 1970:173-174). But the same can be said of most communities studied by anthropologists. For example, a Mexican peasant village has little if any more autonomy than a community hospital, and very little "power" is exercised by its citizens. Although Freidson admonishes us not to overdraw the analogy, it is, in fact, on the basis of the small community model, with lines of authority and interacting roles, that hospital analyses are made.

Hospitals are of many types. One common classification compares the *voluntary* community or religiously supported nonprofit hospital, with the *proprietary,* privately owned, profit-oriented hospital, and with the *publicly owned,* often charity-oriented, hospital. But the distinction that is most apparent in the behavioral science literature is the distinction between the *general* hospital and the *mental* hospital. Although the function of the general hospital, as a type, is to treat and if possible, restore patients to health and society, many of them have *teaching* and *research* as major functions, since patients are critical to the advancement of both. These are the hospitals associated with medical schools and universities. As a rule, they are more easily studied than general care hospitals. The reason why is fairly clear, as Coser points out. "An outside observer can enter more unobtrusively into a teaching hospital where third- and fourth-year medical students, interns, residents, visiting doctors, resident-psychiatrists, registered nurses, student nurses, aides, volunteers, frequently laboratory and X-ray technicians and social workers throng the corridors and the wards. A 'new person' or 'stranger' on the ward, as long as he wears a white coat, is readily accepted. His title of 'researcher' is sufficient to explain his presence" (Coser 1962:xix). Anthropologists, by training, believe that the best studies are made where the people being studied are least disturbed by outside influences, including that of a surfeit of researchers.

As between sociologists and anthropologists, an interesting dichotomy can be noted: anthropologists largely have limited their studies to mental hospitals. Although some sociologists (especially when working with psychologists or psychiatrists, as in the case of Stanton and Schwartz 1954) have worked in mental hospitals, most of their interest has been directed toward general hospital. How can we explain this division of effort? One possible answer has to do with the concept of culture. Hospitals, as small societies, are appropriately viewed as having "cultures." But the "general" or total culture of a hospital is difficult to characterize, and the units of study are more commonly "subcultures." Although we may speak of the subculture of the ward, of the laboratory, of the operating theater, and of the other units of a modern hospital, two basic subcultures always are apparent: the "patient" or "inmate" culture, and the "professional" or "staff" culture of all of the people who work in a hospital. Staff cultures appear to be fairly similar, regardless of the type of hospital. Patient or inmate cultures differ more significantly. If, as most anthropologists believe, cultures take time to develop, people who interact daily for many years, are more likely to develop a viable culture than are those whose contacts are transitory.

We are suggesting that, because of the continuity of interaction between their members, inmate cultures in mental hospitals are more fully developed than in general hospitals. In general hospitals, where the average stay of patients is now only about a week, only under special circumstances, such as in rehabilitation wards or wards for the chronically ill, does time permit the development of true patient cultures. It seems possible that one reason anthropologists have been drawn to the study of mental hospitals is because of the congeniality of what they have found: a real, ongoing culture that can be studied by the methods they have used in studying other cultures.

Staff cultures have, of course, been studied by behavioral scientists in many kinds of hospitals. But the life-style of most hospital professionals — elusively active on duty, and private and inaccessible off duty — makes the study of staff cultures difficult. Even when in the hospital, busy doctors and nurses, unless personally interested in research, are apt to regard the presence and questions of a behavioral scientist as intrusive nuisances. In contrast, inmate cultures are 24-hour a day, seven-day a week propositions. Moreover, patients are a captive audience, especially in mental hospitals, where they have little to do besides passing time; the ear and tongue of a sympathetic behavioral scientist often are welcome intrusions in an otherwise monotonous existence. "Rapport," the basis of all participant observation, is much easier to establish in a situation like this than with members of a staff culture.

There may be another reason that turns anthropologists to mental hospitals. As one of us has recently pointed out (Foster 1974:3), anthropologists historically have studied the "underdogs" of the world, powerless peasant communities and small tribes. Consciously and subconsciously they empathize with people cast in the role of underdog. In the context of the hospital, this means the patient, depersonalized and reduced to the social role of child and, to a lesser extent, the lower, nonprofessional functionaries in the health care system. Frankel, for example, in a study of the emergency care system of a large California city, got on well with emergency room physicians (who feel themselves near the bottom of the status hierarchy in medicine) and other hospital personnel, but it is clear that his real sympathies lay with the hardworking, underpaid ambulance crews, whose roles in this monograph are the most clearly delineated of all emergency care personnel (Frankel 1976).

Whatever the reasons, anthropologists have been drawn to the study of the mental hospital. Salisbury has described the research attractions; he found the state mental hospital he studied to be a relatively self-contained community "from which few patients return to the outside world, in which many people live large portions of their lives, and in which the behavior of all categories of persons is influenced as much by the behavior of other members of that 'community' as it is by the standards of 'society at large' " (Salisbury 1962: v-vi). The size of the hospital (about 3000 patients plus supporting staff) made necessary such things as private bus services, laundries, and class groupings among patients. "In short," he writes, "*the problems are those traditionally treated by the social anthropologist, problems for the study of which his modes of analysis are designed" (Ibid.,* vi. Emphasis added). These include the analysis of small-scale social structures in which each relationship has implications for all other relationships; the analysis of what people believe about their social structures that influence their behavior; and concern with positive and negative sanctions that keep the system functioning, or produce change, and the like.

STRUCTURE AND FUNCTION IN HOSPITALS

A hospital is, at the everyday working level, a highly authoritarian organization. It has been compared to the army. Orders and instructions are to be executed without question, often with great rapidity. To the extent that hospital activities are life and death in nature, it can hardly be otherwise, for a delayed or badly executed act may jeopardize the life of a patient. Yet a hospital is not a hierarchical, authoritarian structure in the usual sense of the word, with direct lines of control extending from top to bottom in an ever widening root system. Behavioral scientists have been struck by the fact that a hospital has a *dual* administrative system in which the lay authority system (the board of trustees, the hospital administrator, and his staff members paid by the hospital) often is in conflict with the professional authority vested in the medical doctors (Smith 1955). The doctors, the most prestigious of all personnel, are in the anomalous position of being "guests" in the hospitals in which they practice; their payment comes from patients and not from the hospital itself. Their authority is of the type Weber called "charismatic" authority, based on the recognition by followers of special attributes or powers vested in them. Whether medical or religious, charisma defies lay authority structures. And, in fact, "there is almost no administrative routine established in hospitals which cannot be (and frequently is) abrogated or countermanded by a physician claiming medical emergency — or by anyone acting for the physician and similarly claiming medical necessity" (*Ibid.,* 59).[1]

CONFLICTING LINES OF AUTHORITY

Conflicting lines of authority do not enhance the stability of any organization, and many workers in hospitals are torn by conflicting demands of physicians and administrators. The most vulnerable is the nurse who often finds herself as the proverbial "[man] person-in-the-middle." Duff and Hollingshead noted the problem facing the head nurse of each patient care unit in the hospital they studied. "Two lines of authority converged in her role. She was the hospital's representative on the floor, responsible for following policies, rules, and procedures laid down by the administration of the hospital . . . and she was the physician's representative on the floor, responsible for carrying out his orders for individual patients" (Duff and Hollingshead 1968:67). Since these lines of authority were not articulated, they presented the nurse with a dilemma that, to be solved, meant satisfying four groups: the nursing hierarchy; hospital departments other than nursing; private physicians and house staff; and patients. This was not always possible.

Coe has noted the same thing. "As the recipient of the doctor's orders for his patients," he writes, "the nurse is obligated to carry out those orders in a professionally competent manner, but at the same time, she is a hired employee of the hospital and consequently subject to all the rules and regulations of the administrative organization. Often the demands of patient care, especially when they are of an emergency nature, cannot be accomplished within the framework of administative rules; thus the nurse is caught in a conflict between the expectations of the physicians that his orders be carried out and the expectations of the administrator that administrative procedures will be complied with" (Coe 1970:272).

BLOCKED MOBILITY IN HOSPITALS

Another structural characteristic of hospitals is what has been called "blocked mobility." Patient care in a modern hospital requires the services of a wide variety of professional, subprofessional, and unskilled personnel. In a study of an East Coast hospital Wessen delineated 23 major occupational groups, quite apart from administrative personnel (Wessen 1972:316). Not only is there a multiplicity of roles in a hospital, but most of them are sharply separated from each other in a rigid status hierarchy outwardly reflected by things such as dress, dining privileges, and other perquisites. In the hospital studied by Wessen there are "at least twelve different uniforms" on a typical ward, as well as three separate dining rooms, one for doctors, a second for nurses, and a third for all other employees (*Ibid.,* 317).

The consequence of rigid role separation is that vertical mobility within a hospital is limited, and only rarely does an incumbent advance from a lower to a higher status role without taking additional formal training. Role separation seems largely a function of the variety of special competences essential to patient care, each of which tends to be compartmentalized. As Smith says, "the skills which are developed in one small component of the hospital, for example x-ray or pathology or housekeeping or administration, are not readily transferable to other departments." Consequently, "When the question of promotion to another department comes up, persons within the hospital who merit consideration often do not actually possess the skills needed to occupy the new position" (Smith 1955:30).

In his study Wessen found that "communication tends to be for the most part channeled within occupational lines, giving rise to a tendency for those who work together on the wards to know and associate principally with those of their 'own kind' " (Wessen 1972:331). Since the primary loyalty of employees tends to be to their professional or status peer groups, the functional teams marked by easy communication that are in the best interests of patients sometimes are not achieved.

THE PATIENT'S VIEW OF HOSPITALIZATION

In addition to the structural characteristics of hospitals, behavioral scientists have also been concerned with what happens to patients after admittance. What they have found is a *process* remarkably akin to *culture shock* (Brink and Saunders 1976), an ordeal of *depersonalization* (Coe 1970:313), a *loss of self-identity* (Brown 1963:119), and a *loss of control over body and physical environment* (Coser 1959:173). When Americans (and presumably also people from other countries) experience the stress of living and working abroad for the first time, they often suffer what has come to be called "culture shock," occasioned by loss of the familiar cues as to appropriate behavior, problems of language, and lack of familiarity with new cultural items. Brink and Saunders believe that the hospital patient often experiences similar stress reactions. They are, for example, faced with hospitalese, a language they little understand: "Did you *void* this morning? When did you have your last BM? You are scheduled for EEG and when you get back we will call GNY for a work-up, and then we will prep you for X-ray" (Brink and Saunders 1976:134). The hospital patient, too, must learn to manipulate new items of material culture such as pushbuttons, bedpans, and other routine hospital artifacts, and he must learn new patterns of interaction with the people about him.

Brown sees admission to a hospital as the beginning of a "stripping" process for the patient. "He is expected to check most of his individualized wants and desires and his long-standing habit of making decisions for himself and others. . . . However, as the stripping process continues and its effect on him becomes cumulative, he often feels as if he were losing one layer after another of his self-identification" (Brown 1963:119). The patient's roles in normal life recede into the background; he becomes a "case" in a numbered room, his identity certified by a plastic bracelet with his name, the same identification used for a newborn baby. The analogy with infancy and childhood is not farfetched; in loss of control the patient *does,* in many ways, regress toward childhood. Even captains of industry, professionals, and other "important" people may be astonished to find that nurses address them by their first names, and perhaps even as "honey."

Coser has noted how the patient must submit to the authority of the hospital staff 24 hours a day. Everything is planned for him, from time and menu of meals to bathing to medication. "He is under continuous supervision and his full day is scheduled for him" (Coser 1959:174). Hospitals, says Coe, reduce the natural differences between patients "to make it more convenient to handle large numbers of patients" (Coe 1970:300). This is accomplished by issuing standard clothing, such as nightgowns unlike those ever slept in elsewhere, which facilitates staff access to the body. Wallets and purses are checked "for safekeeping," and the patient is left with the absolute minimum of personal belongings. "Every distinctly personalizing symbol, material or otherwise, is taken away, thus reducing the patient to the status of just one of many" (*Ibid.,* 300). Coe also notes patient restrictions such as deprivation of information, especially about himself, restriction of mobility, and forced dependence on others.

The problem is not that hospital personnel are heartless and unfeeling. Rather, patient status and patient care seem largely a consequence of the real or imagined need of bureaucratic efficiency. As Lorber notes, "Hospital rules and regulations are for their [hospital personnel] benefit, not for the convenience of patients" (Lorber 1975:213). Not surprisingly, patients who make it easy for doctors, nurses, and other hospital personnel are classified as "good" patients; those who do not are "problem" patients. In her study Lorber found that "Patients who were considered cooperative, uncomplaining, and stoical by the doctors and nurses were generally labeled good patients," whereas patients who were "uncooperative, constantly complaining, over-emotional, and dependent, were frequently considered problem patients whether they had routine or very serious surgery" (Lorber 1975:218-219). "Ease of management" proved to be the basic criterion for a "good" patient, while patients "who took time and attention felt to be unwarranted by their illness" were "problem" patients (*Ibid.,* 220). Analyzing hospitals and "the cult of efficiency," Taylor describes a good patient as one who answers when questioned, accepts treatment, swallows pills, and eats what he is given to eat" (C. Taylor 1970:97). Researchers have found some tendency for "problem" patients to receive less attention from hospital personnel or to be discharged slightly earlier than might otherwise be the case. Sometimes they are turned over to nursing homes and, not infrequently, psychiatric care is ordered for really troublesome cases.

The anthropologist Brown, viewing the problem from, so to speak, the patient's bed, notes the human tendency to assume that others see a human situation in the same way as ego. "Staff often take it for granted that patients think and feel much as they do about many matters" (Brown 1963:123). Hospital personnel, from doctors on down the line, who are familiar with all aspects of hospital life and their meaning and purpose, tend to forget that hospital patients, other than chronic repeaters, know very little about routines that they take for granted. And the unknown is always potentially threatening. "Perhaps," suggests Brown, "if medical and nursing students and prospective hospital administrators were given a ten-day experience as bed patients, they would be better able to recall later how patients feel; perhaps they could express more understanding and interest themselves in making changes wherever possible that might reduce patients' boredom, frustration, and worry" (*Ibid.,* 124).

The very act of admittance to a hospital can become so ritualized as to create serious apprehensions for patients and their families about which the hospital staff may be wholly oblivious. Carol Taylor gives a gripping account of Mrs. Brown, a 59-year-old woman brought to the clinic waiting room by the married son with whom she lived. Without either of them understanding hospital procedures, she was spirited away by attendants and some hours later hospitalized without again seeing her son. It was three weeks before a graduate student in clinical psychology and the nursing student he was dating unraveled the mystery of what was "bothering" Mrs. Brown, who had finally written her silent family but hadn't a stamp to mail the letter. For their part, the worried family, unsure how to penetrate the complex world of the hospital, awaited word from *someone*. They had been taking turns manning a telephone, met the mailman every day, and made special preparations to receive telegrams at unusual hours (C. Taylor 1970:97-99).

The overwhelming regimentation of hospital existence is often acutely felt by patients to whom the depersonalization of the sick role is contrary to all the mandates of their cultures. A reserved people trying to negotiate in a foreign situation, Mexican-American patients often shut down communication altogether upon receiving a negative response from the staff. When, in a children's hospital, the nurse informed a Mexican-American mother that she could not remain with her son the night before his operation, the woman did not confront her. But the resentment was there, and the bitterness was transferred to the entire staff when the boy died following surgery (personal communication).

Anderson and Hazam report an unfortunate clash between traditional Mexican-American and Western health care practices when a mother, palpating the stomach of her hospitalized child to determine whether he was suffering from *empacho*, was discovered by a Mexican-American nurse and subjected to a thorough interrogation. The disdain felt by the nurse for her more traditional sister was painfully obvious both to the shamed mother and to the witnesses of the incident (Anderson and Hazam 1978).

Too often in the context of hospital life, nonverbal cues of fear, disorientation, and the need for reassurance on the part of patient and kinsmen seem to go undiscovered and unresolved.

ALTERNATIVE FORMS OF HOSPITALIZATION

As we will see in a later chapter Americans, including those in medical fields, tend to assume that American institutional norms are fixed, immutable, and rational. They find it difficult to believe that significantly different forms and practices may be equally conducive to goal achievement. Although very little research has been done by Americans on hospitals in developing countries, the observations of a few are highly provocative in suggesting that alternative approaches are feasible and even desirable. In one such study, in four mental hospitals or psychiatric wards in Lima, Peru, it was found that effective custodial care was combined with a humanistic atmosphere, in spite of the fact that lower-echelon personnel had highly authoritarian views. "Modes of coercion are lacking in the Peruvian mental hospital ward. Subordinates, including the most subordinate of all personnel, the patients, tend to accept and follow the requests and orders of superiors. The Peruvian mental hospital is not insulated and isolated from its surrounding culture, as the North American custodial hospital or prison is screened from its context of institutional democracy" (Stein and Oetting 1964:282). In one hospital, patients were even allowed to carry matches and have their own razors. One has the impression that a relaxed approach to custodial care is beneficial to staff and patients.

In a well-known study of a rural Greek hospital, Friedl favorably compares the small four-bed ward she observed, in which patients bring their own bedding and clothing and where they are constantly attended and fed by family members, with the supportive care given patients at home. In Greece, hospitalization traditionally has symbolized desertion of the patient by his family. Greeks further, and in contrast to most Americans, feel that human companionship is just as important to critically ill people as it is to the healthy. Under these circumstances, the informal, messy, and crowded hospital practices that would be anathema to many Americans (patients and hospital personnel alike) probably are highly therapeutic in the context of Greek culture (Friedl 1958).

CHANGING AMERICAN PRACTICES

Fortunately for patients, a small but growing number of progressive American hospitals has been relaxing many of the rigid rules that have made them such unattractive places in which to receive therapy; they have been experimenting with dramatic shifts from conventional patterns of care. Visiting hours have been extended, menus provide choices, and cocktails and wine may even be permitted, within limits, if there are no medical contraindications. Beyond these cosmetic improvements, greater changes are beginning to be seen as, for example, integrating mental patients within general care hospitals, combining the very young and the old on a single ward, and even (in the case of a veterans' hospital) allowing ailing couples to remain together. In Texas one of us (Anderson) has had opportunity to observe what may well become a major trend in child care: the restructuring of hospitals to incorporate parents more intimately into hospital life. In one example, a hospital for disabled children, a new and larger building has been designed with specific innovations in mind: live-in arrangements for parents who come great distances, increased involvement of parents in routine hospital care and consultation, and programs of paramedical training for parents of chronically ill children.

A second hospital has developed facilities and a budget for regular workshops and seminars that involve all employees, from telephone operators to pediatric cardiologists to consulting social and behavioral scientists. A major focus of these seminars is the free exchange, across usually rigid hierarchical lines, of ideas for improved patient care, particularly with respect to the needs of the ethnic minority groups served by the hospital. Under consideration is an intensive Spanish language training program, underwritten by the hospital, and for which staff would receive work credit. In Chapter 16 we will examine other innovations in contemporary, progressive hospital care.

Innovative hospitals are of particular interest to medical anthropologists. We suspect that most anthropologists are unlikely to become interested in hospital economics and in the roles of Blue Cross and Medicare. But in the changing culture of the American hospital, in the processes of innovation and improvement in health care, there is much where the anthropological point of view should contribute to our understanding of this institution and its ability to meet the needs of its clients.

Several areas come to mind where this new research has already begun or where it should prove profitable. The structure and role of the outpatient clinic, for example, is a neglected but highly promising research topic. Recently Carole Browner has found, in a study of an outpatient clinic in a San Francisco hospital, that the clinic plays a major role as a social center or club for elderly neighborhood residents who drop in to visit with friends with a frequency that has little to do with their immediate medical needs, but that certainly contributes to their psychological needs (communicated by Dr. Browner). Emergency medical services likewise seem a promising research area, to judge by the wide spectrum of insights obtained by Stephen Frankel in his study of emergency room procedures in a Pacific Coast hospital (Frankel 1976). Illustrative of still a different kind of hospital research are the preliminary findings of Barbara Koenig on the personal value and emotional conflicts faced by nurses who care for dying children (Koenig 1977). And all of Kübler-Ross' work on the subject of death and dying (to be reviewed in Chapter 16) presages a more patient-sensitive and effective approach to the terminal care of hospitalized patients of all ages.

NOTES

[1] The structural and personality aspects of the frequent conflict between hospital administrators and physicians — and the power of the latter to slow change and reform — recently has been described by Ingman in a medium-sized hospital in Appalachia (Ingman 1975).

chapter 10

Professionalism in Medicine: Doctors

INTRODUCTION

It is to anthropologists, joined in recent years by increasing numbers of psychiatrists, that we owe most accounts of non-Western therapists and their associated personnel. They are the ones who have defined the field, determined the topics that have received primary attention, and provided the vast bulk of the data from which we draw conclusions. When we turn to the study of physicians and associated personnel (especially nurses) in our own society, we find that sociologists and, to a lesser extent, psychologists have played an equivalent role. It is they who have defined the field, determined the principal problems to be studied, and provided the current hypotheses and models as well as the data from which they are constructed.

Although there is some overlap in the research foci of anthropologists and sociologists, the differences in emphasis are more notable. Whereas anthropologists have been primarily interested in the therapeutic techniques of curers, in their personality characteristics, and in their roles as social arbiters as well as health therapists, sociologists have been particularly interested in physicians as exemplars of a social category, the professional. Although some sociologists have been interested in the structure of medical care and the relationship of the physician to society at large (Eliot Freidson's *Professional Dominance* [1970] comes to mind), it is striking how much of the sociological literature deals with medical education and the nature of professions. These are the topics that will particularly concern us in this chapter.

THE CONCEPT OF PROFESSION

That medicine, as Everett Hughes has written, is "the prototype of the professions" (E.C. Hughes 1956:21) has long been recognized. Not surprisingly, it was early recognized by sociologists as an especially fruitful field in which to explore their broad concern with issues such as occupations and the division of labor in American society. One of the first major studies of a medical school, for example, was the outgrowth of an interdepartmental Seminar on the Professions established at Columbia University in 1950. Seminar participants noted the lack of systematic knowledge about the sociopsychological environments of professional schools and the ways in which these environments influenced the learning process. They concluded that a sociological study of a medical school would provide the needed prototype for similar studies in other fields. The result was the classic *The Student-Physician* (Merton et al. 1957), the first major study of medical professionalization.

In examining the literature on physicians and medical practice (and also on nursing), we find that the integrating theme of *profession* is almost always present. So, we ask, what is a profession, and how does an aspirant become a professional? The concept of profession implies content, clients, organization, and control. A profession is based on, or organized around, a body of specialized knowledge (the *content*) not easily acquired and that, in the hands of qualified practitioners, meets the needs of, or serves, *clients*. Many definitions of profession stress the centrality of theoretical knowledge and continuing research to add to this knowledge, certainly a primary characteristic of the medical profession.

With respect to the structure of professional fields we note that relationships are marked by a *collegial organization* of equals in contrast to a hierarchical bureaucratic organization (Coe 1970:191). Through this horizontally phrased community of conceptual equals professionals maintain *control* over their field. Within it they cooperate to promote their common interests, maintain the monopoly of their knowledge, protect themselves from the incursions of others, set the qualifications for admission to the profession and, not always with full vigor, police the competence and ethics of members of the group.

A profession may also be seen as a "special status in the division of labor supported by official and sometimes public belief that it is worthy of such status" (Friedson 1972:187). In the words of Everett Hughes, a profession has a *license* and a *mandate* to carry out its work, partially validated by law, and partially validated by society's informal approbation, or agreement, that the claims to professional status are indeed justified. The members of a profession also normally have a high degree of autonomy in their practice, including control over the training given those aspiring to the profession. Finally, most professionals view their work as a fulltime, lifelong undertaking.

MEDICAL EDUCATION

Entrée into a profession — and certainly into medicine — is gained by an aspirant undertaking long-term training as a member of a group or class of similar people in which (under the direction of qualified professionals serving in the capacity of teachers and by a dual learning process) he acquires the technical knowledge essential to the role as well as the values, the sense of identity, the norms of behavior appropriate to the role, and the like. Very important, as Coe points out, is learning to collaborate with fellow professionals.

The attention sociologists (and psychologists) have given to medical education is a reflection of this basic point. In the research that has been done two main approaches to the study of medical education may be noted: the psychological and the sociological (Merton 1957:53). The former, which appears earlier in time, focuses on the individual and searches for personality characteristics that will influence, or be reflected in, his perception, thinking, acting, and feeling. Many of these early psychological studies were practical in nature, designed to aid medical school selection committees in choosing candidates that they believed most likely to succeed in their medical studies. Psychological studies have also dealt with the factors that influence medical students in their selection of specialty fields or their decision to enter general practice.

The sociological approach devotes primary attention to the medical school viewed as a social system whose structure, function, and processes are set in a cultural environment. Sociologists have been interested in the development of a student "culture" as an adaptive device that helps students to cope with the heavy stresses of their studies and in the changes in values and outlook that mark medical students as they progress from freshmen status to that of young doctors. The two approaches, as Merton points out, are complementary, not competitive; through them we gain greater understanding of medical education than either alone could give us (Merton 1957:54). From the many studies that have been made of the medical education process, we have selected four principal themes for discussion: recruitment to medical school, student culture, "detached concern" and the loss of idealism, and career specialization.

1. Recruitment

The characteristics of medical students differ considerably, depending on the geographical location of their school, the racial and religious composition of the populations from which they are drawn, and the rural-urban ratios of these populations. Thus, medical schools in New York City draw a significantly higher proportion of Jewish students than state medical colleges set in predominantly Protestant rural areas in the Midwest. Yet, in considering the gross characteristics of medical students, the similarities are more striking than the differences. They have high IQs; they tend to be recruited from the upper socioeconomic strata of our society; and a high proportion are children of college graduates in business and the professions. Although there is increasing democratization in selection processes, medical students still probably reflect the highest socioeconomic level of any group of students in the country. Bloom reports that in a sample of 14 medical schools, college graduate fathers ranged from 26 to 54 percent of the total, and 18 to 38 percent had "more than college" training (i.e., graduate school or professional training) (Bloom 1973:-65). In the Downstate Medical Center of the State University of New York, in New York City, Bloom found that two-thirds of the students came from a professional, managerial, or proprietor background (*Ibid.,* 62).

Other studies of the background of medical students conform to Bloom's findings, although the definition of sociocultural status varies from region to region. Thus, Becker and his colleagues found that "a sizable majority" of medical students at the University of Kansas in the late 1950s were "young, white, male, Protestant, smalltown native Kansans" (Becker et al. 1961:59), quite a different group than that found at Downstate, but an advantaged body in the context of Kansas.

Sociologists have also been interested in the factors that have influenced students to seek a medical career. In an early paper Hall spoke of the process of "generating an ambition" (Hall 1948:327). He found that in most cases family and friends were not only major forces in awakening interest in medical careers, but that they also played major roles in making such careers possible by supportive behavior including encouragement, aid in establishing study routines, and provision of privacy to facilitate study. It is not surprising, he concluded, that such a high proportion of medical students come from professional (and other upper socioeconomic backgrounds), since they possess to a greater degree than other groups "the mechanisms for generating and nurturing medical ambition" (*Ibid.,* 328). In contrast, families from lower socioeconomic levels may stimulate the urge, but lack the means and understanding to keep alive and strengthen that ambition through supportive behavior.

A later study of about 750 students in six successive classes at the University of Pennsylvania Medical School analyzes the factors that led these students to select medicine and their ages at the time the decision was made. Less than 20 percent, it was found, reached their decision prior to the age of 16, but these students had fewer doubts than later deciders about the "rightness" of their decision and, more than the others, they expressed the feeling that medicine was the only career that could satisfy them. Fathers played a major role in the choices of early deciders while, not surprisingly, peer group members, and particularly friends already in medical school, played more important roles for later deciders. Finally, early deciders appeared more motivated by humanitarian factors, the desire to help people and to receive their appreciation, than did older deciders, who were relatively more attracted to intellectual medical problems (Rogoff 1957).

2. Student culture

Sociological studies of medical schools have raised a major theoretical and practical question not yet fully answered: the *status* of the medical student. "Is he most essentially a student, required to prove himself in a rite-of-passage that emphasizes a trial by intellectual ordeal? Or is he a physician-in-training, a junior colleague to the medical profession, and therefore already the partial beneficiary of rights and privileges of membership in the profession, which are gradually increased to full measure on a graduated scale?" (Bloom 1965:152). The titles of two of the most important medical school studies graphically pose this question. In the Kansas study Becker and his colleagues studied *Boys in White,* while in the New York Cornell Study, Merton and his colleagues were concerned with *The Student-Physician.*

The contrasting points of view illustrate how models influence interpretation. Students and teachers are, obviously, fairly dichotomous statuses, with many mutual interests, but with separate lives. For those who find the concept of subcultures helpful in understanding complex societies, as anthropologists do, it is logical to see both students and their professors as members of distinct cultures. This is the approach taken by Becker and his colleagues, who define a student culture as "the body of collective understanding among students about matters related to their roles as students" (Becker et al. 1961:46). These authors note several connotations of this term. First, there is coherence and consistency in the "perspectives" (the ways of thinking, feeling, and acting in problematic situations) of students. Second, the term emphasizes that the perspectives held by the student body are closely related to the fact that they are students and not yet professionals. Finally, although the students are preparing for medical careers, "the decisive influences on their perspectives are not medical" (*Ibid.,* 46). They act not as young doctors, but as students.

Student culture, like other cultures, comes into being because a body of people share a common environment, face comparable problems, engage in similar or identical activities, and live under the same stresses. And, just as anthropologists view culture generically as an adaptive mechanism enabling human groups to cope with the problems of existence, so can student culture be envisaged as a coping device that teaches, guides, and leads medical students through the maze and pitfalls of medical education, helping them to make the decisions and take the actions that maximize the likelihood of successfully completing their training. As Bloom sums it up, in the Kansas study students were found "to organize a world within the school but separate from it. This student culture is, at least to some extent, a secret society whose members 'play it cool' — that is, they present one face to the faculty, that of acquiescence and co-operation, acting in the interests of academic survival; in their own private world, they are more independent and critical" (Bloom 1965:155).

In contrast to the Kansas study, the work by Merton and his colleagues suggests a more egalitarian student-faculty relationship in which the younger members are viewed as budding colleagues soon to be full professional partners. The student society they found seems to fulfill different functions from that in Kansas. Whereas the Kansas student society stresses the separation of the student-faculty worlds, in New York student society works to maintain the communications network of the school, "clarifying standards and controlling behavior based on norms that are mutually held by students and faculty" (Bloom 1965:155).

Some critics suggest that the differences in the two interpretations reflect real differences between the two schools. Becker and his colleagues deny this explanation and argue that Kansas is a typical medical school whose differences from Cornell are not significant on this point. While to an anthropologist it is difficult to believe that racial, religious, economic, and rural-urban differences between New York and Kansas will not be reflected in medical school learning environments, Bloom's Downstate Medical Center study suggests that student-faculty opposition also exists in New York City. Students were disappointed because their expectations of an advanced and adult educational experience were not realized. Both faculty and students exhibited "*a defensive type of withdrawal behavior*" that, for the faculty, meant an emphasis on research "where achievement can be rooted in the clear standards of one's own discipline and not [as in teaching be] subject to the vagaries of an unclear set of institutional standards" (Bloom 1973:2). Teaching activities, he found, were narrowed to the goal of fostering technical competence in students. They, in turn, also withdrew, manifesting a "passion for anonymity" and a strategy of "don't make waves" (*Ibid.*).

However one wishes to conceptualize student-faculty relationships, it is clear that in all medical schools student "cultures" or "societies" exist that fulfill a variety of functions in helping aspiring doctors through their training years.

3. Detached concern and the loss of idealism

Most beginning medical students see themselves as idealistic; they are more interested in "helping people" than in making money. Yet as they progress through medical school, they find that they must avoid excessive emotional involvement with patients. The harsh realities of death, chronic invalidism, and physical disabilities make it difficult if not impossible for the doctor routinely to be closely attached to patients. Beginning with their first exposure to cadavers in freshman anatomy courses, sometimes presented in deliberately brutal fashion by teachers, students begin to learn what has been called "detached concern" (Fox 1959). To be objective in diagnosis and treatment of patients, physicians feel it best that they not be caught up in the patient's suffering; concerned, yes, but not emotionally involved. Perhaps this is why doctors rarely treat members of their own families, delegating this task to a trusted colleague.

Some researchers feel that the acquisition of "detached concern" is accompanied by increasing student cynicism. Eron, for example, found that as medical students progress through their 4 years of training, they score higher on a "cynicism" scale and lower on a "humanitarian" scale (Eron 1955). This view has been widely shared within and without the profession. Almost from the beginning, however, it has been questioned, and mounting evidence suggests that it is not really valid today. The results of the Kansas study in the late 1950s suggested that the apparent cynicism of the medical student is more situational than generic, and that the students never lose their original idealism about the practice of medicine. The student "tends to ignore death and human suffering because, being a student and not a practicing physician, he is not in a position to do anything about either. Thus, he tends to regard patients as objects from which he can learn" (Becker and Geer 1963:173). As time passes, students become more realistic in what they can and cannot do as practicing physicians, thus modifying their original nonspecific idealism. The authors conclude that, "while students may (from the layman's point of view) acquire a cynical veneer during the four years of medical school, they also acquire specific notions of how to implement the underlying idealism with which they entered medical school and propose to do this when they do become practicing physicians" (*Ibid.,* 173. See also Becker and Geer 1958).

A much more recent study utilizing attitude and value scales administered to two classes of students at the beginning of their freshman and end of their senior years suggests that the humanitarian-cynicism scales convey a false impression of what actually happens (Perricone 1974). Rather, the new evidence suggests that medical students become *more* socially concerned as they progress through medical school, and not the other way around. "In fact, it appears that many medical school faculties have been 'humanized' by their students; that is, they have begun to offer courses in the social and behavioral sciences which meet this new demand for a more relevant and committed approach to the problems of health care delivery" (*Ibid.,* 546).

4. Medical career specialization

Although most students entering medical school either expect to go into general practice or have not yet made up their minds about possible specializations, a majority decides on the latter course prior to graduation. In part, this is a reaction to the realization that it is impossible to acquire all of the medical knowledge they would like to control, and that it is better to go deeply into a single field; also in part, it is because of the intellectual challenge of a particular medical specialty. Psychologists and medical doctors have been particularly interested in the prediction of specialty selection, including general practice. Two types of data, regarded as influencing decisions, have been used in their studies: the personal characteristics of students who choose different specialties and student perceptions of the attractions of different specialties, together with the personalities of doctors in these specialties. Illustrative of the former approach is a study of 630 students entering six medical schools in the fall of 1967. It revealed that half of those choosing general practice came from towns with populations of less than 10,000, while only one-fifth of those choosing other careers were "small town boys." The general practitioner group also had the highest percentage of Protestants. In contrast, only 1 percent of the aspiring general practitioners were Jewish, a correlation that presumably reflects the fact that a majority of the Jews had a big city background. The choice of psychiatry as a specialty correlated with big city background and, perhaps surprisingly, with Catholicism or no religious affiliation (Paiva and Haley 1971). Students selecting surgery or internal medicine were found to differ from the others in two important ways: more had previously worked in medical settings, and nearly three-fourths had personal contact with a physician who influenced their image of medicine and career choice (*Ibid.*).

Another study searches out the correlation between subjects studied in college and medical specialty selected. It was found, among other things, that future psychiatrists had significantly less college science, and future pediatricians significantly more, than their classmates (Geertsma and Grinols 1972). The "personal characteristics" approach to understanding specialty selection raises interesting policy questions. If the variables and correlations identified prove to be widely consistent, then it should be possible, through the selection process for admission to medical school, to manipulate the percentages of students entering the several specialty fields. For example, by selectively discriminating against applicants whose characteristics suggest that they may chose surgery, the rapid increase in numbers of surgeons during recent years might be slowed or brought to a halt. That there are ethical as well as policy dimensions to this way of looking at medical school admissions is obvious.

Illustrative of student perception of characteristics of physicians in different specialties is a widely quoted article by Bruhn and Parsons. In this study, based on questionnaire research at the University of Oklahoma, it was found that the general practitioner was perceived to be deeply interested in people, patient, and had a friendly personality. The surgeon, in contrast, was judged to be domineering and arrogant, aggressive and full of energy, and mainly concerned with his own prestige. The internist was characterized as sensitive to a wide range of factors when evaluating a medical problem, but only modestly interested in intellectual problems. Student perceptions of the psychiatrist were not unlike those of the general public: emotionally unstable and a confused thinker (Bruhn and Parsons 1964). Not surprisingly, students who had already decided to enter a specialty saw their chosen specialty in a more favorable light than students at large. More students planning to enter psychiatry, for example, "see the psychiatrist as interested in intellectual problems and fewer see him as emotionally unstable and a confused thinker than do students not electing psychiatry as a specialty" (*Ibid.*, 45).

In a more recent study entering freshmen medical students at the University of Colorado were asked to rate five medical specialties — psychiatry, pediatrics, general practice, internal medicine, and surgery — with respect to (1) status, (2) "social attractiveness" (of the personalities of typical practitioners), and (3) "believed similarity-to-self." The results conform in a general way to findings from other studies. Surgery was given the highest status, followed in order by internal medicine, pediatrics, psychiatry, and general practice. But "status" and "social attractiveness" are not the same thing. On the social attractiveness scale general practice was rated first, pediatrics second, internal medicine third, psychiatry fourth, and surgery in last place. This is a striking expression of the ambivalence toward surgery felt by medical students. Finally, with respect to perceived "similarity-to-self," pediatricians were in first place, followed by general practice, internal medicine, psychiatry, and surgery. Breaking down the groups, it is found, as in the Bruhn-Parsons study, that each specialty group sees itself in the most favorable light: in the Colorado study each specialty group perceives higher status, social attractiveness, and similarity-to-self in its chosen specialty than do any of the other specialty groups (Fishman and Zimet 1972).

CONCLUSIONS

In bringing this chapter to a close, two disparate points may be made. The first is that, obviously, medical anthropologists have had very little to do with the study of medical education in the United States. Yet, interestingly, anthropological *research methods* have proven to be highly suitable for this kind of research. In Merton's early work, *The Student-Physician,* for example, we read that "Particularly in the early part of the present investigation, and to some extent throughout its course, field observers have been conducting what is tantamount to *a social anthropological study* of the medical school and of associated sectors of the teaching hospital. The field workers have observed the behavior of students, faculty, patients, and associated staff in the natural, that is to say, the social setting. They have made observations in lecture halls and laboratories; have, upon invitation, accompanied physicians and students on rounds to note the social interaction there; have spent time observing the kinds of relationships which develop between student and patient, and between student and teacher. These many hours of observation have been recorded in several thousand pages of field notes, making up a detailed account of recurrent patterns of students' experience" (Merton et al. 1957:43. Emphasis added).

Similarly, in *Boys in White,* Becker and his associates describe research that is purely ethnographical: "We had no well-worked-out set of hypotheses to be tested, no data-gathering instruments purposely designed to secure information relevant to these hypotheses, no set of analytic procedures specified in advance" (Becker et al. 1961:17). Furthermore, "We concentrated on *what* students learned as well as on *how* they learned it. Both of these assumptions committed us to working with an open theoretical scheme in which variables were to be discovered rather than with a scheme in which variables decided on in advance would be located and their consequences isolated and measured" (*Ibid.*, 18). Participant observation was the principal research method, and the emphasis was on "student culture."

Much more recently Bloom, describing his research for *Power and Dissent in the Medical School,* writes that "The most salient question, it was decided, concerned the collective character of the institution, and not its separate, more readily measurable assets" (Bloom 1973:11). "To answer such questions," he continues, "the first step logically appeared to be *in the tradition of ethnography* — to observe, interview and participate — to become immersed in the environment and follow the flow of its currents of opinion and behavior" (*Ibid.,* 12. Emphasis added).

The research experience of these sociologists suggests that the problem to be studied, and not narrow professional identification, dictates the appropriate research methodologies, and that in spite of their past lack of interest, medical anthropologists can profitably participate in studies of American medical institutions.

The second point, which should also be obvious, is that most of the classic sociological studies of medical education were made from the mid-1950s to the mid-1960s (Fox 1974:198). Yet between the mid-1960s and today, dramatic changes have been made in medical education: particularly, it is now more flexible in its incorporation of multiple "tracks," allows more electives and free time, and is generally more concerned with social aspects of medical practice. Fox asks the question, and answers if affirmatively, as to whether there is a new type of medical student as well. We believe it worthwhile to quote at length from her sympathetic portrait.

"Despite the efforts being made to recruit young persons into medical schools from minority groups and nonprivileged social class backgrounds, the new medical student is likely to be a white, middle-class man. He arrives in medical school garbed as he was in college, in blue jeans or modishly colored sports slacks and tieless shirt. His hair is long, though usually not unkempt, and he may have grown a moderate beard. When he begins to see patients, he often starts wearing a tie and sometimes a jacket. He may also cut his hair on the short side of long and shave more often.

"Although he is fiercely intent on being accepted by a medical school, unlike his counterparts in the 1950s, the new medical student is generally a 'late decider.' It is not uncommon for him to have committed himself to becoming a doctor in the second half of his college career. Because of his 'delayed' decision, he may have had to take his premedical courses in summer school or in a concentrated postundergraduate year. In any case he worked hard and competitively as a college student in order to earn the very high grade point average that made him eligible for admission to medical school. Although aggressively achievement oriented, he deplores it in himself, his classmates, his teachers, the medical profession, his parents, and in American society more generally. . . .

"Such a student is likely to have come to medical school with declared interests in fields like community medicine, public health, family medicine, psychiatry, and pediatrics (pediatrics, he feels obliged to explain, because it is 'holistic' medicine and entails caring for 'new and future generations'). In the end, these may not be the fields that he will actually enter. But they express the interpersonal, moral, and societal perspective on physicianhood that he brings with him from college. He is actively committed to such humane and social goals as peace, the furtherance of civil rights, the reduction of poverty, the protection of the environment, population control, and improvement in the 'quality of life' for all. He extends the principles that underlie these commitments to medicine and the role of doctor. In his view, health and health care are fundamental rights that ought to be as equitably distributed as possible. For this reason, as he sees it, the physician should care for the psychological and social, as well as physical, aspects of his patient's illness. He should have a 'genuine concern for the total health of mankind.' He should take initiative in dealing with some of the factors at work in the society that adversely affect health and keep the medical care system from functioning optimally to maintain and restore it. Although the doctor's social dedication should be universalistic, the new student believes, he has special obligations to those who are disadvantaged or deprived.

"The new medical student is also staunchly egalitarian in his conception of the doctor, the doctor's relationship to patients, and to non-physician members of the medical team. The student disapproves of 'all-knowing' or 'omnipotent' attitudes and behavior on the part of physicians. . . . He maintains that physicians should approach patients 'as human beings' with 'respect for their feelings and opinions' rather than as 'diseased specimens' or persons incapable of understanding their own medical condition and the treatment prescribed for it. . . .

"A 'detached concern' model of relating to patients is not one that the new medical student admires or would like to exemplify. Rather, he places the highest value on feeling with the patient. Although he recognizes the need for maintaining some objectivity in this relationship, he does so with regret. For him, to feel is to be human and compassionate, it dignifies and heals; and the more one feels, the better. However scientifically and intellectually inclined he may be, the student believes that it is all too easy to distance one's self from patients (and from one's own humanity) by approaching the problems for which they seek the doctor's aid in an overly conceptual and technical way. . . .

"Finally, although the new medical student would not downgrade the importance of training, knowledge, skill, and experience for competent physicianhood, he also insists that the doctor's values, beliefs, and commitments are a critical part of his ability to help patients, reform the health care system and 'improve society.' . . . And so, the physician must be more than just a 'good human being.' He must also concern himself with the 'philosophical' problems of life and death, suffering and evil, justice and equity, human solidarity and ultimate meaning in which his chosen profession and the human condition are grounded.

"This is the simultaneously critical, activist, and meditative ideology or world view that the new medical student brings to medical school. How predominant it is, whether it will prevail, and whether in interaction with the medical school environment and the social climate of the seventies it will produce a new type of physician will be revealed in time, the professionalization process, and, perhaps, studies of it" (Fox 1974:217-219).[1]

NOTES

[1] Reproduced from *Ethics of Health Care,* pp. 216-219, with the permission of the National Academy of Sciences, Washington, D.C.

chapter 11

Professionalism in Medicine: Nursing

THE REVOLUTION IN NURSING

The field of nursing is of interest to anthropologists for at least two major reasons. First, like any other sociocultural system, it offers its own research opportunities, some of them more or less unique and others shared with medicine and other fields: training for a professional role, professional role interactions, the dynamics of an entire profession seeking higher status and greater independence, and women's liberation as played out in a particular profession. Second, nursing provides one of those rare instances in which a sociocultural system studied by anthropologists is itself providing anthropologists who bring their special insights into the culture of the group from which they come, who can correct and refine the interpretations made by outsiders, and who can make their own studies in the best anthropological tradition. For methodological reasons, then, nursing is of exceptional importance to anthropology.

This is a recent development. Although one of the earliest studies of nursing was made by an anthropologist (Brown 1936), only in recent years have nurses and anthropologists shown much professional interest in each other. As late as 1969 Leininger could find only 19 published articles on anthropology and nursing (Leininger 1970:38). She also found only eight full-time anthropologists teaching in schools of nursing in 1968 (*Ibid.,* 41). The picture is changing rapidly, however. Increasing numbers of anthropologists now seek careers in association with the nursing profession and, as we have just pointed out, more and more nurses turn to masters and doctoral programs in anthropology and other behavioral sciences to broaden their traditional horizons. An indication of this rapid growth is the subsection on anthropology and nursing in the

Society for Medical Anthropology, which is one of the largest and most active units in the Society. Whereas formerly, most studies of nursing were made by sociologists and psychologists, and even physicians, today we find nurses with behavioral science backgrounds working as full partners in the ongoing study of the profession. If we include professional nursing journals and other publications as well as behavioral science literature, as we must certainly do, the bulk of the contemporary work on nursing comes from the pens of nurse-researchers.[1] The solid underpinning of such research is made clear in a recent article by Leininger who, in a survey of U.S. nursing schools, found that in 1976, 14 offer some kind of Ph.D. degree, with an additional 21 planned by 1980. As of March 1976, 437 nurse-faculty members in these programs held a doctorate (Leininger 1976).

The profession of nursing obviously is undergoing a revolution undreamed of a few years ago. Nurses today are better educated than their counterparts of a generation ago, they are more concerned about their professional roles, they aggressively seek greater independence in offering health care, and they are achieving a recognition and status not part of traditional roles. These changes are partially a natural consequence of better education, of devolution of some of the physician's traditional tasks to nurses, and of higher career aspirations. And, in part, changes reflect the feeling of women that for too long they have played roles subordinate to those of men: women's liberation, in a word. The latter position is eloquently stated by Martin. "To my mind, nursing is now involved in a major battle. The primary issue is power. The cause for which the battle is pitched is greater nursing influence and control over the nature and delivery of health services. Our adversaries are predominantly medicine and health facilities administration. Certain segments in nursing are in the front lines and carry forth the fight; others are in supply lines and support the battle; yet others are in the adversaries' camp. It is an undeniably sexist conflict, for nurses are mainly women while physicians and health facilities administrators are mainly men. The opposing segments within nursing are mainly conditioned sexist women, effectively socialized in their own inferiority" (Martin 1975:95-96).

The rapid changes in nursing make it difficult to paint an up-to-the-moment picture of the contemporary profession, and many of the "classic" behavioral science studies of nursing are now in greater or lesser degree out of date. At the same time, they are interesting as a part of the history of the study of professionalization; they also provide invaluable baselines from which to measure the changes that are taking place, and they suggest problems for contemporary and future research. Faced with this dilemma we propose to call attention to some of the "classical" problems that first focused behavioral science research on nursing and then point out how this picture, still found in a great deal of the literature on nursing, is changing under contemporary pressures.

The themes in nursing that have attracted behavioral science research (and to a considerable extent still do) to some degree parallel those of medicine: recruitment processes, student backgrounds, motivations, education and educational experiences, career patterns, and professional roles and specialties. But they also include other themes that seem peculiar to the role of nurses, especially viewed in historical perspective: the frequent frustration experienced by nurses caused by the difference between their image of what they are supposed to do (give bedside care) and what they often end up doing (administration); the strained relationship between nurses and doctors; and the anomalous position of a profession, many of whose members lack major attributes usually associated with professional status.

NURSING EDUCATION

To understand the professional and behavioral science problems that have been identified in nursing education, it is important to know the kinds of settings in which nursing education takes place. In point of time the oldest institution is the hospital-based, 3-year training program that leads to a nursing diploma. The first three *diploma programs* in the United States appeared in 1873; their numbers mushroomed for the next half century: 15 in 1880; 35 in 1890; 432 in 1900; and 1023 in 1910 (Bullough 1975a:8). Although they represented a major advance over previous nursing education, with the passage of time and as levels of education rose in the United States, their defects became more and more apparent. Although some diploma programs in major hospitals undoubtedly gave (and give) fine training, diploma programs proliferated in hundreds of hospitals that had neither staff nor other resources adequate to the task: a hospital nursing school more often than not was valued as a cheap supply of labor for patient care.

From 1910 to 1920 nursing schools began to be established in major universities. These 4-year courses are called *collegiate* or *baccalaureate programs,* and they lead to the Bachelor of Science degree in nursing. In contrast to diploma programs, university programs stress the scientific base of nursing, including both physical and behavioral sciences. Formal university affiliation and university-level courses obviously placed nursing on a significantly higher professional level than was possible when there were no such programs. Teaching staffs, trained to teach, many of whose members hold advanced degrees, including the Ph.D., emphasize basic and theoretical knowledge to a degree impossible in hospital diploma programs.

A third type of nursing education, known as the *associate degree program,* is given in 2-year community colleges. This is a relatively recent program, dating only from 1952, and less behavioral science research has been done on it than on the other two. Yet it is now the most numerous type of program, as the following comparative figures (Knopf 1975:1) show.

Year	Diploma	Associate	Baccalaureate
1955	963	19	156
1965	821	177	198
"Most recent"	461	598	313

In other words, during the past 20 years, diploma programs have fallen by half, baccalaureate programs have doubled, and associate degree programs have increased by an astonishing 3000 percent!

These changes in relative numbers of each of the three types of educational institutions are, of course, reflected in changing admission and graduation figures (A.N.S. 1976:63, 67).

Admission Changes

Year	Diploma (%)	Associate (%)	Baccalaureate (%)
1963-64	72	8.5	19.5
1972-73	28.5	42.4	29.1

Graduation Changes

1962-63	81.6	4.6	13.8
1972-73	36.1	41.8	22.1

Clearly, associate degree programs have become the dominant type of nursing education in less than a generation, and this growth at the expense of diploma programs will continue in the future.

With respect to recruitment of nursing students, Corwin and Taves some years ago summarized the results of a number of studies that give a good "profile" of beginning nursing students. They found that a quarter of students were rural in origins, and that as a group they appeared to be more religious than the population at large. Just as considerable numbers of medical students follow physician fathers, so were a good many nursing students daughters of nurses. Nursing students differed from medical students, however, in that they made their career decisions at an earlier age, and at an earlier age than university students in general. They also appeared to come from families lower on the socioeconomic scale than medical students. This evidence was misleading, however, since even then baccalaureate program students tended to come from middle- and upper-class families (as did other university students), while those in diploma programs, considerably more numerous as a group, came from somewhat lower socioeconomic backgrounds (Corwin and Taves 1963: 197-199).

A more recent analysis reveals changes in this profile, although socioeconomic level continues to correlate positively with the type of nursing education sought. Knopf has found that associate degree students (not dealt with in the Corwin/Taves study) are "more heterogeneous as regards sex, marital status, age, and ethnic group than those in the other two programs. These entrants probably were capable high school students, may very well have had some nursing school experience before admission to the associate degree program, and came from families of moderate means. The diploma students were relatively homogeneous as regards sex, marital status, age, and ethnic group. They were more likely to be Roman Catholic than students in the other programs, were good students in high school, and came from families of moderate means. Entrants to baccalaureate degree schools were young, white, and single, probably very good students in high school, and may have come from families where the father had a higher educational level and income than fathers of students in the two other groups" (Knopf 1975:9-10).

One of the most interesting changes in recruitment patterns is the relatively larger number of men entering nursing programs. While in absolute terms the numbers are small, the trend is apparent. Type of program correlates with percentages of males, associate programs most attractive (or open?) to males, and baccalaureate programs least open. Knopf's study shows that in associate degree programs 4.2 percent of students are males; in diploma programs, the figure drops to 1.3 percent; and in baccalaureate programs, a mere 0.7 percent are men (Knopf 1975:108, Table A-1).

THE EDUCATIONAL EXPERIENCE

Olesen and Whittaker have given us one of the most complete and insightful accounts of nursing students in a baccalaureate program: the School of Nursing of the University of California in San Francisco. In origins, students conformed to the profiles just given for baccalaureate candidates; they were found to be from middle- and upper-class families. Almost half of their fathers were in professional, managerial, or other white-collar jobs, and only a few were from genuinely blue-collar backgrounds. Most of the students were white and Protestant. A majority had begun to consider a nursing career at a surprisingly early age: 28 percent between the ages of ten and fourteen and an additional 27 percent between the ages of fourteen and sixteen. Very much as with medical students, career choices were influenced by family members and health professionals, particularly practicing nurses. For many, a boyfriend played an important role, not in selection of a nursing career, but as a "legislator of student plans" (i.e., the decision as to whether to continue or not in nursing, following the first tentative proposal) (Olesen and Whittaker 1968: 95).

A well-marked student culture was found in the San Francisco school and, as in medical schools, its role was adaptive, to provide strategies for enabling students to meet the challenges of their training and to provide norms of behavior calculated to strengthen the position of the class as a whole. Although the faculty was younger than most medical faculties (more than two-thirds were not yet forty), a great deal of suspicion of faculty intentions underlay the forms taken by student culture. Students often were uncertain of what was expected of them and of the criteria used in judging their performance. Consequently, students attempted to "psych out" each instructor (i.e., to define what might be asked on examinations and determine what other general forms of behavior brought approbation). As early as their first year, a majority of students decided that important areas of manipulation meant knowing when to seek advice from a faculty member, being able to understand and discuss one's feelings about the patient with the instructor, and being able to present new and interesting material on the patient to the instructor. In the intensely interactional setting of the nursing school, students feared that they were being judged "offstage" as well as "onstage," that behavior and action in settings not normally defined as appropriate to the evaluation process were noted by faculty members and used in judging their overall performance. Consequently, students came to feel that they must be constantly on guard against revealing facets of their personality or behavior that might be used against them.

When the importance of what Goffman has called "impression management" became clear to students, and when they realized that they would be judged in a variety of settings, they developed the technique of "fronting" to present themselves in the best possible light to each instructor. "After determining what the instructor wanted, the students tried to assume the appearance of the identity, which was not necessarily an integrated part of the self, although they expected the faculty to believe that it was" (*Ibid.,* 173). To achieve a basically successful "front," a student "had to blend the correct mixture of assertiveness, humility, and awkwardness" (*Ibid.,* 177).

As in other student cultures, there was much pressure on the individual to cooperate with and maintain solidarity with her colleagues. Interestingly, as in peasant society, the common pressures acted as a performance leveler, with ostracism as a threat against those students who attempted to exceed academic standards, to practice "rate-busting." Students expected each other to do well, but not to stand out significantly. "Displays of superiority, of underhanded methods of attaining good grades, and other similar tactics served only to isolate the offender from her fellows" (*Ibid.,* 188). The effort put forth by a student, and her grades, were carefully scrutinized by her peers. At the same time, students who fell behind, who were deemed worthy of help, received assistance from their more successful colleagues. In spite of the pervasiveness of the leveling ethic, some students were driven to excel, so they sought ways to do this without threatening their classmates. Usually this consisted of denigrating any rewards that suggested extra effort, such as announcing a high grade by saying, "What a surprise, I made an A." Bedside nursing also offered opportunities to stand out, without threatening the basic academic standing of the majority of students. Yet, while competition flourished in private, student culture on the whole "outwardly discouraged the education for excellence which faculty in their fondest hopes desired for students" (*Ibid.,* 195).

NURSING DILEMMAS

Benne and Bennis have pointed out three "dilemma" areas in nursing that have received major behavioral science attention: (1) the nurse's frustration caused by the difference between her image of what she feels she ought to do and what she actually does; (2) nurse-doctor friction; and (3) the many problems of the drive for professionalization (Benne and Bennis 1959:380). These three topics will be considered in turn.

1. The nurse's role: ideal and actual

Schulman has coined the happy phrase "mother surrogate" to describe the ideal, bedside, ministering stereotype of the nurse's role (Schulman 1958). He finds this role to be feminine, characterized by affection, intimacy, physical proximity, and identification with and protective care of a "ward" (i.e., the patient). Certainly the lay public's traditional image of the nurse's role is that of the ministering angel who smooths sheets and fluffs pillows, who places a cool and reassuring hand on a feverish brow, and who through an air of professional competence quiets the patient and promotes the healing process. Historically, at least, this Florence Nightingale image of the "real nurse" has been in the minds of a high proportion of young women who enter this career.

   Perhaps nurses really did fulfill this role at an earlier time. But in the context of the modern hospital, which employs three-fifths of all nurses, this time is well past. As Schulman says in a subsequent article, "There is no longer any doubt that professional nursing has left the patient's bedside and that a majority of professional nurses have resolved the mother surrogate-healer role conflict by abandoning, circumventing or sublimating the mothering functions of the nurse's role" (Schulman 1972:233). Nurse's aides and other less well-trained personnel now in fact do the bulk of "nursing" care in modern hospitals, because it has been found to be more economical to use the skills of nurses in supervisory and managerial positions. Yet the mystique of patient care lingers on; "The power of the bedside imagery," says Strauss, "is such that nurses who work away from the bedside (notably administrators and educators) must justify their activities in terms of ultimate benefit to patients" (Strauss 1966:96).

Many nurses like, or believe they like, bedside care, and so often try to avoid administrative responsibility. Yet "One of the ironies of the profession is that the administrators (along with the educators) have gotten most of the prestige and power, and the bedside nurses have gotten little of either" (*Ibid.,* 97). The reward system of the modern hospital — except in special ways that will be mentioned shortly — discourages patient care by nurses because most of the formal rewards are for skills that involve little patient contact. As Hatton puts it, "in order to advance in the hierarchy of any institution they [nurses] had to take administrative posts, drawing them away from patients. This situation often left the patients without optimum nursing care, and the nurses frustrated about pushing paper and attending committee meetings" (Hatton 1975:118).

2. Nurse-doctor relationships

Although conflicts and tensions between nurses and other health personnel exist, "Few who have talked under free conditions with nurses will deny that the nurse-doctor relationship is the one most pregnant with tensions and misunderstandings on both sides" (Benne and Bennis 1959:381). Barbara Bates attributes this to the fact that the physician is "the last of the autocrats," a person who regards nurses and other allied health personnel as nonprofessionals whose task is to work for him rather than for the patient. If he considers these people at all, he considers them as his servants, not as associates or colleagues (B. Bates 1970:130).

This appears not always to have been the case. At the time Florence Nightingale defined the nurse's role as rigorously subordinate to the physician, sex relationships were so structured that it would not have occurred to nurses that this was not entirely appropriate. With growing sexual egalitarianism in the United States, the way in which nurses formerly worked encouraged a team approach to patient care, although the role of the physician was, of course, clearly dominant. Until the 1930s, most nurses served as "private duty" nurses in homes, where they were on 24-hour duty, often for weeks at a time. The nurse, between the physician's home visits, was his eyes and his ears; it was important for her to report to him on his calls all of the details of the case since his prior visit, and the physician who had confidence in his nurse felt that he had a major ally in promoting recovery. "Regardless of individual exceptions, relations between the doctor and nurse appear to have been generally warm and friendly" (Brown 1966:178).

But with the transfer of most nursing services to hospitals, with increasing division of labor, the nurse lost control of the patient's environment and came to be little more than one among a number of cogs in an increasingly impersonal health care system. Yet, as Brown points out, "Private duty nursing, prior to its decline, is the model against which nurses, physicians, and patients — consciously or unconsciously — still continue to measure their expectations of what nursing is or should be" (*Ibid.,* 181).

The rigidly superordinate-subordinate physician-nurse relationship is what perhaps rankles nurses the most. While recognizing the physician's greater training in skill and diagnosis, they feel that they often are inordinately restrained in what they can do to make the patient more comfortable, to recognize medical needs that escape the physician, and to communicate these needs to the physicians. Nurses were, at one time, taught how to relate to physicians: to be respectful, to recognize their greater knowledge, and to obey their instructions, even to stand as they entered a room. Physicians, in turn, assumed such deference from nurses.

Carol Taylor describes the often inflexible role into which the nurse has sometimes been forced in what she calls "the approach ritual," the process by which the patient is "prepared" by the nurse for the physician. She gives the account of a woman who had arranged to have the wax washed out of her ears in a physician's office. The patient is led by the nurse (who is acting under the physician's instructions) through a relentless sequence of taking weight, temperature, pulse, and blood pressure. The woman's repeated protestations that "I'm only here to have my ears washed out" are just as repeatedly met with: "Doctor wants all patients prepared in this way." Finally, after being asked to lower her dress to the waist and finding the blood pressure cuff refastened around her arm, the patient explodes: "You don't need to take it again, for heaven's sake. My blood pressure does not go up when I strip to the waist." To which the nurse responds: "Doctor wants all patients cuffed in case *he* wants to take their blood pressure" (C. Taylor 1970:109).

However, as in every interpersonal situation, there are both formal and informal channels of communication. When informal channels are recognized and utilized in good faith and mutual respect, the doctor-nurse relationship can be highly effective. Stein has described the "doctor-nurse game" and the unwritten rules that permit the nurse to make subtle recommendations to the doctor, recommendations that would rarely be made overtly. The technique, says Stein, is for the nurse to make her suggestions appear to originate with the physician. He gives the following vignette as illustrative of the process. A nurse calls the resident on hospital call at one o'clock in the morning to report that Mrs. Brown, who has just learned of her father's death, cannot sleep. The nurse is giving facts and also hinting that because of grief she should be given a sedative. The doctor recognizes the cue, and asks what has been helpful to Mrs. Brown in the past. The nurse replies that Pentabarbital mg. 100 was quite effective the night before last. This "disguised" recommendation is what the doctor has been waiting for: "Pentobarbital mg. 100 before bedtime as needed for sleep; got it?" he asks, a note of authority in his voice (L. Stein 1971:187).

"A successful game," says Stein, "creates a doctor-nurse alliance; through this alliance the physician gains the respect and admiration of the nursing service. He can be confident that his nursing staff will smooth the path for getting his work done. His charts will be organized and waiting for him when he arrives, the ruffled feathers of patients and relatives will have been smoothed down, and his pet routines will be happily followed, and he will be helped in a thousand and one other ways" (*Ibid.*, 188). The nurse, in return, enjoys a reputation as a "damned good nurse," and her status and prestige rise accordingly. But in spite of the possibilities of the doctor-nurse game, the contest is uneven; its rules do not permit the professionally motivated nurse to achieve the prestige for herself and for her discipline that she may wish.

3. The drive toward professionalization

Nursing, along with medicine, has attracted the attention of behavioral scientists concerned with the broad theme of "the professions." Students of the professions have, at least until recently, considered nursing's claim to professional status to be anomalous. For the past century nurses have considered themselves to be professionals, and they are so considered by the lay public. Yet compared to other occupational groups normally considered to be professional, they have displayed significant differences in education, distinctive specialized knowledge, autonomy, and career commitment. Most registered nurses, for example, have lacked a bachelor's degree, normally considered a minimal requirement for professional status, and they have lacked the autonomy of action thought characteristic of a profession, since most have worked under the supervision of medical doctors and in hospitals in accordance with the rules of these institutions. Nursing also has struggled to identify a body of specialized knowledge not borrowed from medicine to distinguish its practitioners. It has been suggested, too, that a majority of nurses have appeared to lack the career commitment that is the mark of a profession. Surveys of women nursing students have revealed that most of them desire and expect marriage fairly early in their careers, and that marriage and motherhood will have priority over nursing in their life choices (e.g., Glaser 1966:25). Career ambivalence has also been read into undergraduate withdrawal rates, since about one-third of nursing students failed to complete their education (Corwin and Taves 1963:201). Finally, it has been suggested that career ambivalence is apparent in the average hospital turnover rate, which has been appreciably higher than in other "industries," and in the high percentage of nurses that work only part-time.

It is important to stress, however, that many of the features of nursing that led to these interpretations have changed dramatically in recent years, and it is also possible to interpret many of the data in a quite different, and positive, light. It can be argued, for example, that in a complex society, with multiple life choices and with the sex role problems of women in choosing between or combining a traditional career as wife and mother with a profession, nursing is a remarkably adaptive occupation, a happy compromise which permits women to have the best of several worlds. Good nurses are always in demand, and basic office and hospital nursing skills (but not those needed for intensive care units) are sufficiently standardized so that very little learning time is required in taking up a new job. Hours are flexible, so that wife-mother-nurses have more options in seeking full- or part-time work outside the home. In short, nursing seems to be an occupation admirably suited to the many women who want to combine working with home roles.

Traditional *undergraduate* nursing withdrawal rates also are not an accurate reflection of career commitment, since comparison normally is made with withdrawal rates of medical students who are in *graduate* status. The data may, in fact, be interpreted to mean a strong commitment to nursing. As Knopf recently has written, "Withdrawal before completion is not a phenomenon peculiar to nursing schools. In fact, in comparison with other post-high school education, nursing may be on the plus side in retaining its students" (Knopf 1975:15). Today, as the figures we have given indicate, more and more nurses hold a baccalaureate degree, and increasing numbers are taking masters and doctoral degrees.

Turnover rates in nursing also appear to be significantly lower than those used in earlier interpretations of professionalism in nursing. In 1972, 69 percent of registered nurses were employed, 65 percent of these on a full-time basis. Of employed nurses, 72 percent were married. Not surprisingly, more unmarried nurses (84 percent) were working than married nurses (66 percent) (A.N.S. 1976:2).

To a point, the profession of nursing can be analyzed in terms of the same variables used in analyzing other professions, such as medicine, law, and the ministry. Yet there is one variable — sex — that has been noted but muted in earlier analyses of nursing, which more than any other factor explains the frustrations, anger, and perplexities often felt by nurses, and especially by the leaders in the field. Nursing is, and has been since the time of Florence Nightingale, a sex-segregated occupation based on a sex role stereotype that relegates the woman to a subordinate status in a male dominated society. In a lively and perceptive analysis, Ashley describes the fears of earlier generations of American physicians that nurses might become too well educated and hence pose threats to their control of medicine. She traces the "sexist and paternalistic attitudes toward nursing" that can be traced through the public pronouncements of eminent medical authorities during the past three generations, attitudes expressing the belief that good nurses are born, not made, that the nurse exists to be a doctor's helper, and that overeducation, not undereducation, is the greatest threat to the performance of the nurse (Ashley 1976; Chap. 5). Particularly galling has been the past assumption that members of the medical profession should not only control medical education, but nursing education as well. Increasing numbers of nursing leaders and authors now see the drive for professionalism and the attempt to raise the status of the profession as inextricably bound to the women's rights movement (e.g., Cleland 1971; Lamb 1973; McBride 1976).

EXTENDED NURSING ROLES

A great many circumstances, the women's rights movement among them, are encouraging the development of new and expanded nursing roles marked by increasing autonomy and professional responsibility. These changes are apparent within hospitals and in so-called "extended roles" in the community. In both settings we find a renewed emphasis on patient care. Within hospitals the new roles are best exemplified by the "clinical specialist," whom the Bulloughs describe as "a well-trained nurse (often with a masters degree) who gives bedside care to seriously ill patients" (Bullough and Bullough 1971:1). Clinical specialists offer bedside care in intensive care units where neonatal, pulmonary, and coronary patients require constant monitoring; the presence of medical personnel capable of, and authorized to, make split-second decisions about courses of action that may spell the difference between life and death is vital. The skills required in these units require 6 months to a year of preparation before competence is achieved. Because of this additional education and the autonomy that these nurses exercise, they enjoy high professional status and commensurate monetary remuneration (Bullough 1975b:56).

The magnitude of the changes inherent in physician-nurse relationships in intensive care units — and specifically in coronary care — are made clear by Berwind. "Once the nurse became recognized as the essential figure in the coronary care unit, the physician increasingly deferred to her in matters related to the technical details of the unit, and to her expertise and knowledge, collaborating with her in the best interest of the patient. This new collaboration and interdependence between medicine and nursing has led to increased delegation to the nurse of authority to act in the absence of the physician, and has made it difficult to determine where the doctor's function stops and the nurse's begins" (Berwind 1975:86).

Other systems of improving patient care are also being devised. In one, known as "primary nursing," the nurse assumes responsibility for a patient, usually from admission to discharge. The nurse cares for the patient when on duty and leaves a care plan for others to follow when she is not present. This approach can be combined with intensive care units as, for example, in pediatrics (communicated by Barbara Koenig).

In one recent development nurses have emerged with special skills that place them as participants in the training of physicians. This is in the context of Pediatric Cardiology Associate, a new medical role inaugurated at Driscoll Foundation Childrens Hospital of Corpus Christi, Texas that normally requires 18 months training beyond the nursing degree. The Pediatric Cardiology Associate fills the vital function of relieving busy cardiologists of many of the routine but highly sophisticated aspects of patient examination and patient care. Interns and residents in pediatric cardiology at the hospital are currently instructed in basic heart care delivery as working members of a heart team of which the Pediatric Cardiology Associate is a respected and important member.

Outside the hospital the expanding roles of nurses may be seen in part as a function of inadequate numbers of general practitioners (specialists now outnumber general practitioners more than three to one) to meet patient need and in part as a response to new health care demands arising from longer life spans, the rise of chronic illness, and greater recognition of the importance of mental health care. Today increasing numbers of nurses work as "nurse practitioners," a role viewed by at least one writer as "the most significant event in nursing during the last 30 years" (Mauksch 1975:1835). Nurse practitioners deliver a variety of community-based services such as pediatrics and other family care, psychiatric care, and the like. A few practitioners are self-employed, others work as partners in interdisciplinary groups, and still others are institutional employees. The common denominator in all cases is that they assume major responsibilities that transcend those of most hospital work apart from those of nurse-clinicians.

Nurse practitioners sometimes are mistaken for the parallel new role of "physician's assistant," a movement that nurses view with ambivalence. On the one hand, as Bullough points out, "the highly visible physician's assistant movement was an important factor in the development of nurse practitioners. It demonstrated that the delegation of a significant number of medical tasks was possible" (Bullough 1975b:57). Nurses who work as physician's assistants usually have had at least 2 years of education beyond basic nursing, and they perform commensurately more specialized tasks. But it is a role that still maintains the traditional physician-nurse superordinate-subordinate relationship, which growing numbers of nurses find distasteful. For this reason a small but growing number of nurses are turning to community-based health services in which they are licensed in their own right; they are therefore legally accountable for their own acts and authorized to engage in private practice.[2]

To summarize, the nursing profession is changing at a rate unparalleled in its history. After a long period of concentration of their work in hospitals, this trend has been arrested; in the future more nursing services will be provided outside institutions. Nurses who remain in hospitals will require increasingly specialized patient care skills, so that prestige and status will not be exclusively dependent on administrative roles. And health maintenance in ambulatory settings will absorb larger numbers of nurses.

All of these trends favor the efforts of nursing leaders who, for many years, have skillfully worked to bring to nursing full recognition as a mature profession. For example, the phasing out of hospital-based diploma programs in favor of associate degree and baccalaureate programs is not accidental; it represents a conscious part of a broadbased strategy to achieve full professional status for nursing. Specifically, the Committee on Education of the American

Nursing Association has pushed to make nursing an academic and not an apprentice type of education.

Another aspect of the professionalization drive has been apparent for a longer time. Glaser notes the "sociological axiom that every occupation in achievement-centered societies tries to enhance its public image and self-image, and a common method is to acquire prestigious tasks from a previously more respected occupation" (Glaser 1966:27). Most nurses not primarily concerned with the prestige quest look to medicine and their technical roles within the practice of medicine for prestige. But the leaders of nursing recognize that the crumbs that may be allowed them from medicine's table are insufficient for a distinctive professional status. They have turned instead to other high-status fields that until recently were marginal to medicine, namely the behavioral sciences.

Some years ago Benne and Bennis noted that "Nurses, in rooting their profession in universities and academic life, have tended to form alliances with the social and behavioral sciences much more fully than the medical profession generally has done" (Benne and Bennis 1959:381). This alliance is particularly apparent in the case of medical anthropology and medical sociology. For example, fully one-fourth of all applicants seeking admission through Berkeley to the new Medical Anthropology doctoral program of the University of California in 1976 were registered nurses, and three of the six successful applicants were nurses! In contrast, only one medical doctor applied (and was accepted). Nursing is perhaps the only occupation a major part of whose claim to professional status is based on the mastery and creation of theory and data not traditionally thought of as central to that occupation.

As we have pointed out, anthropologists have devoted relatively less attention to the topics discussed in this chapter than to those in the remainder of this book. Yet it is clear that anthropologists are eminently suited to the kinds of research involved and that in the future they will play more active parts in institutional analysis. In fact, the striking thing is, as pointed out in Chapter 10, that when sociologists have studied medical institutions (i.e., entire "systems" in which the interrelations of the parts are equally if not more important than the relationships between several variables), they have made major use of anthropological research techniques. Many frankly speak of their "ethnological" orientation.

NOTES

[1] The research of nurse-anthropologists is not, of course, limited to nursing alone; it includes a wide variety of health topics such as delivery of health care to minority groups and folk medical beliefs and practices.

[2] For more information on the wide range of contemporary nursing roles see Davis et al. 1975.

part 4

ROLES FOR MEDICAL ANTHROPOLOGISTS

chapter 12

Anthropologists and Medical Personnel

INTRODUCTION

In the preceding chapters we have been largely interested in the substantive topics with which medical anthropologists have dealt. We have defined the field, told a little about its history, shown the relationships between biological and sociocultural factors in health and disease, and looked at man's health behavior in both the traditional and contemporary worlds. Our concern has been to examine medical systems and medical institutions and see what conclusions anthropologists and other behavioral scientists have drawn from these analyses.

In this and the following three chapters we shift our emphasis. We ask not just what medical anthropologists have learned, but also what practical roles they have and may play in programs designed to bring better health care to the world's people. These are questions of application of knowledge and its consequences. We are interested in the role of anthropologist in the planning and execution of international health programs and in nutritional problems at home and abroad. We are also concerned with the role of anthropologist as constructive critic, one who asks searching questions about the appropriateness of many contemporary American medical practices, one who searches for alternative approaches to serve the same end.

To return to the distinction made in Chapter 1 (between the anthropology *of* medicine and anthropology *in* medicine), we are now "in," viewing ourselves as health workers as well as anthropologists, concerned with how, and to what ends, we can most effectively work with other health personnel. A continuing relationship between professionals from distinct fields can be maintained only if the relationship is seen to be mutually advantageous by both parties. Anthropologists have benefited greatly from their association with physicians, nurses, health educators, and public health planners over a generation or longer; their factual and theoretical bases have been enlarged, and they have enjoyed the personal contacts. Anthropologists feel that the health sciences have learned a great deal from them and that it can learn much more. It is to these two themes that we turn in this chapter.

CONTRIBUTIONS OF THE HEALTH SCIENCES TO ANTHROPOLOGY

1. Access to rich and varied research sites

The comedian Bert Lahr once remarked that in order to be a successful dog trainer, a person needs courage, skills, intelligence, resourcefulness — and, of course, dogs. In order to be a successful medical anthropologist, a person needs good basic anthropological training, research experience, a sense of problem, empathy for other human beings — and, of course, access to the medical world and medical people who are willing to have anthropologists around. In the Western world, "medical people" may mean the dean of a medical school, a hospital superintendent, a private physician, or the occupants of numerous other medical roles including, of course, patients. The health sciences offer to anthropology specific research areas directly comparable to traditional subjects such as tribes and villages. There are schools of medicine, nursing, and public health; there are mental and community hospitals; there are health centers, ambulance services, emergency rooms, endemic disease control programs, birth control projects, and health education programs. The same research methods the anthropologist uses in traditional work usually can be applied to these settings. When studied, reports on these cultural and social systems vastly extend the range of data on which we draw in developing our basic hypotheses about human behavior. Few if any institutions so permeate life as do those concerned with disease, the healing of the sick, and the maintenance of health. In all societies, and certainly in contemporary American life, they influence almost all aspects of culture. Health institutions, using the term in the widest sense, are enormously productive research settings for anthropologists.

But it is not enough that there be medical institutions to be studied. The anthropologist must have *access* to such institutions. In the past anthropologists have gained their own access to tribal communities, peasant villages, and urban slums. The study of tribal and peasant medical systems has required relatively little cooperation from other professionals, other than the basic permissions that enable the anthropologist to visit a foreign country. To gain access to a peasant community, an anthropologist tries to obtain a letter of introduction from a higher authority that explains to the village leaders what he is interested in. From then on it is up to him. If the anthropologist can persuade the villagers of his good intentions, he will be permitted to remain. If not, doors will be closed in his face, and he has no alternative other than to leave.

The picture is quite different in contemporary medical institutions. A letter of introduction will not alone do the trick. The anthropologist, to work in a hospital or a medical school, *must be accepted by the establishment.* Access to these rich research areas is controlled by members of the establishment. Only if they feel that the anthropologist (or other behavioral scientist) will, in the course of research, be able to provide them with information they consider useful, or at least will upset no apple carts, will they be sympathetic to his presence. In a tribal community or peasant village an anthropologist is rarely in the way in a physical sense. Space normally is not at a premium. This is not so in a hospital. Space is costly and buildings are designed for specific tasks that do not include provision for an anthropologist in operating theaters, examination rooms, laboratories, and wards. The anthropologist can easily be in the way, his presence resented because of this. Patients, too, may not fully understand his presence and may communicate their discomfort to nurses and physicians. There is also the matter of records, usually confidential, that are not stored in public archives. There must be guarantees of confidentiality if anthropologists are to be given access to such sensitive material.

There are other problems associated with research in contemporary medical institutions. The director of a hospital or the dean of a medical school may be fully supportive of research within his institution. But personnel much farther down the ladder of importance may not be persuaded. They may feel, for example, that the researcher is in fact an efficiency expert, studying their role performances with a view to making recommendations that will be injurious to their interests. Although their positions may be humble, their resistance can seriously interfere with behavioral science research.

For example, in the hospitals and clinics where the anthropologist French worked as a member of a multidisciplinary team, only "nurses and social workers were considered [by other team members] to be reasonable candidates for the task of interviewing" (French 1962:223). Other interviewers, she reports, were only slowly and often grudgingly accepted. They found "no natural allies already established in the institution. In contrast, physicians, nurses, and clerical workers coming into the medical school and hospitals find other persons already present in positions like their own. . . . In circumstances in which there is structural ambiguity, fairly persistent stresses may develop, particularly if there is competition for any 'commodity' e.g., patients, time, or space" (*Ibid.*).

2. Intellectual stimulation

Like other sciences, anthropology is not self-sufficient in generating new hypotheses and research topics. We are stimulated by the data and ideas from other fields. Yet in today's universities — the home of a majority of anthropologists who do research — the degree of intellectual contact we experience with colleagues in other fields is probably less than a generation ago, when departments and universities were smaller. To the extent that our professional contacts are limited to the university setting and to anthropological and other behavioral science colleagues, we cut ourselves off from a great deal of exciting thought and work.

Medical and public health specialists are interested in many of the same things that interest anthropologists: human behavior, how behavior changes, and the relationships among disease, environment, and culture. But in most instances they approach these matters in somewhat different ways from anthropologists; they ask different kinds of questions, whose significance the anthropologist may readily appreciate once his attention is called to them. Association with able medical and public health personnel provides stimulation comparable to that anthropologists find from their own colleagues, and often such contact opens whole new vistas not only for thought and research, but also for permanent professional involvement.

CONTRIBUTIONS OF ANTHROPOLOGY TO THE HEALTH SCIENCES

We believe the utility of anthropology to the health sciences lies within three major categories. First, anthropology offers a distinctive way of looking at both whole societies and their individual members; it uses a holistic, or systemslike, approach in which the researcher constantly asks how all of the parts of the system fit together and how the system itself works. Anthropology's "distinctive way" also stresses the importance of cultural relativism in evaluating ways other than our own, the need to interpret indigenous forms within the context of the culture in which they are found instead of judging them against Western or supposedly universal standards.

Second, anthropology offers an operationally useful model to explain the processes of social and cultural change and to aid in understanding the conditions under which members of "target groups" respond to changed conditions and new opportunities. Anthropologists have not formulated "laws" that predict accurately all individual and group behavior under specified conditions, but they are able to foretell quite accurately the probable range of choices that will be exercised when people find themselves in new situations that permit or force on them new behavior forms.

Third, anthropology offers the health sciences a flexible and effective research methodology for exploring a wide range of theoretical and practical problems that are encountered in medical programs. As one element in this methodology, anthropology offers the concept of "premises" or "assumptions" that underlie behavior; these premises afford an important key to understanding the rationale of acts that, when viewed from vastly different cultural assumptions, often seem irrational.[1]

1. The anthropological perspective

Although the "anthropological perspective" embraces many points and sub-points, two main concepts are particularly appropriate to the health sciences: a "holistic" approach based on the idea of cultural integration, and "cultural relativism." Both of these concepts will be discussed in turn.

(a) THE HOLISTIC APPROACH
Anthropologists, as should be clear by now, are systems-oriented; they emphasize the whole at the expense of the parts. Unlike other social scientists, anthropologists have been little interested in the discrete units within the system for their own sakes and the influence of specific independent variables on dependent variables. The anthropologist's holistic view of cultural and social phenomena is a logical outgrowth of the history of the discipline. Initially it was a historical rather than a social science, and its task was seen to be the recording and preserving of as much as possible of the way of life of primitive (or preliterate) peoples prior to the great changes brought in them by contact with the Western world. During the first third of the present century, anthropologists were trained to visit tribal groups, live with or near them, observe, and question the oldest people about life in their youth: in other words, to find out everything possible about the full cultural spectrum. Since there were few trained anthropologists and many tribes, there was no room for specialization; anthropologists had to be generalists, recording and interpreting data on geography, material culture, economic life, social organization, religion, art, folklore, recreation, language — everything people did or could remember having done.

This early definition of problem, with its attendant research conditions, molded the basic assumptions that underlie our research today. By the reality of culture, early anthropologists were led to appreciate that the boundaries of cultural institutions are not precise, that one institution cannot be studied alone but only in the context of all other institutions that bear on it and on which it bears in turn. Religion, for example, was quickly found to be intimately related to mythology and folklore, magic, world view, the family, economic life, art, and beliefs about death, sickness, and curing. Economic activities were found to be closely tied to environment, game animals or agricultural products locally available, cooperation and competition, division of labor within the family and within the village, interethnic relations (through markets and other exchange relationships) and, often magic, religion, and witchcraft. The same network of relationships was found to hold for all other topics and institutions.

So, almost automatically, when engaged in research or data analysis, anthropologists direct their attention to the entire system. They speak of the "functional interrelationships" of the parts of a culture, of its "integration." By these expressions anthropologists mean not only that the distinct parts of a culture are intimately associated with each other but that this is a functional, purposeful association, in very much the same sense that an automobile engine is a purposeful association of discrete parts, a dynamic system. The units are integrated one with another so that there is logic, coherence, and pattern in the total assemblage.

From this, a basic corollary, already discussed in an ecological context in Chapter 2, follows: *no change within the system can occur in isolation.* Any change in the nature, structure, or role of a unit implies corresponding changes in the units most closely associated with it. Just as an increase in the diameter of the cylinders of an automobile engine calls for larger pistons, a heavier flywheel, a redesigned carburetor, and many other modifications, so a new village health center — to operate successfully — requires changed village attitudes toward the role of government (usually seen as exploitive instead of beneficial), the sharing of health care services with new nonlocal specialists, more complex decision-making processes when someone in the family falls ill, and many other adaptations.

Furthermore, any major change produces secondary and tertiary changes, so that innovations defined as beneficial in one respect may carry social and ecological costs that outweigh anticipated benefits. In the abstract, abundant inexpensive power is desirable. Yet the price includes things such as air pollution, destruction of the land over coal seams, contamination of the oceans from tanker spills, the damming of wild rivers, and the innundation of mountain valleys. Modern superhighways are efficient ways of moving freight and passengers, and most of us appreciate them. But their price has proved to be more than financially high: destruction of urban neighborhoods, withdrawal of large amounts of land from productive purposes, a discouraging effect on rapid transit, billboard blight in scenic areas, noise, and pollution. And many Americans have come to limit daily exercise to a round trip between the front door and the carport.

The basic lesson, so often learned the hard way, is that a single innovation such as may be considered by a public health office, an agricultural program, or an educational organization, defined in narrow professional terms, should never be evaluated solely in this narrow context. It must be evaluated only in the context of all of the potential advantages *and* costs in the form of undesirable changes. Only if the proposed change appears to offer more positive than negative features is a program justifiable.

The problem, simply stated, does not seem difficult to solve. In fact, it is usually *enormously* difficult, at least in a complex society, where the primary interests of different groups of people are not the same. The interests of conservationists are to maintain nature as it is, to stop the building of dams or atomic power plants. But the nature loss may seem of secondary importance to local residents who will benefit from construction in the form of employment, increased local sales, perhaps future tourist trade, and the like. Residents near large airports are jeopardized by airport expansion: more noise, more automobile traffic, and greater danger from accidents. However, wider metropolitan needs make more and larger airports essential, and their utility increases in proportion to their nearness to the centers of the populations they serve.

In short, we usually are not dealing with simple costs and benefits; our decisions are not of the either-or variety. Instead, we are faced with a new (for most of us) type of decision: the *trade-off* decision. The questions are: How much air pollution is acceptable for the convenience of the private automobile? How much risk can we take with nuclear power plants in order to meet future power needs? How much high-cost medical expense for relative rare and exotic diseases can society afford, at the cost of less than adequate care for millions of other people? More and more the decisions that society must make will be of the trade-off variety. And we are not well equipped to make these decisions. How do we balance the legitimacy of varied interests? How do we determine the maximum social good? What, in fact, does such an expression mean? We do not know. But, if we recognize that planned changes have costs as well as benefits, and if we accept that we must try to evaluate every proposal in the widest possible context, we will avoid many of the mistakes of the past.

(b) CULTURAL RELATIVISM
The second element in the anthropological perspective that we believe to be critical to the health sciences is cultural relativism, a willingness to look sympathetically on the cultural forms of other societies and not judge them against the "norm" of our own. In greater or lesser degree all peoples are ethnocentric; at heart, they believe that their values and attitudes, their ways of living, are the best. Even primitive people who concede the superiority of steel knives over stone knives, who admire the European's material mastery of environment, still feel, for the most part, that the essence, the ethos, the spirit of their cultures are best. Pride in one's culture is a good thing. It provides a sound psychological identity to the individual and assures him of a respected place in life. It is only when ethnocentrism is carried to extremes — generally a sin of "civilized" peoples more than of peasants or tribal peoples — that it becomes dangerous. Hitler's racial ethnocentrism was an exceptionally destructive manifestation of this ill but, in lesser degree, members of the white race, since they began exploring the world and establishing hegemony over the native peoples of America, Asia, and Africa, have assumed that their technological achievements and political and military power also made self-

evident their moral and intellectual superiority. Condescendingly, they have thought of the "lower races" of mankind as peoples needing leadership and moral guidance from the West. They viewed their position as the end product of a long period of cultural evolution, the advance from savagery through barbarism to civilization. Being most evolved, they took it for granted that the merit or moral value of any custom of the lesser peoples should be measured against their institutions: The family? Monogamy. Religion? Monotheism. Economics? Free enterprise. Art? The Impressionists. Tribal peoples often were regarded as children with potential, but needing time to learn the ways of adults before fully participating in life. Many people also believed that less complex civilizations were indicative of lesser intellectual ability in a racial sense, just as within European countries members of the upper classes assumed that they were on top because, "as cream rises to the surface," superior genetic endowment had placed them where they belonged.

Since their earliest days, anthropologists have played a major role in breaking down these stereotypes of cultural and racial differences. They have been sensitive to their influences in programs of planned change. Many able and well-meaning technical experts in the fields in which aid is most commonly given — health, education, agriculture — genuinely believe that they have no ethnocentric feelings about the peoples with whom they work. Yet subconsciously these feelings are there, as revealed in the belief that the job is to transplant the American answer to a problem to countries where the socioeconomic and cultural context is drastically different, and where the American solution may be entirely unsuited. In nutrition, for example, the National Reseach Council has, for many years, drawn up recommended diets for Americans, specifying caloric intake, vitamins and minerals; these recommendations are based on foods available and commonly consumed in the United States. International nutrition programs have been based on the American National Research Council recommendations, including abundant milk, animal protein, fresh fruits and vegetables, and grains. The assumption has been that, in improving diet, it is necessary to abolish what already exists and to start from scratch with the superior American pattern. Foreign nationals trained in the United States sometimes have unquestioningly accepted the American patterns and have also assumed they must eradicate their local food patterns in order to build better ones. Yet Heyneman points out how powdered milk sent in vast quantities from Canada and the United States to malnourished peoples has caused violent diarrhea among many Indians and Africans. "Tropical and Asian people unaccustomed to milk often undergo severe intestinal upset or develop allergic reactions to it. The response is rejection, and A.I.D. powdered milk has been thrown away by the ton, fed to animals, used for fertilizer, even paved airplane runways" (Heyneman 1971:305).

The anthropologist's emphasis on cultural relativism is not simply a broad-minded plea for tolerance of the ways of others; it is an essential foundation for successful technical aid, in health and in all other fields. The operational rule underlying the principle of cultural relativism is that before attempting to implement change, one must learn the reasons why the traits under attack are present, the roles they fulfill, and their meanings to the people. Usually there is a very good explanation for the presence of any trait, and to evaluate it in narrow, Western professional terms may do more harm than good. Thus, frequent attempts have been made by well-meaning agricultural experts to replace the simple wood or iron-tipped "scratch" plow of the Mediterranean, Latin America, and parts of Asia with the moldboard plow that cuts deeply and turns over soil from a depth of several inches. Often it has been found, however, that on the thin, stony soils where scratch plows have been used for hundreds and thousands of years, the moldboard cuts too deeply, bringing gravelly soil to the surface, to the detriment of crops. The traditional plow's shallow furrow has proven to be ecologically more sound than the "improved" deep cut.

By the expression "cultural relativism" anthropologists do not mean that all customs are equally adaptive in the contemporary world: they are not. Customs and cultural forms that arose in past generations as adaptive and hence realistic responses to local conditions often survive long after they cease to be effective or during a period when they become less and less adaptive. No culture, including our own, is able to adapt its cultural forms to new conditions as soon as they appear; there is always a lag. In the United States the present ancient system of measurement based on inches, feet, yards, miles, ounces, pounds, tons, and so forth clearly is less adapted to the contemporary world than the metric system, which is now generally used in the "underdeveloped" world. However, our conversion can come — if possible at all — only at enormous financial and social costs.

In the developmental context an awareness of cultural relativism simply means that it is usually wise to find out what already exist and then try to build on the strengths of the present system instead of trying to wipe it out and begin anew with an imported solution. This principle is well illustrated by dietary problems in Brazil. There, relatively small amounts of meat, when combined with the ubiquitous bean, provide a combination of animal and vegetable protein entirely adequate to nutritional needs, at far less expense than the "more meat" American approach. In Mexico the mineral lime used in making tortillas is an excellent substitute for the lime Americans find in milk. Primitive and peasant diets also often include seasonal fruits, herbs, grubs, and insects that are highly nutritious; their continued use should be encouraged, not discouraged just because they may seem repulsive to foreign experts. Where population pressure or poverty is not too great, nutritional deficiencies in traditional diets usually can be remedied by relatively small changes in or additions to what is available. The nutrition specialist who is trained to look for the good in what already exists finds a far simpler task than the one who sets out, National Research Council handbook in pocket, determined to bring good diet, American style, to benighted people.

2. Change: process and perception

The topic of change is implicit and explicit in most chapters in this book. Here we wish to talk especially about perception and the ways in which the concept has been used (and misused) in health programs.

Rising standards of health and increasing longevity both in the West and in developing countries have, until now, been achieved through improved health care services, and particularly through legislation promoting environmental sanitation, compulsory immunization, and specific campaigns aimed at diseases such as smallpox and malaria. Now, however, we are reaching the limits of these approaches, and more and more we see better health as dependent on individual changes in health behavior. Increasingly the responsibility for good health is thrown on the individual instead of the state or the medical profession. With infectious disease almost conquered, our attention turns to the "diseases of civilization" that are caused or aggravated by excessive use of tobacco and liquor, obesity, immoderate consumption of foods believed to cause arteriosclerosis, and just plain unhealthy personal life-styles. As life spans lengthen, the diseases of old age become more frequent; although they cannot be cured, their onset can be delayed and their progression slowed down. The war against these kinds of diseases requires a distinct strategy: through education people must learn what is involved, and they must be motivated to take the steps that will mean better health.

The field of health education has developed to meet this need and, in Western countries at least, it has had a considerable impact on health habits. At the same time, health educators often seem to take an overly simplistic view of their problem: communicate successfully with people so they will understand their health problems (usually as we, not they, define them) and they will want to change their behavior. It is assumed that an understanding of the danger attendant on not changing, or the health advantages to be obtained from changing, are sufficient to motivate people to modify their behavior. Following this assumption, health campaigns make extensive use of audiovisual materials in the form of movies, dramas, skits, film strips, posters, flipchart presentations, and the like. *Perception* is seen as the critical variable. Effective audiovisual techniques require that the pictures or symbols used must be perceived, or understood, or interpreted in the same way by both health educators and audience. When both are members of the same or similar socioeconomic and cultural groups, it is reasonable to assume that this will happen. But it is not reasonable when the work is carried out in a cross-cultural setting, where the mode of presentation and the symbols used are a function of advanced educational systems, and the audience is from a distinct culture.

The literature is replete with cases where lack of awareness of differential perception across cultural boundaries negated the effect of well-intentioned health campaigns. One of the best-described, and in many ways successful, efforts to bring better health to non-Western people through the use of scientific medicine and public health education is that of the Institute of Family and Community Health of Natal, South Africa (Kark and Steuart 1962). One program was set up in a planned community for Africans in Durban. Since, by Western standards, many of the African women were overweight, a campaign against obesity was launched. One poster showed a broken-down, heavily overloaded truck with a flat tire, beside which stood a very heavy African woman. The caption read "Both carry too much weight." Most Westerners would get the message without difficulty. Not so the members of the target group. Two African women on whom the poster was tested, both literate in English, "felt that the poster depicted a rich woman with her own truck loaded with possessions. This they said was the reason for her being fat. They added that she must also be happy" (Gampel 1962:301). Like other African women, these two interpreted obesity according to their cultural norms to mean prestige, wealth, and happiness. In this community it was felt that "a man of importance should be broad of girth and that a woman who is fat bears testimony to a husband's care and attention. A thin woman is said to be unhappy and neglected" (*Ibid.*). Other women agreed it was bad to be overweight, but none noted the analogy of the overloaded truck.

A second poster with the caption "Who do you prefer to look like?" showed a thin, radiant woman with a broom and a badly overweight woman with her hand on a table. The intention of the European artist was to compare the energy and vitality of a slim woman who could sweep and dust easily with the inactivity and discomfort of a fat woman who had to lean on a table for support. There were diverse African interpretations, none correct. "One person thought that the fat woman was the mistress of the home and that she was insisting that certain work be done by the other woman. She was fat because she had a servant. . . . Another individual thought that the fat woman was ordering the other woman to polish the table. . . . Fatness was associated with prestige, and the obese and slim women were seen in the role of mistress and servant respectively" (*Ibid.*, 301-302).

If the symbolic meaning of obesity had been known to the artist, the campaign might have taken a different, and perhaps more successful, approach. On the other hand, it is equally possible that it would have failed, for unless a health problem is perceived as such by the members of the group, they are going to feel that the exhortations of the public health workers are silly. Health problems are defined in two ways: by health workers and by the population at large. Unless or until there is congruence in definition, health behavior is not apt to change.

The problems associated with a novel medium may also make audiovisual materials incomprehensible to some audiences. In an antimalarial campaign among the Bush Negroes of Surinam, films proved to have great drawing power, but most viewers missed the messages. One woman complained that when she watched the movie she could not understand the talk, and when she concentrated on the voice she could not follow the pictures. A village leader constantly asked to have the film turned back to the preceding scene: "It was good," he said, "Why do you make it change so fast?" (Barnes 1968:25). Clearly, rapid comprehension of a sound film required experience that the Bush Negroes had not had.

3. The anthropological research methodology

In contrast to other behavioral scientists, anthropologists carry out their research in a relatively unstructured, wide-ranging, exploratory fashion. Anthropologists are less concerned to isolate tight little research problems for which they can work out aesthetically satisfying research designs than to hit on general, broad problems that will lead the worker along many lines of discovery. Although a narrow, controlled focus is recognized for some studies, the anthropological research methodology stems not from the laboratory or from statistical correlations, but from a natural history type commitment to field investigation where the essential mandate is to go out and find what is there. In medical programs and in other directed culture change programs, where the social, psychological, and cultural factors are almost infinite and are not clearly known, this exploratory, open-ended approach yields important dividends. The investigator is much more likely to uncover the critical elements in any specific situation than the researcher who has drawn his design in more circumscribed fashion. Determination of medically significant categories *follows* rather than precedes research, and subsequent quantification can be based on relevant findings. Even medical sociologists, as we have seen, when studying whole "systems" such as hospitals or medical or nursing schools, often turn to the anthropological approach for at least part of their data.

The primary data-gathering technique evolved by anthropologists is "participant observation." Ideally this means that the anthropologist lives in a community, participates in many aspects of its life, and observes firsthand the behavior of most, if not all, of the members of the group. The term often has been carelessly used. An anthropologist can "participate" in the life of a community in many ways, but he is never a full participant. Most people, Middleton has pointed out, "have no particular reason to be pleased that we are there and. . . . have the power to ignore us, to snub us, or simply to get rid of us if they wish to do so" (Middleton 1970:2). At best, the anthropologist lives with a village family and thus has access to a great deal of what is normally private behavior. More frequently perhaps, the anthropologist rents a house or has constructed a native hut for himself, thus achieving a bit of badly needed privacy. He visits in many homes, talks with many people, attends many of their public and private ceremonies, perhaps becomes a godparent to the children of close friends, exchanges goods and services with the local people, and otherwise develops a more or less intimate acquaintance with the community and its people. One of us, as a consequence of election to a small town school board, was able to participate in wide-ranging discussions of cafeteria menus, health programs, and other matters in a working-class community otherwise suspicious of "outsiders." The information so obtained about values and attitudes could not have been gathered in any other fashion. In comparison to most sociologists, political scientists, geographers, and psychologists, the intimate knowledge that the anthropologist acquires about a community is phenomenal. But the anthropologist, even under the most favorable conditions, never becomes a full member of the study community, and "going native" by adopting local costume and customs will not make him so. Rather, a sustained challenge is the anthropologist's need to live as a human being with other human beings and yet also have to act as an objective observer (Middleton 1970:2).

The anthropological holistic approach to the interpretation of social and cultural forms and primary dependence on participant observation to gather data and generate hypotheses are outgrowths of, and closely related to, the usual anthropological research sample (i.e., a community). Communities are, however, of many different types, and when anthropologists work in communities that reflect their own socioeconomic background — as is increasingly true in health studies — they face new or augmented difficulties not usually found in traditional work. These include, as Ablon recently has pointed out, the increased visibility of the anthropologist because of diminution of the cultural gap, the problem of maintaining objectivity when one is both an outsider *and* insider, and the heightened possibilities of value conflict between anthropologist and informants (Ablon 1977).

In spite of these difficulties, the traditional focus of the community well equips anthropologists to contribute to developing trends in medical education and practice. "With the rapid expansion of community medicine, beginning in the 1960s, a significant new dimension has been added to the medical system — one that will hopefully develop new links between medical schools, health practitioners in communities, and social and/or behavioral scientists" (Pelto and Pelto 1978:403). Anthropologists, by training and experience, are eminently suited to research the wide range of problems inherent in community medicine.

Anthropologists, while not strangers to survey research, tend to be suspicious of some of its results, especially in traditional communities where the question "What do you think about . . . ?" from a total stranger at the door arouses suspicion. Often people dissimulate; at other times they genuinely do not know what they think. And at still other times what people are sure they believe is belied by their actions. Foster once observed an episode in survey research in Tzintzuntzan. When a knock was heard on the patio door that leads to the street, one of the grown daughters answered. She talked for perhaps 10 minutes, and returned so convulsed with mirth that she could hardly talk. A university student was making an "economic study" of several villages in the region. He was going from door to door asking questions such as "What is the income of this family for a day? For a week? For a month?

How much is spent on food? On clothing? On other items." "Just imagine," said the daughter, stiffling her laughs, "that he thinks we would tell such things." She had given him the first figures that had popped into her mind, figures that had nothing to do with reality, but he had gone away happy, and his data, along with similarly "good" data from other village householders (in the event they did not slam the door in his face), would be fed into a computer and emerge accurate to the third place beyond the decimal point. Not only did the daughter not give the correct figures; she could not have given them even if she had wanted to, since village families do not think in these terms, and bookkeeping and budgeting city style are unknown. Some doors are *never* opened to strangers. Many rural French houses, for example, characteristically have high walls topped with jagged pieces of glass, locked gates set in spike-tipped fences, and vicious dogs. It is not an atmosphere amenable to casual doorstep data collection.

Anthropologists who engage in urban research inevitably find that they must engage in more complex methods of data gathering and analysis than their colleagues in villages. The nature of the sample, the conditions of city life, and the research problems call for more sociological methods. Coded responses, scales, indices, ratings and scores derived from examiners' observations, tests and measurements of subjects' reactions or performances, and quantified content analyses often derived from computerized programs — any or all of these approaches (e.g., Clark and Anderson 1967) are legitimately used. But when research involves an essentially integrated system — a tribe, a village, or a medical institution — then the loosely structured, flexible, exploratory approach is indispensable, at least for part of data gathering and analysis.

4. Premises

Anthropologists want not only to observe and describe the behavior of members of a group, but also to explain *why* people behave in the ways they do. Why are peasant villagers often uncooperative and critical of each other? Why do physicians often seem to lose interest in, or avoid, dying patients? Why do non-Western peoples often "irrationally" spend money on fiestas instead of accumulating much-needed capital? We have found that one very important way to understand better the "why" of human behavior is to search for the deep-seated premises, or assumptions, or "postulates" that underlie and, we believe, determine behavior. The premises or assumptions of which we speak characterize individuals but, as diagnostic tools, they are more profitably thought of as applying to groups such as tribes, peasant villages, entire nations, minority ethnic groups, bureaucracies, and professions (cf. Foster 1969:67-70, 97-105; 1973:18-21, 179-180).

All of the members of a group share a series of common cognitive orientations, a comprehension, an interpretation, an ordering of the phenomena of the world about them that set the conditions under which they feel life is lived. Some of these premises lie at a conscious level, while others are deeply subconscious. Middle- and upper-class Americans can verbalize premises such as "hard work brings its own reward," "there's always room at the top for able people," and "opportunity expands with each passing generation." In contrast, not many Americans are aware that the jocular remark, "You only live once," reflects a primary premise underlying our life strategies — a premise so deceptively obvious that its true meaning is unappreciated. It is only when we contrast the "one-life" strategy of Americans with the "many-lives" strategy of Buddhists, who think in terms of countless reincarnations, in which present behavior influences future life experiences, that we can understand much of our behavior. And only when we realize the Buddhist premise can we understand how their "irrational" economic behavior in squandering money on temples and on the support of monks is, in fact, economic rationality of the highest order (Spiro 1966).

Speaking specifically of health, the widespread African belief that death and illness are always caused by sorcery is a premise that explains to non-Africans much African health and interpersonal behavior; it stands in contrast to the premise of scientific medicine that, whatever the specific cause, it can be understood in naturalistic terms.

Premises (or assumptions or postulates) must be thought of as lying on a continuum from overt and conscious to covert and subconscious. Whether the former or the latter, they play enormously important roles in determining individual and group behavior, since all behavior seems to be a response to or a function of the premises that, whatever their degree of consciousness, characterize an individual.

(a) Professional premises

The behavior of health personnel (and some of the consequences of this behavior) can often be better understood if we think of it as a function of professional premises. Public health personnel often justify their activities on the ground that the enjoyment of good health is the maximum value to most people. Yet, as we saw in Chapter 8, illness may have a variety of social roles that to some people under some circumstances make it highly attractive. "Health is good: Period!" is another statement frequently heard. But when we see the consequences of "good" health — the population explosion — we realize that perhaps it is good only in relation to other factors, such as food, space, employment, and population control. The concern of public health specialists to sanitize and immunize probably has had more to do with bringing about overpopulation than the efforts of any other group. Yet only within the last decade have they realized their responsibilities in population control. Even while acknowledging past unconcern with a serious problem, new rationalizations are sought to excuse this unconcern. With population problems, the rationalization takes the form of saying that "human beings are the primary form of capital for every country," thus implying that what is happening is really not bad. But, obviously, human capital, like other forms of capital, is desirable only if it can be used productively. Human life is hardly "capital" in the slums of the great cities of the world where unemployment is high and poverty is extreme.

A basic assumption of nursing is that patients want to leave the hospital as soon as possible. For most patients this is probably correct. But it overlooks the fact that for some people the hospital is a haven, a refuge from the unpleasant facts of life; the last thing on earth these patients want to do is to leave the hospital.

Medical doctors practice on the basis of a whole series of premises. The most comprehensive is that human life is sacred and that no effort should be spared to save or prolong it. This premise, noble as it is, has led us to today's debates as to what constitutes death. The technical devices that permit "heroic measures" in sustaining life sometimes make it almost impossible for a human shell to stop functioning gracefully. Often, it seems to outsiders, medical premises play overly important roles in justifying the physician's work to himself and to other physicians. At times, one feels that the patient is little more than the battlefield in which the physician and his mortal enemy — death — play out the struggle. To the extent the physician can ward off death, he is the winner; the patient, however, is often the loser. It is when we realize the physician's frequent view of death, the asumption that it is the primary enemy, that we appreciate why physicians often seem to lose interest in the dying patient, avoid his room, and leave him to the attention of nurses. The enemy has at last won the battle; it is now time to turn to other fights, where perhaps the odds will be better.

Other premises of physicians include things such as: health problems are those so defined by medical doctors; the good physician personally attends to the health needs of his patients; auxillary health personnel exist largely to conserve the doctor's time; a patient dying on the operating table is a greater blow to the surgeon's self-image than one who expires in the recovery room. The behavioral consequences of this last premise are well known to all medical people.

Premises may be fairly accurate reflections of social reality, or they may be far from the truth, badly outmoded by the passage of time and change in or disappearance of the conditions that brought them into being. The "human life must be saved at all cost" was a reasonable premise at a time when physicians had few therapeutic resources; outcomes were quickly decided. But it must be questioned when, with the passage of time, the conditions that brought it into being have vanished. Our point, however, is not to express our assessments of contemporary medical premises. Rather, we are concerned to make known that there are "ways" of looking at human behavior shared by professional groups and to urge that we be aware of these underlying premises when judgments about human behavior are made.

NOTES

[1] Ragucci recently has discussed the anthropological approach to problems of the health sciences, particulary in the context of nursing research (Ragucci 1978).

chapter 13

Anthropology and Medicine in a Changing World I: Lessons from the Past

In the next two chapters we discuss international public health, an area in which anthropologists and health personnel have had a fairly long, and in many ways mutually satisfying, relationship. In the present chapter we describe some of the things that anthropologists have learned about the dynamics of introducing scientific medical practices into societies that previously have been dependent largely or entirely on traditional services. Our orientation is essentially the past, and our definition of "problem" is narrowly that of health personnel engaged in international work.

Although in Chapter 14 we continue with some of these same topics, our orientation changes to the present and future. We are particularly concerned with contemporary trends that seem to us to be not fully appreciated, and with their implications for health planning and policy. Among these trends are, on the one hand, the growing success of scientific medicine in winning acceptance and, on the other hand (and perhaps anomalously), the rapid growth of alternate or alternative medical systems, particularly in urban areas. Thus the problem (as viewed by formal health personnel) is no longer that of scientific versus traditional medicine. Instead, the question has become one of roles, or possible roles, for scientific, traditional, *and* alternative medical systems in meeting health needs as defined not only by health personnel but also as perceived by the consumers, the patients.

THE PUBLIC HEALTH "PROBLEM"

In its ability to prevent or cure infectious diseases, to eliminate the scourges of the past, such as malaria and smallpox, to prevent infant mortality, and to mend through surgery, scientific medicine has no peers. Almost all peoples who have been exposed to scientific medicine, whatever their cultural levels, acknowledge its superiority, at least with respect to some illnesses. Most would like greater access to scientific medicine. In spite of such instances as the Indian government's support of Ayurvedic academies, the health care programs of all of the countries of the world are based largely on scientific medicine.

In view of this widespread, if not unanimous, appreciation for scientific medicine, one wonders why there should be problems, beyond those of trained personnel and money, in universalizing modern medicine. Yet almost always when scientific medical programs, and particularly preventive programs, have been introduced into areas where indigenous systems are yet strong, there have been great resistances. The initial high hopes of international medical specialists time after time have been dashed, as they have found to their astonishment that seemingly technologically sound programs have failed completely or achieved only partial success. Westerners are highly ethnocentric; we assume that the superiority of our civilization over technologically less complex societies is obvious, and we assume that, given the chance, peoples in "less fortunate" countries would like to adopt our ways. Western medical personnel have been, if anything, even more ethnocentric about the superiority of scientific medicine, finding it difficult to believe — despite evidence to the contrary — that given the opportunity, all peoples will not accept it in its totality.

As a consequence, for nearly 50 years, international public health programs and their medical specialists operated largely on the assumption that better health depended on the design and execution of scientifically sound programs, in which the people to be benefited would be enthusiastic participants. In 1916, after having demonstrated in the southern United States how hookworm could be controlled and ultimately eliminated, the Rockefeller Foundation turned to Ceylon for a massive demonstration of how disease control methods could be applied in other parts of the world. The *technical* part of the program appears to have been sound: a census, sanitary surveys to locate sources of infection, microscopic examination of feces and blood samples of everyone in the trial area, treatment of infected persons, and latrine-installation campaigns. But 6 years later, when the program was brought to an end, hookworm was still widespread, and even today it is endemic. The clinical superiority of Western hookworm control and treatment proved inadequate to the elimination of the disease. Far from winning the gratitude of tea plantation workers, active opposition was incurred (Philips 1955).

Many years later, in 1942, when the Institute of Inter-American Affairs (a forerunner of the Agency for International Development) began public health programs in cooperation with Latin American governments, the same ethnocentrism prevailed. Better health for Latin Americans, it was assumed, would result from the adoption of U.S. practices, especially the dichtomy between clinical, curative, private sector medicine, and preventive, public health, public sector medicine. That uniquely American institution, the public health center, offering pregnancy and postnatal services to mothers and infants, immunization programs, communicable disease control, dental services, environmental sanitation services, and similar activities, was adopted as the keystone of the program. To the surprise of the Americans, public acceptance of the new programs was far from enthusiastic. Many eligible people genuinely in need of the services failed to come at all; others, after initial visits, skipped appointments or dropped out. Utilization of available services was far below planned capacity (cf. Foster 1952 for detailed discussion of these programs).

With the post-World War II establishment of the World Health Organization and the development of a vast international health bureaucracy designed to bring modern medicine to all of the world's countries, similar mistakes have been made. Regardless of country of origin, specialists trained in scientific medicine, when first exposed to cross-cultural health problems, have found it difficult to believe that the "obvious superiority" of their methods is not alone sufficient to win total acceptance.

During recent years, fortunately, we have learned a good deal about what happens when people who previously have relied only on traditional medicine are afforded the option of seeking scientific help. We know the cultural, social, psychological, and economic barriers that have often made them reluctant to try the new; and we also know the kinds of experiences that make them full or partial converts to scientific medicine. A part of the resistance to change, we have discovered, lies in the social and cultural forms of the people themselves. More recently we have also realized that both the quality of scientific medicine and the institutional forms set up to deliver it have not always been characterized by the excellence that wins confidence.

Nevertheless, for all of the problems and shortcomings that have been described for scientific health programs and services, the fact remains that scientific medicine wins converts every day, and traditional medicine, however effective it may be in some areas, is losing its hold. Villagers who, 25 years ago (as in Tzintzuntzan) rarely if ever consulted a physician, today routinely seek his services, turning to traditional curers only for minor problems or (in an interesting reversal of an earlier pattern) if the physician does not bring the immediate cure they have come to expect of him. In the pages that follow we describe what anthropologists and medical specialists have learned about the complex process of bringing scientific medicine to the world's peoples. Some of the "problems" discussed are problems only in an historical sense; today they have largely disappeared. Other "problems" (e.g., the frequent poor quality of health services) require solutions before optimum use is made of scientific medicine.

RESISTANCES IN COMMUNITIES RECEIVING NEW HEALTH SERVICES

In their value and belief systems, in their social structures, and in their cognitive processes, tribal and peasant peoples display forms that sometimes inhibit their acceptance of scientific medicine. All peoples are ethnocentric; they are attached to their traditional ways and beliefs, and they assume that these ways are the equal to, and probably better, than the ways of others. With respect to that complex of beliefs and values associated with food, health, and illness, this seems particularly true. Health beliefs, body imagery, and concepts of illness are parts of a wider world view. And, just as this wider world view is rarely questioned, so too are individual elements that make up its totality accepted unquestionably. If ghosts, witches, and forest sprites are a part of the supernatural environment of a people, the lecture of a scientifically trained health educator is hardly going to convince them that these are not causes of disease. People whose basic view of health and illness is based on humoral pathology, on the hot-cold equilibrium that they have been taught to strive for since infancy, are no more likely to abandon this interpretation of the health environment than are educated Americans to give up the germ theory.

In a clinical sense it is easy to argue (as we have done in Chapter 7) that scientific medicine is superior to non-Western medicine. But, as Young points out, it is incorrect to say that non-Western medicine does not "work," at least when viewed through the lens of its believers. In defining "work," Young makes the important distinction between resulting in what people *hope* will happen, and producing what people *expect* may happen. The two meanings sometimes are congruent: treatment, as hoped and expected, restores the patient to health. Sometimes it does not. But treatment has "worked" in the sense that it has met the expectations of family and friends as to what should be done, and it has perhaps produced expected clinical evidence that the diagnosis has been correct (Young 1976:7). Traditional medicine has played a powerful positive role in maintinaing the psychological and physical well-being of those who believe in it.

1. The "adversary model"

In short, the health and illness views of every people are a part of their innermost being, not to be cast aside lightly until overwhelming evidence indicates that there are better explanations. It is not, to quote Polgar, a question of the "empty vessels" model, the erroneous assumption that the "new wine" of scientific health information and practice can be poured into minds essentially devoid of illness beliefs (Polgar 1963:411). In trying to understand the changing health behavior of tribal and peasant peoples and in trying to help change traditional views, anthropologists have made use of an adversary model, the "conflict" between primitive and folk medical systems, on the one hand, and scientific medicine, on the other. We have tended to see traditional medicine as the defender, under attack by scientific medicine, which little by little forces the traditional medicine to give ground, contesting every inch of the way. As a general rule, we can say that when scientific medicine first becomes available to people whose previous experience has been with traditional systems, therapeutic practices that are interpreted to be in direct conflict with traditional beliefs about health and causes of disease will encounter the most resistance. Richard Adams has given us a classic example from a Guatemalan Indian village, where blood is viewed as a finite good, as a "non-renewable" or "nonregenerative" substance. Blood is seen as the source of strength, but when it is lost through injury or disease, a person's resistance to disease weakens forever. When medical doctors on a health team wished to take blood samples from children for a health survey, they met great resistance. Villagers simply could not understand how outsiders who obviously were weakening their children could claim to be bettering their health (R. Adams 1955:446-447). The view that blood is nonregenerative is common in much of the world. In Latin America it seems to be one of the reasons why blood banks and blood transfusions are less successful than in the United States: people are most reluctant to part with their precious blood.

In societies in which belief in witchcraft is strong, people are careful to conceal their excreta and other bodily wastes so that evil doers cannot find materials on which to work contagious magic. To such people, the thought of advertising the presence of excreta in a sanitary latrine, advocated by public health workers, is the height of folly. In a pilot project in social medicine among the Zulu of Durban, South Africa, projects such as home gardening and compost pits were modestly successful, but pit latrine programs less so. "Adults and children are found to micturate in the immediate vicinity of their huts, but defecation, except in the case of infants and young children, always took place some distance from the homestead. Bushes were preferred, but as long as a place was found that offered protection from the public gaze it was considered satisfactory. Modesty, and perhaps even more important, the desire to conceal the identity of the persons defaecating, demanded this protection" (S. and E. Kark 1962:26). In response to questions as to why pit privies were not used, answers showed clearly the fear of witchcraft. "People do not want to defaecate in one place because they still think that someone can bewitch them through their faeces. Because of this belief it is hard to get them to build pit privies" (*Ibid.*).

2. A cognitive dichotomy

Physicians unacquainted with the popular medical beliefs of their patients often are puzzled by the apparently erratic decisions sometimes made in the face of illness. In Vellore, Tamil Nadu, India, for example, it was found that young children suffering from diarrhea and severe dehydration were sometimes brought to the hospital, but other times they were not, or they were brought too late to save them. Research revealed that there are two distinct types of diarrhea, *bedhi* and *dosham*. *Bedhi* is viewed as a "natural" diarrhea caused by an excess of heat in the body, commonly caused by eating foods classed as "hot" according to the Ayurvedic system. To go to the hospital is viewed as an appropriate decision in cases of *bedhi*. *Dosham* diarrhea, in contrast, has its origin in views about ritual pollution; it occurs most commonly when a mother feeds her infant after seeing a woman who has suffered a miscarriage. Children who are believed to be suffering from *dosham* are treated with elaborate purification rites that are not, of course, a part of the treatment received in the hospital; hence, they are rarely taken to physicians (Lozoff et al 1975).

Diarrhea in Vellore is a modern illustration of a cognitive dichotomy first noted more than a generation ago. In the early 1950s anthropologists studying public health programs in Latin America discovered that traditional peoples who had access to scientific medical services felt that illnesses with certain etiologies could be cured or prevented by physicians so that, in spite of initial distrust, they sought such services. Illnesses with other etiologies, however, were felt best treated by home remedies or by *curanderos,* since it was believed that physicians did not recognize, and hence could not be expected to cure, such cases. Illnesses with magical or emotional etiologies, such as the evil eye or *susto* (fright), were the ones most frequently judged to be unsuitable for treatment by the modern physician (Foster 1952). Infectious diseases quickly relieved by antibiotics or surgery fell into the other category. Erasmus found in Ecuador that even *curanderos* admitted that the physician was best qualified to treat things such as diphtheria, tuberculosis, venereal disease, and appendicitis, and that they had "nothing but praise for the yaws campaign and a complete conviction that yaws was a disease which the doctor alone was capable of curing" (Erasmus 1952:416, 417).

This basic dichotomy between illnesses the physician can cure and those he cannot cure has subsequently been found in widely separated parts of the world. Thus, in North India Gould found that "critical incapacitating dysfunction" (i.e., usually infectious diseases) were taken to the physician, while "chronic nonincapacitating dysfunctions" (i.e., degenerative, recurrent diseases) tended to be treated in the village (Gould 1957).

A second type of cognitive dichotomy, that between "our" diseases and "their" diseases, has also been noted. Madsen quotes a Mexican-American *curandero* from south Texas who makes clear this distinction. "I do not know why God has afflicted only us with the evil eye, *empacho,* fallen fontanel, fright, and many other diseases. But God is merciful. He sends us these afflictions but he also taught us how to cure them . . . . They come to us and only we understand them. Only we of *La Raza* can cure them. . . . God sends disease to punish us but he also lets us learn to repent and undo the suffering. His great concern must reflect a very great love for *La Raza.* You punish most the erring children whom you love best. Therefore, it is not strange that the Anglos never suffer these divinely sent afflictions" (Madsen 1964:79).

The Pima Indians of Arizona have a similar belief. The *kà:cim mùmkidag,* or "staying sicknesses," are "Indian sicknesses that afflict only Pimans, are diagnosed only by Piman shamans, and are cured by native ritual curers" (Bahr et al. 1974:19). These are the sicknesses associated with the moral order; beliefs about their etiology encourage correct behavior. Staying sicknesses are caused by the "strength" of sacred or dangerous objects whose "way" has been violated by an evil or thoughtless human act. "In trespassing against a danger-ous object's 'way,' the patient is said to have committed an impropriety against rules which were set down for Pimans at the time of creation. The *kà:cim* sicknesses were intended specifically for Pimans as a race of chosen People" (*Ibid.,* 21).

The Scot missionary-physician Barker found the same pattern among his Zulu patients: a strong belief that their diseases were African diseases, thus hidden from foreign eyes. "After all," says Barker, "it is human enough to believe our problems to be unique. We speak of *our* gall-bladders, *our* stom-aches, *our* appendices, as if we owned them like so many lap-dogs to be pampered and fed" (Barker 1959:88). During the early years of his practice, most diseases that patients recognized in themselves were considered to be peculiarly African. "You wouldn't have been able to help," women would tell him, in commenting on the deaths of their children. "The child had one of the sicknesses of the people." The usual symptoms of these "people's diseases" were diarrhea, vomitting, coughing, high fever, which "indicated nothing very mysterious yet the belief persisted that such symptoms were an exclusively African privilege" (*Ibid.,* 88-89). Little by little Barker and his physician wife gained the confidence of his patients, who brought more and more "African" diseases to him for treatment. However, this did not indicate a weakening of belief about their exclusiveness; instead, it was a testimonial to Barker for his skills in having learned to treat African diseases!

3. Resistance to hospitalization

Sometimes people resist hospitalization, not only because hospitals have been perceived historically as places people go to die, but because hospital practices often conflict with traditional patient care. Many tribal and peasant peoples ritually dispose of the placenta following childbirth, burying it beneath the ashes of the hearth or placing it in a running stream. In Tzintzuntzan the placenta beneath the three hearth stones symbolically ties the child to its ancestral home. When first offered the opportunity to deliver in hospitals or clinics, a number of mothers refused, because they were worried about the placenta disposal. In some hospitals whose clients share these beliefs, the placenta is delivered to the relatives of the mother for ritual disposal.

Other hospital procedures may be frightening. Clark tells of an elderly Mexican-American woman in a California hospital who, when past the acute phase of her illness, was forced by a well-meaning nurse to take a shower. Returning to her bed, she was struck by "bad air"; to the dismay of the hospital staff, she then insisted on going home where she could receive "proper care" (Clark 1959a:202). For this woman, as in Tzintzuntzan, bathing was not to be taken lightly; it was safe only when she was fully recovered. Clark also tells how postpartum food taboos discourage Mexican-American women from accepting hospitalization for delivery. The postpartum period among village Mexicans is a dangerous time for mother and child; the mother's diet is strictly limited, emphasizing chicken and excluding things such as fruit juices and certain vegetables, which are too "cold" to follow immediately after the heat of pregnancy and childbirth. Some mothers are worried that in hospitals they will be asked to eat foods that they believe are dangerous to them (*Ibid.,* 167, 227).

4. Differing perceptions of role behavior

When scientific medicine is first made available to people who previously have relied on traditional methods, one of the most important initial resistances stems from differing expectations between patient and physician about appropriate role behavior. These differences, and the frequent mutual bewilderment that results, have been partially explored in the section on the "Therapeutic Interview" in Chapter 6. Other examples further illustrate the problem. Clark, for example, in discussing health problems of Mexican-Americans in California, points out how Anglo doctors are taught that impersonal objectivity, professional "efficiency," an authoritarian manner (which connotes confidence?), and a right to "lecture" patients on what they should do are appropriate behavior for their roles. Mexican-American patients' expectations, however, are quite different. They routinely visit doctors accompanied by family members who, it is assumed, participate in all deliberations; this situation is reassuring to the patient, but hardly contributes to "efficient" use of often cramped space and busy schedules of doctors. Since Americans assume that at least some sickness is the result of the patient's failure to take routine precautions, physicians may suggest that a condition has resulted from failure to exercise proper precautions. Mexican-Americans, however, do not feel guilt or responsibility for illness. "A medical worker who implies that a sick person is at fault and is somehow responsible for his condition may find his statements received with indignation or hostility. To the patient and his family such a view is unjust or even malicious" (Clark 1959a:230). A leg ulcer responds to the penicillin, and not to the hand that injects it; the patient, however, responds to the person who injects, and even if the results are seen to be beneficial, an unpleasant therapeutic encounter will discourage future visits.

In this context Alland's comments on the Abron of the Ivory Coast are pertinent. "Confidence in Western drugs seems greater than confidence in doctors. . . . There is little ritual associated with Western medical treatment. The paraphernalia of the examination room is seldom seen, and examinations are usually cursory; thus the doctor often appears to be an unnecessary adjunct to the distribution of medicine" (Alland 1964:720). In other societies traditional peoples accept Western medicines, but view their dispensers with distaste. In North India Gould found that modern medical practitioners "are rarely able, because rarely inclined, to establish the kind of rapport that would win acceptance of *themselves* in the village" (Gould 1965:202). In developing countries physicians often feel that they are degrading themselves and their science if they listen sympathetically to recitals of magical or supernatural causes of illness. Sometimes they heap scorn on traditional beliefs, thus alienating patients who would like to turn to them because of their obvious clinical skills.

Most medical anthropologists believe that therapy in intercultural or interclass situations is most effective when the physician has an understanding of the medical beliefs and treatment expectations that the patient brings to consultation. Smithsonian Institution anthropologists studying public health programs in Latin America in the early 1950s stressed the importance of knowing folk medicine. "If public health personnel are acquainted with prevailing concepts of folk medicine, in many cases these beliefs can aid rather than hinder the doctor — the good or the useful can be separated from the bad and the useless, and programs planned with this in mind" (Foster 1952:10). The anthropologists pointed out that an understanding of folk medicine would aid health personnel in phrasing curative and preventive measures so that they would be intelligible to patients accustomed only to traditional medicine, and that confidence in the new would be instilled in patients if it were apparent to them that health personnel understood *their* beliefs (*Ibid.*).

More recently anthropologists working in intercultural and interethnic settings in the United States have come to the same conclusion. Harwood, speaking of Puerto Ricans in New York, writes that "To communicate effectively with a patient about his illness or treatment regimen, a physician must know something about how the patient conceives of disease, its etiology, and therapeutics in general. . . . In order to treat patients of a different sociocultural background effectively, the physician must . . . develop a special understanding of their medical beliefs and practices" (Harwood 1971:1153). Snow voices similar thoughts with respect to American minority ethnic groups. "It is important that the physician know what the patient has been using to combat the illness — if it is harmless, it might be left in the treatment plan and the physician's own suggestions added" (Snow 1974:94-95). And Wintrob, a psychiatrist-anthropologist, writing of American blacks specifically and minority groups in general, believes that "Sensitivity to the culturally determined beliefs and practices of patients whose ethnic and social class background is different from that of the treatment personnel is essential in the assessment of those patients' illnesses, whether medical or psychological. And in evaluating the data one must take account of folk beliefs and folk medicine, no less than interpersonal stresses and intrapsychic factors" (Wintrob 1973:325).

5. Preventive medicine and the maintenance concept

Whatever the specific etiological views of traditional peoples or their image of the therapeutic interview, they share one major premise: illness is manifest through pain or discomfort. They find it difficult to believe — faintly ridiculous, in fact — that unknown to a victim, a serious illness can appear and develop slowly, making itself known only when it is too late to help the sufferer. When a person feels well, when his body functions normally, that is all one can ask. The time to seek medical aid is when one does not feel well, when one's body is not functioning normally. Since much of preventive medicine is based on the philosophy of taking action before illness appears, through immunization that prevents it, or through early detection that increases the likelihood of successful treatment, traditional peoples are not the best candidates for this branch of medicine.

In this premise about health, traditional peoples — probably all preindustrial peoples — reflect a much wider world view: maintenance, Western style, is little valued. Europeans and Americans have had two centuries in which to learn the importance of maintenance. Routine but elaborate care of machinery is basic in industry. In our private lives we have learned that automobiles must be serviced at regular intervals, that houses last longer if periodically painted, and that clothing can profitably be mended. Although we sometimes ignore or delay such prescriptions, there is concensus that we do so at our peril. We have aphorisms that, from childhood, impress on us the importance of maintenance: a stitch in time saves nine; never put off until tomorrow what you can do today; an ounce of prevention is worth a pound of cure; and so forth. With this basic premise about the importance of maintenance deeply engrained in us, we are good candidates for the proposition that maintenance of the human body (i.e., preventive medicine) is a sound idea. Preventive medicine is consistent with our wider world view, and we take it for granted that it is a wise policy.

In traditional and developing societies just the opposite is true; the maintenance of machinery in new factories is always a struggle, house roofs are repaired after they begin to leak, highways are rebuilt more often than they are repaired and, in some areas such as Africa south of the Sahara, the mending of worn clothing is conspicuous for its absence. Lacking basic agreement that maintenance is essential to a smoothly running society, it is not surprising that preindustrial peoples are less receptive to maintenance of the human body through preventive medical activities than are people whose ancestors began the practice generations ago. Major forms of preventive medicine are not consistent with the wider world view of traditional peoples, and they will not accept it with the same relative alacrity with which Europeans and Americans have done so.

RESISTANCES IN SCIENTIFIC MEDICAL BUREAUCRACIES

When international public health workers first began to think in cultural terms, to realize that indigenous peoples do not necessarily perceive the benefits of Western medicine in the same ways that they did, they jumped to the conclusion that "cultural" and "social" barriers such as those just described were rooted in the ways of the target group members. Anthropologists working in early international public health programs shared this view. We believed that if the social and cultural forms of recipient peoples were studied, then it would be possible to design health programs that could clearly be understood by the people concerned. We assumed that people failed to understand Western medicine, and that if it could be presented to them in such a way that they could perceive its obvious advantages, they would be happy to accept it. Posparturient Mexican mothers fear many of the foods normally given to American women? Find out the foods that they feel are safe and construct a nourishing diet around these foods. Salvadorean village women believe that their husband's shirt, inside out, under the mattress, facilitates delivery? By all means allow them to have the shirt in the hospital. Physician's instructions are not phrased in ways that conform to, or build on, traditional interpretations of illness? Proper rephrasing is a reasonable goal that does little or no violence to the integrity of scientific medicine.

Public health and other medical personnal generally have been receptive to what anthropologists have told them about the customs and beliefs of the people with whom they work. After all, the problem is identified as being "out there," among the patients. Physicians, like most other people, prefer to believe that shortcomings in their performances are due to outside factors. Unquestionably public health and medical programs designed with an awareness of cultural factors, and the beliefs and attitudes of the target groups, have been more successful than those based only on the assumption that scientific medicine is best, and only a people's stupidity prevents their acceptance of it.

Yet as time has gone on we have slowly come to accept a disquieting thought: *at least as many of the resistances encountered in the promotion of scientific medicine are rooted in the medical profession and in health bureaucracies as in the target peoples.* Medicine's clinical assumptions, the statuses of its practitioners, its bureaucratic organization, the hours of its services — all of these, and many more factors of its own creation, inhibit the acceptance of scientific medicine. [1]

1. Erroneous planning assumptions

Much international planning continues to be based on the assumption that the ways that have worked best in Western countries are the model to be followed in developing countries. Rifkin lists things such as "the belief that increased facilities constitute improved health. . . . ; that highly trained manpower is the only method by which to deliver health care; that medical care is exclusive of social factors including health education and preventive activities; and that disease and hospital-based systems are, without reservation, the most appropriate to meet health needs" (Rifkin 1973:249). Similarly, Bryant asks questions about medical schools in developing countries, giving the case of the University of Dakar in Senegal. Many basic facilities are excellent. Yet French influence, which accounts for much of this basic excellence, also raises disquieting questions; for example, the size and composition of the entering class is determined by the same rigorous examination system used in France. Consequently, in the 1964 entering class, only three of the 28 students were Senegalese. Moreover, the entire medical curriculum is planned in France and conforms to the same plan determined by the Ministry of Education for French medical schools. Bryant asks: "Is a curriculum designed for an advanced, industrialized country appropriate for a far less advanced, nonindustrialized country? Are the attitudes, skills, and concepts needed by a physician to direct the health affairs of a sector of Senegal sufficiently different from those required for France (or the United States or England) to warrant designing an educational program more specifically for that situation?" (Bryant 1969:63-64).

Bryant obviously believes that the answer lies in developing curricula adapted to the local needs. To illustrate his point, he describes a day in the life of a Western-educated Senegalese physician in charge of a hospital in which he, aided by a nurse and auxillary personnel, and by seven dispensaries, each with a nurse, serves 100,000 people! The doctor sees perhaps 150 patients every day. Five or six patients are admitted weekly to the hospital, and about ten women come for delivery. There is no midwife, no X ray, no running water, no facilities for simple surgery, and insufficient medicine. Time must be taken occasionally to visit the dispensaries, where services are rudimentary in the extreme. It seems clear that to maximize his utility, a Senegalese physician in a rural area must have many skills that are unnecessary in urban Europe.

Bryant believes that the "health team," led by a physician and composed of a variety of health workers especially trained for specific tasks and to work together as a unit, is the answer to health problems in developing countries. The major problem, he says, is that the physician simultaneously wishes to retain his traditional role as primary diagnostician and therapeutist, a role that obviously cannot be combined well with team direction. Instead, says Bryant,

"He must fill a role in which he manages limited resources to meet the comprehensive health needs of large numbers of people rather than serving as personal physician for a few. But there is widespread reluctance to accept this concept — it is in fundamental conflict with much of current medical education and professional thought as to what the physician's role should be" (*Ibid.*, 141-142).

A part of the greatness of the good physician, says Bryant, is his acceptance of responsibility to give unstintingly of himself to those who need his help. But this is also the basis for the physician's reluctance to share his activities with others, because it is intertwined with the feeling that no one other than a physician can provide that help. "A curious side of this concept is the value the physician places on the particular acts of diagnosis and prescription of treatment. Physicians are anxious to use every level of health worker in furthering a health program . . . but the words 'diagnose' and 'prescribe' evoke the strongest feelings of professional possessiveness" (*Ibid.*). The concept that the physician must attend personally to his patients actually determines the form of most health services, says Bryant, and it can obstruct efforts to change the design of health systems. "Thus while logic tells us that the physician's role should be determined by the health needs of the entire population, implementation of this logic is obstructed by the insistence of the medical profession that only physicians can evaluate and treat the sick. This stand of the medical profession has a paralyzing effect on the design and implementation of health services and is one of the most serious obstacles to the effective use of limited health resources" (*Ibid.*, 143).[2]

2. Clinical versus preventive medicine

Still another example of the imposition of inappropriate Western models on developing countries is the American distinction between clinical, curative, private sector medicine, and preventive, public health, public sector medicine. Considering American history, emphasis on private enterprise, numerous medical schools, and large numbers of patients who can pay for medical services, this dual system seemed reasonable for many years. It developed as a function of the reality of the total American cultural and economic pattern. But it was not God-given, inherent in nature, an answer for all peoples in all times. In most developing countries relatively few people have the means to consult private physicians. The curative needs of most of them must be met through government clinics, free or subsidized, through social security benefits, and in other ways in which curative and preventive services are combined.

Yet, more than 30 years ago, when the first cooperative programs with American aid began in Latin America, they were based on the assumption that health centers with maternal and child health and preventive services such as environmental sanitation and immunization were what was most important.

Whatever the merit of a health program based on preventive medicine, the average Latin American is primarily interested in doctors and nurses because he hopes they can cure his, or his children's, ills. When people for whom health centers were designed discovered the limited range of services and the relative neglect of curing activities, they were strongly critical. Criticism was particularly bitter when, in some instances, it was discovered that sick children would be examined by a doctor only if they had previously been registered in the so-called "well baby clinic" and were under health center "control."

Preventive medicine undoubtedly has contributed more than curative medicine in promoting longevity and high health standards. Certainly in the developing world major improvements in health levels will owe more to public health measures than to clinical services. But the prevention and the cure of illness are part of the same process and, through successful curing, people can be led to appreciate the importance of contemporary preventive measures. To assume that American institutional models of health care hold the solution to health problems of other countries is the height of ethnocentrism. Fortunately, the health services of most developing countries now realize this, and *their* personnel, not Americans or Europeans, are in the vanguard in the development of "social" or "community" medicine.

3. Personal priorities of health personnel

A third major problem in health programs based on scientific medicine is the frequent assumption of health personnel that their *personal* priorities are also those of the target group. Time after time we find that medical personnel fail to realize that they confuse their personal values in research and health goals with those of the people they hope to serve. Moreover, when we consider the total spectrum of problems faced by everyone, it is clear that health problems "compete" for priority ratings with economic problems, family problems, and a host of other kinds of problems. Busy Americans, thoroughly convinced of the importance of an annual medical examination, often postpone the visit to the doctor because they place a higher priority on other activities that compete for precious time.

A public health physician notes the frequency of cancer of the cervix among American women, and he knows that with regular Pap smears and early surgery, a high percentage of deaths can be avoided. He wonders at the apathy of most women, who do not share his consuming passion for control of cancer of the cervix, and he despairs of reaching his goal: annual examinations for all women. However, if one makes a list of immediate priorities for the average housewife — grocery bills, children not doing well in school, teenage truancy and perhaps brushes with the law on marijuana, a husband whose ardor has cooled, or a mother-in-law who does not hesitate to give advice — it is clear that an annual checkup for something that in any event is not apt to strike is of very low priority.

Even within the list of individual health priorities, the physician's own personal priority may be far down the list. In developing countries, public health personnel, not unreasonably, have stressed preventive measures. But without exception, on the priority list of the average person preventive measures fall below curative measures, i.e., immediate attention to their health needs as *they* perceive them. In the Rockefeller Foundation antihookworm campaign in Ceylon this became clear: "Some villagers were irritated by the concentration on hookworm disease in view of their other overwhelming medical needs. . . . The villagers were more interested in having their wounds and abcesses dressed and their miscellaneous acute illnesses attended than continuing in the dull routines of anti-hookworm work" (Philips 1955:289). Despite a home-office warning not to scatter their energies by engaging in such activities, field directors found they had to treat all kinds of complaints in order to gain support for the hookworm work.

The story of an attempt to bring pure drinking water to the village of Arenal, in Peru's Ica Valley, illustrates the same point. The regional health department, concerned with developing economical and technologically simple ways to achieve a protected water supply, offered to provide a concrete cover for the village well and add a hand pump. A health department sanitary engineer made the simple installation and turned the maintenance over to the villagers. A year later the village had returned to the use of a rope and pail to draw water. The problems of maintenance had proved insuperable. Various reasons account for the failure. Perhaps the overriding problem was that of priorities. "To be sure, Arenal could conceivably have used its meager funds for pump repairs and even for paying a stipend to a well-custodian. Had it done so, however, this would have meant diverting available resources from the important town celebrations (the patron saint's fiesta, the Independence Day celebration, and others). Much as Arenal favored the new hand pump over the former rope-and-bucket arrangement, the town fiestas were even more important than the pump" (Wellin 1966:123-124).

A similar story comes from a tribal group in Orissa state in India, where the National Malaria Eradication Program met with scant success. "They are pre-occupied with other aspects of their daily life, related to agriculture, construction of roads, and drainages which they view as problems. Though they mentioned 'fever' in interviews, they did not consider it a problem to worry about and, therefore, were not motivated to cooperate" (Dhilon and Kar 1963:20-21).

It is clear that unless the members of a target group share or come to share similar health priorities with the specialists who wish to help them, interest and cooperation in specific projects will be difficult to achieve.

4. Erroneous assumptions about decision making

A continuing problem in the doctor-patient and health educator-client relationship in the developing world is the tendency of medical people to assume that the patient or potential patient makes the decision about what kind of medical help to seek. In fact, medical decisions in the traditional world usually are group decisions, and matters such as status, rank, age, sex, and traditional roles may be involved. To illustrate, today in Indonesia family planning is a major government activity, with services provided through the regular health clinic network. In spite of apparent technical excellence, the program has been only moderately successful. Among the reasons for a low rate of acceptance of family planning has been the assumption, in the face of all evidence to the contrary, that it is the woman who decides to take this step. Hence, family planning education and propaganda are largely directed toward the wife, although she is the person whose desires are least important in the family. Major decisions are made by the husband and, on matters such as children and grandchildren, the views of grandparents are also highly important.

The same erroneous assumption about who makes decisions often has characterized maternal and child health services in new health centers in developing countries. Mothers and mothers-to-be seem like the obvious educational targets. But the older women in traditional families often consider themselves to be the repositories of wisdom on pregnancy, childbirth, and infant care, and their role as experts on these matters is widely accepted. Not surprisingly, to many of them a new health center may be seen as a direct competitor, an intrusive government activity that threatens their status and power within their families; therefore they oppose it vigorously. In families where the elderly women's roles are accompanied by real power they, as well as the young mothers, must be won over to the new system.

5. Deficiencies in health services

Still other factors discourage the acceptance of scientific medicine and preventive programs. Sometimes the reaction is negative because, in fact, the scientific medicine is not very good, its mode of delivery does not meet the needs of the people, or it is accompanied by side effects that are viewed adversely by the peoples concerned. For example, one of the most successful of all preventive measures (if we discount possible long-term consequences) has been residual spraying with DDT to eliminate the *Anopheles* mosquito vector that spreads malaria. Large parts of the world have been rendered completely free of malaria as a consequence of this activity. Yet opposition to spraying often has been intense. In many places cats have died in large numbers; they rub against DDT-sprayed walls, lick their fur, ingest DDT, and die. Since cats play the role of mousers in traditional societies, rat and mice populations increased, causing damage to food supplies. In tribal areas of Orissa state in India there were additional complaints: the spray gave a bad odor to the unventilated rooms in which people sleep; bedbug populations were believed to explode after spraying; and whitish DDT deposits disfigured colorfully painted house walls (Dhilon and Kar 1963:22-23).

WHO-UNICEF personnel found similar resistances in an antimalaria program among the Bush Negroes of Surinam; not only cats, but dogs and chickens also died from the effects of DDT and dieldrin. Furthermore, the cockroach problem increased drastically after spraying; the insects bit sleeping children and ate stored rice, cassava, and bananas. The head of one antimalaria team sprayed a box of cockroaches with insecticide, confidently expecting them to be dead by morning. The cockroaches, however, had become DDT-resistant and were alive and active when the box was opened. This demonstration did nothing to increase the villagers' confidence in the program's effectiveness. Finally, the Malaria Eradication Program workers, all Surinam nationals, were comparatively well paid by local standards. Consequently, they were both envied and feared by the local men; their relative affluence made them attractive to some married women who preferred them to their own less affluent husbands (Barnes and Jenkins 1972).

On other occasions it has been noted that vaccines have lost their potency because of inadequate refrigeration. When children fall ill of the diseases against which they were presumably protected, parents lose confidence not only in immunization but also in other modern medical procedures. Health personnel, too, may be lax about their duties. In the Indian villages that he and his colleagues studied, Banerji found general (but not universal) acceptance of smallpox vaccination. However, "The number of children who are left unvaccinated due to lapses of the parents appear to be a very small fraction of those who remain unvaccinated due to the lapses of the vaccinators and their supervisors" (Banerji 1974:11).

Other bureaucratic practices that at first thought appear to have no bearing on health services utilization can be viewed as deficiencies in those services. Family planning in Indonesia appears to have suffered because of pill procurement practices: the sizes, shapes, and colors change from time to time as the government, with U.S. support, gives succeeding contracts to the lowest bidder. The unexplained changes in what seems like a standard product make village women distrustful of the program.

These examples illustrate the kinds of factors that have often inhibited the acceptance of modern medicine among traditional peoples. They are not intended to convey the impression that traditional medical systems stand largely unchanged, fiercely defended by their supporters, that representatives of scientific medicine have learned nothing about the delivery of health care to traditional peoples. Just the opposite is true; in spite of the historic and continuing problems that characterize the introduction of scientific medicine to traditional peoples, more and more people are turning each day to the trained physician instead of to the indigenous curer. In turn, physicians who practice among patients from social or ethnic backgrounds quite different from their own are far more aware than a generation ago of the implications of this gap in expectations. New therapeutic role expectations can be, and are being, learned both by physicians and patients; in many instances well-trained doctors show remarkable sympathy and understanding in dealing with patients from lower socioeconomic classes or different cultural backgrounds. Increasing numbers phrase their questioning and instructions to conform, as nearly as possible, to local concepts and terminologies.

In a recent study in rural Thailand, Goldschmidt points out that "Experienced doctors agree upon [the necessity of] trying to use vocabulary which is adapted to their patients' level of understanding," even though it distresses them that some of the words they must use are "impolite." They have learned, however, that "polite words may easily lead to mistakes confusing patients" (Goldschmidt 1972:11). Goldschmidt also found that many of the Thai doctors he observed showed great understanding of the sociocultural problems of their poor patients, and that they often went to considerable lengths to try to help them with these problems (*Ibid.,* 16).

Presently in Tzintzuntzan, villagers often express distrust for physicians in the abstract while at the same time they describe satisfactory encounters with them, often praising individual doctors for their skill and for the kindnesses they have shown to their patients.

6. Professional role conflicts

Cohen has called attention to an ethical and policy dilemma that, although of a somewhat different order from the "bureaucratic barriers" just described, can nonetheless be considered as a part of the wider problem of providing good medical care to all those who need it. Large numbers of illegal aliens live and work in the United States: 2 million, and perhaps many more. They are poor, they speak little or no English and, in self-defense, they maintain a low profile, avoiding agencies and services where their illegal status might be detected. Many of these people are hard workers; they have come to the United States to better themselves economically. They are lawbreakers, but they are not criminals.

Their health problems are at least as great as those of low-socioeconomic-class Americans but, in addition to the barriers that often prevent the latter from seeking medical help, the illegal aliens are also deterred by fear of exposure and deportation. The situation, says Cohen, "provokes fundamental questions regarding the expression of altruism and forms and functions of giving towards such groups" (Cohen 1973:184). Americans subscribe more and more (although far from universally) to an ideology of equal access to health services for all people. Yet they wonder if they should be taxed to provide such services for people who have violated American laws by coming to this country.

Cohen describes how many health professionals cope with the ethical dilemma that faces them. They recognize the moral obligation of the health professional to aid those in need; they are also circumscribed in their actions by agency regulations that distinguish between eligible and ineligible clients. Cohen believes that the low-profile behavior of illegal immigrants tends to protect "the health care giver from potential conflict between the ideals of his calling, and the societal norms embodied in agency guidelines. The hidden status of these potential clients appears to have relieved health personnel from accountability for the full exercise of professional ideals. It contributed to the avoidance of conflict with the regulations which govern the health systems under consideration" (*Ibid.,* 188).

Since aliens tend to limit their contacts with public health agencies, health personnel are relieved in considerable measure of the compulsion to practice the "Good Samaritan principle." Professionals who express frustration because follow-up home visits often are fruitless because of the high mobility of illegal aliens are, in fact, relieved of the responsibility of justifying their (legally) questionable actions. These are ethical and policy problems, and answers satisfactory to all concerned are not easily found.

NOTES

[1] See Foster (1976a) for a discussion of this point in the historical context of international health planning.

The tendency to assign problems encountered in health programs to the target peoples instead of looking for possible problems in health bureaucracies is not limited to international health programs. In a study of an underutilized neighborhood health clinic in a large eastern U.S. city, Jones found that "the health practice of many people in the area could be explained in part by the poor treatment people received in public health clinics — a common complaint" (D. Jones 1976:225). The problem initially was seen by health personnel as rooted in attitudes shared by the target population. But, "as it turned out, part of the problem was traced to the attitudes of health professionals toward the poor" (*Ibid.,* 226). And part of the problem simply resulted from lack of thought of health professionals about how the health world looks to the poor. The clinic was located in what was known as a "fancy" hospital; many people, not believing that there could be a free outpatient clinic in the hospital, made no attempt to patronize it. Others tried unsuccessfully; there were no signs directing patients to the part of the hospital containing the clinic, and some receptionists either did not know of the clinic or were reluctant to speak of it (*Ibid.* 226).

[2] Many observers in health roles, physicians included, may feel that this picture, while undoubtedly true in an earlier era, is overdrawn for today. More and more, medical doctors are not only willing, but anxious, to delegate much

of the diagnosis and treatment of patients with both acute and run-of-the-mill medical problems to other medically qualified personnel. In the discussion of changing nursing roles (Chapter 11) we saw how clinical nurse specialists have assumed responsibilities in intensive care units that would have been exercised only by physicians in an earlier period. "Physician assistant" programs, too, have been established at a number of medical schools, and the employment of men and women in this new role is gaining increasing acceptance by physicians who are hard pressed to keep up with the demands on their time. Medical practice, like nursing, is undergoing rapid change, and this will unquestionably be reflected in planning for health needs in developing countries.

chapter 14

Anthropology and Medicine in a Changing World II: Trends and Dilemmas

In the preceding chapter we have dealt with some of the problems of international health (largely as defined by health personnel) as they have been observed and studied by anthropologists. Our approach has been historical; we have been concerned with what anthropologists have learned and done up to now. In this chapter we continue with the same basic theme of international health, but we change our emphasis from the past to the present and future, asking questions about problems and policy dilemmas that concern the consumers and the providers of health services. We are particularly anxious to present data and ask questions that seem to us to have been ignored or passed over lightly in advocating specific courses of action. The topics we consider in this chapter include the patterns that lead to the acceptance of new medical systems (more properly, the curers representing systems); how choices are made in seeking health care; the recent successes of scientific medicine in winning converts and the problems this has caused in providing primary health care for all who need it; the policy question of the use of traditional medicine and traditional curers in meeting primary health care needs; and the growth of so-called "alternate" medical systems and their relationship to all of the foregoing.

PATTERNS OF ACCEPTANCE OF NEW MEDICAL SYSTEMS

In considering the problems of international health, of bringing better care to needy peoples, there is a tendency to think in terms of a simple conflict between traditional and scientific medicine, and/or possible collaboration between the two systems. In either case, the fundamental assumption is that we are dealing with only two systems, the traditional and the modern. This is a serious oversimplification. If we reflect a moment, we realize that there are multiple medical systems available to many, if not most, of the world's people, and the options available to any specific group are growing rapidly. In the United States, for example, we have not only what we can call "establishment" medicine, but also osteopathy, chiropractics, a wide variety of ethnic folk medicines, acupuncture, spiritualism, and many forms of faith healing, including Christian Science.

The acceptance of any, or a combination of these forms of therapeutic help, will depend on a variety of factors. Regardless of what patient or what group is changing from one medical system to another or is exercising a specific option from among the choices available, it seems that a single paradigm explains what is happening, and that it is the same paradigm which accounts for all kinds of individual and group innovation. Specifically, we believe people will modify preexisting practices if:

1. They perceive economic, social (e.g., status), psychological (e.g., ego-gratification), health, or other advantages in so doing.

2. The economic costs are within their capabilities.

3. The social costs do not outweigh the perceived advantages.

It should be noted that this simple paradigm deals with changes in *overt behavior,* in practices and customs, but it does not necessarily explain (or require) changes in *belief systems.* In fact, as we will see, a remarkable thing about changing health practices is the extent to which this can occur in the absence of understanding of the underlying scientific rationale for so doing. Traditional peoples are skillful in reconciling new practices with old beliefs.

In our consideration of the acceptance of new medical systems (and practices) we are, for the moment, particularly concerned with the successes of scientific medicine in the Third World. This is because, in spite of the "barriers" of which we have spoken in the preceding chapter, this kind of medicine is winning converts at an ever-accelerating rate. It is, in fact, this success that in significant measure underlies the emerging consideration of the use of traditional methods and healers to augment scientific medicine, since it appears unlikely that the latter will be able to keep up with the demand. Later in this chapter we describe some of the "successes" of alternate medical systems, and we discuss the implications of the growing popularity of such therapies.

1. Perception of advantages — pragmatism

In all societies people are remarkably pragmatic in testing and evaluating new alternatives, in deciding whether it is to their advantage to innovate. This is true of health behavior, where we can almost speak of a cost-benefit mode of analysis. When, on the basis of empirical evidence, traditional peoples see that scientific medicine is more effective than their own, and when they can have scientific medicine on terms they deem acceptable, they are very apt to turn to it. Speaking of the acceptance of curative medicine in Ecuador, Erasmus many years ago pointed out that, as far as tradition was concerned, "folk beliefs in themselves are offering no resistance to modern medical practices *in so far as those practices may be judged by the folk on an empirical basis*" (Erasmus 1952:418. Emphasis added). In contrast, Erasmus found that preventive medicine was resisted because its comprehension is essentially theoretical, not lending itself to easy empirical observation.

Subsequent studies among other groups reveal the same pattern. In a study of 108 lower-class women in Cali, Colombia, it was found that although "the traditional or folk beliefs about fertility, pregnancy and abortion remain important" a full 55 percent of births during the study took place in health centers or government hospitals (Browner 1976:51). Similarly, in Mexico City Casillas Cuervo found among urban migrants in poor barrios near the University of Mexico campus that, although they had brought with them a "heap" of [traditional] beliefs and knowledge, which continued to guide health practices, when offered other types of medical services they accept them and put them to the test. They do not in all cases continue to use the new services, but they show open-mindedness and pragmatism in trying them out (Casillas Cuervo 1978). Even among the Navaho, traditional people with complex traditional curing ways in which they have great pride, Wagner finds that they "have a very open, pragmatic, and non-discriminatory attitude toward the various medico-religious options available in time of need. White medicine, traditional chantways, Peyotism, and even the various Christian sects on the reservation tend to merge in their minds into alternative and somewhat interchangeable avenues for being cured" (Wagner 1978:4-5).

The evidence presented here deals largely with therapy, suggesting that, as far as individual decision making is concerned, curative medical services are embraced much more readily than preventive services. The reason is obvious: the results of scientific curative medicine are much more easily demonstrated than the results of preventive medicine. Few people suffering from yaws or other dangerous infections that have been cut short by an injection of an antibiotic question that this is indeed a miracle medicine much superior to any they have previously known. Cause and effect are easily comprehended when serious illness gives way to no illness in a few hours or days. Cause and effect are less easily seen when, in the case of immunization and environmental sanitation programs, no disease is followed by no disease. The implication that is drawn from this evidence is that the traditional American separation of most clinical from most preventive medical measures is, in other parts of the world, counterproductive. Experience suggests that preventive measures are more apt to be accepted if they are "blanketed in" with or sold as a part of a "package deal" along with curative medicine, whose advantages are so much more easily demonstrated.

2. The economic costs of innovation

Motivation is by no means the only factor in innovation; the goal must be seen as feasible, or worth the cost. A university professor may be persuaded that a Mercedes-Benz is a highly desirable automobile, but he may consider its ownership an unobtainable goal because of the cost. Economic factors likewise explain a great deal about the acceptance or rejection of scientific medicine. Although it has been argued that medical services are often more attractive to users if "value" is placed on them in the form of at least a token fee (e.g., Foster 1962:128-130), it is clear that when medical costs are deemed to be too high in relation to perceived advantage, they will discourage innovation. Recognizing this, health services in many developing countries are free to users, or formal charges are modest. However, services offered gratis or for a nominal fee are often anything but "free" to the user.

(a) "FREE" SERVICES

A classically simple example of "free" services failing to attract all patients who needed care is that of tuberculosis control in Kenya, where it was found that the bus fare kept many patients from going to the clinic (Ndeti 1972:408). In Indonesia family planning services, free in the strict sense of the word, are sometimes underutilized because of social customs requiring expenditures. Most mothers are interested in birth control only after they have four or five children. Often they have no one with whom to leave these children so that when they decide to visit a clinic in response to the urging of a family planning worker, at least the younger children must trail along. This usually means bus fare for all. But a trip on a bus is, by definition, an "outing," and on such an occasion people buy food snacks, to which Indonesians are much addicted. Therefore a mother with three or four small children may spend a day's income on a simple visit to the free family planning clinic.

Other kinds of attendant services also sometimes make free services prohibitively expensive. In a village near Bandung in western Java, at the bottom of a steep valley reached only by a poor dirt road, a woman seeking family planning help pays a 200-rupiah round-trip fare to ascend to the health center in a truck or old bus that requires nearly an hour for the 5-mile trip. There she finds that, prior to being given pills or fitted with an IUD, she must take a pregnancy test, which carries a laboratory fee of 150 rupiahs. The woman is asked to return three days later, again at a cost of 200 rupiahs for transportation, to learn the laboratory results. If the 200 rupiahs in wages lost from absence from work for two days are added in, it costs a woman 750 rupiahs simply to find out if she is eligible for family planning. Small wonder that few of these village women are interested in this kind of service.

(b) HOURS OF SERVICE

Non-Western peoples may not consciously realize that "time is money"; nonetheless, they are entirely rational in the ways in which they allocate their time to maximize attainment of goals. They fully realize that time spent on one task slows the completion of other tasks. Thus, when patronizing a government health service for prenatal or postnatal care, or any of the other services that in themselves may seem desirable, means loss of a major chunk of valuable working time, we can speak of the economic costs to the potential user. A widespread complaint of villagers in developing countries is that government clinics offer their services only at inconvenient hours. Since almost all bureaucracies schedule their services to meet the convenience of their employees instead of that of the people served, clinics customarily are open only during the morning, or perhaps into the early afternoon.

Potential patients who would be happy to utilize services later in the day — and there are many of them in developing countries — are simply out of luck. Unless they are faced with a real medical emergency, women who are busy with shopping, preparing meals for their families, and getting the children off to school are reluctant to sacrifice their busy morning hours for routine checkups whose value they may not fully accept. Many years ago one of us found in San Salvador that the free government morning prenatal clinics were badly underutilized. Yet in the same city a private fee-for-services clinic offering comparable services in the evening had a crowded waiting room. Women questioned said they could come for their examinations only when their husbands had returned from work and could care for the children during the mother's absence. In a slightly altered version of the same problem, it has been noted that Moroccan women who will not leave their homes for medical treatment during the day, for fear of being seen by prying eyes, will happily slip out to attend evening birth control clinics with women doctors.

3. Social costs

"Social costs" refers to the restructuring of personal relationships, customary exchange patterns, and friendship ties that often accompany innovation. A young woman may be convinced that the government health center in or near her village, with its pre- and postnatal care and delivery services by a doctor and nurse-midwife team, is more desirable than delivery with the aid of a village midwife. But if the midwife is her mother's sister, failure to turn to the aunt may be seen as a personal rejection, an act that may cause major family rifts. Marriott describes the results of a similar "social cost." The father and father's brother of a Brahman girl ill with malaria asked for and received quinine from the physician. Three days later the physician found that none of it had been used: an elderly aunt, the supreme authority in the household, had objected, and the whole matter of Western treatment was dropped (Marriott 1955:243). To have overriden the aunt would have produced family discord that would be more serious than the illness.

When these kinds of social costs are seen by traditional peoples as too high a price to pay for the perceived advantage of Western medical treatment, change does not occur. Yet in the contemporary world it is more and more the economic cost, not the social cost, that affects health behavior. In Thailand, for example, in a major study of doctor-patient communication, it was found that "The decision to go to a hospital depends less on the gravity of the disease than on the financial resources" (Hinderling 1973:74).

CHOICES IN SEEKING MEDICAL CARE

When new forms of medical care, scientific medicine included, are made available to people whose health problems previously have been met solely or largely by an indigenous system, the basic decision they have to make is not whether to accept the new or adhere to the old. Instead, they have now a variety of options open to them that can be, and almost always are, exercised on a situational basis (i.e., the course of action that seems the most appropriate for the particular problem at hand). The strategies that underlie these decision-making processes have come to be called the "hierarchy of resort in curative practice" (Schwartz 1969). The ways in which people structure their personal hierarchies of resort and the factors that enter into their calculations tell us much about how scientific and other new "alternate" (and largely urban) forms of medicine are crowding out a great deal of traditional practice.

1. Variety of health care options

Until recently both anthropologists and international health personnel have viewed medical care decisions as involving only two variables: the patient either turns to the physician or continues with the traditional curer. We now realize that with growing frequency both scientific and traditional medicine are only two options among a dazzling array of alternatives. For example, in Puntarenas, a Pacific coastal town of 20,000 in Costa Rica, a patient can choose between "orthodox physicians, who operate as resident doctors in a charity hospital, as clinicians in a governmental clinic, or as private physicians in their own offices. He can request aid from members of the minor orthodoxy, the pharmacist, the licensed midwife, or her unlicensed colleague. He may go outside orthodoxy and seek heretic curers, the homeopath or the naturist. Finally he may seek to complement the efforts of humans and call upon supernatural healers. Available to him are spirits, saints, and God" (Richardson and Bode 1971:261).

Similarly, in Lusaka, Zambia, the choices open to the sick "are of bewildering complexity. They include . . . dyadic consultation with kin; with white, Indian, or fellow African employer; with fellow employees of diverse tribal and linguistic origin; with neighbours and friends . . . 'western' doctors operating privately, or through government hospitals or clinics, and nurses, medical assistants and the like," all in addition to traditional healers, the *ng'angas* (Frankenberg and Leeson 1976:227-228).

And in Vellore, Tamil Nadu, Indian patients may choose between physicians in the Christian Medical College Hospital, those in the Government Hospital, local trance curers and exorcists, sidewalk and village herbalists, and an enormous spectrum of private practitioners of varying degrees of training, ranging from apprenticeships to Ayurvedic and Western-type medical colleges (Montgomery 1976:274).

Not only have anthropologists underestimated the variety of health care options available in the contemporary world, but they have also been guilty, as Press has pointed out (1971), of clinging to a stereotype of the traditional curer that, at least as far as urban counterparts are concerned, is far from accurate. The stereotypical picture of the traditional curer is known to us all: a wise and skilled person who knows not only the patient but also the family, who is aware of the social and personal tensions of the patient's life, who sees relief from interpersonal stress as essential to relief from physical symptoms. The stereotypical curer is, in short, a social pathologist, able and willing to spend unlimited time with a single patient, little concerned with payment.

Press' research on "urban" *curanderos* in Bogotá reveals not only the wide variety of diagnostic and curative techniques they use, culled from traditional, folk, and modern sources, but also how far they depart from the stereotypical model. Many urban *curanderos,* Press found, see up to 70 patients a day in consultations lasting from 5 to 10 minutes, of which only 1 or 2 minutes involve conversation. This is hardly a social pathologist at work; "If illness is indeed the cue for a social drama of sanction, cultural identity, escape from responsibility, etc., the city curer is *not* a principal actor nor is his office the stage" (Press 1971:752). Moreover, "With few exceptions, the Bogotá curers are professionals for hire, are viewed as such, and charge a fee" (*Ibid.,* 753), often a large one.

2. Medical systems are not competitive

Individual hierarchies of resort in making health care decisions must be viewed against this background of variety of medical systems, and the personalities and characteristics of the practitioners in each. On the latter point it is increasingly clear that in cities, at least, alternative system practitioners are more like physicians than like their traditional counterparts. Over the years both anthropologists and international health specialists have tended to conceptualize medical systems — particularly scientific and traditional systems — as competitors. But this is an ethnocentric conceptualization that exists largely in the mind of the Western-oriented observer. In fact, most patients, and not necessarily those in Third World countries alone, see nothing inconsistent in patronizing curers from two or more systems, often simultaneously. They want the widest possible variety of opinion and advice, and they assume that it is good judgment to select from this advice the elements that most nearly fit their perception of how to deal with a particular illness episode. They are quite aware of the differences between the medical systems they have been exposed to and of the representatives of each, and they have noted that while one tactic works well on one occasion, another "resort" seems more desirable for another occasion. Often, of course, strategies are sequential or progressive, the patient trying one therapist after another in the hope of finding a cure. Competition, to the extent that it can be viewed as playing a role in the hierarchy of resort, lies more between individuals than systems. Therapists — Western, indigenous, or alternate types — will be consulted for the problems for which they are believed to be competent.

Not all medical judgments are made with cool objectivity, after weighing the relative strengths of each type of curer against all others. Hasan describes how in rural India villagers often depend on the advice of neighbors, relatives, fellow caste members, and village elders, sometimes in a haphazard manner. He tells of a young mother in Lucknow district who, when her infant son began to pass blood in his stool, set out for the nearby clinic. En route she met village women who urged her not to go there, saying that her child was suffering from sorcery that the doctor's medicine could not cure. Swayed by this advice, she returned to the village where the services of an exorcist were obtained. In spite of treatment, the child died. However, no one blamed the exorcist or the women who had persuaded the mother against consulting the physician (Hasan 1967:161).

3. The reconciliation of indigenous beliefs and scientific practices

Although busy physicians in the United States often take little or no time to explain why a particular prescription or injection is suitable for the patient's complaint, much preventive medicine is based on the assumption that if people understand "why," their health behavior will become more rational. Thus we "educate" people to understand the "dangers" of cigarette smoking, of obesity, of lack of exercise, and the like. Health education is also an important part of health programs in developing countries, but the evidence indicates that it is the perception of desired results — recovery or improvement — and not the understanding of Western disease theory that leads traditional people to modern medicine. In India Gould found that acceptance of modern medical help for the critical incapacitating illnesses had no relationship to a comprehension of scientific etiologies or appreciation of the germ theory (Gould 1965:202).

In fact, traditional peoples show great ingenuity in reconciling scientific medical practices with their own etiological systems. In Tzintzuntzan Doña Micaela Gonzalez is a great believer in scientific medicine. The lives of her two daughters have been saved by surgery, and her own life has been prolonged, first through discovery of incipient diabetes, and second through prompt and excellent medical care following a near fatal stroke. In the late 1950s during the World Health Organization-Government of Mexico antimalarial campaign, health workers drew blood samples of people suspected of harboring malarial parasites for laboratory analysis and left the patient three pills to be taken, presumably in case of discomfort. The pills, says Micaela, who strongly supported the campaign, are to prevent "cold air" from entering the body through the tiny aperture left by the needle. Her hot-cold belief system is not shaken by modern medicine; instead, it is called on to justify the new, thereby strengthening itself. Although there is a growing awareness of *microbios* in Latin American villages, there is a considerable tendency to understand by the term those things that cause the illnesses that scientific medicine can cure. But they are not thought to have any relationship to the evil eye, or illness caused by anger, fright, envy or jealousy. Certainly they do not threaten the basic concept of the hot-cold dichotomy that underlies much illness.

Faith in the correctness of one's own medical and health beliefs probably characterizes all people; it is one of the most important symbols around which the group organizes its perception of its ethos, its uniqueness, its vital essence. Therefore to abandon traditional health beliefs is a far greater step than to accept a new mode of therapy; it means relinquishing a major support to a group's sense of identity and view of itself. Hence, all kinds of accommodations are made and all manner of rationalizations appear, to justify continuing faith in the old system while simultaneously accepting the new. In Tzintzuntzan most people who enjoy the economic means to do so now routinely turn to physicians, but their belief in the correctness of their own system's etiology and treatment is almost as strong as ever. "If you are sure the traditional remedies are best, why do you rush to the physician?" Foster has often asked. "Because," they explain, astonished at his naiveté, "once the body has been opened up to the physician's medicines, through injections and pills, it no longer responds to the traditional remedies." The physician's treatments have destroyed the body's ability to react properly to traditional remedies, and people have no option other than continuing with the new. But their faith in the old remains unshaken. DeWalt has noted a similar rationale in another community in the State of Mexico where the physician has become the health practitioner most often consulted. Faith in the old therapy remains strong but, informants explained, "The illnesses have now changed; the herbs are no longer obeyed" (i.e., no longer continue to have the effect they were believed formerly to have had) (DeWalt 1977:11).

THE SUCCESS OF WESTERN MEDICINE

A good deal of the medical anthropological literature dealing with the introduction of Western medicine into traditional societies is either out of date or no longer very relevant. While anthropologists have been documenting cultural resistances to the acceptance of modern medicine and finding flaws in the assumptions on which such services are based, millions of people have quietly accepted this medicine. When good or reasonably good scientific medicine is available on economic and social terms that patients deem acceptable, these services are avidly sought. For example, a 1970 survey of 250 college students in Taipei and 60 workers and peasants in southern Taiwan revealed a strong preference for "Western" medicine. Among the college students 77.5 percent reported that they called first on the Western medical system, or that they resorted to both systems, but predominantly the Western. Among workers and peasants the preference was even more striking: 92.2 percent favored Western medicine (Unschuld 1976:312).

The same trend is reported from Hong Kong, where traditional (and unlicensed) practitioners abound. Here Lee, clearly partial to traditional medicine and critical of modern medicine, reports that "most residents prefer to consult Western-trained doctors" (Lee 1975:400). Patients report believing that Western drugs and other remedies are more effective than Chinese herbs in preventive and curative medicine, but not in "tonic care." A clear preference for Chinese medical care is expressed only for rheumatism, sprains, and fractures — hardly the great historic killers! (*Ibid.,* 400).

Similarly, in Kota, an Indian town of 9000 people on the Indian Ocean north of Mangalore, "The present trend is for most physically ill patients to consult a modern doctor first and soon follow it up with consultation with a traditional healer if the doctor's medicine does not take effect immediately" (Carstairs and Kapur 1976:66). The reasons underlying this choice include the rationalism taught at school and the impact of health workers, "but most of all the beneficial effects of modern medicine make people question the efficacy of traditional healers more and more . . . not many agree that the traditional healers are best agencies of help in case of illness" (*Ibid.*). This pattern appears to characterize much of India; in a major survey Banerji and his colleagues found "that the response to the major medical care problems is very much in favour of the western . . . system of medicine, irrespective of social, economic, occupational and regional considerations. *Availability of such services and capacity of patients to meet the expenses are the two major constraining factors"* (Banerji 1974:6. Emphasis added). Furthermore, although he found numerous examples of people who consulted practitioners of indigenous or homeopathic medicine, "Among those who suffer from major illness, only a very tiny fraction preferentially adopt these practices, by *positively rejecting* facilities of the western system of medicine which are more efficacious and which are easily available and accessible to them" (*Ibid.,* 7).

A similar pattern has been found in Thailand where in cities, and especially in Bangkok, the physician is the first curer to be consulted; only if he is unsuccessful will a traditional healer be consulted (Boesch 1972:34). In contemporary Tzintzuntzan the picture is the same. Thirty years ago physicians were essentially unknown; today most people — even at significant financial cost — turn first to the physician, returning to the *curandero* only if the physician is unable to work the miracle they have come to expect from modern medicine.

Among the Bono of Ghana hospitals and clinics are more and more utilized for a variety of reasons. Frequently the services and conveniences of the hospital are deemed superior to those of the traditional system. For one thing, since indigenous curers often specialize, a patient may have to travel a long way to find the curer who can treat his ailment. In contrast a conveniently located hospital, because of its complete range of services, alleviates the need to travel long distances to find indigenous specialists. Again, a priest-curer can work only on those days specified by his deity, usually two or three days a week. In contrast, the hospital is available every day and, in an emergency, at night as well. Hospital medicines have other attractions; they are already prepared so that, in contrast to a common indigenous practice, the patient or family members avoid trips to look for herbs, barks, and roots that may be difficult to find and are always time-consuming in preparation. Finally, the hospital patient can avoid making public personal matters that might be probed by the traditional curer (Warren 1974-1975:33-34). For all of these reasons Bono patients often prefer scientific treatment to traditional therapy.

Among Latin Americans the same trend is apparent. For example, in the conservative corn-farming Yucatecan village of Pustunich, most villagers have been treated by indigenous *curanderos*. Nevertheless, "there is no wholesale use of their services. Villagers pay more calls to M.D.s than to curanderos over a year's period, even though curanderos charge less than the combined physician-prescription fee" (Press 1975:196). Perhaps more surprising, research on mental illness of Mexican-Americans in East Los Angeles indicates that, in spite of a deep-rooted faith in the use of traditional *curanderismo* for such afflictions, "its importance has diminished greatly. Both ethnographic observations and formal interviews indicate that for Mexican-Americans in East Los Angeles, the preferred treatment resource for mental illness is the general physician, not the curandero" (Edgerton et al. 1970:133).

To summarize, when good scientific medicine is available to traditional peoples, delivered by friendly and sympathetic personnel, at a price patients can afford, and at convenient times and places, scientific medicine is more and more the first choice for traditional peoples.

POSSIBLE ROLES FOR TRADITIONAL HEALERS

So general is the acceptance of Western medicine becoming in developing countries that the "problem" (as defined by ministry of health personnel) no longer is "How can people be persuaded to patronize government clinics and hospitals?" Instead, the problem is insufficient supply to keep up with growing demand. Not now, nor in the foreseeable future, will there be sufficient fully professional personnel to meet health needs. Part of the solution to the problem lies in the expanded use of auxillary health workers. In the former British and French colonies local men were trained as "dressers" or *infirmiers auxiliaires* to staff rural clinics and, depending on level of training, to perform a variety of therapeutic duties, including simple laboratory analyses. Among the Navaho Indians the "health visitor" works under the supervision of the public health nurse, significantly extending her capacity to fulfill her role. And in contemporary China rural "barefoot doctors" offer a primary level of treatment in a referral system that sends seriously ill patients to more highly trained health personnel.[1]

In these and in other comparable instances, the subprofessional worker is (or was) a member of the formal health establishment, trained by qualified teachers, and paid by and formally incorporated into colonial, tribal, or national health services. But insofar as traditional healers and traditional therapies have been concerned, official attitudes of those concerned with developing national health services have ranged from neglect to outright opposition. Only occasionally, as with Ayurvedic medicine in India, has an indigenous medical system and its practitioners been formally encouraged by government. Even in India the vast substratum of "folk" medicine not recognized as Ayurvedic is ignored by government.

Now, however, this traditional neglect of or opposition to indigenous therapies and practitioners is giving way to renewed interest in possible utilization of traditional elements and personnel in government health services. Beginning in the early 1970s, the World Health Organization and other United Nations organizations such as UNICEF began to explore the use of traditional midwives as aids in family planning programs and to consider the inclusion of indigenous curers in formal programs to extend primary health care to all people. This interest was formalized in a resolution passed by the 29th World Health Assembly in May 1976, requesting that member nations take steps to develop primary health care programs that include traditional medicines and curers where appropriate. Further formal attention was given to these questions at a Pan American Health Organization-sponsored workshop held in El Paso, Texas in January 1977, in which medical anthropologists from Mexico and the United States were asked to examine alternate therapeutic systems with respect to their roles and utility in meeting some of the health needs of the populations concerned (B. Velimirovic 1978).[2]

The question of recognition of traditional healers is important because, in addition to the man power problem, the fact remains that no scientific medical system completely satisfies all health needs of a nation. Even in countries with highly developed health care systems, many people, under certain conditions, will turn to nonestablishment forms of medical help such as chiropractors, faith healers, and herbal doctors. "Alternate" forms of medical care fill social, psychological, and perhaps organic health needs that for some people, at least, remain unmet by physicians and associated care services.

Viewing particularly the supportive sociopsychological functions of the indigenous curer, anthropologists generally have been impressed with many positive aspects of non-Western medicine. Medical doctors, on the other hand, point to the dangers of some traditional remedies and to the fact that traditional curers may delay referral to medical doctors until routine therapy has become vastly more complicated, with consequent danger to the life of the patient.These divergent views are described by Harrison, who believes that "retrained" traditional healers can be important integral parts of the health delivery system of Nigeria. However, he notes that, except for psychiatrists — relatively favorably disposed toward traditional healers — most Nigerian government personnel with whom he discussed the problem were skeptical of the value of traditional healers (Harrison 1974-1975:12).

In spite of the prevailing negative view of the wisdom of incorporating traditional healers into formal state medical services, some specialized uses have been made of them, especially indigenous midwives. Because most births are "normal," it is reasoned, the primary problem is to (1) encourage the midwife to practice hygienic methods, and (2) refer difficult cases to government health services. Since at least the early 1950s, village midwives in El Salvador have been recognized and trained by government personnel; among the Navaho Indians similar training of indigenous midwives has reduced infant and maternal mortality. Indigenous midwives also are incorporated into government health services in Tanzania (Dunlop 1974-1975:138) and Liberia (Dennis 1974-1975:23), and doubtless in many other countries as well.

Mental illness is a second area in which formal recognition has been given to traditional healers. The Nigerian psychiatrist Lambo has described the therapeutic "villages" to which patients are sent that he and colleagues established in Nigeria. Speaking of his "unorthodox collaboration" with traditional healers, he writes: "We have discovered throughout long practice in Africa that it is essential to the scientific understanding of man and his social environment to work in close collaboration with other disciplines and even to establish some form of interprofessional relationship on a fairly continuing basis — even with those who, by Western standards, are not strictly regarded as 'professionals' " (Lambo 1964:449). Lambo feels that cooperation with indigenous curers has contributed to his understanding of the psychopathology and psychodynamics of mental illness in Nigeria, especially with respect to social and cultural variables. Moreover, the traditional healers employed in the project have had considerable experience in managing patients. "They supervise and direct the social and group activities of our patients in the villages under our guidance" (*Ibid.,* 450).

In spite of the success of some countries in integrating native midwives into national health services, and in spite of the evidence of beneficial results to be obtained from the use of indigenous mental curers, the problems of the blanket inclusion of native curers into scientifically based health services are formidable. Midwives constitute a special case; they cannot serve as a model for other indigenous health personnel. With pregnancy there is no problem about diagnosis. Both indigenous midwife and physician agree about the cause of the onset, the course, and the outcome of the "illness." If indigenous midwives can be taught hygiene and can be induced to refer difficult deliveries to more highly trained medical personnel, they obviously contribute to low-cost health services. Since the treatment of nonorganic mental illness in Western society is much less a science than surgery or the treatment of acute infection, it is reasonable to assume, as found by Lambo, that indigenous curers may have a role to play in formal health services.

For other kinds of illness, collaboration between indigenous curer and physician presents more difficult problems, but examples of successful cooperation do exist. Among the Navaho, the National Institute of Mental Health has spent a quarter of a million dollars financing a training school for medicine men, and there seem to be documented cases of "singers" curing blood poisoning and rattlesnake bites with herbal treatments (McDowell 1973). Nevertheless, the strength of Navaho traditional medicine lies in the area of psychiatry. Many Navaho happily accept the physician's treatment of their physical symptoms while simultaneously turning to singers to restore them to harmony with nature. The physician is concerned with the first level of causality — to him the primary level — and the singer is concerned with the second level. As long as each is tolerant of the other, the patient benefits. But if the singer had primary responsibility for, let us say, treating tuberculosis, it is not certain that the patient would do so well. This is the major problem in making extensive use of indigenous curers in primary health care services. When physician and native curer hold drastically different ideas about etiology, prognosis, and appropriate treatment, how do the two collaborate, except in special and nontypical cases such as that of the Navaho? When the indigenous curer says "evil eye" or "spirit possession" and recommends rubbing the patient's body with a raw hen's egg or recommends ritual dances or demon expulsion, and the physician suspects a strep throat or a blood disorder, how do the two join forces?

Whatever the potential merit of making formal use of the medical talents of indigenous curers, the idea has made little progress in practice. We suspect the question may never need be resolved, since it is based on two assumptions that have neither been explored nor their implications considered.

1. Traditional healers will continue to be produced in the same numbers and with the same skills as in the past.

2. Traditional healers *want* to be incorporated into formal government health programs.

With respect to the first assumption, we suspect that social, economic, and educational change in most of the world is coming so rapidly that the children and grandchildren (figuratively speaking) of today's traditional healers will take up the roles of their parents and grandparents with less and less frequency. Instead, they are already faced with two more attractive choices. Some are studying modern medicine and are trained in health care in medical schools, schools of nursing, and other government health institutions. Others are becoming what, for want of a better term, we can call "alternative" healers. Although many variants of the latter are emerging, the most important categories seem to be faith healers (particularly spiritualists) and "injection doctors," people usually without formal medical training who, in countries where controls over prescription drugs are weak, specialize in hypodermic injections.

Recent evidence substantiates our belief that traditional medicine is less and less attractive as a career in Third World countries, and that traditional curers are not being, and will not be, turned out in the same numbers as in the past, or in numbers sufficient to make them viable major additions to health care services. The loss of attraction of traditional medicine as a career, for example, is clearly seen in Kota, India, where for 19 of the 23 practicing healers medicine was a hereditary profession that their children might reasonably expect to follow. These healers acknowledge the achievements of modern medicine, but they also express the belief that their treatments can "strengthen" the physician's drugs, and hence feel that they have a useful role to play. "None of them, however, wanted his sons to follow in his footsteps. 'Times are changing', they said" (Carstairs and Kapur 1976:65).

An actual decline in numbers of indigenous curers is beginning to be well documented in the anthropological literature. Thus, in 1941 in San Pedro La Laguna, on Lake Atitlán in Guatemala, there were 15 shamans; all but three had died by 1974 and only one man, with uncertain credentials, had begun practice in this 33 year interval (Paul and Paul 1975:718). In nearby San Lucas Tolimán the situation is the same. Woods and Graves, conducting research in 1966, reported that while "elderly informants were able to supply a list of 36 native curers practicing twenty-five years ago, only 13 shamans were active in 1966," none on a full-time basis (Woods and Graves 1973:12). Similarly, among Nubians resettled in Egypt below the Nassar High Dam, the number of indigenous midwives is declining and when a midwife dies, "There is no desire on the part of her daughters, relatives, or others to take over" (Fahim 1975:15). And in Botswana recruitment to the role of traditional healer is threatened by formal education, which is incompatible with traditional medicine as an occupational choice (Ulin 1974-1975:123). In Tzintzuntzan a number of young people have entered medicine and nursing during the last 15 years, but no new midwives or *curanderos* have appeared for more than 30 years.

Doubt as to the availability of traditional curers for contemporary health services is also cast by the findings of Casillas Cuervo in the lower-class urban neighborhood she studied in Mexico City. Full-time curanderos proved to be less numerous than is frequently assumed; women practicing on a part-time basis were the most common type of traditional curer. The remarkable thing, she feels, is not so much the fairly limited demand for curanderos, but the high degree of interest these poor, little-educated mothers show in the services of physicians, and their advice about the care and feeding of children (Casillas Cuervo 1978).

The evidence as to whether traditional curers want or do not want to be incorporated into formal government programs is less substantial. Indigenous midwives, as we have noted, appear to be willing, and sometimes anxious, to join forces with their more highly trained counterparts. Even in Texas some (of Mexican-American background) have participated in programs designed to institutionalize and upgrade the practice of midwives (Schreiber and Philpott 1978). In contrast, Cheney and Adams found in a study in Houston that *curanderos* voiced major concerns about possible demeaning attitudes health care professionals might show toward them, and showed considerable skepticism about the idea of collaborative efforts (Cheney and Adams 1978). Alvarado, who is highly sympathetic to indigenous practitioners in the American Southwest, believes that most indigenous practitioners, by the nature of their system, must have private or individual practices instead of becoming incorporated into state systems (Alvarado 1978).

An important argument in favor of making use of indigenous curers is that they are (generally) older people, highly respected in their communities, and trusted by the people they serve. But even this assumption must be questioned. When the National Indian Institute began its rural health work among Tzeltal and Tzotzil Indians in Chiapas, Mexico, it was assumed that the local shamans would be the logical candidates for training and incorporation into the new health services. But to the surprise of both anthropologists and medical people planning the new program, great resistance to this idea was encountered in the population at large, as well as among the shamans themselves. Elderly people of high status, including the shamans, turned out *not* to be the most effective intermediairies in introducing sociocultural change. Ultimately — as in the case of barefoot doctors in China — the program came to rely on young, literate, health auxillaries as "health promoters" (Aguirre Beltrán 1978).

THE INCREASING ROLE OF ALTERNATE MEDICAL SYSTEMS

In both the anthropological and medical literature there is a strong tendency to view the "problem" of health care as involving two systems only: Western and traditional medicine. The "problem," as we have seen, gives rise to many questions: how can traditional peoples be converted to Western medicine, how can the two systems be coordinated, and should, and if so how, can non-Western curers be incorporated into official health systems, and the like. This view of the problem, is, in fact, highly simplistic; consequently, policy decisions based on the assumptions that underlie it may be unrealistic.

One of the most striking things about the contemporary health care scene is the vitality displayed by traditional systems and their practitioners, not in carrying on in unchanged fashion, but in adapting their etiologies, therapies, and rituals to meet the expectations of their traditional (and new) clients who are also adapting to the modern world and its ways. Of the contemporary alternate health care systems spiritualism and other forms of faith healing are perhaps the most important. Modern New World spiritualism (and spiritism), as Macklin recently has pointed out, springs from ideological elements long present in Europe (Macklin 1974a). In its Latin American form spiritualism appears to have been shaped almost in its entirety by the influence of a Frenchman, Leon Denizarth Hippolyte Rivail (1804-1869) who, under the pen name of Allan Kardec, published a series of books widely distributed, and today still available, in the Spanish-speaking world (*Ibid.*, 388).

Although spiritualism cannot be described as an outgrowth of shamanistic practices, the similarities (belief in spirit possession, a medium who enters trance to communicate with a familiar, etc.) are notable. In this sense spiritualism can be viewed as civilization's attempt to structure and pattern and validate the near-universal belief in spirits that harm human beings, who can be dealt with by means of human intermediaries. Particularly in Latin America, but also in other parts of the world, spiritualistic practices have increased dramatically in recent years, at least in part as a response to the health and psychic needs of newly urbanizing populations (e.g., Harwood 1977; Kearney 1978; Kelly 1961; Koss 1975; Macklin 1967, 1974a, 1974b, 1976; Rogler and Hollingshead 1961).

The growing importance of spiritualism as *the* alternate health care system along the Mexican-American border is apparent in a number of the papers read at the 1977 El Paso workshop. Thus, in Tucson, Arizona, among Mexican and Mexican-American residents the most renowned curer is not a traditional *curandera:* it is a black woman, Chloe,[3] who practices voodoo medicine (Kay and Stafford 1978)! In the El Paso-Ciudad Juarez border area, spiritualists and other faith healers have become the dominant alternate health resource (Aguirre 1978). Recent research on alcohol counseling in minority groups in south Texas also testifies to the importance of faith healing. Although the authors use the term *curanderismo,* it is clear that they are not speaking of traditional Mexican curers, since therapy involves contacting spiritual beings by a trance medium, channeling mental energy from the healer's mind to the affected part of the patient's body, and ritual sweeping of the body to remove "negative vibrations" (Trotter and Chavira 1978).

The reasons for the growing importance of spiritualism, faith healing, and other religion-based therapies, at the apparent expense of *curanderos,* root doctors, *spilatos,* and the other traditional curers of American ethnic groups, and at the expense of herbal and home remedies that conform to naturalistic etiologies, are not entirely clear. We see, however, two possible factors that may influence this trend. First, we suspect that syncretism has resulted in the substitution of aspirin, vitamins, Geritol, and other nonprescription drugs for the herbs and other home remedies of an earlier generation.

Second, and paradoxically, we believe the success of scientific medicine goes a long way in explaining the success of contemporary supernatural therapies. That is, we believe that scientific medicine has demonstrated its capabilities, to the satisfaction of the great majority of Americans, in the areas of the common infectious diseases, of the afflictions of childhood, and of initial malaise of most types. The physician is the first recourse for most people when they fall ill and, for most illnesses, the physician's treatment is successful. But not always. For many chronic illnesses, psychosomatic complaints, and mental problems, the physician's answers are not always satisfactory. It is this residual category of complaints that refuse to yield to physical therapy that falls to the supernatural healers. Traditional naturalistic therapies are of little use in treating these symptoms, so they too are forced to leave the field to curers offering more powerful remedies. As Malinowski long ago pointed out, the less the degree of control, the greater the tendency to resort to magic. This seems to be what is happening in contemporary American supernatural curing.

Although the evidence of the decline in absolute numbers of indigenous curers in many parts of the world is impressive, many who continue have been successful in holding patients by incorporating real or feigned elements from scientific medicine into their practice. In much of the world local curers routinely patronize licensed pharmacies for patent medicines; where antibiotics are sold without prescription they, too, are prescribed and administered by traditional curers and village "injectionists" who have mastered the technique. The term "injection doctor," coined by Cunningham in Thailand, is coming to be a standard expression to describe this updating of traditional therapies. In that country Cunningham finds injection doctors to be "mobile village or semi-urban people" in origin, rarely connected with traditional medicine. Their power lies in the magic of antibiotics; their clients are pragmatic and note the frequency with which they cure. Older "modern" physicians and "ancient doctors" (i.e. traditional curers) often respect each other and recognize each other's areas of competence, but both resent the injection doctors for the trade lost to them. The magnitude of this competition is apparent in a village studied by Cunningham where a sample of 133 people in 82 households over a 4-year period revealed 102 treatments at the government health station, 101 treatments by injection doctors, and only six treatments by "ancient doctors" (Cunningham 1970:6-8). More striking evidence of the decline of traditional medicine and the increase in the use both of modern and alternative forms of medical care can hardly be imagined.

Injection doctors armed with antibiotics both save and kill patients; in either case, they have something that goes beyond psychological support. This cannot be said of a charming "charlatan" encountered by Vargas in Mexico City who, recognizing the impact that X rays have made on Mexican popular medical views, concocted his own apparatus from an old automobile. Patients stood in front of the lights, the motor was accelerated to produce maximum noise, and the "exposed plates" were taken dripping from another apparatus and hung beside the patient in front of the car (Vargas 1978).

Landy suggests the term "role adaptation" to describe this process whereby traditional therapies are updated by the incorporation of real or feigned elements from scientific medicine. The concept of role adaptation has anomalous aspects. On the one hand, "adaptation" implies ability to change. At the same time, as Landy points out, however flexible some curers may be, they tend to remain cultural conservatives: the more closely their roles approximate those of scientific curers, the more vulnerable they become to extinction. Hence, the indigenous curer's adaptive strategy for role preservation in the face of changing conditions "consists in selecting only those changes that will preserve his role while at the same time minimally disturbing his already intruded culture" (*Ibid.,* 118). There is, however, an alternate strategy that in at least one instance has proven to be dramatically successful: master scientific medicine, but then continue to practice a modified traditional medicine. This is what has happened in Japan where *Kanpo,* the Japanese variant of traditional medicine, flourishes. Perhaps one reason for its success is that its practitioners "must first learn modern medicine and pass the state examination" (Otsuka 1976:335). "Traditional" curers such as these can hardly be compared to the Mexican *curandero,* the Siberian shaman, or the spiritualist.

The pattern of replacement of traditional medicine by both modern and alternative forms — such as those described here — seems to be worldwide. Thus, to ask about the possible use of traditional healers in national health services is to ask an incomplete or partial question. The real question is, should any (or all) forms of alternate health care systems and their practitioners be recognized as legitimate, and efforts be made to incorporate them into government health services? *All* health care systems meet at least some of the needs and expectations of sufferers who seek them out; otherwise they would not survive. Just as good a case can be made for the supportive, therapeutic value of spiritualistic therapy as for more traditional therapies; a case can even be made for the Mexican X ray specialist. If, then, therapies and curers that come from outside modern medicine are to be considered for incorporation into formal health care services, it seems arbitrary to exclude one system with demonstrably good results in favor of another, just because the other is older or more traditional. Yet this, we suspect, is what will happen. Planners who will seriously discuss the roles of traditional medicines and therapies in meeting primary health care needs will probably reject out of hand spiritualism and other alternate forms. The reason? At the planning and policy level the manifest function of traditional medicine is quite distinct from its latent function. In Third World countries today traditional medicine has become one of the most potent symbols of nationalism, evidence of the antiquity of cultures and of the ingenuity of their carriers. Traditional medicine is therefore attractive. Modern alternate therapies lack this symbolic value, so they have nothing — beyond helping people in need — to offer.

In conclusion, we hazard the guess that a good deal of lip service will be paid to traditional therapies and curers in future years, but that the impact on the development of national health services will be minimal.

NOTES

[1] Contrary to a common belief in the United States, the Chinese barefoot doctor is usually not a traditional curer. He (occasionally she) is a young person selected by the community on the basis of ideological commitment and willingness to work extra hours, as needed, who is given a few weeks or months of elementary health training. Barefoot doctors are, however, encouraged to make use of traditional as well as scientific remedies (cf. Hsu 1974; Sidel 1972). There is disagreement as to whether the model is suitable for other developing countries. [Cf. "Is the Chinese 'Barefoot Doctor' Exportable to Rural Iran?" (Ronaghy and Solter 1974).]

[2] The present world status of indigenous medicine and curers in formal health services is reviewed by Boris and Helga Velimirovic in the volume that incorporates the El Paso papers (B. Velimorovic and H. Velimirovic 1978).

[3] This is the same woman who is the subject of an article by Snow (1973).

chapter 15

Anthropology and Nutrition

THE PROBLEM OF ADEQUATE NUTRITION

Of the world's 4 billion people, hundreds of millions are malnourished and undernourished. Exact figures do not exist; there is no census of the hungry, and the distinction between adequate and inadequate nutrition is a broad band, not a sharp line. Whatever our criteria, hunger (and often starvation) stand as the greatest of all barriers to improved health in most of the world's countries. Malnutrition lowers the body's ability to resist infection, it leads to chronic illnesses of many kinds, and it makes sustained hard work impossible. Moreover, many specialists believe that protein-calorie deficiencies in the post-weaning period lead to permanent brain impairment. Much of the problem of malnutrition stems from the inability of nonindustrial countries to produce enough food to meet the needs of their burgeoning populations. Only major increases in world food production, through better agricultural methods, can reduce malnutrition and undernutrition that come from an absolute lack of calories and protein. But much of the problem also depends on widespread but erroneous beliefs about the relationships between food and health, and on beliefs, taboos, and rituals that prevent people from making the best use of the foods that are available to them. Malnutrition caused by poor dietary habits is, of course, not limited to the Third World; it is found in abundant measure in our own country. Because of recognition that worldwide nutritional problems are based on cultural forms as well as agricultural shortfalls, all of the major international and national developmental organizations are concerned not just with increasing food production, but also with changing traditional diet habits to achieve maximum nutritional advantage from the foods that are available.

This is an extraordinarily difficult task, since food habits have proven to be among the most resistant to change of all habits. Our likes and our dislikes, our beliefs as to what is and what is not edible, and our convictions as to diet in relation to health states and ritual calendars are set early in life. Only with great difficulty do most people break the bonds of food habits of their early years to embark on a greatly changed dietary course. Since food habits, like all customs, can be understood only in a total cultural context, effective nutritional education programs that may lead to improved dietary habits must be based on an understanding of food as a social institution that fulfills many functions.

The study of diet in its cultural context, pointed toward these practical problems, is an obvious role for anthropologists; as with medical beliefs and practices, anthropologists, since the earliest days of field research, have gathered information on the dietary practices and food beliefs of the peoples they have studied. And, just as interest in medical beliefs and practices, when coupled with practical concerns about health, led to medical anthropology, so has interest in food beliefs and practices, when coupled with practical concerns about world nutritional problems, led to the new field of *nutritional anthropology* (cf. Pelto and Jerome 1978). The Chairman of the Committee for Nutritional Anthropology (within the Society for Medical Anthropology), Norge Jerome, recently has defined this new field. "Nutritional anthropology encompasses the disciplines of nutritional sciences and anthropology. The field is concerned with those anthropological phenomena which impinge upon the nutritional status of humans. Thus, man's evolution, history and culture, and his adaptation to nutritional variables under various environmental conditions represents the focal materials in nutritional anthropology" (Kotona-Apte 1976:8).

In this chapter we are concerned with two important aspects of nutritional anthropology: (1) the social, cultural, and psychological attributes of food (i.e., the sociocultural roles of food, as distinct from its nutritional roles), and (2) the ways in which the sociocultural and psychological dimensions of diet relate to the problem of nutritional adequacy, especially in traditional societies. Thus, our approach reflects an anthropological instead of a strictly nutritional, science point of view.

FOOD IN A CULTURAL CONTEXT

Anthropologists view eating habits as a whole complex of culinary activities, likes and dislikes, folk wisdom, beliefs, taboos, and superstitions associated with the production, preparation, and consumption of food — in a word, as a major cultural category. And, as a major cultural category, they see food impinging on and related to many other cultural categories. Although they recognize that food is essential to life, that it is ultimately a physiological phenomenon, cultural anthropologists at least are particularly interested in the role of food in culture as an expressive activity that reaffirms social relationships, sanctions beliefs and religion, determines many economic patterns, and governs a large part of the daily round of life. In other words, just as medical systems play roles that transcend health and illness so, too, do dietary customs play basic social roles that far transcend mere nourishment of the human body. It is to some of these roles, and to certain cultural characteristics of food, that we first turn our attention.

1. Culture defines food

At first thought it seems odd to ask, "What is food?" Food is what grows on farms, what comes from the sea, what is sold in markets, and what appears on our tables at mealtime. Yet the question is basic to an understanding of the problem of nutrition. As a cultural phenomenon, food is not simply an organic product with biochemical qualities that may be utilized by living organisms, man included, to sustain life. Rather, to the members of every society, food is culturally defined; for an item to be consumed, it needs a cultural stamp of approval, of authenticity. No group, even under conditions of extreme starvation, utilizes all available nutritional substances as food. Because of religious taboos, superstitions, health beliefs, and historical accident, some nutritionally sound items are excluded from every diet; they are classified as "not food." In other words, it is important to distinguish between *nutriment* and *food*. Nutriment is a biochemical concept, a substance capable of nourishing and keeping in good health the organism that consumes it. Food is a cultural concept, a statement that in effect says "This substance is suitable for our nourishment." So strongly held are our beliefs about what is and what is not food that it has proven extremely difficult to persuade people to modify their traditional diets in the interest of improved nutrition.

In the United States we have access to an astonishingly wide variety of foods because of our multiethnic origins and an abundantly productive food system. Perhaps there is no other society in the world in which, at least among the middle and upper clases, so many different food items are consumed. But there are many nutritious items highly esteemed by the members of other cultures, and known to us, that we normally do not define as edible: horses, dogs, small birds such as larks and warblers, frogs, salamanders, sea urchins, octopus, seaweed, acorns, armadillos, rattlesnakes, dragonflies, ants, grubs, grasshoppers, maguey worms, and the Mexican "flying bedbug," the *jumil*. The list could be extended many times over and it is possible, in fact, that a nutritionally acceptable diet could be constructed of "foods" that most Americans never eat.

Personal preferences further reduce the variety of foods that every individual consumes, since none of us enjoys absolutely everything our culture approves as food. Childhood experiences, as we have noted, have much to do with our adult preferences; the foods we knew as children continue to attract us, while those we have come to know as adults are more apt to be rejected. Although some people delight in new food experiences, most seem happiest with familiar menus. In the United States studies indicate that the "most disliked" foods include buttermilk, parsnips, eggplant, caviar, hominy, oysters, turnips, Limburger cheese, pig's feet, and internal organs such as brains, liver, kidneys, heart, and tripe (e.g., Hall and Hall 1939; Wallen 1943).

Americans are not alone in their reluctance to exploit fully their nutritional environment. As Jelliffe and Bennett point out, "Man everywhere, even under adverse conditions, eats only part of the actually edible material available." As an example they cite the case of the "nutritionally hard-pressed Hadza hunters of Tanganyika" (Tanzania) who "will not eat the blood of animals and meticulously discard the apex of the hearts of animals they have shot" (Jelliffe and Bennett 1962:175).

2. Appetite and hunger

Not only is food culturally defined, but also the concept of a meal, when it is eaten, what it consists of, and the etiquette of eating. Among well-nourished people, culture dictates when they are hungry and what and how much they should eat in order to satisfy this hunger. Upon arising in the morning most Americans feel the need for more food than do continental Europeans. The stomachs of most Americans send insistent hunger signals around noon — in spite of hearty breakfasts — whereas in Mexico stomachs lie passively until three or four o'clock in the afternoon. Then they send up similar distress signals. The same Mexican stomach again asks for a light meal at nine or ten o'clock in the evening "because," its owner explains, "of the altitude" (7200 feet in Mexico City). In Bogotá, however, most stomachs cry out for a heavy meal at the same hour "because of the altitude" (8700 feet), the visitor is told.

In other words, *appetite* and *hunger* are related, but distinct, phenomena. Appetite, and what is needed to satisfy it, is a cultural concept that may vary greatly from one culture to the next. In contrast, hunger represents a basic nutritional deprivation and is a physiological concept.

In many societies the full definition of food cannot be made without reference to the concept of meals and mealtimes. In the United States we usually think of any item with recognized nutritional value as being food, regardless of when it is consumed, although midmorning and midafternoon coffee — even with nutritious cream and sugar — may not normally be seen as involving "food." In other societies the contrast may be more marked. In rural Mexico, for example, "food" is what is consumed at mealtime. Between-meal snacks, such as seasonal fruits, peanuts, candied squash, and other delicacies, which are placed on a table and offered to visitors who may call, are "not food," something eaten and enjoyed, but conceptually distinct from mealtime dishes. In early nutritional surveys in Mexico this rural distinction was not always appreciated. When asked what foods they had eaten during the preceding day, informants dutifully listed the items eaten at regular mealtimes. Consequently, many nutritious and important items, including delicacies such as grubs and insects, were omitted from analyses, and diets appeared to be less well balanced than was, in fact, the case.

3. All societies classify foods

In every group foods are classified in a wide variety of ways: what is appropriate to each formal meal, and as between-meal snacks; and according to ideas of status and prestige, social occasions, age, illness and health, and symbolic and ritual values. Americans, for example, hold very strong beliefs about what is appropriate at each meal. Although a few hearty souls enjoy a beef filet at breakfast, even they would turn down soup, salad, and chocolate pudding as inappropriate. Although eggs are suitable for all meals, their mode of preparation is not. Fried, they are acceptable only with breakfast, but as an omelette, they go well with any meal. So strongly held are American beliefs about breakfast that we, perhaps uniquely, have coined the expression "breakfast foods."

Status concerns play important roles, especially in changing food habits. Rural Mexicans, for example, prefer maize tortillas when they want something to stick to their ribs, but white bread is more and more seen as a status food, particularly to be eaten with breakfast. Cussler and deGive have pointed out how among lower-class whites and blacks in the southeastern United States, light-colored foods have more prestige than dark-colored foods (Cussler and deGive 1970:112), a phenomenon that has been noted in many parts of the world, and not just among class-conscious people. The wide preference for polished rice, for example, which is nutritionally less desirable than unpolished brown rice, seems due to prestige ideas. Refined, packaged, highly advertised foods seem to have irresistible appeal for people in the developing world, even though many of these foods are nutritionally inferior to traditional dishes. Developed countries, too, reflect status ideas that are divorced from nutritional reality, as, for example, the nearly universal preference for beef as compared to pork or lamb.

Probably all peoples classify food in relationship to health and illness and to stages in the life cycle. Pre- and postnatal food restrictions have been noted by anthropologists in the societies they have studied, and diet limitations are the rule at times of illness. In the United States we recognize "light" and "heavy" foods, the former suitable for the sick and the convalescent, the latter a luxury in which a person in good health may indulge. In France and, to a lesser extent in Italy, there is a notion that qualities of "virility" and "non-virility" attach to certain foods. Virility may be identified by color, spiciness, or "heaviness," or by some attributed ability to "excite" the body; they are, of course, particularly appropriate to males. Nonvirile foods are the opposite: "light," pale, or tender as, for example, in the case of veal and white wine, in contrast to beef and red wine. They are more appropriate to women and children.

Perhaps the most widespread of all food classifications, and particularly significant with respect to health, is the "hot-cold" dichotomy described in the discussion of humoral pathology in Chapter 4. Whatever the local qualities ascribed to each food, the common theme is that through judicious balancing of foods and the avoidance of excessive amounts of heat and cold, health is most apt to be maintained. Thus, in a north Indian village, hot foods include split peas, raw sugar, buffalo milk, eggs, and fish, and the especially hot foods of meat, onions, and garlic. Milk, it is believed, must not be taken with either meat or fish because of the heat produced. Regular and habitual consumption of the extra hot foods produces a "hot" temperament and a readiness to anger. Cold foods include leafy vegetables, carrots, water chestnuts, and curd (Hasan 1971:62). As we will see later, the taboos associated with the hot-cold dichotomy sometimes present serious nutritional problems during illness, infancy, pregnancy, and the postnatal period.

4. The symbolic roles of food.

Food is, obviously, essential to life. It is also essential to social intercourse. Were it not for the ways in which food is symbolically manipulated to express the perception of the relationships between individuals and groups, and within groups, it is hard to see how social life could exist.

(a) FOOD AS AN EXPRESSION OF SOCIAL TIES

Probably in every society to offer food (and sometimes drink) is to offer love, affection, and friendship. To accept proferred food is to acknowledge and accept the feelings expressed and to reciprocate them. To withhold food (as when a mother threatens a naughty child) or to fail to offer food in a context in which it is expected culturally is to express anger or hostility. Equally, to reject proferred food is to reject an offer of love or friendship, to express hostility toward the giver. In English we formalize this symbolism in the phrase "to bite the hand that feeds one." People feel most secure when eating with friends and loved ones and, in most societies, public and private meals symbolically express these feelings. Normally we do not share a meal with our enemies; on the rare occasions when we do, the mere act of dining together signifies that at least for the moment antagonisms are laid aside.

In Tzintzuntzan a mother once expressed regret that her eldest daughter had married out of the village and that she saw her only occasionally. Her youngest daughter lives only a few houses away, and it is a source of great comfort to her continually to be able to send bits of food, delicacies, and special items to her daughter. And, on occasion, and at the cost of an entire day's trip, she feels compelled to make something special and take it to her distant elder daughter.

In Tzintzuntzan dreams, too, seem to illustrate preoccupation with the expressive dimensions of food. Among housewives, one of the most common of all dreams is to have guests in the house, to struggle to prepare food but, in the end, to be unable to complete the meal and serve the visitors. Self-doubts of social adequacy may be expressed in this theme. In another common dream women tell of eating, but the food has no taste and cannot be felt in the stomach. One wonders if the dreamer is not expressing her fear that she cannot fully accept the love and affection offered to her by others.

Among rural Mexicans foods of known origin, content, and preparation, offered by someone the diner knows and likes, symbolize security; strange and different foods of unknown content, prepared by strangers (such as villagers encounter on short trips to big cities), symbolize insecurity and danger. When villagers as yet unfamiliar with big cities make occasional visits to them, one of their greatest preoccupations has to do with food. If they find a small restaurant or market stall in which the cook or proprietor seems friendly or comes from their part of the country, they will return to this place again and again, often at considerable inconvenience, because of the sense of security it offers them. A common theme of villagers' stories of city visits is the finding of parts of the bodies of babies in tamales and soups served in strange restaurants. This cannibalism motif seems to reflect a basic apprehension that afflicts people when they are removed from their known environments.

(b) FOOD AS AN EXPRESSION OF GROUP SOLIDARITY.
In America we recognize the role of food in maintaining family and friendship ties. Ideally, at least, to eat together, gathered around a big table, symbolizes the cohesiveness of the family; in an earlier and simpler America, Sunday dinner after church services, with grandparents, parents, and children, was consciously felt to emphasize family unity. On a wider level foods are often esteemed as symbols of ethnic or national identity. But not every food has this kind of symbolic value; those of greatest affect are foods native to, or believed to be native to, the group itself, and not those eaten commonly in many different countries or shared by many ethnic groups. As a symbol of national unity, the American Thanksgiving dinner illustrates this point: we *must* have turkey, a bird native to North America and hunted by our Pilgrim ancestors; cranberries, which grow in bogs near Plymouth; corn pudding, from the New World staple that the Indians taught the first immigrants to plant; and pumpkin pie, made from a native American squash. We would be just as satiated with roast beef and potatoes and gravy, but it would not be Thanksgiving. American ethnic and age groups also search out foods that serve them as identity symbols: soul food for blacks, maize-based Southwestern dishes for Chicanos, and health foods, natural foods, and macrobiotics for many young people.

In the contemporary world the symbolic use of indigenous foods frequently is a device to reaffirm national and ethnic ties. In Mexico turkey with *mole* sauce, served with tortillas, beans, and mashed avocado *guacamole* is notable as a ceremonial meal, in that all of the elements are native to the New World, and most of them to Mexico. The *mole* sauce is particularly interesting; it includes vanilla and chocolate (both indigenous to the Gulf Coast), peanuts (from the West Indies), and tomatoes and chile peppers, preconquest Mexican domesticates. Other symbolic foods include lamb in Arab countries, palm wine in West Africa, hot peppers, native maize *choclos,* and local fish pickled in lime juice (*ceviche*) in Peru, and *couscous* in Saharan Africa.

(c) FOOD AND STRESS

Specific foods, more than other cultural artifacts, come to reflect the identity of those that use them; consequently, they are vastly reassuring in stress situations. To the extent possible, many immigrants to the United States continue home dietary patterns, often at considerable cost and effort. In turn, Americans living overseas are much happier when they have access to an American commissary with all of the frozen, canned, and packaged foods they use at home. The psychological security value of food is also evidenced by a common tendency to eat more than normal and to snack between meals when a person is unhappy or otherwise under great stress.

Burgess and Dean suggest that attitudes toward food often reflect perception of danger as well as feelings of stress. One way to cope with the internal stress of threats to life or emotional security, they say, is to overestimate external dangers; another is to attribute internal threats to external influences. Magical attempts of various kinds are made to evade or appease an external threat or to balance one type of threat against another. "The practice of giving 'heating' or 'cooling' foods in particular kinds of clinical conditions may be a form of this kind of balancing technique; similarly, avoiding certain foods may unwittingly be a magical technique for evading what are regarded as threatening influences—not of a nutritional kind" (Burgess and Dean 1962:68).

Currier also has interpreted the Mexican hot-cold dichotomy in a covert, symbolic, as well as an overt, health-related sense. "Cold," he writes, "is associated with threatening aspects of existence, while warmth is associated with reassurance" (Currier 1966:256). In this vein it is worth noting that most Americans equate hot food with better nourishment than cold food, even though there is no apparent nutritional correlation with this belief. Nonetheless, we go to considerable trouble to make sure that we have at least one hot meal a day, and many people feel better able to face the rigors of the day if they start out fortified with a hot breakfast.

(d) FOOD SYMBOLISM IN LANGUAGE

In varying degrees languages reflect deep-seated psychological correspondences among food, perception of personality, and emotional states. In English, to an extent perhaps unrivaled in other languages, the basic adjectives used to described the *qualities* of food are used equally to describe the qualities of people: cold, warm, sweet, sour, bitter, salty, peppery, acid, spicy, tart, tough, tender, crisp, bland, strong, weak, fresh, spoiled, and so on. The words used in English to describe the *preparation* of food (a temporal process with a beginning and an end) also are words commonly used to describe moods (which are temporal, in contrast to enduring basic personality characteristics): boil (as in "boiling mad"), simmer (as in "simmering with anger"), steam (as in "all steamed up" about something), burn (as in "burned up" about something), stew (as in "stewed," intoxicated, or to "stew" over some worry), bake (as in "half-baked"), and coddle (as in "to coddle" or overly protect a person). Other food terms that describe personal characteristics include a "milk-and-honey" complexion, a "meat-and-potatoes man," and a "milk-toast."

The English language is also rich in other linguistic forms that express the symbolic ties between food and eating and emotional state. We can, for example, be "hungry for love" or "hungry for human companionship," just as we are hungry for food; one recognized cause of obesity is the substitution of food for love and friendship by lonely people. When we are shamed or embarrassed by being proven wrong, we "eat our words," "eat crow," or "eat humble pie." When obviously pining for something, we are asked, "What's eating you?", or it may be observed that we are "eating our heart out." When disappointed we "swallow a lump in our throat," and we "swallow our pride" in the face of a humbling situation about which we can do nothing. Gullible people "bite" or "take the hook [in their mouths]," and when we are "fed up" with something, we may be guilty of a "biting" remark or answer.

The extent to which food symbolism is used in other languages to describe character and temperament is uncertain, since neither anthropologists nor linguists appear to have paid attention to this usage. From our field notes we have a few examples from Indonesian and Spanish. In the former language there are expression that mean "nice, tasty to be looked at," "to be as enthusiastic as fermented soya beans" [or cassava (i.e., to be indolent, lazy)], "a cold person," "to have a sweet face," "to have a sour face," "to have already eaten much salt" (i.e., to be mature), and "the little chile pepper" (to describe a clever, little person). In Spanish a person may be described as *dulce* (sweet), *agrio* (sour), *amargado* (embittered), *saleroso* (from *sal,* salt: happy, smiling), *salado* (from *sal,* salt; plagued with bad luck), *desabrido* [tasteless (i.e., dull)], *frío* (cold), *caluroso* (warm), *tierno* (tender), and so on.

CULTURAL LIMITATIONS TO NUTRITIONAL ADEQUACY

Except where population pressures are excessive, tribal and peasant peoples long settled in the same place usually have done a remarkably good job in exploiting their environment to achieve a balanced diet. Although they may not define as "food" all nutritious resources available to them, they have, through trial and error, learned what they need to maintain strength and health. Utilizing a combination of staple foods and seasonal delicacies such as fruits, herbs, berries, grubs, and insects, they often have achieved a satisfactory diet. What tribal and peasant peoples frequently *have not* learned is the relationship between food and health and between diet and pregnancy, and the special food needs of children after weaning. Although much malnutrition in the world is due to absolute shortages of food, the problem is exacerbated because of cultural beliefs and taboos that frequently restrict the use of foods that *are* available. In health planning the problem is thus not limited to finding ways to provide more foodstuffs; ways must also be found to make sure that the foods that are available are used in the most effective way.

1. Failure to recognize the relationship between food and health

The basic conventional wisdom about food noted in the preceding paragraph is marked by major gaps in understanding as to how food can best be used. Perhaps the most important of these gaps is the frequent failure to recognize the *positive* relationship between food and health. Adequate diet tends to be thought of in terms of quantity, not quality, of sufficient staple foods, not a balance of many foods. Consequently, malnutrition may exist where the potential exists for an adequate diet.

To illustrate, Sharman found that among the Adhola of eastern Uganda, "there is no conception of the differential nutritional value of foodstuffs. The Adhola see no link between nutrition . . . and health . . . There is no Adhola belief that illness can be caused by *lack* of a particular type of food" (Sharman 1970:81). And in the north Indian village of Chinaura, Hasan found that people "generally believe that it is the adequate quantity of food that is important. The idea of quality is restricted to certain foods recognized to be 'strengthening. . . . ' No distinction is made between protective and energy producing foods" (Hasan 1971:57). Jelliffe and Bennett, who have had wide experience with nutritional problems in the tropics, speak of the problem of "superfoods" (i.e., staples that, unless supplemented by other items, may fill the eater but leave him malnourished). In Buganda, they point out, "Sufficient nutrients are available to prevent malnutrition, but despite this, protein-calorie malnutrition of early childhood is common because people do not make full use of the nutritious foods available" (Jelliffe and Bennett 1962:174-75). Failure to use what is available, they say, is often due to the belief that only the "superfood" (i.e., the staple plantain) is really food, and that other items are of no serious consequence.

Curiously, although traditional peoples frequently fail to appreciate the *positive* relationship between good diet and good health, they often see what can be called a *negative* relationship between food and illness. That is, in times of illness the foods most needed may be withdrawn from the patient. Solien and Scrimshaw, in describing the perceived relationship between food and health in the Guatemalan village of Santa María Cauqué, probably express a very widespread misconception: good health *allows* a person to eat a wide variety of foods, but poor health *restricts* a person's choice. "People in Santa María" they write, "feed their children well not to make them healthy, *but because they are healthy.* A good appetite is associated with health. . . . Almost any degree of sickness, however, results in the withdrawal of part of the food from his diet. Unfortunately for the child this is most often the part of his diet furnishing protein of good quality and may include nearly all of his protein of any sort. Thus, a child who has been receiving meat and milk along with beans and tortillas, will, if he develops diarrhea, have these withdrawn from his diet, and be given instead an *atole,* or gruel, consisting almost entirely of carbohydrate" (Solien and Scrimshaw 1957:100. Emphasis added). Protein-rich foods, especially meat and milk, may be eliminated from the diets of children with intestinal worms because they are believed to "cause the worms to rise." Although food is not considered a direct cause of illness, certain foods may aggravate conditions. Thus, "Even during pregnancy and the postpartum period, foods are selected carefully not because of their positive health-giving qualities, but because they will not 'hurt' the mother or the child (through the mother's milk). Thus, 'harmful' foods are excluded, 'harmless' ones permitted" (*Ibid.*).

In many societies the age or condition of a person may be given as the reason for prohibiting certain foods. In parts of West Africa, for example, eggs are denied to young children because it is believed that they delay closure of the fontanelle (e.g., the Yoruba in Nigeria), that boys who eat eggs become thieves (also Yoruba), and that girls who eat eggs will be marked by moral laxity (Ghana) (Hendrickse 1966:344). In one instance it was noted that the father of a child who suffered from severe protein malnutrition was a successful poultry farmer who sold hundreds of eggs a week, but it had never occurred to him to feed eggs to the child. (*Ibid.*).

For the east coast Malays in Malaysia, the postpartum woman is considered to be highly vulnerable, especially to "cold" coming from air or "cold" foods. Consequently, all "cold" foods are prohibited during the 40-day "roasting period" that follows delivery. These include almost all vegetables, all raw fruits but the "hot" *durian,* all sour and all uncooked foods, all fried foods, many kinds of fish, curry, gravy, and other sauces. The postparturient woman is limited to eggs, honey, yeast, tapioca, cooked bananas, roasted fish, black pepper, and coffee (i.e., "hot" foods). Because of these restrictions, her diet is less adequate than desirable (C. Wilson 1973).

2. Failure to recognize the special nutritional needs of children

The second major gap in the traditional dietary wisdom of tribal and peasant peoples is their frequent failure to recognize that children have special nutritional needs, both before and after weaning. Too often children are considered, for nutritional purposes, simply as little adults. Hendrickse points out the problem in tropical Africa. "The fact that a toddler may receive little meat or fish or eggs occasions little concern as there is no recognition of the special needs of young children for protein foods, and in any case, local taboos may place restrictions on the consumption of these items by young children" (Hendrickse 1966:344). Speaking specifically of the Adhola in eastern Uganda, Sharman writes that "It is not thought that children need special foods and none are prepared for them" (Sharman 1970:82). And Jelliffe and Bennett note the same thing. "In many places the ideas that young children need specially prepared foods and three or four meals a day are practically unheard of; people do not make the Westerner's customary association between growth and food, between malnutrition and lack of certain foods" (Jelliffe and Bennett 1962: 175).

Other childhood nutritional hazards stem from the frequent belief that children should not be forced to do anything against their will. In much of the world, in the absence of the idea of special childhood and postweaning foods, mothers rarely if ever force children to eat certain foods "because it is good for you." Children, like adults, are permitted to select what they want and to reject what they do not want. This barrier to upgrading infant nutrition is well illustrated by a Guatemalan case. "A new food for infant feeding . . . will win acceptance for well children *if it is liked by them* and if its use is not associated with any consequences which the parents regard as unfavourable. If, on the other hand, *the child does not like it*, or if vomiting, diarrhoea, or pains of any sort coincide with its introduction, the new food will no longer be given" (Solien and Scrimshaw 1957:100. Emphasis added.).

Nutritional blind spots like these — and particularly those that result in major protein deficiency in children's diets — frequently lead to the protein-calorie deficiency disease known as *kwashiorkor*. The symptoms of kwashiorkor, which was first identified in Ghana in the early 1930s by the British physician Cicely Williams, are (among African children) reddish hair, growth failure, edema, pallor, and apathy; unless the condition is skillfully treated, the ill child usually dies. The name itself comes from the Ga language of coastal Ghana and means "the sickness which the older child gets when the next baby is born." Curiously, in spite of William's early work, the gravity of the problem was not widely recognized until the 1950s (Cook 1966:330). In clinical and subclinical forms kwashiorkor has now been found in most other parts of the tropics, and today it is considered to be one of the greatest, and perhaps *the* greatest, of all health threats to infants in developing countries.

Jelliffe, who encountered a great deal of kwashiorkor and other nutritional deficiencies in children in West Bengal, India, has described some of the cultural "blocks" he found that aggravate the basic dietary limitations of that region due to poverty. Among these "blocks" is a delayed *mukhe bhat* or rice-feeding ceremony that should occur at about the age of 6 months for boys and 7 months for girls. Until the ceremony an infant subsists largely on its mother's milk, perhaps augmented with a little cow's milk, sago, or barley, which are adequate for its nutritional needs, including protein, for the first 6 or 7 months of life. But if supplemental foods are not then gradually added to this basic diet, the infant's health may suffer. The *mukhe bhat* is a social and family function of great importance; it is also expensive. The main feature of the ceremony consists of laying the infant on the lap of a maternal uncle or grandfather who places in its mouth small bits of boiled rice mixed consecutively with curries containing a bitter food, a sour food, green vegetables, and fish. These are *shokri,* or ritually dangerous, foods, and they include most of the items that the growing child needs.

If the child does not undergo the *mukhe bhat* ceremony at the appropriate time, its health obviously is endangered. Why, then, is the ceremony not always carried out on time, and why are children who undergo the ceremony sometimes not immediately fed *shokri* foods? Sometimes the delay is occasioned by poverty, lack of an auspicious day, or because of the absence of appropriate family members. Some mothers whose children have undergone the ceremony say they do not yet feed them *shokri* foods because the infant has no teeth. Among the most orthodox Hindu women the nuisance of pollution seems to play a role. The stools of infants not fed *shokri* foods are ritually clean, so the mother has merely to clean the infant after it defecates. But *shokri* stools are ritually unclean; the mother must therefore always change her sari after cleaning the baby and, if bedclothes are soiled, *all* bedding must be washed. For mothers who have little understanding of the relationship between diet and health, all of these seem like good reasons for not feeding *shokri* foods.

Other "blocks" to adequate infant nutrition in West Bengal are based on the classification of foods as "hot" and "cold". Foods classes as *garam* ("hot"), which include eggs, meat, milk, honey, sugar, and cod liver oil, are not given to children during hot weather (which lasts during a large part of the year) or when children are suffering from illnesses classified as *garam.* In all of these ways cultural practices add to the already serious limitations in nutritional possibilities open to poor village mothers in West Bengal (Jelliffe 1957).

Similar cultural "blocks" prevail in many other parts of the world. Wiese, for example, has found that in Haiti humoral pathology beliefs severely restrict the foods available to lactating mothers. Because of poverty, the staple foods available to women are severely limited at best but, because of hot-cold restrictions, a high proportion of the staples normally available are denied to nursing mothers. Health workers seeking to alleviate nutritional problems in rural Haiti seem to be oblivious of the nature of these "blocks" (Wiese 1976).

It is important to note that the onset of kwashiorkor most commonly occurs following weaning, when the mother is again pregnant. Until this point the infant has probably had fairly adequate protein from its mother's milk. But now, thrown out on its own, the child is in trouble. This problem is aggravated even further by the widespread custom whereby the father and older sons are served before the women and small children. They select the protein-rich items from what is available, leaving the less nutritious parts of the meal to the women and small children. The consequences of prolonged protein deficiency, even if the child ultimately recovers from kwashiorkor, are frightening; medical scientists now generally believe that loss of protein following weaning may result in irreversible brain damage resulting in lifelong lowered intelligence.

Proper treatment of kwashiorkor is sometimes inhibited because of the belief that its cause is psychological. This is clear in the meaning of the Ga term itself, which implies sibling rivalry, in which the older child loses. The explanation of *chipil* in Mexico and Central America (see page 66) is the same. When the recently weaned knee baby becomes irritable and displays apathy, indifference, weeping, petulance, or temper tantrums — all part of the kwashiorkor syndrome — mothers explain that they are *chipil,* angry at their mother who no longer gives them the breast and envious of the younger sibling they sense to be on the way. In Uganda this behavior, which doctors recognize as due to kwashiorkor, is called *obwosi;* it is explained in a slightly different way, although sibling rivalry remains the basic psychological explanation. "It is believed that *obwosi* is caused by the jealousy of the unborn child, and the weaning of the child who is already born is necessary because the unborn child will poison the [mother's] milk" (Burgess and Dean 1962:25).

There are, undoubtedly, elements of psychological deprivation in many cases of kwashiorkor. In research in Uganda it was found that in more than half of the cases of children admitted to the hospital because of kwashiorkor, there was a record of mother-child separation. Moreover, those hospitalized children whose mothers took the greatest interest in them and who stayed with them recovered faster and more completely than those whose mothers were indifferent (Geber and Dean 1956).

With respect to improving health levels, the question is not whether kwashiorkor interpreted as *chipil* or *obwosi* is due to sibling rivalry, protein deficiency, or a combination of both. The problem is that in the local etiologies, the illness is defined *entirely* in psychological terms, and diet is not recognized as relative to the problem. One therefore wonders whether mothers will be able to accept a nutritional explanation and be willing and able to change their traditional child-feeding practices significantly.

THE NUTRITIONAL PROBLEMS OF CULTURE CHANGE

When the lives of long-settled rural peoples who have achieved reasonably satisfactory diets are disrupted by the introduction of cash crops, wage labor, or migration to cities, dietary deterioration frequently occurs (Foster 1973: 61-63). The findings of Burgess and Dean describe the general rule. "Although there is a general tendency for diets to improve with increased income, they may also deteriorate, especially during a change from a subsistence to a cash economy. When cash crops, such as cocoa, cotton or tobacco, replace the traditional food crop, or when families abandon traditional tasks for paid employment, inferior foods such as cassava, or foods that can be bought, replace the better usual diet" (Burgess and Dean 1962:17). In the South Pacific, for example, nutritional levels fall when copra prices are high because islanders buy tinned beef and fish, sugar, and refined wheat flour instead of catching fish and growing food (*Ibid.*).[1]

A common relationship between cash crops and nutritional levels has been described by Marchione for Jamaica, with an unusual twist that drives home the point. In the parish he studied in the early 1970s, total reliance on subsistence agriculture was rare, and incomes were augmented by wage work and sale of cash crops. With countrywide soaring food prices, households were forced to spend 70 to 90 percent of their income on food, an economic situation that led to increased semisubsistence farming. This return to a more "primitive" economic system was widely expected to worsen an already serious malnutrition problem. In fact, Marchione found, malnutrition in poorer semisubsistence-oriented rural households significantly decreased, especially among children. That an increase in subsistence farming largely or entirely explains this improvement is evidenced by urban malnutrition rates which, in the absence of significant changes in food procurement patterns, remained constant (Marchione 1977:66-67).

Dubos describes dietary deterioration as a concomitant of economic "progress" in terms of a "loss of biological wisdom" which, he points out, characterizes both the Western and non-Western worlds. "There is no such thing," he writes, "as an instinct of good nutrition. There is only the kind of empirical learning that comes from trial and error, from experiences gained subconsciously under a given set of conditions. *But this kind of subconscious nutrition wisdom is lost as soon as conditions change, in particular if they change too rapidly*" (Dubos 1971:55. Emphasis added).

As we have seen in Chapter 2, this loss of wisdom is nowhere more apparent than in the tendency of mothers who have moved from village to city or who remain in the village but have access to city products to be swayed by commercial advertisements for baby foods. In much of Africa, for example, "Education and increasing urbanization have weakened the hold of custom and tradition on the present generation . . . the period of breast feeding is seldom as long as in traditional society . . . an ever increasing number of African women are undertaking paid employment and have to curtail or abandon breast feeding in order to meet the requirements of their work" (Hendrickse 1966:343). Infants are left with relatives, often totally untrained and unprepared for the task of bottle feeding. "The consequences of mismanagement of feeding are very apparent if one visits the wards of hospitals in Africa. These artificially fed infants seldom receive their correct dietary requirements and become malnourished, while faulty hygiene in the preparation of their feeds determines that they are the victims of recurrent attacks of gastro-enteritis, which can lead to nutritional failure and death. Few African women appreciate the risks involved in abandoning breast feeding for artificial feeding and, because of economic pressures and the steadily increasing influence of glamorous advertisements of proprietary brands of 'baby food', the practice is growing" (*Ibid.*). Jelliffe has found the same thing in West Bengal where, among lower-socioeconomic-class mothers, there is a growing tendency to "waste" money on widely advertised, powdered carbohydrate-milk baby foods (Jelliffe 1957:137).

An odd variant on the frequent pattern of dietary deficiency being associated with culture change has been noted in the north Indian village of Chinaura. Here the desire to enjoy a higher status in the caste ranking of India has led members of some of the lower castes to turn to vegetarianism — the custom of the highest castes — with consequent negative effects on their nutritional status (Hasan 1971:58).

SOME IMPLICATIONS OF THE CULTURAL CORRELATES OF FOOD

It is clear that for those who are interested in improving nutritional levels of malnourished people, the clinical analysis of dietary deficiencies is just the first step. Unless the nutrition educator also knows the social functions of food, its symbolic meanings, and the beliefs associated with it, little progress can be made. It is hardly helpful to recommend balanced diets if recommended foods violate in major fashion beliefs about the hot-cold restrictions that many people associate not only with normal eating, but especially with life crises such as pregnancy, the postpartum period, and illness. Nor does it do much good, for example, to prescribe milk for people who do not define it as food or who, because of lactase deficiency, are unable to drink it, at least beyond infancy. On the positive side, knowledge of local beliefs can be used in planning improvements. Cassel has shown how the identification of good diet with their ancient diet appealed to the Zulu among whom he worked and who, with this nationalistic motivation, were willing to accept numerous changes that improved their current diet (Cassel 1955).

Poverty and an absolute lack of adequate food set limits to the degree of nutritional improvement possible among hundreds of millions of malnourished people. However, it is discouraging to find how frequently cultural practices exacerbate basic shortages. Awareness of these practices and knowledge of the "barriers" that must be overcome to change them are essential to helping people maximize the food resources that are available to them. It is here that anthropology has much to offer nutritional science in research and instruction.

NOTES

[1] As with all cultural "rules" there are, of course, exceptions. Gelfand found, for example, that among the Mashona of Rhodesia hospital patients suffering from nutritional diseases most commonly came from rural villages, not urban townships. Survey research also indicated that urban Shona consumed more first-class protein and other nutritionally desirable foods than rural Shona did (Gelfand 1971:193-204).

chapter 16

Bioethics: Birth, Old Age, and Death

INTRODUCTION

In the preceding three chapters we have dealt with aspects of the anthropologist's role as an associate of other health personnel and the ways in which an anthropologist's knowledge and skills can be used to help raise health levels. In this final chapter we turn to a different anthropological role: that of constructive critic who asks questions about the appropriateness of medical assumptions in our own society that have long been taken for granted. These questions stem mostly from the conviction on the part of many Americans — professional and nonprofessional — that a chasm has grown and widened between medical goals and some very basic human values, that scientific advance in the maintenance and extension of life has not been without its cost in personal autonomy. For many (theologians, jurists, philosophers, and a concerned citizenry), there is a call for more lay involvement in decisions previously regarded as the inviolate prerogative of physicians and hospitals: decisions as to who is treated and where, how, by whom, and for how long?

Behavioral and social scientists are exploring health behavior to ask new questions. We want to know, *What does this mean* to the woman in pain, to the father separated from his family, to the child who has yet to come to terms with chronic illness? We ask subjective questions such as, How good a job does our society, and our medical system, do in dealing with universal human crises? To explore the ways in which anthropologists examine such questions and the grounds on which they base their answers, we turn to three areas of particular and growing criticism: the ways in which we, as a nation, handle the "problems" of birth, of old age, and of death. We ask, along with many critics of contemporary medical practices, whether there is an inherent "wisdom" in non-Western ways of accepting illness and of accepting the inevitable progression through life. We are not reopening the question of the relative efficacies of Western and non-Western medicine; we are asking philosophical questions dealing with attitudes, values, and goals, and we are asking if, in these areas, modern man may learn from his more traditional brethren.

The three topics we have selected are appropriate to the discussion that follows, since a great deal of contemporary research has been carried out on all of them both in Western and non-Western societies; they therefore lend themselves admirably to comparative treatment. They are not the *only* topics that might have been selected: alcoholism, drug abuse, alienation, and mental illness might also be profitably explored. But birth, old age, and death have the added appeal that they are universals, problems which all of us have experienced or will experience, while many of the other topics studied by anthropologists, although widespread, do not necessarily touch directly on the life of everyone.

THE INSTITUTIONALIZATION OF LIFE CRISES

When we look at the practices of birth, care of the aged, and the activities associated with dying in non-Western societies and compare them with those of contemporary United States, we find a great contrast. In the United States these life crisis have been fully — overly is a better term — institutionalized; in nonindustrial societies they are intimate parts of family experience. The fundamental question, then, has to do with the relative merits of an institutionalized approach to social and human problems versus a family-oriented approach. Increasing complexity of society historically is marked by institutionalization of ever-widening circles of human activities. Is this inevitable? Is it desirable, if not inevitable? Are we losing in human values much of what we assume we gain in efficiency and quality of care? Let us begin by looking at the Western-non-Western contrast in birth.

In traditional societies birth usually takes place in or near the home with the assistance of a midwife, more often than not a friend and neighbor. Old age, too, means the continued integration of the individual into the ongoing life of the group, with shifting role responsibilities and diminishing obligations suited to the mental and physical abilities of the people in question. Almost always there is some useful task an aged person can engage in, that helps give a continued feeling of worth; except in rare instances, usually dictated by harsh ecological conditions, old people expect care until they die. Death, when it comes, also occurs in or near the home, hidden from no one, not even the youngest child.

Until well into the twentieth century, this pattern was also the norm in the United States. Then, with the rapid development of medical technologies, of elaborate life-saving and life-prolonging equipment, the home seemed to become less and less suitable for birth and death. And, with increasing mobility, migration to cities, and the search for work where it was offered, the stability and rootedness of the family began to weaken. The care of the aged within the family became more and more of a chore, something to be avoided, if possible. In short, birth, old age, and death are less and less home-based; they have become institutionalized. It is this common transformation, their removal from the traditional setting, that ties them together. And it is the phenomenon of institutionalization that we increasingly question, asking, Have we gone too far?

Particularly striking is the contrast in children's knowledge about and participation in the rites of birth and death and the affairs of the aged in traditional and contemporary societies. In communities where there are few opportunities and less impetus to remove children from the full gamut of human experience, less apprehension and ambivalence attach to the stuff of life. Parents and old people, in health and in pain, are models that provide the appropriate cues for one's own behavior and the interpretation of birth and death. The wonder and mystery of life, the costs and rewards of human status, and the recognized limitations of man's control over life and health are subjects of little reticence, their nature known to all. As we have seen, non-Western peoples have their share of mental illnesses; still, it is hard to believe that the frank and open way in which life crises are usually handled in these societies is not advantageous to the psychological stability of most individuals.

In contrast, children in our society have come to be sheltered from these incorporative, even routine parts of daily interaction in traditional societies. Where birth and death occur in sealed-off, sanitized, alien places, we are all denied the opportunity to learn to accept them as predictable, inevitable, and normal dimensions of human life. When pregnancy and old age come to be regarded as pathological conditions warranting hospitalization, apprehension about or denial of the fundamental nature of life can easily follow.

We must not assume that families and homes always and everywhere are supportive, warm, feeling, concerned groups of people; often they are not. But they *can* be and, in the traditional setting, they frequently are. Nor must we assume that hospitals, clinics, and convalescent homes are never supportive, because they sometimes are, but the structural characteristics of bureaucracies militate against this as a general rule. The personal qualities so critical to birth, old age, and death attach to human actions rather than to institutions and resources. In the field of medicine, as elsewhere, impersonal priorities that reify the cult of efficiency tend to take precedence over personal rapport and psychological needs.

It is against this background that anthropologists, and concerned citizens at large, ask questions such as: Have contemporary birth practices caused us to loose sight of basic values and experiences that are part of the creation of new life? In institutionalizing the aged and insisting that they no longer have constructive roles in life, are we depriving them — and ultimately ourselves — of an important part of the full human experience? And in asserting that human life is sacred and that no effort must be spared to save and prolong it, are we the victims of our own ingenuity and technical skills? Have we confused the dignity of life — and of death — with the technical goal of increasing control over life? Questions like these can be researched. Not everyone will agree on the answers, but study can give us deeper understanding of what is happening, help us to form our own views and, to a point, shape the decisions we make then faced with these issues.

BIRTH

The mystery of life evokes awe and concern; it is an auspicious period as man compensates for his mortality through his powers of procreation. Birth completes the nuclear family, provides the considerable "staff" that keeps large extended families viable and insures the continuity of man himself. In traditional societies children offer the best promise that old ways will be continued, land retained, and parents cared for when they can no longer care for themselves. At the same time, birth is not, as is often asserted, normally regarded as a casual, nonthreatening experience. There are, of course, societies in which birth occurs with remarkably little fuss. Chance tells the case of an Eskimo woman "traveling by boat to Point Hope who asked to be put ashore 'to go to the toilet.' She gave birth after the boat had moved on without her, cut the cord, and scraped sand over the afterbirth. Putting the child in her parka, she ran along the beach to catch up with the boat" (Chance 1966:20). But these accounts are the exception, not the rule. Downs, analyzing the life cycle of American Indian groups, questions the stereotype of the primitive mother who disappears into the jungle to return shortly thereafter with a child, ready to continue her chores as if nothing unusual had happened. "Although this may be true in some parts of the world," he writes, "it does not apply to the Washo or any of their neighbors. The birth of a child was an event of enormous importance surrounded by ritual acts" (Downs 1966:42). In their analysis of delivery in some 200 traditional village societies, Mead and Newton conclude that unattended childbirth does occur, but "it is a rare event to be gossiped about in the same manner as an American birth taking place in a taxi cab" (Mead and Newton 1967:169).

In most non-Western societies, childbirth creates a running tug-of-war with spirits that are attracted by female emissions and the birth scene. Also, the fetus, not yet fully human, can easily be lured to the supernatural world from which, often, it is regarded as not yet freed. Birth is a time of pain and suffering, of bleeding and loss of bodily fluids with the threat of death always present. These are the characteristics of illness. Not surprisingly, pregnancy and childbirth are semantically tied to illness in many societies. In Tzintzuntzan a pregnant woman *está enferma,* she "is sick." And when the child is born, *se alivia,* the mother "gets well." Both expressions are the same as those used for illness and recovery of all other types. Similarly, the Araucanian Indians of South America, who carefully bar outsiders from the birth scene, feel that "most certainly all children should be there, now when mama is sick" (Hilger 1957:14). In societies lacking a sense of asepsis, and with very limited knowledge about the functioning of the entire human system, including gestation, pregnancy and childbirth may quite understandably be pervaded with fear. The high maternal and infant mortality rates of many non-Western societies corroborate the logic of such fears and the inefficiency of essentially magical precautions against real dangers.

In voicing the criticisms of many Americans about childbirth practices we are not, obviously, holding up those of tribal or peasant groups as ideal models — effortless and safe approaches that we have abandoned at our peril and urgently need to reinstall as standard childbirth procedures. In our view the problem, rather, is how to build more satisfying patterns of childbirth that utilize advanced gynecological skills to the point that they are needed (but not beyond) without depersonalizing the birth experience.

For the majority of Americans, medical bureaucracies are the final arbitors of life, in birth as in death. The prescriptions for a "normal" delivery vary little in their patterning, from the signing of forms for hospital admittance (when labor pains are a prescribed number of minutes apart or when the "water breaks") to the synchronized activities of the obstetrical team. Resistance by many to hospital-dictated forms of childbirth is part of a mounting disenchantment in the United States with what is regarded as the generally impersonal and mechanized treatment of fundamental human needs by the medical system. Among many the conviction is growing that the life cycle basically is a social and not a medical phenomenon and, where medicine has asserted dominant control, we have paid a generous toll in psychological, and sometimes even physical, well-being.

Part of the problem is that, with modernization and urbanization, medicine has increasingly taken over the functions not only of family care (Parsons and Fox 1952), but also of family authority and "conscience". Hospitals, in particular, have insulated society against coping with once familiar family crises. Life-and-death-affecting decisions that in the traditional world remain the province of morals and religion and the social group have, in Western culture, fallen within the health field domain. "In fact," says Mechanic, "we take it so for granted that seeking medical care is the rational and natural thing to do . . . that we are frankly surprised at the persistence of folk and religious concepts in what we view as the legitimate province of medicine" (Mechanic 1975:50).

It is probably fair to say that with regard to the most predictable of human conditions — birth, aging, and death — there is an enormous lag between scientific and cultural interpretations of what gives them special significance, makes them a basis for joy or despair, and facilitates or inhibits their orderly progression. Consequently, in their failure to recognize the chasm that so frequently exists between *their* perceptions and desires and those of the individuals and families they serve, medical personnal have often unwittingly created new crises as they have resolved old ones.

For Americans who are dissatisfied with the usual forms of hospital delivery, the search for alternate forms is based on three convictions, which will now be discussed in turn.

(1) *Western medicine has complicated and mechanized the process of normal birth.* Since the vast majority of human beings alive today were born at home, how does it happen that in the United States 90 percent of births take place in hospitals? Why are mothers not routinely delivered at home?

Essentially because it would be inconvenient for doctors, some critics contend. If the doctor can persuade his maternity patients to go to the hospital, he can see them there without seriously interrupting his other professional activities. "In the hospital the obstetrician doesn't even have to be present when the baby is born. If he can manage to be present, well and good, but if he happens to be elsewhere when the baby is about to be born, an intern or any nurse on the service will do just about as well" (Hazell 1969:139-140). This occurrence, however, violates such a strong medical taboo — none but the doctor may or is indeed capable of delivering a baby — that it is rarely disclosed, and the official assumption (U.S. Statistical Abstracts, U.S. Bureau of the Census) is that *all* births in hospitals are attended by a physician (Mead and Newton 1967:195). Since birth certificates are customarily signed by the physician, the fiction is easily sustained (*Ibid.*).

But isn't hospital delivery safer for the mother and baby and, realistically, shouldn't the time of the busy doctor be considered, defenders of the present system ask. The labyrinthian coldness of hospitals, the pain orientation of these institutions structured essentially for the sick or dying, anxiety-provoking delivery rooms with their awesome array of lights and instruments, the tangential involvement of husbands and families (when they are permitted at all), and the engulfing sense of being an outsider in a strong but privileged world — these factors are regarded by many as contributing not only to the mother's psychological discomfort, but to actually harmful routinization of an event that should be allowed its ordained progression.

The medical activist Arms argues that there is often premature and excessive use of drugs with the onset of hard labor (often against the expressed wishes of the mother) and that this inhibits effective contractions, needlessly promotes forceps deliveries, and endangers mother and child (Arms 1975:54-58).

Not all criticism is by nonmedical personnel. "I'm not sure," says obstetrician William J. Sweeney, that "the position we use for hospital deliveries in America is really the best one." If a woman gives birth in bed, he points out, everything is more relaxed and she is less likely to tear than she is when she is in the prescribed delivery room position — up in stirrups. "Most primitive people deliver in a squatting position or use an obstetrical chair, thus taking advantage of the force of gravity. Or they lie on their side. A woman in labor turns on her side if you leave her alone because the pain is less severe." In England patients are delivered in that way. "But, he concludes, "it doesn't fit in with U.S. hospital routine. Of course it's easier to work on a patient when her legs are up" (Sweeney 1973:304-305). In short, the rationale of the present system is the well-being of the mother and child, but the determining factor in maintaining it seems to be the convenience of the doctor. It is "*because* of the insistence of the doctors," says Cosminsky, that one of the changes occurring throughout Northern Mexico "is the increasing use of the supine or horizontal position" (Cosminsky 1974:12. Emphasis added). Midwives are taught that it is unbecoming to follow the Indian kneeling position (*Ibid.*).

(2) *Childbirth should be returned to the home from the hospital.* Although there is strong medical conviction that the more scientifically advanced the level of maternal and infant care, the more effective the prevention of mortality, injuries, and birth defects, an eminent medical sociologist in a review of the literature finds there is "no clear evidence that this is the case" (Mechanic 1975:56). It is probable that a higher percentage of childbirth occurs in hospitals in the United States than in any other country but, popular beliefs to the contrary, this country is by no means the safest in which to be born. In fact, we are approximately in fifteenth place, trailing countries such as Sweden, France, Holland, Japan, New Zealand, and Australia.

In some situations home delivery has been found to be safer than hospital delivery. The Frontier Nursing Service of Appalachia, made up largely of English-born nurse-midwives, for many years traveled the most rugged hills, sometimes on horseback, to deliver babies in isolated homes under the simplest conditions. In Kentucky they did not lose a mother in 12 years. "Unfortunately, the modern age caught up with the Kentucky mountains" writes Montagu. "Home deliveries were discontinued by the Frontier Nursing Service because patients' hospitalization policies ceased paying for them. Now the women must drive many miles over tortuous mountain roads in uncertain automobiles to get to the hospital. Otherwise, they can't afford to have the baby." (Montagu 1962:113-115). Even under urban slum conditions, the Chicago Maternity Center, in 30 months, lost not one of the more than 8000 mothers its staff delivered. As Montagu also points out, this compared impressively with our national average of maternal loss of 1 per 1000 live births (*Ibid.*).

Advocates of home childbirth make their case, however, not on numbers but rather on the richer quality and rewards of having children born in homes instead of in hospitals. "It is my conviction that childbirth is a family affair, everyone being strongly affected by its outcome," write Hazell (1969). This attitude is strongly reminiscent of that expressed to Wylie by the villagers of Peyrane, France, who know that there are "beautiful new maternity hospitals," but feel strongly that hospital care "is necessarily inferior to home care because you can not expect 'strangers' to devote themselves to you as members of the family would . . . . The birth of a baby is the most important event that can occur in a family. Both the mother and the baby deserve the best care the family can give them" (Wylie 1957:37).

The conviction is also strong that home arrangements allow the feelings of achievement at birth to center around the mother and not around the actions of the obstetrician. The priority accorded the accomplishments of the physician is reflected in medical parlance. Mead and Newton point out that the obstetrician says, "I delivered Mrs. Jones," using the active voice. Reciprocally, Mrs. Jones acknowledges that "Dr. Smith delivered me," using the passive voice (Mead and Newton 1967:174). It is the obstetrician, not the mother, who routinely is thanked for a successful birth.

Home birth also affords the husband a more therapeutic role in labor; in some instances he actually participates in the delivery. Finally, pain expectation is thought by many to be reduced and delivery facilitated in the familiarity of the home situation under conditions which, like those that prevail in most traditional societies, allow women to engage in normal physical activity up until birth, often between labor contractions.

(3) *The midwife, not the physician, is the logical person to assist at delivery.* Suzanne Arms is perhaps the most vociferous advocate of legalized midwifery in the United States. She has strong support from a number of medical anthropologists who have worked on the subject of "birth culture," underscoring the side effects of overregulated hospitals (Mead and Newton 1967; Scheper-Hughes 1974; Hazell 1969; Newman 1965). Civilization, Arms contends, brought on conditions and attitudes that complicated childbirth, and then doctors to deal with these problems, and more doctors and *hospitalization* to deal "with the problems the first doctor had caused." Arms' assumption that nonindustrial childbirth is "uncomplicated and inherently safe" is, as we have seen, highly questionable, but it is an argument that many people want to believe, so that it is enormously influential. "If we believe today that childbirth is dangerous, risky, painful, and terrifying, it is only because as a race of people, we have made it so. If we turn to the doctor and the hospital as the only authorities on childbirth available, it is because we have turned away from the built-in authority of our own bodies" (Arms 1975:23).

Ideally the midwife functions in the home in a bedroom that she has helped the family to prepare for the event. Some midwives work in consulation with sympathetic obstetricians who make themselves available in the event of an emergency, such as a Caesarean section or a difficult presentation of the fetus. In a few instances they have been integrated into hospital staffs to cooperate in alternative forms of childbirth that better simulate home delivery conditions within the hospital structure. However, unlike most of Europe, the United States has yet to allow the midwife to become a part of the integral medical or social structure of the community.

Only in the District of Columbia and 14 states is the midwife now licensed to practice, and then only as a member of an obstetric team. In states where laws are permissive but actual legal recognition is withheld, midwives who work independently simply take the chance that they will not be challenged. In California, where home birth has achieved phenomenal popularity, laws ambiguously state that midwives may function if they carry a certificate which, in effect, has never been issued by the State Board of Medical Examiners! With legal crackdowns occurring more and more frequently, the home birth "underground" has been forced into the open, and obstetrical restrictions are being challenged by parents and practitioners.

Natural childbirth and its offshoot, the Lamaze method, are the best known and most widespread of formal attempts to modify hospital delivery practices that have prevailed during recent decades. They arose as vigorous attempts at the demystification of medical obstetrics and of birth itself. Basically, however, they are compatible with the hospital environment, which they do not reject. The obstetrician, Frederick Leboyer, *has* rejected much of conventional delivery-room procedure and advocated "birth without violence," a general softening and enhancement of the birth experience for mother and infant (Leboyer 1975). More radical in concept are the views and practices of some members of the "counterculture" who seek the "remystification" of birth as a spiritual experience of awesome potential. Anthropologist Nancy Scheper-Hughes has described this birth counterculture in the San Francisco Bay Area. Some adherents do not reject outright hospital delivery; they accept it if their terms are met. A small Marin County hospital, for example, has wholly revamped its maternity-wing environment and its delivery procedures to accommodate the expectations and rituals of its large population of "birth freaks" (communicated by Dr. Scheper-Hughes). Delivery is now allowed to take place in labor rooms that the mother and father have decorated in any way they choose. Soft music, chanting, and colored lights are permitted, as are eating and drinking in moderation during the long hours of labor. The laboring woman is not confined to bed, and doctors and nurses are expected to adapt themselves as fully as possible to her wishes. Finally, the infant is not separated from the parents who, after a brief period of observation, are allowed to decide when they wish to return home. The dividends of these innovations have been felt as significant by the hospital staff in actually facilitating delivery and in improved interpersonal relationships.

Other members of the birth counterculture feel that, except under extraordinary provocation, birth *must not* take place in a hospital, where the depersonalized approach is antithetical to the fragile and transcendental quality of new life. Whereas natural childbirth enthusiasts mistrust and fear the mechanization of natural processes, "birth freaks" fear, in their own words, the "poisoning" of psychic resources and the "violation of the body at the hands of a blundering medical profession." Despite some excesses of enthusiasm, the two groups — natural and counterculture — have forced a reexamination of some of the assumptions that underly obstetrical care and accepted medical management of the body through pregnancy and labor.

Proponents of midwifery and home delivery regard these alternatives to conventional hospital care as psychologically, socially, and medically beneficial. Opponents see them as fadistic, Rousseauan, unrealistic, and essentially perilous undertakings. The former see midwifery as upgrading the quality of medical care, the latter, as diluting it. Patients, and a growing number of physicians and social scientists, find themselves somewhere between the two camps, seeking redress from medical excesses, but wary of abdicating conventional safeguards.

"The point is," says William Silverman, in a taped talk reported by Arms, "that we do not need blanket rules. In our plural society there are different value systems, and the standards of risk vs. benefit in birth and death are not the same for everyone; this must be accepted" (Arms 1975:114). For those committed to the desirability of home birth, health care funding and services should be provided. "With both birth and death we face the question of how far we are willing to go from the natural process just to protect us from risk. The agonizing experiences of having to make difficult decisions is part of life. The whole quality of life today is interfered with because we avoid experiencing parts of life, and try to lay down blanket rules about what is and is not an acceptable risk" (*Ibid.*).

OLD AGE

One segment of the life span that is now widely experienced by Americans is old age. Few men and women, however, have come to value this part of life; instead, they have learned to hold late life in invidious comparison with "young life." Anthropologists and other social scientists are asking why this should be the case. Why in the United States today can one as happily entertain the suggestion that he is growing old as he can the early indications of malignancy? It is otherwise in many non-Western societies. Describing his childhood in Mongolia, Onon writes, "According to the thinking of our people, honors and riches are bestowed by mere men, but ripe old age is a gift from Heaven" (Onon 1972:9). For this reason, he says, no one makes any attempt to conceal advancing years. "On the contrary, all could look forward to that golden autumn period of life when, full of years and rich experiences of living, they would receive that special respect and consideration which would be their greatest reward" (*Ibid.*). What is less emphasized, of course, is that few aspirants lived to reach the golden years.

It is difficult to tell whether anthropologists, in their studies of traditional communities, have overdrawn the picture of respect accorded to the aged. Certainly in many communities, as in the "closed corporate" Indian and peasant villages of Spanish America, the major ritual activities of the year provide a "ladder" or an avenue by which men, through continuing service to the community, gradually achieve the status of "principal," or distinguished elder, an individual rich in merit and prestige, no longer ambitious for worldly rewards. Yet in one of these communities, Tzintzuntzan, Foster found attitudes toward the aging remarkably similar to those in the United States. Old people who continued to show interest in and participate in community affairs — people who demonstrate their continuing commitment to the village — are respected *for their interest,* but not because of earlier activities. Once they relax, respect rapidly slips away.

Other cultural forms make one wonder about the totally satisfactory role of elders in traditional societies. In Korea, for example, it is believed that God allots humans a life span of 60 years. Those who continue to live past this age do so at the expense of others; in true "limited good" fashion, their extra years come out of the allotment of someone else, who will die as much before the age of 60 as the old person surpasses it. What, one wonders, are the feelings of guilt attached to old age in such a situation?

Whatever the nature and range of attitudes toward old age in non-Western societies, the perception of the value of late life in the United States seems qualitatively different. "Old age" is not a role to which many aspire, and possible honors and esteem more often than not are outweighed by family and community lack of interest and concern. Older men and women too often live and die "in despair, feeling only that there is nothingness, they are nothing, death is nothing" (Curtin 1972:228).

The ethic of the relative worthlessness of late life, as compared with youth or young adulthood, is a recent cultural phenomenon in the United States; it is linked with medicine's success in pushing the expectable life span from 47 to 70 years in little more than a half-century. As recently as 1900, only 1 person in 25 reached the age of 65. Today the figure is 1 in 10. And the man who reaches the age of 65 can today expect to live to 78; the average women to about 80. As long as there were few old people, relative to the rest of the population, we could accommodate them socially. We could absorb with particular pride the exceptional few — elder statesmen, seasoned artists, heads of commercial empires, wise judges, theologians, and professors. These were still active, productive people and therefore highly esteemed in a work-oriented society. But, by the 1970s, we had created an age group of awesome proportions — 21 million people — the bulk of whom, like the bulk of Americans, were not so gifted. What was *not* created was a prescription for their viable incorporation in a youth-oriented society.

The very concepts of aged and old have become ambiguous and damning, because they merge distinctions (made in most cultures) between healthy longevity and that helpless, near-moribund stage that often just precedes death. The consequence is a curious anachronism: long life accompanied by social attitudes appropriate only toward the dying. We have, in brief, succeeded in substituting a formal instead of functional definition of aging, obviating the need for logical assessment of what the old are indeed capable of doing.

Our cultural stance has had deep implications for the psychological and physical well-being of the old and for their medical treatment, not only in the U.S. but also in whatever traditional systems Western culture makes inroads. Viewed as a diseased or dying minority (Clark 1973:80-81), their care has fallen more and more routinely to "rest homes" and "convalescent" hospitals. When actually mentally or physically ill, the aged frequently face a medical rationale of therapeutic nihilism; psychodynamic treatment is considered a waste of time and, as Sudnow and others have reported, the aged are less likely to be regarded as salvageable when they enter a hospital in serious condition (Sundnow 1967; Knutson 1970:51). In the Caucasus, on the other hand, sickness is not considered a normal or natural event, even in very old age, and it has to be counteracted. Everybody, including the patient, expects recovery. "One never hears the expression of the fatalistic view, 'Well, what do you expect at that age?' " (Benet 1974:14).

The consequence of our assessment of aging has also been unfortunate for health research, because as long as the aged are so readily cast into the sick role, there is little impetus to separate the course of many diseases from the as yet little understood, little explored aging process. But, as Clark points out, "in the United States it is becoming clear that what we have thought as inevitable biological characteristics of old age — sensory loss, learning deficits, confusion, memory loss, incontinence, etc. — may be reversible or controllable symptoms of disease process that are separable from 'normal' aging" (Clark 1973:81).

1. Social interpretations of aging

The need to explore the nature of normal, "healthy" aging was first recognized by sociologists. Tentative proposals such as the "disengagement theory" (Cumming and Henry 1961), the "quasiminority theory" (Barron 1961; Kiefer 1971), and the "subculture theory" (Rose 1965) had distinct implications for the delineation of standards of mental and physical health and for appropriate care as aging "progressed" (Cowgill and Holmes 1972). The most influential of these has been the disengagement theory — derived from the study of healthy, middle-class Kansans — which postulates not only that mutual withdrawal on the part of aged persons and society is normative, but that both are better adapted after this joint withdrawal has taken place. Subsequent testing of this theory by sociologists and psychologists in the United States and to a very limited extent crossculturally (Havighurst, Neugarten and Tobin 1968) has raised questions about the "normalcy" of this kind of social attrition in late life, and suggests that activity, not disengagement, is correlated with psychological well-being in late life.

Until the late 1960s anthropologists had given the emerging field of social gerontology (and its medical sister, geriatrics) only passing attention. As Cowgill and Holmes have pointed out, "This is not to say that anthropologists had ignored the field; merely that in their field work and in their publications the process of aging and the condition of old people were treated along with many other facets of the cultures being studied. Rarely was aging made the focus of such studies, although elders often served as key informants" (1972:vii). That situation has changed, and the last decade has seen some provocative anthropological explorations of the phenomenon of aging and of the cultural dilemmas that have accompanied it. Jacobs (1974), Byrne (1974), and Johnson (1971) have utilized conventional field techniques to analyze "communities" of elderly within the United States and the psychosocial dividends and liabilities of these alternate life-styles. Benet (1974) holds up the Abkhasians of the U.S.S.R., with their commitment to moderation and their rejection of age discrimination, as a model for stress-free physical and social adaptation. On the basis of cross-cultural data, Cowgill and Holmes (1972) challenge some existing propositions on the inevitably of alienation and diminished ego-strength with modernization. And, in a landmark article, Clark has defined the concepts of aging in the United States that identify the old in our society "as dependent and cast many of them in the sick role — one of the only socially sanctioned roles that they are permitted to play" (Clark 1973:81).

2. Ways of coping: two basic strategies

Most of the foregoing accounts contain at least implicit suggestions on how to cope with existing inequities. Essentially two basic strategies, or models, are advanced by anthropologists and other behavioral scientists.

(a) THE "CONFRONT-THE-SYSTEM" MODEL

Clark and Anderson espouse a "confront-the-system" approach with a five-task model of aging adaptation. This model emerged from a 3-year longitudinal study of 1200 old San Franciscans, half of whom had developed age-linked mental illnesses severe enough to have caused hospitalization. The "tasks" derived from an assessment of strategies that had proved successful in keeping the normal half of the sample from reaching the psychiatric ward after the age of 60 (Clark and Anderson 1967:398-414). These tasks — all of which need to be "worked through" if "successful aging" is to occur — include the acceptance of aging itself, the reorganization of "one's life space" in order to preserve a continued optimum level of control, substitution of alternative sources of need satisfaction as old ones become inappropriate or disappear, a modification of one's basis for self-evaluation and, finally, a reintegration of values in order to evolve a new life-style. The latter often demands aggressive personal action to wrest a legitimate place in society. "It appears to us," the authors conclude "that the alienation of the aged from American life is not wholly barred from any creative solutions." (Ibid. 429). Those who survive best in their later years are "simply those who have been able to drop their pursuits of the primary values (as their culture has required them to do) and to go on to pick up, as workable substitutes, the alternative values which have been around all along: conservation instead of acquisition and exploitation; self-acceptance instead of continuous struggles for self-advancement; being rather than doing; congeniality, cooperation, love, and concern for others instead of control of others" (*Ibid.* 429).

Admittedly this shift from one set of value orientations to another has imposed serious, stressful discontinuity for some persons. But the ability to substitute, to stay within the arena of life, is "the crucial skill." Social withdrawal, they underscore, is physically and emotionally maladaptive, despite the fact that American culture (as it is constituted today) regards it as normative for its old people. They oppose the sociological theory that "disengagement" of the individual from society is an integral part of "normal," healthy aging. Recently Anderson has further refined the five-task model into a series of action formulas for spearheading the cultural reintegration of the aged (Anderson, 1978).

(b) THE "ESCAPE-THE-SYSTEM" MODEL

More and more, older Americans are attracted either to communities exclusively designed for them, as in the euphemistically named "adult-living communities," or to settings such as mobile-home parks, where less affluent retired individuals congregate. In both types of settings retired people build life-styles around leisure pursuits instead of around work. Anthropologists have studied both, reporting on their relative success in compensating for the psychological and physical supports denied their residents in the larger community.

"Ignoring" old age by emphasizing a cult of pseudoactivity created within the communities seems to work for some people; it provides the basis for a healthier self-image and insulates them against disquieting changes "on the outside." The fundamental source of appeal, however, writes Susan Byrne of Arden, a pseudonym for a wealthy California retirement community, "lies in its provision of an environment that permits residents to live much as they did in earlier years" (1974:151). For some people adaptation in these high-density, age-segregated communities apparently requires less drastic behavior modification than growing old in the urban or suburban areas from which they had come. But few men and women escape the insidious reminders that golden age worlds are, at best, a compromise refuge from a society that has little regard for them. "Unlike the urbanized peasant who has entered the mainstream of his society and may wholeheartedly adopt new ways, the emigrant to a retirement community is, in a sense, weakening his bonds to the wider society and is reluctant to admit that he is doing so" (Byrne 1974:139). A large measure of the appeal of trailer parks among the elderly is precisely because their relatively small and more integrated structure provides critical psychological reinforcement, making them feel "we are all like one big family" (Johnson 1971:173).

Predictably the most recurrent stress reported for all such communities is the fear of illness and death within their midst. "Such deaths seemed to depress them and they generally avoided attending the funerals," writes Johnson of a Berkeley, California, working-class mobile home community. In the more select community of Arden, a retired professor of public health describes "an unwritten rule that you don't talk about it (death), just within little circles of acquaintances if one of them is stricken. Otherwise it's six months later that you ask, 'Where's so and so?' and someone says that he died" (Byrne 1974: 148). Byrne reports an incident wherein a man died of an apparent heart attack at a large clubhouse meeting. "The ambulance arrived, silently, within five minutes of the telephone call, and the moderator resumed his speech as the ailing man was lifted into it." On the terrace the overflow crowd "reacted with remarkable disinterest. A woman standing in a group of four people near me remarked that the stuffy air inside must have caused the man to faint, a second woman replied that she was glad they had not arrived in time to be seated inside, and all murmured assent and laughed. They then began talking about gardening" (Byrne 1974:149).

DEATH

Preparation for dying involves the projection of a condition without precedent in our experience. Americans especially are conditioned from early childhood to live as though they were immortal, protected from evidence that such a position is untenable.

In most of the traditional world this fiction cannot be maintained. Death crowds the streets of Calcutta in daily overdisplay, as it does the scrubby villages of Africa's Sahel. Children live with the ultimate toll of malnutrition and disease, mothers lose as many babies as survive into adulthood, and it is the rare family that remains intact for many years. Even in those peasant areas where life is better and health and maturity may be reasonable expectations, the presence of dying people in the house, the large attendance at funerals, and the daily contact with aging people prepare the young for the fact of death and teach them how to die.

In the United States, on the other hand, it is common to reach maturity without ever having seen someone die. The occasional, chance exposure to death through violence, accident, or suicide only reinforces our fear of it as a random mutilating event, from which, with any luck, we will somehow be exempt. In our unconscious minds we cannot die. We can only be killed. "Therefore death in itself is associated with a bad act, a frightening happening" (Kubler-Ross 1969:2).

In death, even more than in birth, Americans have abdicated care and decision making to hospitals and physicians. The trend away from medical fiat so evident in the new birth culture has not been evident in any complementary approach to death, unless the present ventilation of concern about inordinate prolongation of life in our hospitals represents some kind of overture. Hospitals continue to insulate homes and families from the rigors of coping with the dying. Death takes place in the anonymity of "white-sheeted habitats" that, in the judgment of some critics, too often reduce patients to "room numbers" and their parents and children to "visitor" status. Few of us even conceive of alternative ways of dying.

1. The art of dying

The art of dying (*ars moriendi* in the words of medieval writers) is perhaps most nearly approached today in the peasant world where naturalistic interpretations of life and health foster a greater sense of the legitimacy of death, however reluctantly accepted. The process of growing up in the relative timelessness of village life, in stable, often three-generational households, in daily interaction with old and young, sick and well, and where wakes and funerals are common — these experiences provide models for aging and dying that are essentially absent elsewhere. There develops a sense of the legitimate programming of life and the fulfillment of a drama whose inexorable denouement has been witnessed a dozen times before and brings few surprises.

Frances Adams tells how in the Mexican village of Santo Tomás Mazaltepec children become aware from an early age of the process of getting old and dying. "They run errands for old people who are weak or tired, and they help to nurse older relatives when they are ill" (F. Adams 1972-112). They learn that death comes within the supportive arc of the entire family in the one-room house in which children and grandchildren will continue to live as visible evidence of man's continuity. Death, seen through the eyes of a 13-year-old Indian child of the community, is not denied, nor is the reassuring prospect of reward and afterlife. "The old man is dying in the house. All the family is inside, the children too. The parents tell the children that they are going to say goodbye to the old man because they are never going to see him again. He is going to eternity. Some weep. One says . . . 'I am never going to see you again' and then he cries. The neighbors visit, and also the compadres. . . . The children say to the old man, 'Many thanks for taking care of us, for not leaving us.' The old man says farewell to his family" (*Ibid.*).

In the United States, on the other hand, coping with death usually is much less straightforward. When death is imminent, enormous care is taken by medical personnel to draw a curtain around the drama, to remove the afflicted (even those already hospitalized) to private "dying rooms" where a stalwart relative may take on the burden of the deathwatch.

These precautions seem as much designed to alleviate the anxieties of the medical staff and relatives as they are those of the patient, for whom these tactics have been demonstrated as far from therapeutic. Carol Taylor, in her study of hospital culture, found that the dying welcomed the opportunity to talk out their concerns about living and dying, that many wanted to know as soon as possible that they are going to die, and that they were frustrated in their desires for a proper farewell to family and friends. A young hospitalized woman protested: "They (the nurses) wheeled me out, and I said goodbye. I wish the kids could have come to my room; it was rough on them with strangers hanging around watching and listening" (C. Taylor 1970:187). And, in the same institution, a Cracker woman spoke wistfully of the rural South and an older tradition within our culture that would have permitted a different goodbye. "If I were at home all my kin would sit up and see me through" (*Ibid.*, 186).

In much of the traditional world, hospitalized dying patients are returned to the family. When this decision is not made promptly, kinsmen often are much distressed. "We are upset," explained an Indian informant to Taylor, "when members of our family die among strangers" (C. Taylor 1970:187). In Wissous, France, the villagers make no secret of the fact that their readiness to return dying relatives from the distant hospital in time to die in their homes is not wholly a sentimental gesture. If death takes place in the hospital, a sizable "death tax" is levied on the families of patients who come from outside the administrative department in which the hospital is located. And, as one informant explained, families prefer to spend the money to bring scattered relatives home for a last goodbye and to feed and house them during the funeral period. Only a few indulge in the "plumed funeral" that, for an additional $30, provides black velvet draperies across the house of the deceased and a richly feathered headdress for the horse that pulls the hearse to the familiar cemetery by whose walls children fly kites in the spring. Most were content to walk behind an austere hearse with friends who had seen the black-bordered announcements posted in store windows, and who would return with the family to minister to the needs of the survivors.

2. The management of the dying patient

The medical community, Kübler-Ross tells us, has not chosen to take on the moral responsibility to the dying patient and his family abdicated by society. Doctors, in fact, often are acutely uncomfortable in the face of death, divorcing themselves insofar as possible from intimacy with the dying person or his relatives. Too frequently Americans who die in institutions are left alone to come to terms with themselves in the face of inevitable death. In a sensitive analysis of death and dying, Kübler-Ross describes five sequential stages that characterize the patient's struggle. The first stage is denial of death; the person simply refuses to believe the mounting evidence of his own impending demise. In a second stage, denial is replaced by anger and rage at the injustice and unfairness of it all. The third stage is the bargaining stage, during which he tries to make a deal with God or fate in return for his life (promises of being a better person, showing more concern for others). When the futility of this is realized, the person moves into a period of depression and preparatory grief over the loss of life and loved ones. Finally, in the last stages, a level of acceptance is reached — a quiet expectation of death and a lessening of interest in the outer world, including loved ones (Kübler-Ross 1969).

A powerful barrier to straightforward talk about dying is the double-talk that characterizes hospital dialogs about death. "Thus," says Carol Taylor, "the central character in the death drama is told that although it is possible he will die, it is possible that he may live to die at another time. Those closest to the dying person are told that it is probable that he will die . . . the nurses are told that barring a miracle death is inevitable." Although from time to time the nurses have seen miracles, the miracle most anticipated is "the one that pushes the death scene into the next shift" (C. Taylor 1970:186-187).

Many physicians and social scientists are critical of "the management of the dying" and the medically created conditions of death (Krant 1972). In the hospital, death comes quietly and with sedation. So silently does death arrive that detection of death has become a "delicate affair" (M. Richardson n.d.:2). Inexperienced nurses often have strenuous problems. In one case, described by Sudnow, the man being attended "had been severely burned and was almost totally wrapped in gauze, with the exception of his eyes. A young student spent several minutes trying to get him to drink some juice through a straw." Frustrated in her efforts, she reported to her instructor for help. "The instructor said, 'Well, honey, of course he won't respond, he's been dead for twenty minutes' " (Sudnow 1967:87).

Spiegel (1964:297) has explained a growing American tendency to view death as a technical failure. "The implication is that someone slipped up or that research simply has not yet got around to solving this kind of thing." Thus, despite the lengthening process of dying [which Duff and Hollingshead (1968) now estimate as medianly 29 months], "dying is covered over with optimistic or reassuring statements and the dying person is scarcely given the opportunity to make the most of his position" (Spiegel 1964:297). The medical miracle that will snatch the deteriorated, terminal patient from the brink of death is often encouraged by medical personnel, who secretly chafe at their inability to produce them.

No less a person than the physician is caught up in the dilemma of just how far he must go in his role as "healer." In the face of death, he may find himself in need of defending his expertise. "We have done all we can and now it is just a matter of waiting," is a phrase that provides the conviction that if death occurs unannounced, the physician knew of its coming. On the other hand, if the patient clings to life, the physician can refer to the patient's "indomitable spirit" (Richardson n.d.:2).

The most empathetic physician has problems in the face of death. One of us (Anderson) has had the opportunity to work with dying children and to observe the frustration of pediatricians and surgeons who can not continue, and do not know how to end, an often long relationship marked by trust and dependency on the part of the child. Sometimes the doctor sees no alternative but to withdraw gradually (or sometimes abruptly), ending the protective camaraderie and creating in the child a sense of abandonment and in the parents confusion and resentment.

3. Definitions of death

As death approaches, families take their cues from the physician, nurse, and staff, whose treatment of the person shifts almost imperceptibly from treating the person like a patient to treating him like a corpse. There is, however, a serious lack of agreement as to just when this transition actually takes place. It is a significant decision for, as Knutson points out in a cultural assessment of the dying patient, "By formal and common law and by professional ethical standards, the treatment due living persons differs markedly from that accorded the dead" (Knutson 1970:44).

Although "brain death" is under test and may serve the purpose, its validity as a gauge is clouded, since it is entirely possible, especially with modern technological advances, for the "plugged-in" patient to continue to breathe and provide a discernible heartbeat even after ostensible brain death. Sudnow distinguishes: "clinical death," or the appearance of death signs on physical examination; "biological death," the cessation of cellular activity, which is not easily established; and "social death," not a diagnostic implement, but the point at which the living individual is accorded treatment appropriate to a corpse. Kalish's "anthropological death" (the point at which one is rejected or cut off from his social world) does not help the designation of physical death, but all definitions attempt to cope with the critical medical designation of when an individual ceases to be defined as human (Knutson 1970:44).

4. Proposals for change

What of the future? Dissatisfaction has grown more and more widely with the organized care of dying patients and the technological developments that have removed death from the province of family, conscience, and God to that of medicine. "On one level," says Avorn, the controversial physician-philosopher, "we medical professionals can claim better results than our predecessor. What priest could measure up to a well-placed defibrillator, what man of God could infuse the breath of life with the efficacy of a Bird Mark IV Respirator? We can even raise the dead, if we get there fast enough." On the other hand, he argues, medicine has somehow in the process "made death another mass-produced, impersonal commodity controlled by expert providers rather than by the consumer." Narrow attention to the preservation of vital signs, he concludes, is not enough (Avorn 1973:58).

Krant and his co-workers believe that "helping someone to die *well* should be conceived as a positive part of health care," and they propose, in addition to a new and empathetic hospital atmosphere, moving beyond the walls of the hospital room to work with family and friends in eliminating camouflage from the care of the dying and the needs of those who survive them (Krant 1972: 101-108). A more therapeutic approach, augmenting drugs and general medical theory with personal counseling in meeting death and its burdens of intractable pain and anxiety, has been movingly argued by Kübler-Ross, based on her work with over 200 dying patients. She places the problem squarely in the cultural arena. The development of a social ethic about death must precede the development of a medical one. "If we could stop our pursuit of more and more material things, if we could reflect for a while on what really counts, if we had the courage to think and reflect about life *and* death, we would raise our children differently. We would not allow 80 percent of the population in the United States to die in institutions. We would not allow our children to be excluded from visiting sick and dying patients in hospitals. We would make death and dying a part of life again. We would then be able to raise a generation that would say with peace, 'I have lived and therefore I will be able to die' " (Kübler-Ross 1973:159).

Avorn urges a new basis for trust between medical personnel and dying patients, and he would like to see mind-expanding drugs used to accomplish it. "What these drugs . . . appear to do is provide access to a form of reality that challenges bedrock assumptions of Western culture, assumptions about the nature of man and the purpose of life that have been carried to often grotesque extremes in contemporary America" (Avorn 1973:59). Few physicians, however, would be likely to consider such an implementation of hospital treatment, even if it were possible. Most have displayed caution and conservatism in innovating changes in time-tested procedures. At the same time, however, medical technology — almost as an independent science — continues to open up new options in the control of death; and doctors, patients, and their families are being forced as never before into difficult areas of decision making. The complexity of these and their influence on life and death are only beginning to be felt, and (if medicine and man abdicate control) may force answers from our courts as to how and when Americans should be allowed to die.

SUMMARY AND CONCLUSIONS

Although the great majority of Americans continue to be born and to die in hospitals; growing numbers of them question *how* they are brought into the world and *how* they leave it. In significant ways physicians and hospitals do not meet the needs of "patients" and their families in what many regard as the basically nonmedical phenomena of childbirth, aging, and death. Even where these do not run their "normal" course, major questions arise on the consequences of their relegation to medically prescribed supervision and care. Particularly volatile ethical issues stem from the extraordinarily high value placed on life (and the birth experience) in our culture, and from ambivalence about the treatment of the aged and the consequences of prolongation of life at any cost. A limited but spirited amount of research has suggested that traditional approaches to these issues often provide important emotional and social supports, perhaps as critical for health as the technological and clinical advances to which we point with so much pride. Home childbirth, communal supports for the aged, and a more open approach to death have been proposed.

Although it would be wrong facilely to conclude that the problems surrounding childbirth, aging, and death in our culture can readily be solved by good will and a new dose of socialization, it may well be, as Garceau says, that "medicine suffers the discontents of its very virtues" (1966:61).

REFERENCES CITED

Ablon, Joan
1977 Field Method in Working with Middle Class Americans: New Issues of Values, Personality, and Reciprocity. Human Organization 36:69-72.
Ackerknecht, Erwin H.
1945 Malaria in the Upper Mississippi Valley, 1760-1900. Bulletin of the History of Medicine, Supplement No. 4. Baltimore: The Johns Hopkins Press.
1971 Medicine and Ethnology: Selected Essays. Baltimore: The Johns Hopkins Press.
Adair John, Kurt Deuschle, and Walsh McDermott
1969 Patterns of Health and Disease Among the Navajos. *In* The Cross-Cultural Approach to Health Behavior. L. R. Lynch, ed., Pp. 83-110. Rutherford, N.J.: Fairleigh Dickinson University Press. [1957].
Adams, Frances McAleavey
1972 The Role of Old People in Santo Tomás Mazaltepec. *In* Aging and Modernization. D.O. Cowgill and L. D. Holmes, eds. Pp. 103-126. New York: Appleton-Century-Crofts.
Adams, Richard N.
1953 Notes on the Application of Anthropology. Human Organization 12(2):10-14.
1955 A Nutritional Research Program in Guatemala. *In* Health, Culture, and Community. B. D. Paul, ed. Pp. 435-458. New York: Russell Sage Foundation.
Aguirre, Lydia
1978 Alternative Health Practices In the Western Texas Border. *In* Modern Medicine and Medical Anthropology in the U.S.-Mexico Border Population. B. Velimirovic, ed. Washington, D.C.: Pan American Health Organization, Scientific Publication PAHO No. 359.
Aguirre Beltrán, Gonzalo
1963 Medicina y Magia. México, D.F.: Instituto Nacional Indigenista, Colección de Antropología Social, No. 1.
1978 Training in Intercultural Aspects of Medicine. *In* Modern Medicine and Medical Anthropology in the U.S.-Mexico Border Populations. B. Velimirovic, ed. Washington, D.C.: Pan American Health Organization, Scientific Publication PAHO No. 359.
Ahern, Emily M.
1975 Sacred and Secular Medicine in a Taiwan Village: A Study of Cosmological Disorders. *In* Medicine in Chinese Culture. A. Kleinman, P. Kunstadter, E. R. Alexander, and J. L. Gale, eds. Pp. 91-113. Washington, D.C.: National Institutes of Health DHEW Publ. No. (NIH) 75-653.

Alland, Alexander, Jr.
1964 Native Therapists and Western Medical Practitioners Among the Abron of the Ivory Coast. Transactions of the New York Academy of Sciences 26:714-725.
1970 Adaptation in Cultural Evolution: An Approach to Medical Anthropology. New York: Columbia University Press.
Alpers, Michael
1970 III. Kuru in New Guinea: Its Changing Pattern and Etiologic Elucidation. The American Journal of Tropical Medicine and Hygiene 19:133-137.
Alpers, Michael, and D. Carleton Gajdusek
1965 Changing Patterns of Kuru: Epidemiological Changes in the Period of Increasing Contact of the Fore People with Western Civilization. The American Journal of Tropical Medicine and Hygiene 14:852-879.
Alvarado, Anita L.
1978 Factors to Consider in the Utilization of Ethnomedical Practitioners and Concepts Within the Framework of Western Medicine. *In* Modern Medicine and Medical Anthropology in the U.S.-Mexico Border Populations. B. Velimirovic, ed. Washington, D.C.: Pan American Health Organization, Scientific Publication PAHO No. 359.
American Nurses' Association (A.N.S.)
1976 Facts About Nursing 1974-1975. Kansas City: American Nurses' Association.
Anand, D., and A. Rama Rao
1963 How Well Doctors Communicate with the Patients — A Diagnostic Study. Indian Journal of Public Health 7:152-156.
Anderson, Barbara Gallatin
1978 The Aging Game: Sanity, Sex, and Success After Sixty. Manuscript. Department of Anthropology, Southern Methodist University.
Anderson, Barbara Gallatin and Nancy Hazam
1978 Cultural Factors Influencing Diagnostic and Remedial Heart Care Among Mexican-Americans. Paper Read at the 1978 Annual Meetings of the Society for Applied Anthropology, Merida, Yucatan, Mexico.
Anderson, E.N., Jr., and Marja L. Anderson
1975 Folk Dietetics in Two Chinese Communities, and Its Implications for the Study of Chinese Medicine. *In* Medicine in Chinese Culture. A. Kleinman, P. Kunstadter, E. R. Alexander, and J. L. Gale, eds. Pp. 143-175. Washington, D.C.: National Institutes of Health DHEW Publ. No. (NIH)75-653.
1977 Modern China: South. *In* Food in Chinese Culture: Anthropological and Historical Perspectives. K. C. Chang, ed. Pp. 319-382. New Haven, Conn.: Yale University Press.
Angel, J. Lawrence
1964 Osteoporosis: Thalassemia? American Journal of Physical Anthropology 22:369-371.

Angrosino, Michael V.
1974 Outside is Death: Community Organization, Ideology and Alcoholism Among the East Indians in Trinidad. Winston-Salem, N.C.: Overseas Research Center, Wake Forest University, Developing Nations Monograph Series, Series II, No. 2.

Armelagos, George J., and John R. Dewey
1970 Evolutionary Response to Human Infectious Diseases. BioScience 20:-271-275.

Arms, Suzanne
1975 Immaculate Deception: A New Look at Women and Childbirth in America. Boston: Houghton Mifflin.

Ashley, Jo Ann
1976 Hospitals, Paternalism, and the Role of the Nurse. New York: Columbia University, Teachers College Press.

Avorn, Jerry
1973 Beyond Dying: Experiments Using Psychedelic Drugs to Ease the Transition from Life. Harper's 246:54-66.

Bahr, Donald M., Juan Gregorio, David I. Lopez, and Albert Alvarez
1974 Piman Shamanism and Staying Sickness. Tucson: The University of Arizona Press.

Balint, Michael, M.D.
1957 The Doctor, His Patient and the Illness. New York: International Universities Press.
1966 The Drug, "Doctor." *In* Medical Care: Readings in the Sociology of Medical Institutions. W. R. Scott and E. H. Volkart, eds. Pp. 281-291. New York: John Wiley.

Banerji, D.
1974 Health Behaviour of Rural Populations: Impact of Rural Health Services. A Preliminary Communication. New Delhi: Jawaharlal Nehru University, Centre of Social Medicine and Community Health.

Barker, Anthony
1959 The Man Next to Me: An Adventure in African Medical Practice. New York: Harper & Brothers.

Barnes, Seymour T.
1968 Malaria Eradication in Surinam: Prospects of Success after Five Years of Health Education. International Journal of Health Education 11:20-31.

Barnes, Seymour T., and C. David Jenkins
1972 Changing Personal and Social Behaviour: Experiences of Health Workers in a Tribal Society. Social Science & Medicine 6:1-15.

Barron, Milton L., ed.
1961 The Aging American. New York: Crowell.

Basham, A. L.
1976 The Practice of Medicine in Ancient and Medieval India. *In* Asian

Medical Systems: A Comparative Study. C. Leslie, ed. Pp. 18-43. Berkeley: University of California Press.

Bates, Barbara
1970 Doctor and Nurse: Changing Roles and Relations. The New England Journal of Medicine 283:129-134.

Bates, Marston
1953 Human Ecology. *In* Anthropology Today: An Encyclopedic Inventory. A. L. Kroeber, ed. Pp. 700-713. Chicago: The University of Chicago Press.
1959 The Ecology of Health. *In* Medicine and Anthropology. I. Galdston, ed. Pp. 56-77. New York: International Universities Press.

Beck, Brenda E. F.
1969 Colour and Heat in South Indian Ritual. Man 4:553-572.

Becker, Howard S.
1963 Outsiders: Studies in the Sociology of Deviance. New York: The Free Press.

Becker, Howard S., and Blanche Geer
1958 The Fate of Idealism in Medical School. American Sociological Review 23:50-56.
1963 Medical Education. *In* Handbook of Medical Sociology. H. E. Freeman, S. Levine, and L. G. Reader, eds. Pp. 169-186. Englewood Cliffs, N.J.: Prentice-Hall.

Becker, Howard S., Blanche Geer, Everett C. Hughes, and Anselm L. Strauss
1961 Boys in White: Student Culture in Medical School. Chicago: The University of Chicago Press.

Benet, Sula
1974 Abkhasians: The Long-living People of the Caucasus. New York: Holt, Rinehart and Winston.

Benne, Kenneth D., and Warren Bennis
1959 The Role of the Professional Nurse. The American Journal of Nursing 59:196-198, 380-383.

Berwind, Anita
1975 The Nurse in the Coronary Care Unit. *In* The Law and the Expanding Nursing Role. B. Bullough, ed. Pp. 82-94. New York: Appleton-Century-Crofts.

Black, Francis L.
1975 Infectious Diseases in Primitive Societies. Science 187:515-518.

Bloom, Samuel W.
1965 The Sociology of Medical Education: Some Comments on the State of a Field. The Milbank Memorial Fund Quarterly 43:143-184.
1973 Power and Dissent in the Medical School. New York: The Free Press.

Blum, Richard, and Eva Blum
1965 Health and Healing in Rural Greece: A Study of Three Communities. Stanford, Calif.: Stanford University Press.

Boesch, Ernst E.
1972 Communication between Doctors and Patients in Thailand, I. Saarbrücken: University of the Saar, Socio-Psychological Research Centre on Development Planning.
Bonser, Wilfrid
1963 The Medical Background of Anglo-Saxon England: A Study in History, Psychology, and Folklore. London: The Wellcome Historical Medical Library.
Brink, Pamela J., and Judith M. Saunders
1976 Culture Shock: Theoretical and Applied. *In* Transcultural Nursing: A Book of Readings. P. J. Brink, ed. Pp. 126-138. Englewood Cliffs, N.J.: Prentice-Hall.
Brown, Esther Lucile
1936 Nursing as a Profession. New York: Russell Sage Foundation.
1963 Meeting Patients' Psychosocial Needs in the General Hospital. *In* Medicine and Society. J. A. Clausen and R. Straus, eds. The Annals of the American Academy of Political and Social Science 346:117-125.
1966 Nursing and Patient Care. *In* The Nursing Profession: Five Sociological Essays. F. Davis, ed. Pp. 176-203. New York: John Wiley.
Browne, Edward G.
1921 Arabian Medicine. Cambridge: Cambridge University Press.
Browner, Carole
1976 Poor Women's Fertility Decisions: Illegal Abortion in Cali, Colombia. Ph.D. Dissertation, Anthropology Department, University of California, Berkeley.
Bruhn, John G., and Oscar A. Parsons
1964 Medical Student Attitudes Toward Four Medical Specialties. Journal of Medical Education 39:40-49.
Bryant, John
1969 Health & the Developing World. Ithaca, N.Y.: Cornell University Press.
Bullough, Bonnie
1975a The First Two Phases in Nursing Licensure. *In* The Law and the Expanding Nursing Role. B. Bullough, ed. Pp. 7-21. New York: Appleton-Century-Crofts.
1975b Factors Contributing to Role Expansion for Registered Nurses. *In* The Law and the Expanding Nursing Role. B. Bullough, ed. Pp. 53-61. New York: Appleton-Century-Crofts.
Bullough, Bonnie, and Vern Bullough
1971 New Directions for Nurses. New York: Springer Publishing.
Burgess, Anne, and R. F. A. Dean, eds.
1962 Malnutrition and Food Habits. London: Tavistock Publications.

Burnet, Sir Macfarlane, and David O. White
1972 Natural History of Infectious Disease. 4th ed. Cambridge: Cambridge University Press.
Byrne, Susan W.
1974 Arden, An Adult Community. *In* Anthropologists in Cities. G. M. Foster and R. V. Kemper, eds. Pp. 123-152. Boston: Little, Brown.
Cairns, John
1975 The Cancer Problem. Scientific American 233(5): 64-78.
Carstairs, G. Morris
1969 Changing Perception of Neurotic Illness. *In* Mental Health Research in Asia and the Pacific. W. Caudill and T. Lin, eds. Pp. 405-414. Honolulu: East-West Center Press.
Carstairs, G.M., and R. L. Kapur
1976 The Great Universe of Kota: Stress, Change and Mental Disorder in an Indian Village. Berkeley: University of California Press.
Casillas Cuervo, Leticia
1978 Health and Culture in Urban Marginal Zones. *In* Modern Medicine and Medical Anthropology in the U.S.-Mexico Border Populations. B. Velimirovic, ed. Washington, D.C.: Pan American Health Organization, Scientific Publication PAHO No. 359.
Cassel, John
1955 A Comprehensive Health Program Among South African Zulus. *In* Health, Culture and Community. B. D. Paul, ed. Pp. 15-41. New York: Russell Sage Foundation.
Caudill, William
1953 Applied Anthropology in Medicine. *In* Anthropology Today: An Encyclopedic Inventory. A. L. Kroeber, ed. Pp. 771-806. Chicago: The University of Chicago Press.
Cawte, John
1974 Medicine is the Law: Studies in Psychiatric Anthropology of Australian Tribal Societies. Honolulu: The University Press of Hawaii.
Chadwick, John, and W. N. Mann, trans. and eds.
1950 The Medical Works of Hippocrates: A New Translation from the Original Greek Made Especially for English Readers by the Collaboration of John Chadwick, M.A. and W. N. Mann, M.D. Oxford: Blackwell Scientific Publications.
Chance, Norman A.
1966 The Eskimo of North Alaska. New York: Holt, Rinehart and Winston.
Cheney, Charles C., and George L. Adams
1978 Lay Healing and Mental Health in the Mexican American Barrio. *In* Modern Medicine and Medical Anthropology in the U.S.-Mexico Border Populations B. Velimirovic, ed. Washington, D.C.: Pan American Health Organization, Scientific Publication PAHO No. 359.

Christopherson, Victor A.
1971 Sociocultural Correlates of Pain Response. Social Science 46:33-37.
Chu, H. J., and I. H. Ch'iang
1931 Extracts from Some Old Chinese Medical Books on Worm Infections. National Medical Journal of China 17:655-666.
Clark, Margaret
1959a Health in the Mexican-American Culture: A Community Study. Berkeley: University of California Press.
1959b The Social Functions of Mexican-American Medical Beliefs. California's Health 16:153-156.
1973 Contributions of Cultural Anthropology to the Study of the Aged. *In* Cultural Illness and Health. L. Nader and T. W. Maretzki, eds. Washington, D. C.: American Anthropological Association, Anthropological Studies, No. 9.
Clark, Margaret and Barbara Gallatin Anderson
1967 Culture and Aging: An Anthropological Study of Older Americans. Springfield, Ill.: Charles C Thomas.
Clausen, John A.
1963 Social Factors in Disease. *In* Medicine and Society. J. A. Clausen and R. Straus, eds. The Annals of the American Academy of Political and Social Science 346:138-148.
Cleland, Virginia
1971 Sex Discrimination: Nursing's Most Pervasive Problem. American Journal of Nursing 71:1542-1547.
Clements, Forrest E.
1932 Primitive Concepts of Disease. Berkeley: University of California Publications in American Archaeology and Ethnology 32(2):185-252.
Cockburn, T. Aidan
1971 Infectious Diseases in Ancient Populations. Current Anthropology 12:-45-62.
Coe, Rodney M.
1970 Sociology of Medicine. New York: McGraw-Hill Book Co.
Cohen, Lucy M.
1973 Gifts to Strangers: Public Policy and the Delivery of Health Services to Illegal Aliens. Anthropological Quarterly 46:183-195.
Colson, Anthony C.
1971 The Prevention of Illness in a Malay Village: An Analysis of Concepts and Behavior. Winston-Salem, N.C.: Overseas Research Center, Wake Forest University, Developing Nations Monograph Series, Series II, No. 1.
Colson, Anthony C., and Karen E. Selby
1974 Medical Anthropology. Annual Review of Anthropology 3:245-263.
Cook, R.
1966 The General Nutritional Problems of Africa. African Affairs 65:329-340.

Corwin, Ronald G., and Marvin J. Taves
1963 Nursing and Other Health Professions. *In* Handbook of Medical Sociology. H. E. Freeman, S. Levine, and L. G. Reader, eds. Pp. 187-212. Englewood Cliffs, N.J.: Prentice-Hall.
Coser, Rose Laub
1959 Some Social Functions of Laughter: A Study of Humor in a Hospital Setting. Human Relations 12: 171-182.
1962 Life in the Ward. East Lansing: Michigan State University Press.
Cosminsky, Sheila
1974 The Role of the Midwife in Middle America. Paper presented at the XLI International Congress of Americanists, Mexico City.
1975 Changing Food and Medical Beliefs and Practices in a Guatemalan Community. Ecology of Food and Nutrition 4:183-191.
1977 Alimento and Fresco: Nutritional Concepts and Their Implications for Health Care. Human Organization 36:203-207.
Cowgill, Donald O., and Lowell D. Holmes, eds.
1972 Aging and Modernization. New York: Appleton-Century-Crofts.
Crapanzano, Vincent
1973 The Hamadsha: A Study in Moroccan Ethnopsychiatry. Berkeley: University of California Press.
Croizier, Ralph C.
1968 Traditional Medicine in Modern China: Science, Nationalism, and the Tensions of Cultural Change. Cambridge, Mass.: Harvard University Press.
Cumming, Elaine, and William E. Henry
1961 Growing Old: The Process of Disengagement. New York: Basic Books.
Cunningham, Clark E.
1970 Thai "Injection Doctors": Antibiotic Mediators. Social Science & Medicine 4:1-24.
Currier, Richard L.
1966 The Hot-Cold Syndrome and Symbolic Balance in Mexican and Spanish-American Folk Medicine. Ethnology 5:251-263.
Curtin, Sharon R.
1972 Nobody Ever Died of Old Age. Boston: Little, Brown.
Cussler, Margaret, and Mary L. DeGive
1970 'Twixt the Cup and the Lip: Psychological and Sociocultural Factors Affecting Food Habits. Washington, D.C.: Consortium Press (1952).

Damon, Albert, ed.
1975 Physiological Anthropology. New York: Oxford University Press.
Davis, Marcella Z., Marlene Kramer, and Anselm L. Strauss, eds.
1975 Nurses in Practice: A Perspective on Environments. St. Louis: C.V. Mosby.

Demerath, N.J.
1942 Schizophrenia Among Primitives. The American Journal of Psychiatry 98:703-707.
Dennis, Ruth E.
1974-75 The Traditional Healer in Liberia. Rural Africana 26:17-23.
Devereux, George
1940 Primitive Psychiatry. Bulletin of the History of Medicine 8:1194-1213; 11:522-542 (1942).
1944 The Social Structure of a Schizophrenic Ward and Its Therapeutic Fitness. The Journal of Clinical Psychopathology 6:231-265.
1956 Normal and Abnormal: The Key Problem of Psychiatric Anthropology. *In* Some Uses of Anthropology: Theoretical and Applied. Pp. 23-48. Washington, D. C.: The Anthropological Society of Washington.
Dewalt, Kathleen Musante
1977 The Illnesses No Longer Understand: Changing Concepts of Health and Curing in a Rural Mexican Community. Medical Anthropology Newsletter 8(2):5-11.
Dhilon, H. S., and S. B. Kar
1963 Behavioural Science and Public Health. Indian Journal of Public Health 7:19-24.
Diamond, Norma
1969 K'un Shen: A Taiwan Village. New York: Holt, Rinehart and Winston.
Dohrenwend, Bruce, and Barbara S. Dohrenwend
1965 The Problem of Validity in Field Studies of Psychological Disorder. International Journal of Psychiatry 1:585-605.
Dorson, Richard M.
1952 Bloodstoppers & Bearwalkers: Folk Traditions of the Upper Peninsula. Cambridge, Mass.: Harvard University Press.
1959 American Folklore. Chicago: University of Chicago Press.
Downs, James
1966 The Two Worlds of the Washo. New York: Holt, Rinehart and Winston.
DuBois, Cora
1961 The People of Alor: A Social-Psychological Study of an East Indian Island. Vol. 1. New York: Harper Torchbooks (1944).
Dubos, René
1965 Man Adapting. New Haven, Conn.: Yale University Press.
1971 Mirage of Health: Utopias, Progress and Biological Change. New York: Harper & Row (1959).
Duff, Raymond S., and August B. Hollingshead
1968 Sickness and Society. New York: Harper & Row.
Dunlop, David W.
1974-75 Alternatives to "Modern" Health-Delivery Systems in Africa: Issues

for Public Policy Consideration on the Role of Traditional Healers. Rural Africana 26:131-139.

Dunn, Frederick L.
1965 On the Antiquity of Malaria in the Western Hemisphere. Human Biology 37:385-393.
1968 Epidemiological Factors: Health and Disease in Hunter-Gatherers. *In* Man the Hunter. R. B. Lee and I. de Vore, eds. Pp. 221-228. Chicago: Aldine.
1976 Traditional Asian Medicine and Cosmopolitan Medicine as Adaptive Systems. *In* Asian Medical Systems: A Comparative Study. C. Leslie, ed. Pp. 133-158. Berkeley: University of California Press.

Edgerton, Robert B.
1966 Conceptions of Psychosis in Four East African Societies. American Anthropologist 68: 408-425.
1969 On the "Recognition" of Mental Illness. *In* Changing Perspectives in Mental Illness. S. C. Plog and R.B. Edgerton, eds. Pp. 49-72. New York: Holt, Rinehart and Winston.
1971 A Traditional African Psychiatrist. Southwestern Journal of Anthropology 27: 259-278.

Edgerton, Robert B., Marvin Karno, and Irma Fernandez
1970 Curanderismo in the Metropolis. American Journal of Psychotherapy 24:124-134.

Eisenberg, Leon
1977 Disease and Illness: Distinctions Between Professional and Popular Ideas of Sickness. Culture, Medicine and Psychiatry 1:9-23.

Erasmus, John Charles
1952 Changing Folk Beliefs and the Relativity of Empirical Knowledge. Southwestern Journal of Anthropology 8:411-428.

Eron, Leonard D.
1955 Effect of Medical Education on Medical Students. Journal of Medical Education 10:559-566.

Evans-Pritchard, E. E.
1937 Witchcraft, Oracles and Magic Among the Azande. Oxford: Clarendon Press.

Fabrega, Horacio, Jr.
1972 Medical Anthropology. *In* Biennial Review of Anthropology 1971. B. J. Siegel, ed. Pp. 167-229. Stanford, Calif.: Stanford University Press.
1974 Disease and Social Behavior: An Interdisciplinary Perspective. Cambridge, Mass.: The MIT Press.

Fahim, Hussein M.
1975 Community-Health Aspects of the Nubian Resettlement in Egypt. Pittsburgh: University of Pittsburgh, University Center for International Studies (Mimeo).

Field, Margaret J.
1960 Search for Security: An Ethno-Psychiatric Study of Rural Ghana. London: Faber and Faber.
Fiennes, Richard
1964 Man, Nature and Disease. London: Weidenfeld and Nicolson.
Fischer, Ann, and J. L. Fischer
1961 Culture and Epidemiology: A Theoretical Investigation of Kuru. Journal of Health and Human Behavior 2:16-25.
Fishman, Daniel B., and Carl N. Zimet
1972 Speciality Choice and Beliefs about Freshman Medical Students. Journal of Medical Education 47:524-533.
Fortune, R. F.
1932 Sorcerers of Dobu: The Social Anthropology of the Dobu Islanders of the Western Pacific. London: George Routledge & Sons.
Foster, George M.
1944 A Summary of Yuki Culture. Berkeley and Los Angeles: University of California Anthropological Records 5(3):155-244.
1945 Sierra Popoluca Folklore and Beliefs. University of California Publications in American Archaeology and Ethnology 42(2):177-250.
1952 Relationships between Theoretical and Applied Anthropology: A Public Health Program Analysis. Human Organization 11(3):5-16.
1953a Relationships between Spanish and Spanish-American Folk Medicine. Journal of American Folklore 66:201-217.
1953b "What is Folk Culture?" American Anthropologist 55:159-173.
1962 Traditional Cultures and the Impact of Technological Change. New York: Harper & Row.
1967 Tzintzuntzan: Mexican Peasants in a Changing World. Boston: Little, Brown.
1973 Traditional Societies and Technological Change. New York: Harper & Row.
1974 Medical Anthropology: Some Contrasts with Medical Sociology. Medical Anthropology Newsletter 6(1):1-6.
1976a Medical Anthropology and International Health Planning. Medical Anthropology Newsletter 7(3):12-18.
1976b Disease Etiologies in Nonwestern Medical Systems. American Anthropologist 78:773-782.
Foulks, E.
1972 The Arctic Hysterias of the North Alaskan Eskimo. Washington, D.C.: American Anthropological Association.
Fox, Renée C.
1959 Experiment Perilous: Physicians and Patients Facing the Unknown. Glencoe, Ill.: The Free Press.
1974 Is There a "New" Medical Student? A Comparative View of Medical Socialization in the 1950s and the 1970s. *In* Ethics of Health Care. L. R.

Tancredi, ed. Pp. 197-220. Washington, D.C.: National Academy of Sciences.

Frankel, Stephen Charles
1976 Emergency Medical Care in an Urban Setting. Ph.D. Dissertation, Anthropology Department, University of California, Berkeley.

Frankenberg, Ronald, and Joyce Leeson
1976 Disease, Illness and Sickness: Social Aspects of the Choice of Healer in a Lusaka Suburb. *In* Social Anthropology and Medicine. J. B. Loudon, ed. Pp. 223-258. London: Academic Press.

French, Katherine S.
1962 Research Interviewers in a Medical Setting: Roles and Social Systems. Human Organization 21:219-224.

Friedl, Ernestine
1958 Hospital Care in Provincial Greece. Human Organization 16(4):24-27.

Freidson, Eliot
1970 Professional Dominance: The Social Structure of Medical Care. New York: Atherton Press.
1972 Profession of Medicine: A Study of the Sociology of Applied Knowledge. New York: Dodd, Mead. (1970).

Gajdusek, D. Carleton
1963 Kuru. Transactions of the Royal Society of Tropical Medicine and Hygiene 57:151-169.
1973 Kuru in the New Guinea Highlands. *In* Tropical Neurology. J. D. Spillane, ed. Pp. 377-383. New York: Oxford University Press.

Gajdusek, D. Carleton, and Clarence J. Gibbs, Jr.
1975 Slow Virus Infections of the Nervous System and the Laboratories of Slow, Latent, and Temperate Virus Infections. *In* The Nervous System, Vol. 2, The Clinical Neurosciences. D. B. Tower, Editor-in-Chief. Pp. 113-135. New York: Raven Press.

Gampel, B.
1962 The "Hilltops" Community. *In* A Practice of Social Medicine. S. L. Kark and G. E. Steuart, eds. Pp. 298-308. Edinburgh and London: E. & S. Livingstone.

Garceau, Oliver
1966 The Morals of Medicine. The Annals of the American Academy of Political and Social Science 363:60-69.

Gayton, A. H.
1930 Yokuts-Mono Chiefs and Shamans. University of California Publications in American Archaeology and Ethnology 24(8):361-420.

Geber, Marcelle, and R.F.A. Dean
1956 The Psychological Changes Accompanying Kwashiorkor. Currier 6:-3-14. Paris: International Children's Centre.

Gebhard, Bruno
1976 The Interrelationship of Scientific and Folk Medicine in the United

States of America since 1850. *In* American Folk Medicine: A Symposium. W. D. Hand, ed. Pp. 87-98. Berkeley: University of California Press.

Geertsma, Robert H., and Donald R. Grinols
1972 Speciality Choice in Medicine. Journal of Medical Education 47:509-517.

Geertz, Clifford
1963 Agricultural Involution: The Process of Ecological Change in Indonesia. Berkeley: University of California Press.

Gelfand, Michael, M. D.
1971 Diet and Tradition in an African Culture. Edinburgh and London: E. & S. Livingstone.

Gibbs, Clarence J., Jr., and D. Carleton Gajdusek
1970 IV Kuru: Pathogenesis and Characterization of Virus. The American Journal of Tropical Medicine and Hygiene 19:138-145.

Gillin, John
1948 Magical Fright. Psychiatry 11:387-400.
1956 The Making of a Witch Doctor. Psychiatry 19:131-136.

Glaser, William A.
1966 Nursing Leadership and Policy: Some Cross-National Comparisons. *In* The Nursing Profession: Five Sociological Essays. F. Davis, ed. Pp. 1-59. New York: John Wiley.

Glick, Leonard B.
1967 Medicine as an Ethnographic Category: The Gimi of the New Guinea Highlands. Ethnology 6:31-56.

Goldschmidt, Armin M. F.
1972 Analysis of the Interviews with Doctors. Part I in Armin M. F. Goldschmidt and Bernd Höfer, Communication between Doctors and Patients in Thailand, II. Saarbrücken: University of the Saar, Socio-Psychological Research Centre on Development Planning.

Gonzalez, Nancie Solien
1966 Health Behavior in Cross-Cultural Perspective: A Guatemalan Example. Human Organization 25:122-125.

Goody, Jack
1962 Death, Property and the Ancestors: A Study of the Mortuary Customs of the Lodagaa of West Africa. Stanford, Calif.: Stanford University Press.

Gould, Harold A.
1957 The Implications of Technological Change for Folk and Scientific Medicine. American Anthropologist 59:507-516.
1965 Modern Medicine and Folk Cognition in Rural India. Human Organization 24:201-208.

Gruner, O. Cameron
1930 A Treatise on the Canon of Medicine of Avicenna. Incorporating a Translation of the First Book. London: Luzac & Co.

Gussow, Zachary
1964 Behavioral Research in Chronic Disease: A Study of Leprosy. Journal of Chronic Diseases 17:179-189.

Gussow, Zachary, and George S. Tracy
1968 Status, Ideology, and Adaptation to Stigmatized Illness: A Study of Leprosy. Human Organization 27:316-325.

Guthrie, George M.
1973 Culture and Mental Disorder. An Addison-Wesley Module in Anthropology, No. 39.

Hall, Irene S., and Calvin S. Hall
1939 A Study of Disliked and Unfamiliar Foods. Journal of the American Dietetic Association 15:540-548.

Hall, Oswald
1948 The Stages of a Medical Career. The American Journal of Sociology 53:327-336.

Hallowell, A. Irving
1940 Aggression in Saulteaux Society. Psychiatry 3:395-407.
1963 Ojibwa World View and Disease. *In* Man's Image in Medicine and Anthropology. I. Galdston, ed. Pp. 258-315. New York: International Universities Press.

Hardesty, Donald L.
1977 Ecological Anthropology. New York: John Wiley.

Harley, George Way
1941 Native African Medicine: With Special Reference to its Practice in the Mano Tribe of Liberia. Cambridge, Mass.: Harvard University Press.

Harper, Edward B.
1957 Shamanism in South India. Southwestern Journal of Anthropology 13:267-287.

Harrison, Ira E.
1974-75 Traditional Healers: A Neglected Source of Health Manpower. Rural Africana 26:5-16.

Hart, Donn V.
1969 Bisayan Filipino and Malayan Humoral Pathologies: Folk Medicine and Ethno-History in Southeast Asia. Ithaca, N.Y.: Cornell University, Department of Asian Studies, Southeast Asia Program, Data Paper Number 76.

Harwood, Alan
1971 The Hot-Cold Theory of Disease: Implications for Treatment of Puerto Rican Patients. The Journal of the American Medical Association 216:-1153-1158.
1977 R$_X$: Spirits as Needed. New York: John Wiley.

Hasan, Khwaja Arif
1967 The Cultural Frontier of Health in Village India. Bombay: Manaktalas.

1971 The Hindu Dietary Practices and Culinary Rituals in a North Indian Village. An Ethnomedical and Structural Analysis. Ethnomedizin 1:43-70.

1975 What is Medical Anthropology? Medical Anthropology Newsletter 6(3):7-10.

Hasan, Khwaja Arif, and B. G. Prasad
1959 A Note on the Contributions of Anthropology to Medical Science. Journal of the Indian Medical Association 33: 182-190.

Hatton, Corine L.
1975 The Mental Health Clinical Nurse Specialist in Private Practice. *In* The Law and the Expanding Nursing Role. B. Bullough, ed. Pp. 118-124. New York: Appleton-Century-Croft.

Havighurst, Robert J., Bernice L. Neugarten, and Sheldon S. Tobin
1968 Disengagement and Patterns of Aging. *In* Middle Age and Aging. B. L. Neugarten, ed. Pp. 161-172. Chicago: University of Chicago Press.

Hazell, Lester Dessez
1969 Commonsense Childbirth. New York: G. P. Putnam's Sons.

Hendrickse, R. G.
1966 Some Observations on the Social Background to Malnutrition in Tropical Africa. African Affairs 65:341-349.

Henry, Jules, and Zunia Henry
1944 Doll Play of Pilagá Indian Children. American Ortho-psychiatric Association. Research Monographs, No. 4.

Heyneman, Donald
1971 Mis-aid to the Third World: Disease Repercussions Caused by Ecological Ignorance. Canadian Journal of Public Health 62:303-313.

Hilger, Inez
1957 Araucanian Child Life and Its Cultural Background. Washington, D. C.: Smithsonian Institution Miscellaneous Collections, No. 113.

Hinderling, Paul
1973 Communication Between Doctors and Patients in Thailand, III. Saarbrücken: University of the Saar, Socio-Psychological Research Centre on Development Planning.

Hippler, Arthur E.
1977 On Stein and Kleinman, and the Crucial Issues in Medical Anthropology. Medical Anthropology Newsletter 9(4):18-19.

Hochstrasser, Donald L., and Jesse W. Tapp, Jr.
1970 Social Medicine and Public Health. *In* Anthropology and the Behavioral and Health Sciences. O. Von Mering and L. Kasden, eds. Pp. 242-271. Pittsburgh: University of Pittsburgh Press.

Horton, Robin
1967 African Traditional Thought and Western Science. Africa 37:50-71, 155-187.

Hostetler, John A.
1963-64 Folk and Scientific Medicine in Amish Society. Human Organization 22:269-275.
Hsu, Robert C.
1974 The Barefoot Doctors of the People's Republic of China — Some Problems. The New England Journal of Medicine. 291:124-127.
Huard, Pierre
1969 Western Medicine and Afro-Asian Ethnic Medicine. *In* Medicine and Culture. F.N.L. Poynter, ed. Pp. 211-237. London: Wellcome Institute of the History of Medicine.
Huard, Pierre, and Ming Wong
1968 Chinese Medicine. London: World University Library. Translated from the French by Bernard Fielding.
Hughes, Charles C.
1968 Ethnomedicine. *In* International Encyclopedia of the Social Sciences 10:87-93. New York: Free Press/Macmillan.
Hughes, Charles C., and John M. Hunter
1970 Disease and "Development" in Africa. Social Science & Medicine 3:-443-493.
Hughes, Everett C.
1956 The Making of a Physician — General Statement of Ideas and Problems. Human Organization 14(4):21-25.
Hultin, Neil
1974 Some Aspects of Eighteenth-Century Folk Medicine. Southern Folklore Quarterly 38:199-209.
Hunt, Edward E., Jr.
1978 Ecological Frameworks and Hypothesis Testing in Medical Anthropology. *In* Health and the Human Condition. M. H. Logan and E. E. Hunt, Jr., eds. Pp. 84-100. North Scituate, Mass.: Duxbury Press.
Hurston, Zora
1931 Hoodoo in America. Journal of American Folklore 44:317-417.

Ingham, John A.
1970 On Mexican Folk Medicine. American Anthropologist 72:76-87.
Ingman, Stanley R.
1975 Static Dynamics in Medical Care Organization. *In* Topias and Utopias in Health: Policy Studies. S. R. Ingman and A. E. Thomas, eds. Pp. 121-140. The Hague: Mouton.

Jaco, E. Gartly, ed.
1972 Patients, Physicians and Illness: A Sourcebook in Behavioral Science and Health. 2nd ed. New York: The Free Press.
Jacobs, Jerry
1974 Fun City: An Ethnographic Study of A Retirement Community. New York: Holt, Rinehart and Winston.

Jansen, G.
1973 The Doctor-Patient Relationship in an African Tribal Society. Assen, The Netherlands: Van Gorcum & Comp. B. V.
Jelliffe, Derrick B.
1957 Social Culture and Nutrition: Cultural Blocks and Protein Malnutrition in Early Childhood in Rural West Bengal. Pediatrics 20:128-138.
Jelliffe, Derrick B., and F. John Bennett
1962 Cultural Problems in Technical Assistance. Children 9:171-177.
Jenney, E. Ross, and Ozzie G. Simmons
1954 Human Relations and Technical Assistance in Public Health. The Scientific Monthly 78:365-371.
Jones, Delmos J.
1976 Applied Anthropology and the Application of Anthropological Knowledge. Human Organization 35:221-229.
Jones, Louis C.
1949 Practitioners of Folk Medicine. Bulletin of the History of Medicine 23:480-493.
Johnson, Sheila K.
1971 Idle Haven: Community Building among the Working-Class Retired. Berkeley: University of California Press.
Joseph, Alice
1942 Physician and Patient: Some Aspects of Inter-Personal Relations between Physicians and Patients, with Special Regard to the Relationship between White Physicians and Indian Patients. Applied Anthropology 1(4):1-6.

Kark, Sidney L., and Emily Kark
1962 A Practice of Social Medicine. *In* A Practice of Social Medicine: A South African Team's Experiences in Different African Communities. S. L. Kark and G. E. Steuart, eds. Pp. 3-40. Edinburgh and London: E. & S. Livingstone.
Kark, Sidney L., and Guy E. Steuart, eds.
1962 A Practice of Social Medicine: A South African Team's Experiences in Different African Communities. Edinburgh and London: E. & S. Livingstone.
Kassebaum, Gene G., and Barbara O. Baumann
1965 Dimensions of the Sick Role in Chronic Illness. Journal of Health and Human Behavior 6:16-25.
Katona-Apte, Judit
1976 Nutritional Anthropology. Medical Anthropology Newsletter 7(2): 8.
Kay, Margarita A.
1977 Health and Illness in a Mexican American Barrio. *In* Ethnic Medicine in the Southwest. E. H. Spicer, ed. Pp. 99-166. Tucson: The University of Arizona Press.

Kay, Margarita A. with Anita Stafford
1978 Parallel, Alternative or Collaborative: Curanderismo in Tucson. *In* Modern Medicine and Medical Anthropology in the U.S.-Mexico Border Populations. B. Velimirovic, ed. Washington, D.C.: Pan American Health Organization, Scientific Publication PAHO No. 359.

Kearny, Michael
1972 The Winds of Ixtepeji. New York: Holt, Rinehart and Winston.
1978 Espiritualismo as an Alternative Medical Tradition in the Border Area. *In* Modern Medicine and Medical Anthropology in the U.S.-Mexico Border Populations. B. Velimirovic, ed. Washington, D.C.: Pan American Health Organization, Scientific Publication PAHO No. 359.

Kelly, Isabel
1956 An Anthropological Approach to Midwifery Training in Mexico. Journal of Tropical Pediatrics 1:200-205.
1959 La Antropología, la Cultura, y la Salud Pública. La Paz: United States Operations Mission to Bolivia, The Institute of Inter-American Affairs (Mimeo).
1961 Mexican Spiritualism. Kroeber Anthropology Society Papers 25:191-206.

Kennedy, Donald A.
1961 Key Issues in the Cross-Cultural Study of Mental Disorders. *In* Studying Personality Cross-Culturally. B. Kaplan, ed. Pp. 405-442. Evanston, Ill.: Row, Peterson.

Kennedy, John G.
1973 Cultural Psychiatry. *In* Handbook of Social and Cultural Anthropology. J. J. Honigmann, ed. Pp. 1119-1198. Chicago: Rand McNally.

Kenny, Michael
1962-1963 Social Values and Health in Spain: Some Preliminary Considerations. Human Organization 21:280-285.

Kerley, Ellis R., and William M. Bass
1967 Paleopathology: Meeting Ground for Many Disciplines. Science 157:-638-644.

Kiefer, Christie
1971 Notes on Anthropology and the Minority Elderly. Gerontologist 11(2):-94-98.

Kiev, Ari
1968 Curanderismo: Mexican-American Folk Psychiatry. New York: The Free Press.
1972 Transcultural Psychiatry. New York: The Free Press.

King, Stanley H.
1962 Perceptions of Illness and Medical Practice. New York: Russell Sage Foundation.

Kitano, Harry H. L.
1969 Japanese-American Mental Illness. *In* Changing Perspectives in Mental

Illness. S. C. Plog and R. B. Edgerton, eds. Pp. 257-284. New York: Holt, Rinehart and Winston.

Kleinman, Arthur
1977 Lessons from a Clinical Approach to Medical Anthropological Research. Medical Anthropology Newsletter 8(4):11-15.

Kluckhohn, Clyde
1944 Navaho Witchcraft. Cambridge, Mass.: Harvard University, Papers of the Peabody Museum 22:2.

Knopf, Lucille
1975 RN's One and Five Years after Graduation. New York: National League for Nursing.

Knutson, Andie L.
1970 Cultural Beliefs on Life and Death. *In* The Dying Patient. O. C. Brim, Jr., H. E. Freeman, S. Levine, and N. A. Scotch, eds. Pp. 42-64. New York: Russell Sage Foundation.

Koenig, Barbara
1977 Role Strain in Pediatric Nurses: A Study of the Conflicts in Caring for Dying Children. Manuscript. Department of Anthropology, University of California, Berkeley.

Koo, Linda C.
1973 Traditional Chinese Diet and Its Relationship to Health. Kroeber Anthropological Society Papers 47-48:116-147.
1976 Nourishment of Life: The Culture of Health in Traditional Chinese Society. Ph.D. Dissertation, Anthropology Department, University of California, Berkeley.

Koos, Earl Lomon
1954 The Health of Regionville: What the People Thought and Did About It. New York: Columbia University Press.

Korsch, Barbara M., and Vida Francis Negrete
1972 Doctor-Patient Communication. Scientific American (August). Pp. 66-74.

Koss, Joan D.
1975 Therapeutic Aspects of Puerto Rican Cult Practices. Psychiatry 38:-160-171.

Krant, Melvin J.
1972 The Organized Care of the Dying Patient. Hospital Practice 7:101-108.

Kroeber, A. L.
1925 Handbook of the Indians of California. Washington, D.C.: Bureau of American Ethnology Bulletin 78.

Kübler-Ross, Elisabeth
1969 On Death and Dying. New York: Macmillan.
1973 Life and Death: Lessons from the Dying. *In* To Live and to Die: When, Why, and How. R. H. Williams, ed. Pp. 150-159. New York: Springer-Verlag.

Lamb, Karen T.
1973 Freedom for our Sisters: Freedom for Ourselves: Nursing Confronts Social Change. Nursing Forum 12: 328-352.

Lambo, T. Adeoye
1962 The Importance of Cultural Factors in Psychiatric Treatment. Acta Psychiatricà Scandinavica 38:176-179.
1964 Patterns of Psychiatric Care in Developing African Countries. *In* Magic, Faith, and Healing: Studies in Primitive Psychiatry Today. Ari Kiev, ed. Pp. 443-453. New York: The Free Press.

Landy, David
1974 Role Adaptation: Traditional Curers Under the Impact of Western Medicine. American Ethnologist 1:103-127.

Langness, L. L.
1967 Hysterical Psychosis: the Cross-Cultural Evidence. The American Journal of Psychiatry 124:143-152.

Laughlin, William S.
1963 Primitive Theory of Medicine: Empirical Knowledge. *In* Man's Image in Medicine and Anthropology. I. Galdston, ed. Pp. 116-140. New York: International Universities Press.

Lawick-Goodall, Jane Van
1971 In the Shadow of Man. Boston: Houghton-Mifflin.

Leboyer, Frederick
1975 Birth Without Violence. New York: Alfred A. Knopf.

Lee, Rance P. L.
1975 Toward a Convergence of Modern Western and Traditional Chinese Medical Services in Hong Kong. *In* Topias and Utopias in Health: Policy Studies. S. R. Ingman and A. C. Thomas, eds. Pp. 393-412. The Hague: Mouton.

Leighton, Alexander H.
1969 A Comparative Study of Psychiatric Disorder in Nigeria and Rural North America. *In* Changing Perspectives in Mental Illness. S. C. Plog and R. B. Edgerton, eds. Pp. 179-199. New York: Holt, Rinehart and Winston.

Leighton, Alexander H., and Dorothea C. Leighton
1941 Elements of Psychotherapy in Navaho Religion. Psychiatry 4:515-523.
1944 The Navaho Door: An Introduction to Navaho Life. Cambridge, Mass.: Harvard University Press.

Leininger, Madeleine M.
1970 Nursing and Anthropology: Two Worlds to Blend. New York: John Wiley.
1976 Doctoral Programs for Nurses: Trends, Questions, and Projected Plans. Nursing Research 25:201-210.

Lemert, Edwin M.
1951 Social Pathology. New York: McGraw-Hill.
1967 Human Deviance, Social Problems, and Social Control. Englewood Cliffs, N.J.: Prentice-Hall.
Leslie, Charles
1968 The Professionalization of Ayurvedic and Unani Medicine. Transactions of The New York Academy of Sciences 30:559-572.
1969 Modern India's Ancient Medicine. Trans-action, June. Pp. 46-55.
Leslie, Charles, ed.
1976 Asian Medical Systems: A Comparative Study. Berkeley: University of California Press.
Levy, Jerrold E., and Stephen J. Kunitz
1971 Indian Reservations, Anomie, and Social Pathologies. Southwestern Journal of Anthropology 27:97-128.
Levy, Robert I.
1973 Tahitians: Mind and Experience in the Society Islands. Chicago: University of Chicago Press.
Lieban, Richard W.
1962a The Dangerous Ingkantos: Illness and Social Control in a Philippine Community. American Anthropologist 64:306-312.
1962b Qualifications for Folk Medical Practice in Sibulan, Negros Oriental, Philippines. The Philippine Journal of Science 91:511-521.
1973 Medical Anthropology. *In* Handbook of Social and Cultural Anthropology. J. J. Honigmann, ed. Pp. 1031-1072. Chicago: Rand McNally.
Livingstone, Frank B.
1958 Anthropological Implications of Sickle Cell Gene Distribution in West Africa. American Anthropologist 60:533-562.
Logan, Michael H.
1973 Humoral Medicine in Guatemala and Peasant Acceptance of Modern Medicine. Human Organization 32:385-395.
Looff, David H.
1971 Appalachia's Children: The Challenge of Mental Health. Lexington: The University Press of Kentucky.
López Austin, Alfredo
1974 Sahagún's Work and the Medicine of the Ancient Nahuas: Possibilities for Study. *In* Sixteenth Century Mexico: The Work of Sahagún. M. S. Edmonson, ed. Pp. 205-224. Albuquerque: University of New Mexico Press.
Lorber, Judith
1975 Good Patients and Problem Patients: Conformity and Deviance in a General Hospital. Journal of Health and Social Behavior 16:213-225.
Loudon, J. B.
1976 Introduction. *In* Social Anthropology and Medicine. J. B. Loudon, ed. Pp. 1-48. A.S.A. Monograph 13. London: Academic Press.

Lozoff, Betsy, K. R. Kamath, and R. A. Feldman
1975 Infection and Disease in South Indian Families: Beliefs about Childhood Diarrhea. Human Organization 34:353-358.

McBride, Angela Barron
1976 A Married Feminist. American Journal of Nursing 76:754-757.

McCracken, Robert D.
1971 Lactase Deficiency: An Example of Dietary Evolution. Current Anthropology 12:479-500.

McCullough, John M.
1973 Human Ecology, Heat Adaptation, and Belief Systems: The Hot-Cold Syndrome of Yucatan. Journal of Anthropological Research 29:32-36.

McDermott, Walsh, Kurt W. Deuschle, and Clifford R. Barnett
1972 Health Care Experiment at Many Farms. Science 175:23-30.

McDowell, Edwin
1973 Navaho Medicine Men are Busier Than Ever Bringing Peace of Mind. The Wall Street Journal, March 26.

McKinlay, John B.
1972 The Sick Role — Illness and Pregnancy. Social Science & Medicine 6:561-572.

Mackenzie, Margaret
1978 More North American Than the North Americans: Medical Consequences of Migrant Enthusiasm, Willing and Unwilled. *In* Modern Medicine and Medical Anthropology in the U.S.-Mexico Border Populations. B. Velimirovic, ed. Washington, D.C.: Pan American Health Organization, Scientific Publication PAHO No. 359.

Macklin, June
1967 El Niño Fidencio: Un Estudio del Curanderismo en Nuevo León. Anuario Humánitas.Pp. 529-563. Monterrey, N. L: Universidad de Nuevo León, Centro de Estudios Humanísticos.
1974a Belief, Ritual, and Healing: New England Spiritualism and Mexican-American Spiritism Compared. *In* Religious Movements in Contemporary America. I. I. Zaretsky and M. P. Leone, eds. Pp. 383-417. Princeton, N.J: Princeton University Press.
1974b Folk Saints, Healers and Spiritist Cults in Northern Mexico. Revista Interamericana Review 3:351-367.
1976 A Connecticut Yankee in Summer Land. *In* Case Studies in Spirit Possession. V. Crapanzano and V. Garrison, eds. Pp. 41-83. New York: John Wiley.

Maclean, Una
1971 Magical Medicine: A Nigerian Case-Study. Harmondsworth, Middlesex: Penguin Books.

Madsen, William
1955 Hot and Cold in the Universe of San Francisco Tecospa, Valley of Mexico. Journal of American Folklore 68:123-139.
1964 The Mexican-Americans of South Texas. New York: Holt, Rinehart and Winston.
Mandelbaum, David G., ed.
1949 Selected Writings of Edward Sapir. Berkeley: University of California Press.
Mandelbaum, David G.
1970 Curing and Religion in South Asia. Journal of the Indian Anthropological Society 5:171-186.
Marchione, Thomas J.
1977 Food and Nutrition in Self-Reliant National Development: The Impact on Child Nutrition of Jamaican Government Policy. Medical Anthropology 1:57-79.
Maretzki, Thomas W.
1973 Epilogue. *In* Cultural Illness and Health. L. Nader and T.W. Maretzki, eds. Pp. 135-137. Washington, D. C.: American Anthropological Association, Anthropological Studies No. 9.
Marriott, McKim
1955 Western Medicine in a Village of Northern India. *In* Health, Culture and Community. B. D. Paul, ed. Pp. 239-268. New York: Russell Sage Foundation.
Marshall, Carter L.
1972 Some Exercises in Social Ecology: Health, Disease, and Modernization in the Ryukyu Islands. *In* The Careless Technology: Ecology and International Development. M. T. Farvar and J. P. Milton, eds. Pp. 5-18. Garden City, N. Y.: The Natural History Press.
Martin, Leonide L.
1975 View from the Firing Line: Family Nurse Practitioner in California. *In* The Law and the Expanding Nursing Role. B. Bullough, ed. Pp. 95-117. New York: Appleton-Century-Crofts.
Martinez, Cervando and Harry W. Martin
1966 Folk Diseases Among Urban Mexican-Americans. Journal of the American Medical Association 196:147-150.
Mauksch, Ingeborg G.
1975 Nursing is Coming of Age . . . through the Practitioner Movement: Pro. American Journal of Nursing 75:1835-1843.
Mazess, Richard B.
1968 Hot-Cold Food Beliefs Among Andean Peasants. Journal of the American Dietetic Association 53:109-113.
Mead, Margaret
1942 Anthropological Data on the Problem of Instinct. Psychosomatic Medicine 1:396-397.

Mead, Margaret, and Niles Newton
1967 Cultural Patterning of Perinatal Behavior. *In* Child Bearing: Its Social and Psychological Aspects. S. A. Richardson and A. F. Guttmacher, eds. Pp. 142-244. Baltimore: Williams and Wilkins.
Mechanic, David
1975 The Comparative Study of Health Care Delivery Systems. *In* Annual Review of Sociology Vol. I. A. Inkeles, ed. Pp. 43-66. Palo Alto, Calif.: Annual Reviews.
Mechanic, David, and Edmund H. Volkart
1961 Stress, Illness Behavior, and the Sick Role. American Sociological Review 26:51-58.
Merton, Robert K.
1957 Some Preliminaries to a Sociology of Medical Education. *In* The Student-Physician. R. K. Merton, G. G. Reader, and P. L. Kendall, eds. Pp. 3-79. Cambridge, Mass.: Harvard University Press.
Merton, Robert K., George G. Reader, and Patricia L. Kendall, eds.
1957 The Student-Physician: Introductory Studies in the Sociology of Medical Education. Cambridge, Mass.: Harvard University Press.
Messing, Simon D.
1958 Group Therapy and Social Status in the Zar Cult of Ethiopia. American Anthropologist 60:1120-1126.
Middleton, John
1970 The Study of the Lugbara: Expectation and Paradox in Anthropological Research. New York: Holt, Rinehart and Winston.
Miller, Max J.
1973 Industrialization, Ecology and Health in the Tropics. Canadian Journal of Public Health 64 (Monographic Supplement):11-16.
Moloney, James Clark
1945 Psychiatric Observations on Okinawa Shima. Psychiatry 8:391-399.
Molony, Carol H.
1975 Systematic Valence Coding of Mexican "Hot"—"Cold" Food. Ecology of Food and Nutrition 4:67-74.
Montagu, Ashley
1962 The Humanization of Man: Our Changing Conception of Human Nature. Cleveland: World Publishing Company.
Montgomery, Edward
1976 Systems and the Medical Practitioners of a Tamil Town. *In* Asian Medical Systems. C. Leslie, ed. Pp. 272-284. Berkeley: University of California Press.
Mote, Frederick W.
1977 Yüan and Ming. *In* Food in Chinese Culture: Anthropological and Historical Perspectives. K.C. Chang, ed. Pp. 193-257. New Haven, Conn.: Yale University Press.
Murphree, Alice H.
1968 A Functional Analysis of Southern Folk Beliefs Concerning Birth. *In*

Essays on Medical Anthropology. T. Weaver, ed. Pp. 64-77. Southern Anthropological Society Proceedings No. 1. Athens, Ga.: University of Georgia Press.

Murphy, H.B.M., E. D. Wittkower, and N.W. Chance
1970 The Symptoms of Depression — A Cross-Cultural Survey. *In* Cross-Cultural Studies of Behavior. Ihsan Al-Issa and W. Dennis. eds. Pp. 476-493. New York: Holt, Rinehart and Winston.

Murphy, Jane M.
1976 Psychiatric Labeling in Cross-Cultural Perspective. Science 191: 1019-1028.

Murphy, Jane M., and Alexander H. Leighton
1965 Native Conceptions of Psychiatric Disorder. *In* Approaches to Cross-Cultural Psychiatry. J.M. Murphy and A.H. Leighton, eds. Pp. 64-107. Ithaca, N.Y.: Cornell University Press.

Myerhoff, Barbara G., and William R. Larson
1965 The Doctor as Culture Hero: The Routinization of Charisma. Human Organization 24: 188-191.

Nash, June
1967 The Logic of Behavior: Curing in a Maya Indian Town. Human Organization 26:132-140.

Ndeti, K.
1972 Sociocultural Aspects of Tuberculosis Defaultation: A Case Study. Social Science & Medicine 6:397-412.

Neel, James V.
1970 Lessons from A "Primitive" People. Science 170:815-822.

Nelson, Cynthia
1971 Self, Spirit Possession and World View: An Illustration from Egypt. International Journal of Social Psychiatry 17:194-209.

Newman, Lucile F.
1965 Culture and Perinatal Environment in American Society. Ph.D. Dissertation, Anthropology Department, University of California, Berkeley.

Newman, Philip L.
1965 Knowing the Gururumba. New York: Holt, Rinehart and Winston.

Nolen, William A.
1972 The Making of a Surgeon. New York: Pocket Books.
1974 A Surgeon's World. Greenwich, Conn.: Fawcett.

Nurge, Ethel
1958 Etiology of Illness in Guinhangdan. American Anthropologist 60:-1158-1172.

Obeyesekere, Gananath
1969 The Ritual Drama of the *Sanni* Demons: Collective Representations of Disease in Ceylon. Comparative Studies in Society and History 11:174-216.

Olesen, Virginia L.
1974 Convergences and Divergences: Anthropology and Sociology in Health Care. Medical Anthropology Newsletter 6(1):6-10.
Olesen, Virginia L., and Elvi W. Whittaker
1968 The Silent Dialogue: A Study in the Psychology of Professional Socialization. San Francisco: Jossey-Bass.
O'Nell, Carl W.
1975 An Investigation of Reported "Fright" as a Factor in the Etiology of Susto, "Magical Fright." Ethos 3:41-63.
O'Nell, Carl W., and Henry A. Selby
1968 Sex Differences in the Incidence of Susto in Two Zapotec Pueblos: An Analysis of the Relationships Between Sex Role Expectations and a Folk Illness. Ethnology 7: 95-105.
Onon, Urgunge
1972 My Childhood in Mongolia, Oxford: Oxford University Press.
Opler, Morris
1936 Some Points of Comparison and Contrast Between Treatment of Functional Disorders by Apache Shamans and Modern Psychiatric Practice. The American Journal of Psychiatry 92:1371-1387.
1963 The Cultural Definition of Illness in Village India. Human Organization 22:32-35.
Osborne, Oliver H.
1969 The Yoruba as a Therapeutic Community. Journal of Health and Social Behavior 10:187-200.
Orso, Ethelyn
1970 Hot and Cold in the Folk Medicine of the Island of Chira, Costa Rica. Baton Rouge, La.: Latin American Studies Institute, Louisiana State University, Monograph and Dissertation Series No. 1.
Otsuka, Yasuo
1976 Chinese Traditional Medicine in Japan. In Asian Medical Systems. C. Leslie, ed. Pp. 322-340. Berkeley: University of California Press.

Paiva, Rosalia E. A., and Harold B. Haley
1971 Intellectual, Personality, and Environmental Factors in Career Specialty Preferences. Journal of Medical Education 46:281-289.
Parsons, Talcott
1951 The Social System. Glencoe, Ill.: The Free Press.
Parsons, Talcott, and Renée Fox
1952 Illness, Therapy and the Modern Urban American Family. Journal of Social Issues 8(4):31-44.
Paul, Benjamin D.
1950 Sibling Rivalry in a Guatemalan Indian Village. American Anthropologist 52:205-218.

1955 Health, Culture and Community: Case Studies of Public Reactions to Health Programs. New York: Russell Sage Foundation.

1963 Anthropological Perspectives on Medicine and Public Health. *In* Medicine and Society. J. A. Clausen and R. Straus, eds. Pp. 34-43. The Annals of the American Academy of Political and Social Science 346.

Paul, Lois, and Benjamin D. Paul

1975 The Maya Midwife as Sacred Specialist: A Guatemalan Case. American Ethnologist 2:707-726.

Pearsall, Marion

1963 Medical Behavioral Science: A Selected Bibliography. Lexington: University of Kentucky Press.

Pellegrino, Edmund D.

1963 Medicine, History, and the Idea of Man. *In* Medicine and Society. J. A. Clausen and R. Straus, eds. Pp. 9-20. The Annals of the American Academy of Political and Social Science 346.

Pelto, Gretel H., and Norge W. Jerome

1978 Intracultural Diversity and Nutritional Anthropology. *In* Health and the Human Condition. M. H. Logan and E. E. Hunt, Jr., eds. Pp. 322-328. North Scituate, Mass.: Duxbury Press.

Pelto, Pertti J., and Gretel H. Pelto

1978 Medicine, Anthropology, Community: An Overview. *In* Health and the Human Condition. M. H. Logan and E. E. Hunt, Jr., eds. Pp. 401-406. North Scituate, Mass.: Duxbury Press.

Perricone, Philip J.

1974 Social Concern in Medical Students: A Reconsideration of the Eron Assumption. Journal of Medical Education 49:541-546.

Philips, Jane

1955 The Hookworm Campaign in Ceylon. *In* Hands Across Frontiers: Case Studies in Technical Cooperation. H. M. Teaf, Jr. and P. G. Franck, eds. Pp. 265-305. Ithaca, N.Y.: Cornell University Press.

Pickard, Madge E., and R. Carlyle Buley

1945 The Midwest Pioneer: His Ills, Cures, & Doctors. Crawfordsville, Ind.: R. E. Banta.

Pillsbury, Barbara L. K.

1976 "Doing the Month:" Confinement and Convalescence of Chinese Women After Childbirth. Paper Presented at the 75th Annual Meeting of the American Anthropological Association, Washington, D. C.

Polgar, Steven

1962 Health and Human Behavior: Areas of Interest Common to the Social and Medical Sciences. Current Anthropology 3:159-205.

1963 Health Action in Cross-Cultural Perspective. *In* Handbook of Medical Sociology. H. E. Freeman, S. Levine, and L. G. Reader, eds. Pp. 397-419. Englewood Cliffs, N.J.: Prentice-Hall.

Polunin, Ivan V.
1967 Health and Disease in Contemporary Primitive Societies. *In* Diseases in Antiquity. D. Brothwell and A. T. Sandison, eds. Pp. 69-97. Springfield, Ill.: Charles C Thomas.
1976 Disease, Morbidity, and Mortality in China, India, and the Arab World. *In* Asian Medical Systems: A Comparative Study. C. Leslie, ed. Pp. 120-132. Berkeley: University of California Press.
Potter, Jack M.
1974 Cantonese Shamanism. *In* Religion and Ritual in Chinese Society. A. Wolf, ed. Pp. 207-231. Stanford, Calif.: Stanford University Press.
Pratt, Lois, Arthur Seligmann, and George Reader
1958 Physicians' Views on the Level of Medical Information Among Patients. *In* Patients, Physicians and Illness. E. G. Jaco, ed. Pp. 222-229. Glencoe, Ill.: The Free Press.
Press, Irwin
1971 The Urban Curandero. American Anthropologist 73:741-756.
1975 Tradition and Adaptation. Life in a Modern Yucatan Maya Village. Westport, Conn.: Greenwood Press.
Prince, Raymond
1974 Indigenous Yoruba Psychiatry. *In* Anthropology and Community Action. E. Hegeman and L. Kooperman, eds. Pp. 138-145. Garden City, N. Y.: Anchor Books.

Ragucci, Antoinette T.
1978 The Ethnographic Approach and Nursing Research. *In* Health and the Human Condition. M. H. Logan and E. E. Hunt, Jr., eds. Pp. 314-321. North Scituate, Mass.: Duxbury Press.
Rather, Lelland J., trans.
1958 Disease, Life, and Man: Selected Essays by Rudolf Virchow. Stanford, Calif.: Stanford University Press.
Read, Margaret
1966 Culture, Health, and Disease: Social and Cultural Influences on Health Programmes in Developing Countries. London: Tavistock Publications.
Regester, P. T.
1956 The Study of Primitive Communities and its Relation to Social Medicine — With Particular Reference to the Muruts and Dusuns of North Borneo. Journal of the Royal Institute of Public Health and Hygiene 19:350-376.
Reichard, Gladys A.
1963 Navaho Religion: A Study of Symbolism. New York: Bollingen Foundation Inc. (1950).
Reichel-Dolmatoff, Gerardo
1976a Cosmology as Ecological Analysis: A View from the Rain Forest. Man 11:307-318.

1976b Desana Curing Spells: An Analysis of Some Shamanistic Metaphors. Journal of Latin American Lore 2:157-219.

Reichel-Dolmatoff, Gerardo, and Alicia Reichel-Dolmatoff
1961 The People of Aritama: The Cultural Personality of a Colombian Mestizo Village. Chicago: University of Chicago Press.

Richardson, Miles
n.d. Cultural Responses to Death: A Brief Sketch. Department of Anthropology, Louisiana State University (Mimeo).

Richardson, Miles, and Barbara Bode
1971 Popular Medicine in Puntarenas, Costa Rica: Urban and Societal Features. New Orleans: Middle American Research Institute, Tulane University, 24:249-275.

Rifkin, S. B.
1973 Public Health in China — Is the Experience Relevant to Other Less Developed Nations? Social Science & Medicine 7:249-257.

Rivers, W. H. R.
1924 Medicine, Magic, and Religion. New York: Harcourt Brace.

Roemer, Milton I., ed.
1960 Henry E. Sigerist on the Sociology of Medicine. New York: MD Publications.

Rogler, Lloyd H., and August B. Hollingshead
1961 The Puerto Rican Spiritualist as a Psychiatrist. The American Journal of Sociology 67:17-21.

Rogoff, Natalie
1957 The Decision to Study Medicine. *In* The Student-Physician. R. K. Merton, G. G. Reader, and P. L. Kendall, eds. Pp. 109-129. Cambridge, Mass.: Harvard University Press.

Romano, Octavio Ignacio
1965 Charismatic Medicine, Folk Healing, and Folk Sainthood. American Anthropologist 67:1151-1173.

Ronaghy, Hossain A., and Steven Solter
1974 Is the Chinese "Barefoot Doctor" Exportable to Rural Iran? The Lancet 1(7870):1331-1333. June 29.

Rose, A. M.
1965 The Subculture of Aging: A Framework in Social Gerontology. *In* Older People and Their Social World. A. M. Rose and W. A. Peterson, eds. Pp. 3-16. Philadelphia: F. A. Davis.

Rosenhan, D. L.
1973 On Being Sane in Insane Places. Science 179:250-258.

Rubel, Arthur J.
1960 Concepts of Disease in Mexican-American Culture. American Anthropologist 62:795-814.

1964 The Epidemiology of a Folk Illness: Susto in Hispanic America. Ethnology 3:268-283.

1966 Across the Tracks: Mexican-Americans in a Texas City. Austin: University of Texas Press.

Rubin, Vera

1960 Preface. In Culture, Society, and Health. V. Rubin, ed. Pp. 785-786. Annals of the New York Academy of Sciences 84:783-1060.

Rubin, Vera, and Lambros Comitas

1976 Ganja in Jamaica: The Effects of Marijuana Use. Garden City, N. Y.: Anchor Books.

Ryesky, Diana

1976 Conceptos Tradicionales de la Medicina en un Pueblo Mexicano: Un Análisis Antropológico. México, D. F.: Sep Setentas #309.

Salisbury, Richard F.

1962 Structure of Custodial Care: An Anthropological Study of a State Mental Hospital. Berkeley: University of California Press. University of California Publications in Culture and Society, Vol. 8.

Samora, Julian

1961 Conceptions of Health and Disease Among Spanish-Americans. American Catholic Sociological Review 22:314-323.

Sarton, George

1954 Galen of Pergamon. Lawrence, Ka.: University of Kansas Press.

Saunders, Lyle

1954 Cultural Difference and Medical Care: The Case of the Spanish-Speaking People of the Southwest. New York: Russell Sage Foundation.

Scheff, Thomas J.

1974 The Labeling Theory of Mental Illness. American Sociological Review 39:444-452.

Scheper-Hughes, Nancy

1974 Birth, Culture, and Counter-Culture. Paper presented at the Southwestern Anthropological Association Meetings, San Francisco.

1978 Saints, Scholars, and Schizophrenics: Mental Illness and Irish Culture. Berkeley: University of California Press.

Schulman, Sam

1958 Basic Functional Roles in Nursing: Mother Surrogate and Healer. In Patients, Physicians and Illness. E. G. Jaco, ed. Pp. 528-537. Glencoe, Ill.: The Free Press.

1960 Rural Healthways in New Mexico. In Culture, Society, and Health. V. Rubin, ed. Pp. 950-958. Annals of the New York Academy of Sciences 84:783-1060.

1972 Mother Surrogate — After a Decade. In Patients, Physicians and Illness. 2nd ed. E. G. Jaco, ed. Pp. 223-229. New York: The Free Press.

Schurr, E.
1971 Labeling Deviant Behavior: Its Sociological Implications. New York: Harper and Row.

Schwartz, Lola R.
1969 The Hierarchy of Resort in Curative Practice: The Admiralty Islands, Melanesia. Journal of Health and Social Behavior 10:201-209.

Scotch, Norman A.
1963a Medical Anthropology. *In* Biennial Review of Anthropology 1963. B. H. Siegel, ed. Pp. 30-68. Stanford, Calif.: Stanford University Press.
1963b Sociocultural Factors in the Epidemiology of Zulu Hypertension. American Journal of Public Health 53:1205-1213.

Scudder, Thayer
1973 The Human Ecology of Big Projects: River Basin Development and Resettlement. Annual Review of Anthropology 2:45-55.

Segall, Alexander
1976 The Sick Role Concept: Understanding Illness Behavior. Journal of Health and Social Behavior 17:162-168.

Seijas, Haydée
1972 El Susto Como Categoría Etiológica. Acta Científica Venezolana 23 (Supl. 3):176-178.
1973 An Approach to the Study of The Medical Aspects of Culture. Current Anthropology 14:544-545.

Shaffer, Richard A.
1977 Mastering the Mind: Advances in Chemistry are Starting to Unlock Mysteries of the Brain. The Wall Street Journal, August 12.

Sharman, Anne
1970 Nutrition and Social Planning. The Journal of Development Studies 6:77-91.

Shiloh, Ailon
1961 The System of Medicine in Middle East Culture. The Middle East Journal 15:277-288.

Shreiber, Janet M., and Loralee Philpott
1978 Who is a Legitimate Health Care Professional? Changes in the Practice of Midwifery in the Lower Rio Grande Valley. *In* Modern Medicine and Medical Anthropology in the U.S.-Mexico Border Populations. B. Velimirovic, ed. Washington. D.C.: Pan American Health Organization, Scientific Publication PAHO No. 359.

Shryock, Richard Harrison
1969 The Development of Modern Medicine: An Interpretation of the Social and Scientific Factors Involved. New York: Hafner Publishing (1936).

Shuval, Judith T., Aaron Antonovsky, and A. Michael Davies
1973 Illness: A Mechanism for Coping with Failure. Social Science & Medicine 7:259-265.

Sidel, Victor W.

1972 The Barefoot Doctors of the People's Republic of China. The New England Journal of Medicine 286:1292-1300.

Sigerist, Henry E.

1951 A History of Medicine. Vol. I: Primitive and Archaic Medicine. New York: Oxford University Press.

Simmons, Ozzie G.

1955 Popular and Modern Medicine in Mestizo Communities of Coastal Peru and Chile. Journal of American Folklore 68:57-71.

Singer, Milton

1961 A Survey of Culture and Personality Theory and Research. *In* Studying Personality Cross-Culturally. B. Kaplan, ed. Pp. 9-90. Evanston, Ill.: Row, Peterson.

Smith, Harvey L.

1955 Two Lines of Authority Are One Too Many. The Modern Hospital 84:59-64.

Smith, M. Estellie

1972 Folk Medicine Among the Sicilian-Americans of Buffalo, New York. Urban Anthropology 1:087-106.

Snow, Loudell F.

1973 "I was Born Just Exactly with the Gift": An Interview with a Voodoo Practitioner. Journal of American Folklore 86:272-281.

1974 Folk Medical Beliefs and Their Implications for Care of Patients. Annals of Internal Medicine 81:82-96.

1976 Old-Fashioned "Medicine" is Still with Us. The Osteopathic Physician 43:51-64.

1977a The Religious Component in Southern Folk Medicine. *In* Traditional Healing: New Science or New Colonialism? P. Singer, ed. Pp. 26-51. New York: Conch Magazine Limited.

1977b Popular Medicine in a Black Neighborhood. *In* Ethnic Medicine in the Southwest. E. H. Spicer, ed. Pp. 19-95. Tucson: University of Arizona Press.

Solien, Nancie L., and Nevin S. Scrimshaw

1957 Public Health Significance of Child Feeding Practices Observed in a Guatemalan Village. The Journal of Tropical Pediatrics 3:99-104.

Spencer, Robert F.

1959 The North Alaskan Eskimo: A Study in Ecology and Society. Washington, D.C.: Bureau of American Ethnology Bulletin 171.

Spiegel, John P.

1964 Cultural Variations in Attitudes Toward Death and Disease. *In* The Threat of Impending Disaster. G. H. Grosser, H. Wechsler, and M. Greenblatt, eds. Pp. 283-299. Cambridge, Mass.: MIT Press.

Spiro, Melford E.
1952 Ghosts, Ifaluk, and Teleological Functionalism. American Anthropologist 54:497-503.
1966 Buddhism and Economic Action in Burma. American Anthropologist 68:1163-1173.

Stanton, Alfred H., and Morris S. Schwartz
1954 The Mental Hospital: A Study of Institutional Participation in Psychiatric Illness and Treatment. New York: Basic Books.

Stein, Howard F.
1977 Commentary on Kleinman's "Lessons From a Clinical Approach to Medical Anthropological Research." Medical Anthropology Newsletter 8(4):15-16.

Stein, Leonard I.
1971 Male and Female: The Doctor-Nurse Game. *In* Conformity and Conflict. J. P. Spradley and D. W. McCurdy, eds. Pp. 185-193. Boston: Little, Brown.

Stein, William W., and E. R. Oetting
1964 Humanism and Custodialism in a Peruvian Mental Hospital. Human Organization 23:278-282.

Stekert, Ellen J.
1970 Focus for Conflict: Southern Mountain Medical Beliefs in Detroit. Journal of American Folklore 83:115-147.

Stini, William A.
1971 Evolutionary Implications of Changing Nutritional Patterns in Human Populations. American Anthropologist 73:1019-1030.

Straus, Robert
1957 The Nature and Status of Medical Sociology. American Sociological Review 22:200-204.

Strauss, Anselm
1966 The Structure and Ideology of American Nursing: An Interpretation. *In* The Nursing Profession: Five Sociological Essays. F. Davis, ed. Pp. 60-108. New York: John Wiley.

Suárez, María Matilde
1974 Etiology, Hunger, and Folk Disease in the Venezuelan Andes. Journal of Anthropological Research 30:41-54.

Suchman, Edward A.
1965 Stages of Illness and Medical Care. Journal of Health and Human Behavior 6:114-128.
1968 Epidemiology. International Encyclopedia of the Social Sciences 5:97-102. New York: Free Press/Macmillan.

Sudnow, David
1967 Passing On: The Social Organization of Dying. Englewood Cliffs, N. J.: Prentice-Hall.

Sweeney, William J., III
1973 Woman's Doctor. New York: William Morrow and Co.
Szasz, Thomas S.
1961 The Myth of Mental Illness: Foundations of a Theory of Personal Conduct. New York: Hoeber-Harper.

Taylor, Carl E.
1976 The Place of Indigenous Medical Practitioners in the Modernization of Health Services. *In* Asian Medical Systems. C. Leslie, ed. Pp. 285-299. Berkeley: University of California Press.
Taylor, Carl E., et al.
1973 Asian Medical Systems; A Symposium on the Role of Comparative Sociology in Improving Health Care. Social Science & Medicine 7:307-318.
Taylor, Carol
1970 In Horizontal Orbit: Hospitals and the Cult of Efficiency. New York: Holt, Rinehart and Winston.
Thomas, Anthony E.
1975 Health Care in *Ukambani* Kenya: A Socialist Critique. *In* Topias and Utopias in Health: Policy Studies. S. R. Ingman and A. E. Thomas, eds. Pp. 267-281. The Hague: Mouton.
Time-Life Multi Media
n.d. Witch Doctor. Time-Life Films. New York.
Tinling, David C.
1967 Voodoo, Root Work, and Medicine. Psychosomatic Medicine 29:483-490.
Topley, Marjorie
1970 Chinese Traditional Ideas and the Treatment of Disease: Two Examples from Hong Kong. Man 5:421-437.
Torrey, E. Fuller
1972 The Mind Game: Witchdoctors and Psychiatrists. New York: Emerson Hall.
Trigger, Bruce G.
1969 The Huron: Farmers of the North. New York: Holt, Rinehart and Winston.
Trotter, Robert T., II, and Juan Antonio Chaviro
1978 Discovering New Models for Alcohol Counseling in Minority Groups. *In* Modern Medicine and Medical Anthropology in the U.S.-Mexico Border Populations. B. Velimirovic, ed. Washington, D.C.: Pan American Health Organization, Scientific Publication PAHO NO. 359.
Tryoler, H. A., and John Cassel
1964 Health Consequences of Culture Change — II. The Effect of Urbanization on Coronary Heart Mortality in Rural Residents. Journal of Chronic Diseases 17:167-177.

Udupa, K. N.
1975 The Ayurvedic System of Medicine in India. *In* Health by the People. K. W. Newell, ed. Pp. 53-69. Geneva: World Health Organization.

Ulin, Priscilla R.
1974-75 The Traditional Healer of Botswana in a Changing Society. Rural Africana 26:123-130.

Underwood, Jane H.
1975 Biocultural Interactions and Human Variation. Dubuque, Ia.: Wm. C. Brown.

Unschuld, Paul U.
1976 The Social Organization and Ecology of Medical Practice in Taiwan. *In* Asian Medical Systems. C. Leslie, ed. Pp. 300-316. Berkeley: University of California Press.

Uzzell, Douglas
1974 *Susto* Revisited: Illness as a Strategic Role. American Ethnologist 1:369-378.

Valdizán, Hermilio, and Angel Maldonado
1922 La Medicina Popular Peruana, Vol. 2. Lima: Imprenta Torres Aguirre.

Vargas, Luis Alberto
1978 Acceptance and Rejection of Medical Techniques in Different Cultures. *In* Modern Medicine and Medical Anthropology in the U.S.-Mexico Border Populations. B. Velimirovic, ed. Washington, D.C.: Pan American Health Organization, Scientific Publication PAHO No. 359.

Veith, Ilza, trans.
1972 The Yellow Emperor's Classic of Internal Medicine. Berkeley: University of California Press.

Velimirovic, Boris, ed.
1978 Modern Medicine and Medical Anthropology in the U.S.-Mexico Border Populations. Washington, D.C.: Pan American Health Organization, Scientific Publication PAHO No. 359.

Velimirovic, Boris, and Helga
1978 Utilization of Traditional Medicine and Its Practitioners in Health Services. *In* Modern Medicine and Medical Anthropology in the U.S.-Mexico Border Populations. B. Velimirovic, ed. Washington, D.C.: Pan American Health Organization, Scientific Publication PAHO No. 359.

Von Mering, Otto
1970 Medicine and Psychiatry. *In* Anthropology and the Behavioral and Health Sciences. O. Von Mering and L. Kasden, eds. Pittsburgh: University of Pittsburgh Press.

Wagner, Roland M.
1978 Traditional and Modern Medicine as Reflected in Contemporary Peyotist Practices. *In* Modern Medicine and Medical Anthropology in the U.S.-

Mexico Border Populations. B. Velimirovic, ed. Washington, D.C.: Pan American Health Organization, Scientific Publication Paho No. 359.

Wallace, Anthony G. C.

1961a Culture and Personality. New York: Random House.

1961b Mental Illness, Biology, and Culture. *In* Psychological Anthropology: Approaches to Culture and Personality. F. L. K. Hsu, ed. Pp. 255-295. Homewood, Ill.: The Dorsey Press.

1969 Culture Change and Mental Illness. *In* Changing Perspectives in Mental Illness. S. C. Plog and R. B. Edgerton, eds. Pp. 75-87. New York: Holt, Rinehart and Winston.

Wallen, Richard

1943 Sex Differences in Food Aversions. Journal of Applied Psychology 27:288-298

Warren, Dennis M.

1974-75 Bono Traditional Healers. Rural Africana 26:25-39.

Weaver, Thomas

1968 Medical Anthropology: Trends in Research and Medical Education. *In* Essays on Medical Anthropology. T. Weaver, ed. Pp. 1-12. Southern Anthropological Society Proceedings, No. 1. Athens, Ga.: University of Georgia Press.

Wedge, B. M.

1952 Occurrence of Psychosis Among Okinawans in Hawaii. American Journal of Psychiatry 109:225-258.

Weidman, Hazel Hitson

1968 Anthropological Theory and the Psychological Function of Belief in Witchcraft. *In* Essays on Medical Anthropology. T. Weaver, ed. Pp. 23-35. Southern Anthropological Society Proceedings, No. 1. Athens, Ga.: University of Georgia Press.

Wellin, Edward

1966 Directed Culture Change and Health Programs in Latin America. Milbank Memorial Fund Quarterly 44(Part 2):111-128.

1977 Theoretical Orientations in Medical Anthropology: Continuity and Change Over the Past Half-Century. *In* Culture, Disease, and Healing. D. Landy, ed. Pp. 47-58. New York: Macmillan.

Wells, Calvin

1964 Bones, Bodies, and Disease: Evidence of Disease and Abnormality in Early Man. New York: Praeger.

Wessen, Albert F.

1972 Hospital Ideology and Communication Between Ward Personnel. *In* Patients, Physicians and Illness. 2nd ed. E. G. Jaco, ed. Pp. 315-332. New York: Free Press.

Whitten, Norman E.

1962 Contemporary Patterns of Malign Occultism Among Negroes in North Carolina. Journal of American Folklore 75:311-325.

Wiese, H. Jean C.
1976 Maternal Nutrition and Traditional Food Behavior in Haiti. Human Organization 35:193-200.
Wiesenfeld, Stephen L.
1969 Sickle-Cell Trait in Human Biological and Cultural Evolution. *In* Environment and Cultural Behavior. A. P. Vayda, ed. Pp. 308-331. Garden City, N.Y.: The Natural History Press.
Wilson, Christine S.
1973 Food Taboos of Childbirth: The Malay Example. Ecology of Food and Nutrition 2:267-274.
Wilson, Robert N.
1963 Patient-Practitioner Relationships. *In* Handbook of Medical Sociology. H. E. Freeman, S. Levine, and L. G. Reeder, eds. Pp. 273-295. Englewood Cliffs, N. J.: Prentice-Hall.
Wintrob, Ronald
1973 The Influence of Others: Witchcraft and Rootwork as Explanations of Behavior Disturbances. Journal of Nervous and Mental Disease 156:318-326.
Withers, Carl
1966 The Folklore of a Small Town. *In* Medical Care: Readings in the Sociology of Medical Institutions. W. R. Scott and E. H. Volkhart, eds. Pp. 233-246. New York: John Wiley.
Woods, Clyde M., and Theodore D. Graves
1973 The Process of Medical Change in a Highland Guatemalan Town. Los Angeles: Latin American Studies Series, Vol. 21. University of California.
Wylie, Laurence
1957 Village in the Vaucluse: An Account of Life in a French Village. Cambridge, Mass.: Harvard University Press.

Young, Allan
1974-75 The Practical Logic of Amhara Traditional Medicine. Rural Africana 26:79-89.
1976 Some Implications of Medical Beliefs and Practices for Social Anthropology. American Anthropologist 78:5-24.

Zborowski, Mark
1952 Cultural Components in Response to Pain. Journal of Social Issues 8:16-30.
Zigas, Vincent
1970 II. Kuru in New Guinea: Discovery and Epidemiology. The American Journal of Tropical Medicine and Hygiene 19:130-132.
Zimmer, Henry R.
1948 Hindu Medicine. Edited with a foreward and preface by Ludwig Edelstein. Baltimore: The Johns Hopkins University Press.

Index

Page numbers in *italics* refer to the pages on which the full references appear.

MEDICAL
ANTHROPOLOGY